Literature, Moderns, Monsters, Popsters and Us

BY THE SAME AUTHOR

Love Is War

Sex and Violence: A Love Story

Confessions of a Lady-Killer

George Stade is also Consulting Editorial Director of *Barnes & Noble's Classics* and Editor in Chief of *Scribner's British Writers Series* and *Scribner's European Writers Series*

GEORGE STADE

Literature, Moderns, Monsters, Popsters and Us

PARI PUBLISHING

George Stade is professor emeritus at Columbia University, where he taught in the English Department for forty years and won the Great Teacher's Award. He lives in New York City with his wife of fifty years and his youngest daughter. He is the author of three novels, *Confessions of a Lady-killer, Sex and Violence: A Love Story,* and *Love Is War,* and over fifty articles and reviews. He is currently working on a new novel.

"Start with a high-octane intelligence, add large handfuls of irreverent wit, a capacious literary curiosity, a visceral dislike of the bogus and a lean prose that skewers at the same time it illuminates, and you have the recipe for the kind of marvelous criticism George Stade has been producing for over thirty years. Whether writing about popular fiction or the great modernists, ethology or the joys of football, Stade is never less than entertaining and provocative. It is a treat to have these essays at last collected in a single volume."
Michael Rosenthal is the Roberta and William Campbell Professor of the Humanities at Columbia University.

"Stade's essays are amusing and insightful. His criticism extracts golden nuggets from the text while it informs and delights the reader, who feels privileged to be a part of the process of discovery and who wishes Stade's best essays, like a good novel, would never end. It shows his endearing love of, and commitment to, literature. The fact that these essays and reviews will enlighten and absorb their readers in the pleasure of the text is why I urge readers to read the book; they will be reminded why they love literature."
Norman Loftis, poet, novelist, essayist, philosopher and filmmaker.

Copyright © George Stade 2007

First published in Italy in 2007 by Pari Publishing, Sas

George Stade has asserted his right under the Copyright, Designs and Patents Act 1988 to be identified as the author of this work.

All rights reserved. No part of this publication may be reproduced, transmitted or stored in a retrieval system, in any form or by any means, without permission in writing from Pari Publishing, Sas, application for which must be made to the publisher.

A catalogue record for this book is available from the British Library.
ISBN 978-88-901960-9-6

Book design and cover by Andrea Barbieri
Cover image: © Stephen Coburn - Fotolia
Printed and bound in Italy by Global Print, Gorgonzola (MI)

Pari Publishing

Via Tozzi 7, 58040 Pari, Grosseto, Italy
www.paripublishing.com

TABLE OF CONTENTS

PREFACE I

I

LITERATURE AS EQUIPAGE 3

THE LIBERAL EDUCATION FRONT 27

II

A PARABLE OF THE PEOPLE 33

SNOT, NAVEL-FLUFF, TOE-JAM,
AND THE UNCENSORED BODY OF *ULYSSES* 41

FICTION IN THE MODERNIST MODE 52

A LUMINOUS PARABLE 57

AFTERWORD TO TWO NOVELS
BY FRIEDRICH DÜRRENMATT 63

WILLIAM GADDIS'S FRIGICOM 75

A FICTION MADE OF HISTORY,
WHICH IN TURN WAS MADE OF FICTIONS 82

III

HORROR AND DISSOCIATION 91

DRACULA'S WOMEN,
AND WHY MEN LOVE TO HATE THEM 122

FRANKENSTEIN'S MEN,
AND WHY MARY HATED TO LOVE THEM 151

HIS ALTER EGO IS A KILLER..160

MONSTERS HAVE NEEDS, TOO 163

IV

THRILLERS 169

RATNER'S STAR..179

MYSTERIES OF A HARDCASE 183

COP TRISTESSE AND ONE-LINERS.............................190

V

INTRODUCTION TO A CLOSER LOOK AT
ARIEL: A MEMORY OF SYLVIA PLATH 197

SEX IS EVERYTHING... 224

MANISM IN RETREAT 229

THE 'NICE GUY' WHO TOUCHED OFF
McCARTHYISM 239

VI

INTRODUCTION TO *SIX MODERN BRITISH WRITERS*. 247

FANTASTIC LESSING 256

ROMANCE FOR HIGHBROWS 263

VII

FAT-CHEEKS HEFTED A SNAKE; ON THE ORIGINS
AND INSTITUZIONALIZATION OF LITERATURE 271

K. LORENZ, AND THE DOG BENEATH THE SKIN 288

DESPORTMENT 323

GAME THEORY 331

ON EXPERT WITNESSING 337

ACKNOWLEDGEMENTS 345

PREFACE

This volume contains a selection of my writings from over a thirty-year period. Originally they were essays, reviews, lectures, introductions, and one afterword. Originally they were written for colleagues, for students, for people with a professional interest in literature, in two cases for psychoanalysts, but always and above all, for the general reader. I have arranged them not chronologically, but according to subject matter. Within each of the seven sections the individual pieces deal with matters of overlapping interest:

    I) .... introductory,
    II) .... moderns and modernism,
    III) ...... horror, literary and otherwise,
    IV) ...... a sample of popular genres,
    V) .... recent American writing,
    VI) ...... modern British literature,
    VII) ..... miscellaneous.

The first two pieces are different from those that follow in emphasis, in tone and weight, in the degree of impersonality. They began as talks, in one case to students and administrators who had given me an award, in the other case to alumni of Columbia College and Graduate School. In both cases I meant to introduce myself as well as the ideas and verbal universes in which I live and move and have my being. I do believe, however, that appetizers should contribute to the nourishment of what they lead us into.

Usually, within each section there are essays that deal with a general topic, such as what horror is good for, as well as reviews of books that concretely expose the general topic. In short, the reviews I decided to include are of books that allowed me to move from the individual case to the general condition. These pieces, long or short, are held together by my belief that it is as much a species characteristic of humans to produce and consume literature as it is, say, characteristic of moles to dig underground. Every such characteristic outfits the species that possesses it to survive in its social or natural setting. Literature, I claim, helps us to get by, and not just because it gives us pleasure. If readers come to feel that they can say as much about the pieces of writing that follow, I will have achieved my goal..

LITERATURE AS EQUIPAGE

A talk given to the Columbia College
Alumni on Dean's Day, April 17, 1998.

When last December Katharine Yatrakis[1] asked me to speak to you today, I was at first reluctant. There at the end of the fall term, I felt as though I had spoken myself out; I could hardly stand the sound of my own voice. My mind was a blank screen, nothing but flashes, pops, and squiggles, my interior monologue mere white noise. But as many of you have learned, Katharine's combination of schmooz, charm, moral blackmail, and veiled threats can be very persuasive. I was given to understand that the whole future of higher education at Columbia depended on my saying a few well-chosen words.

"What should I say?" I said.

"Well, you can't say what you always say, because some of your audience will already have heard you," she said, and I have yet to forgive her.

So I took the subway to Chambers Street and began to walk back, for my thinking machinery seems somehow linked to my locomotor apparatus. I think best at about four blocks every five minutes.

As I passed through Union Square, where there used to be a Klein's department store, whence came the suit I wore to my

---

[1] *Dean of Academic Affairs, Columbia College, NYC*

junior high school graduation, I was blind-sided by the realization that my education was about to end, for a teacher is someone who conducts his education in public, for in a month from now, April 14, I will be reading the last blue books from the last class I will ever teach, before a sabbatical followed by retirement. As I passed Times Square, from which I averted my gaze, for I believe that the old scene of hookers and hustlers was more edifying than the current Guilianification[2], I was sucker-punched by the realization that I owed it to Katharine, to Columbia, and maybe even to myself, that I use this occasion to look back, take stock, sum up, and sit in judgment on what I have been doing here these thirty-six years. There would be no chance of my saying what I always say, for I had been careful all this time never to ask myself what I was doing, why I was doing it, and what it is good for. As Nietzsche said, when you look into the abyss, the abyss looks back—or was that Linda Tripp[3]?

As I crossed Fiftieth Street, site of my alma mater, Haaren High, which once led the city in broken windows, but has long since been razed, I was beanballed by the realization that I had committed myself to no less than a defense of literature and an apologia for teaching it. By the time I crossed Ninety-Third Street, where I had attended P.S. 93, which was built right after the Civil War, but which had gone with the snows of yesteryear, never mind Haaren High, I had a limp. And will someone please

---

[2] *Rudi Giuliani when mayor of New York transformed Times Square from a picturesque hangout for all kinds of hustlers into a monument to corporate America.*

[3] *Linda Tripp betrayed her friend Monica Lewinsky by exposing her affair with President Bill Clinton.*

tell me why they are pulling my past out from under me? But I was already formulating phrases in refutation of my businessman brother-in-law, who believes that my profession is at best frivolous, at worst a scam, and in between one more way of contributing to the delinquency of minors. He thereby allies himself with that old reprobate Plato, who banished poets from his Utopia.

Then let either one of them explain this: of the thousand human societies discovered by anthropology and archeology there is none, not one, known to be without a literature, oral or written—without, that is, tales, poems, sayings, myths, chants. Think of it: wherever there are humans, there is literature. It is therefore strictly scientific to say that literature is a species-specific behavioral trait. Literature is as definitively human as opposable thumbs, which enable us to grasp things, and rounded buttocks, which keep us upright (for starters),and it is an axiom of evolutionary biology that every species-specific physiological or behavioral trait is either adaptive or a by-product of an adaptation, as lower back pain is a by-product of bipedalism. For various reasons I prefer to think of literature as an adaptation, rather than as a pain in the tush, for of pains in the tush one can confidently say that we already have far too many.

I see justifications for that preference all around me. Everywhere I look, I see an obsessed humanity, telling, taking in, and talking about tales. It's not only a matter of novels, stories, comic books, comic strips, courtroom testimony, and sermons—in the February issue of *Brill's Content*[4], for example, I read that the "average amount of time that TV is viewed per household per

---

[4]Brill's Content, *a print magazine and website that covered the media, ceased publication in 2001*

day in the U.S." is seven hours and twenty-one minutes. Each day, for about as long as the average workday, that is, the tube is likely to be showing us morning and afternoon tales of buff girls seducing pretty boys and evening tales of Keystone families and cop tristesse. These tales are interrupted by shorter fantasies called commercials, some of which are graced by jingles, or poems without poetry, but still a kind of literature. When father comes home, he is likely to tell mother a tall tale of his hard day at the office, in return for which she will tell him a taller tale of her own hard day at the office, or a tale of her still harder day at home. The point is that when we want to relate an experience we do not break it into topics or categories and tick them off one, two, three, four—we arrange it into a narrative, perhaps because that's how to hook a listener, perhaps because we believe that what happens to us tells a story. In fact, it does not. Only humans tell stories or listen to them. "Fiction rescues history from its confusions," says Don DeLillo, and he's right. I will only add that in the best colleges and universities, including this one, the English Department is always one of the two or three biggest. Then there are all those other departments that teach literature in funny languages like French....

These instances are mere reminders of what you already know: by the time a human enters that zone of dementia we call adolescence, he or she is a supersaturated solution of tales, poems, performances. Now why is that, we may wonder. Part of the reason has got to be that adults indoctrinate the young through cautionary yarns, old saws, old wives' tales, tendentious gossip, bragging, autobiographical anecdotes, religious myths, and inspirational fables. But these only "take," because there preexists in the young a healthy appetite for fictions, the one good thing that does not diminish with age. Here is Charles Darwin writing as an old man:

> I have said that in one respect my mind has changed during the last twenty or thirty years. Up to the age of thirty, or beyond it, poetry of many kinds, such as the works of Milton, Gray, Byron, Wordsworth, Coleridge, and Shelley, gave me great pleasure, and even as a schoolboy I took intense delight in Shakespeare, especially in the historical plays. I have also said that pictures gave me considerable, and music very great, delight. But now for many years I cannot endure to read a line of poetry: I have tried lately to read Shakespeare, and found it so intolerably dull that it nauseated me. I have also almost lost any taste for pictures or music. Music generally sets me thinking too energetically on what I have been at work on, instead of giving me pleasure. I retain some taste for fine scenery, but it does not cause me the exquisite delight which it formerly did. On the other hand, novels which are works of the imagination, though not of a very high order, have been for years a wonderful relief and pleasure to me, and I often bless all novelists. A surprising number have been read aloud to me, and I like all if moderately good, and if they do not end unhappily—against which a law ought to be passed. A novel, according to my taste, does not come into the first class—unless it contains some person whom one can thoroughly love, and if it be a pretty woman all the better.

If I had to say why we have this appetite, or put differently, how literature is in a general way adaptive, I would say this: it stimulates us to do in our imaginations what we can't or won't do in the flesh but that makes life worth living.

In the same spirit of scientific objectivity that has governed all these remarks, however, I should mention those turncoat writers who in their own writing have depicted fiction as maladaptive, as leading people astray. The patron saints of such writers are Heloise and Abelard, who looked up from the book they were reading together to exchange kisses and you know what that can lead to. Abelard's punishment was castration; Heloise had to enter a nunnery, never again to taste the ambrosia of lovemaking, never, never, again to sip the nectar of sex.

Similarly, that old pedophile Dante Alighieri imagines himself descending to the second circle of hell, where souls are beaten, battered, and driven through the murky air by a ferocious storm that will never let up for a second, not through all eternity. The souls are those of "carnal sinners who subject reason to lust," we read. When Dante asks two of them how they got into this fix, Paolo and Francesca tell their story. They were together reading a book about Lancelot and Guinevere. After reading how that knight finally kissed that lady, Paolo kissed Francesca. "A Pandar was that book and he that wrote it," says Francesca; "that day we read in it no farther." It's enough to make Dante the character faint and Dante the author consign the lovers to the most exquisite torment an ingenious deity can devise. Dante! Thou shouldst be living at this hour. I'd tweak your nose for you—or send you to Washington.

And how can we forget Don Quixote? He read chivalric romances until "his wits were gone beyond repair," says Cervantes, whereupon the would-be knight jumped upon a sway-backed nag he dubbed Rocinante and went out to tilt at windmills. Such was his way of doing service to his Lady, a local farm girl he called Dulcinea, who, however, didn't know he existed. The Don thereby became the prototype of all male adolescents, which is probably the only kind of males there are.

Nor can we forget that old libertine Flaubert, whose Emma

Bovary, even during her school days in a convent, was never without a supply of romantic novels in her apron pockets: They were all about love, lovers, sweethearts, persecuted ladies fainting in lonely pavilions, postilions killed at every relay, horses ridden to death on every page, sombre forests, heartaches, rows, sobs, tears and kisses, little boat rides by moonlight, nightingales in shady groves, gentlemen brave as lions, gentle as lambs, virtuous as no one ever was, always well dressed, and weeping like fountains. Such reading moves Emma to cheat on her stick-in-the-mud husband with a jaded aristocrat, who ultimately disses her. She dies a ghastly death from arsenic poisoning administered by her own hand.

Neither should we forget that male equivalent of Emma Bovary, Conrad's Lord Jim. "After a course of light holiday literature," Jim's "vocation for the sea" declares itself:

> He saw himself saving people from sinking ships, cutting away masts in a hurricane, swimming through surf with a line; or as a lonely castaway, barefoot and half naked, walking on uncovered reefs in search of shellfish to stave off starvation. He confronted savages on tropical shores, quelled mutinies on the high seas, and in a small boat upon the ocean kept up the hearts of despairing men - always an example of devotion to duty, and as unflinching as a hero in a book.

Jim's reading takes his eye off the ball; it unreadies him for the actual crisis that occurs. He is like a batter all tense in expectation of a fast ball who is thrown a slow curve. The end result is the breakup of a native village, the death of his best friend, his own death at the hands of the friend's father, the raging despair of his young wife, and a serving of Conrad's high-protein ironies, soul-food for skeptics.

The infernoed spirits of Francesca, Quixote, Emma, and Jim, I hope, wept rueful tears of sympathy when poor Oscar Wilde's Dorian exclaimed "I've been poisoned by a book." The unnamed book, given to Dorian Gray by his mentor no less, teaches him new vices, novel depravities, and original sins. In the end, horrified by what a portrait reveals to him of his inner condition, he stabs it, thereby killing his conscience, thereby sending himself to join those rueful shades in that inflamed crevice of our brains set aside for fictional sinners.

From the careers of these lost souls I extract a lesson not so much of literature's power to lead us astray as of its sheer amoral power, for evil *or* good. Lincoln, after all, when introduced to Harriet Beecher Stowe, author of *Uncle Tom's Cabin*, said "So, you're the little lady who started the Civil War." In any case, from the perspectives of Flaubert and Conrad, and probably of Dante and Cervantes, what led their characters astray was not that they were readers, but that they read *schlock*, which is not what Dante and Cervantes, nor Flaubert and Conrad, thought *they* were writing. Not only did those poor sinners read schlock; they read it uncritically.

And I see, to my surprise, that I have come by a side entrance to a justification of my own existence and that of others like me. One of our jobs is to separate the schlock from the greats. If my fictional dupes had read the same schlock, but read it under critical guidance of one of my colleagues in the English Department (and a more critical gang of literary hitpersons is nowhere to be found), Abelard, Francesca, and Quixote, Emma, and Jim, would have been spared castration, madness, suicide, execution, damnation, and worst of all, chastity.

Because it is the custom nowadays for professors to begin

by confessing the sins they expose in literature, sins of racism, sexism, homophobia, class prejudice, ageism, knowism, and in general fellow-traveling with the oppressor—"situating" oneself it is called—because of all that, I will confess a certain fondness, a preference even, for characters who stray. For one thing, it is the sinful characters who best stimulate us to experience in our imaginations what we deny ourselves in the flesh. And if by morality we mean some public standard of behavior, we need frequent vacations from it, if only in the pleasure gardens of our minds. At the entrance to Rabelais's Abbey of Thelme is a sign that reads "Do What Thou Wilt." That invitation is the implied preface to all works of literature that are not a species of propaganda in drag. In any case, immoral works of literature, when properly read, do not lead us into immorality, or out of it for that matter, but show us what it is. And how to read properly is what professors of English teach, when they are not commissars in disguise.

But once you begin this confessing business, it is hard to stop. I will therefore confess further that I was myself irredeemably led astray during my twelfth and thirteenth years when I read thirty-nine books by Edgar Rice Burroughs, author of the Tarzan novels. My friend Keith and I spent hours in Central Park trying to swing from branch to branch, never realizing that the human shoulder is not designed for brachiation, nor human skin for the abrasions of bark. Nor did Jane ever show up looking to be rescued. Like Francesca and the others, like those many readers of Goethe's *Wilhelm Meister* who committed suicide, like the boy who after reading a Superman comic flew out of a second-story window right into traction at a nearby hospital, like these, Keith and I made the mistake of trying out in the flesh what is better left to the imagination.

But I do not want this orgy of confession to leave you with the idea that I believe literature is only good for imaginative indulgences. Our clever bipedal ancestors were quick to convert new adaptations to uses for which they could not have evolved. Our rounded bottoms, for example, which are unique among mammals, evolved to keep us upright, so far as they are firm, and to store fat, as far as they are flabby. But we also use them to cushion our bones when we sit on those hard office chairs before our computers, unknown to our ancestors, no matter how clever. Similarly, our opposable thumbs evolved so that we could grasp branches or throw the stones and bones that became tools, but we have learned how to use them for the pinching of rounded bottoms. So it is with works of literature, any one of which can cushion us against reality or help us get a grip on it, sometimes both at once. From the core function of stimulating us to experience in our imaginations what we can't or won't do in the flesh evolved numerous other functions of literature, all of which may be grouped in the category of equipment for living.

Let me backtrack a few cautious steps to clarify what I mean. We can safely assume that protohumans had a repertoire of gestures, postures, expressions, of grunts, groans, and whistles by which they could point out to fellow protohumans something in their environment that was perceptible to the senses, an anteater, say. With the acquisition of language, our protohuman ancestor—let's call him Slick—could move from pointing out something in his visible environment to pointing out something visible only to the inner eye, a plan to get that anteater, say. He could move from the grunt and gesture that signified "anteater" to a plan according to which he would make faces and thump his chest to distract the anteater while a conspecific—let's call him Ken—circled around to brain the anteater with his club.

Language became literature around the campfire that night when Slick, picking a shred of cooked anteater from his tooth, told how he warded off the anteater's evil eye by crossing his own eyes and touching the tip of his nose with the tip of his tongue, while Ken stumbled over a clump of poison sumac, nearly braining himself with his club in the process; how he felled the anteater with a single karate chop across its snout, while Ken rolled onto a patch of nettles; how all the way home he fought a rear-guard action against a pack of hyenas, each one the size of a rhinoceros, while Ken scratched himself. He embellished the facts in this outrageous manner in part to put down Ken, who still had seven teeth, three of them in front, and was therefore considered good-looking, but mainly to puff himself up in the eyes of his wives. He wanted to look good to his wives because he was in the grip of an evolutionary pressure to make his genes become fruitful and multiply. It is for reasons such as this that tellers of tales tell them.

But listeners do not necessarily make of tales what the teller had in mind. Wife Number One, for example, was making of Slick's tale a confirmation of her belief that a woman would have subdued the anteater without all that vainglorious fuss, that face making and chest thumping. She remembered the secret lore of women, which holds that an anteater can be put into a trance by a whiff of the perfume that wafts from behind the knees of a beautiful woman. She can then pounce on it and rip out its throat with her fangs, for Wife Number One was too mean to have lost any teeth. Wife Number Two missed the end of Slick's story, for she was already dreaming of how she would borrow Ken's club, so that if Slick pestered her that night by dropping his pants, she could brain him. Wife Number Three, and a very good wife she was, also missed the end of Slick's tale, for she was in a reverie of how she would find the anthill on which the anteater had met its demise, for she knew that Slick liked a stew made of left-over anteater to be spiced by formic acid. Little daughter, on the other hand, was telling herself a story of how if she had an anteater for a pet, she would cuddle it, hand feed it ants, and let it sleep on her feet, to keep them warm, for the Ice Age had not receded. And all the while, the foppish shaman, sitting by his antisocial campfire, supping on bean sprouts and tofu, was listening in, for Slick's voice was loud. Slick's tale evoked in the shaman a vision of an event from just after the beginning of all things, when a giant anteater snuffled all the protohumans up his snout. But the world's first shaman tickled the anteater's nose hairs with his feathered boa until it sneezed the people out. Ever after, protohumans were obliged to abide the demented ravings of their shaman.

The moral of this scientific reconstruction is as follows: before the inner eyes of their audiences story tellers affix to their tales their motto, which reads "This is the way it is"; but audiences supplant that motto with their own, which reads "Do what thou wilt." The professor of English who tries to impose a uniform response has forgotten that the function of a liberal education is to liberate students from all sorts of uniformities, especially those imposed by shamen, tribal taboos, and the *Zeitgeist* itself.

Just the same, not all audiences respond as variously as Slick's, which, after all, was of the kind we call "captive." It's a recurrent trait of humans, bless them, that when pushed one way, they go the other, as with drinking during Prohibition or with smoking among the young during the recent *Kulturkampf* against cigarettes. But outside the classroom, at least, we are free to choose fictions that stimulate our imaginations as we wilt.

What is more, a storyteller less self-involved than Slick

knows how to solicit the response he wants. Everything we mean by "form," for example, guides the reader or listener in one direction, at the same time that it rewards him with a payload of aesthetic pleasure for going along. The deployment of conventions and stock characters arouse familiar expectations that the listener or reader will want to see satisfied, preferably in an unexpected way. Felicitous phrasing puts the listener or reader into an accommodating mood. And finally, writers can devise fictions that satisfy the predictable needs that keep a group together rather than the unpredictable kinks that keep individuals apart, as when heartwarming stories of plucky women who turn domestic tragedy into personal triumph are aired opposite "Monday Night Football."

In a classic essay entitled "Literature as Equipment for Living" the critic Kenneth Burke gives us some instances of how literature helps recurrent types of people get by—or how it can help any of us get through recurrent types of discouraging situations. Burke's stroke of genius was to treat aphorisms as compact works of literature. As an aid to the consolation we seek in our imaginations because it is not available in actuality, for example, he cites the proverb "The wind in one's face makes one wise," something I've never noticed myself, by the way. He also cites "He is not poor that hath little, but he that desireth much"—although that strikes me as a proverb more likely to be said by someone who is not poor himself to someone who in fact is. The proverb "At length the fox is brought to the furrier" affords consolation to those who are not crafty, at the same time that it symbolically enacts vengeance against those who are. Again, the proverb "Straws show which way the wind blows" is good medicine for those who lack style, at the expense of lightweights who think that the latest fashion is the last word. And in the same way, the proverb "The sun is never worse for shining on a dunghill" is good medicine for jilted lovers. Among other things, the proverb "Eagles catch no flies" can confirm a high-flier in his belief that he need not concern himself with those low-fliers buzzing away their lives beneath him.

After his inventory, of which I have given you only a sample, Burke sums up. Proverbs and works of literature, which he describes as "proverbs writ large," should be considered

> Strategies for selecting enemies and allies, for socializing losses, for warding off evil eye, for purification, propitiation, and desanctification, consolation and vengeance, admonition and exhortation, implicit commands and instructions of one sort or another.

What Burke calls "proverbs writ large," poems, plays, and novels, however, are harder to pin down than proverbs writ small. There's all that paradox, irony, and ambiguity that the New Critics used to talk about. Further, how extended works of literature help groups or individuals survive is hard to make out because they are complicated by the contradictions that bedevil life outside of literature, by the "realism" that makes us trust the writer. The adaptive function of James Joyce's *Ulysses*, for example, the most complicated and realistic novel ever written, is to help us accept life with "equanimity," but only after Joyce has shown us how much of life is hard to accept. For all that, there is one extended form of literature that is fairly clear of paradox, irony, and ambiguity; it therefore goes down as easily as ice cream uncontaminated by chunks of Oreos or other detritus. I am talking about popular fiction, also known as craft fiction or genre fiction or formula fiction.

I should explain that by "popular" I do not mean bestselling. I mean a work devised ideally to equip a whole populace or at least a significant subgroup within it. I mean works that ideally cut across boundaries of class, education, occupation or gender, although in modern industrial societies they are hard to come by. I mean our equivalent to the tales told again and again around the cave fire, before the Neolithic revolution ruined everything. I mean the sort of thing initially devised by Mary Shelley, Edgar Allen Poe, James Fenimore Cooper, John Cleland (author of *Fanny Hill*), Charlotte Bronte, Arthur Conan Doyle, H. G. Wells, Owen Wister, and Dashiell Hammett. I mean not the sort of thing chosen for us to read by teachers, but the sort of thing we choose to read outside the classroom. I mean westerns, whodunits, science fiction, adventure yarns, romances, spookeroos, pornography, and the kind of melodramas known in the trade as "blockbusters."

To ask how such fictions help us get by, as with all adaptations, is to ask what forces shaped them, what selection pressures made them the way they are. Because for a long time now, the more immediate human environment has been social rather than natural, popular fictions are shaped by pressures, by needs and desires, arising out of social situations, rather than by climate and geography, by prey and predators, although these needs and desires may indeed also have a biological substratum. Every plot formula, every convention of setting and incident, every stock character, is shaped by the social-psychological equivalent of the natural selective pressures that put beaks on birds and pouches on kangaroos. In that respect they are unlike the art novel, the author of which can make his bones by whacking a convention. What works in a popular fiction is preserved in its successors; what doesn't work becomes extinct. Popular fictions evolve by the small mutations of craftsmen rather than through the catastrophic transformations wrought by the meteoric impact of genius. Sometimes a change in the climate of opinion can cause a popular form to die out or to survive only in a shrinking backwater, as with the western, although Zane Grey was once the world's most popular novelist, although he was the number one best-selling author for nearly ten years straight following World War I.

It doesn't take a full professor in a great Ivy League institution to separate out the adaptive component of your ordinary blockbuster, for example. Think of what Jacqueline Susann's *Valley of the Dolls*, published in 1966, when everyone under thirty was breaking out of the down dudgeon of the fifties, could have done for the middle-aged suburban frump. On the one hand, she could experience in her imagination the glamorous lives of the kind of gorgeous creatures she has read about in gossip columns and glossy magazines; on the other hand she could be reconciled to her condition by the revelation that these same gorgeous creatures are in fact junkies, lushes, lesbians, and suicides-about-to-happen. Similarly, Judith Krantz's *Scruples*, which last time I looked, was world-wide the best-selling paperback ever, satiates in the imagination every sort of greed produced by a consumption-oriented economy. The heroine winds up with not only a closet full of designer dresses, but a whole boutique.

The classic whodunit, as written by Agatha Christie say, is more complicated, or, let us say, more over-determined. But surely there is solace in such of its operative fantasies as that all mysteries have rational solutions; that guilt is strictly individual rather than social; that an outsider is the one whodunit. More specifically, Christie's fictions satisfy, but not in the flesh, longings for prophylaxis against bounders, climbers, and the lower classes; for imaginative indulgence in criminal aggression against members of one's own domestic circle; for relief from guilt for that indulgence and from an anxiety of being found out; for a detective, a stand-in for God the Father and all the other fathers we murdered and murder but want around to assure us that he did not die for *our* sins; for someone to restore the order we desire to destroy. My surmise is that people who obsessively read detective stories want to kill someone—and who doesn't?—but want the other guy to be found guilty. They are also confirmed in their refusal or inability to act on that desire by the demonstration that crime does not pay. People who don't read whodunits at all, I would guess, are too afraid of their impulses to indulge in them, even imaginatively.

But even the tolerant listener who has provisionally gone along with me this far may well be thinking "What about the spookeroo?" What good does it do us to be scared by things that don't exist, such as werewolves and vampires? And certainly the popular genre most condescended to is the chiller. People read horror fiction as they used to read pornography, on the sly. Reviewers with intellectual pretensions titter in print. Academic critics distance themselves with donnish humor and ponderous scholarship. The prevailing tone of the scant discourse about horror fiction is an amused derision that cuts both ways—at the chiller, for being what it is, and at the discourser, for having an interest in it. And yet recent critics, some of them very highbrow, have worked at tidying up overlapping concepts such as the grotesque, the uncanny, and the fantastic. But what we mean when we use the word "horror" remains unclear.

One explanation may lie in certain oddities about the emotion of horror, if an emotion is what it is. Horror, to cite one oddity, is typically a response to something that is not there.

Typically, that is, it attends such things as nightmares, phobias, art and literature, movies, hallucinations, delusions. It attends apparitions of the supernatural, of course, but for me the whole realm of the supernatural is a delusion, alas—although the horror is real. Horror can be distinguished from terror, which is sudden fright in the presence of a material cause, a charging lion, say. Material threats can be dissipated by material causes, a well-placed shot from a .450 Nitro Express, say. The frights of nightmares, daymares, and nightmarish literature cannot by dissipated by a bullet, unless the bullet is silver, unless it is invested with magical, that is delusory, properties.

Phobias at first glance seem to have material causes. But if you have a phobia of earmuffs or peaches, of toadstools or dripping faucets, of dirt on your hands or red-haired men, it is because they remind you of what horrifies you, and not because of what materially they are. Situations that should theoretically produce terror, such as premature burial or shrinking rooms, can turn horrifying if you invest them with psychological meaning, as Poe did.

A second oddity of horror, as distinct from terror or disgust, is that what it evokes is frequently as attractive as it is repulsive; there is as much fascination as dread. The apparitions of horror are attractive because they represent wishes—they do what we want to do or want to have done—but they are dreadful because the wishes are taboo. In that respect the vampire baring his teeth for a kiss is exemplary. Ernest Jones remarked that "morbid dread always signifies repressed sexual wishes," and he might be right. But in some of the classic tales of horror, some of those by Poe and Le Fanu and M. R. James, for example, the sexual wishes, if there at all, are buried so deep that I for one can't find them. The more proximate source of the horror of horror fiction boils down to threats and promises of madness, mutilation, and death. These things are fearful in themselves, but in horror fiction, as in our fantasy lives, there is a special *frisson* about them, for they feel like punishments for sin. Dracula will not come into your house unless you invite him. If you do he rewards you with the kiss of death that is your punishment for inviting it. If his victims seem innocent, it is because they don't, won't, know their own minds.

Tales of mild-mannered men changing to ravening wolves, for example, or timid and lovelorn ventriloquists controlled by their raunchy dummies, of virtuous Jekylls undone by vicious Hydes, of virginal maids and respectable housewives possessed by malicious demons, of twins, one good, one evil (but which is which?), of high-minded doctors like Victor Frankenstein and their low-minded monsters, all look to me like parables of dissociation: the ethical self gives in, loses control to a secret sharer. He goes after what the ethical self doesn't want to know it wants. Looked at from the other side, the ethical self, in an attempt at exorcism, separates off a portion of the personality it no longer wants to live with.

We are now ready to address the question of what horror is good for. We can make the plausible assumption that our emotions were once good for something, that they helped us survive. My guess is that as terror evolved as the emotional concomitant to a material danger to life and limb, horror evolved as the emotional concomitant to the breaking of a taboo. The emotion of horror, then, would be a signal that we are indulging actually or imaginatively in something we have forbidden ourselves in compliance with an internalized group prohibition. The bodily weakness, sense of suffocation, and inability to move, prevent us from indulging ourselves further.

Thinking big, we can suggest a social function for horror

fiction. On the one hand, it stimulates imaginative indulgence in activities we forbid ourselves in the flesh. To that extent the chiller is morally subversive. On the other hand, the indulgence is depicted as monstrous, and the monsters who do all the indulging are finally defanged by the good guy or nice girl or sacrificial hero. Other things being equal, the composer of chillers who performs the social function best, Stephen King for example, will be one whose conscious values coincide with those of the group, whose phobias are also taboo—with the understanding that where there are taboos, there is an itch to violate them. The violation arouses a compulsion to restore them.

I have chosen for my example a passage from *The Vampyre of Moura* by Virginia Coffman, a specialist in gothic romances. As in *Jane Eyre*, which established the form, and as in *Rebecca*, the classic redo, it tells the story of how a woman of low social status, in this case a housekeeper, comes to a great house that is the visible sign of the power and prestige of its master, in this case one Istvan Stavko. One night the damn fool wanders through the house—in a movie she would be wearing a diaphanous nightgown—and blunders into a room full of dazzling lights that make her weak in the knees:

> A pair of hands lifted me to my feet while I shrank away, trying to scream, to cry for help, unable to utter any but muted sounds. The hideous thing was that I could feel myself surrender to the mesmerizing influences of those dazzling jewel lights.
>
> Within the aura of those lights, I felt my wits and my will grow numb. A face shimmered as if seen through many facets of the jewel lights and for an instant I thought it was our nemesis, the evil-eyed coachman, but then, the features rearranged and became the austere, high-boned face of Istvan

Stavko. I was conscious of the faint repulsion I always felt at his close proximity, the remembrance of a creature nearly a century old; yet the man I saw, tantalizingly, through jewel prisms, was barely above middle age. In my present state, lulled to a great calm, I remember thinking, with his head so close above mine, that he was about to kiss me and that I would welcome that kiss. It had never been so during my previous encounters with him. Why had I changed?

His deeply curved lips, which I had found repulsive, were moist and sensuous in the prism light as he bowed his head over me and those lips touched, feather-light upon my throat. A trembling pervaded my flesh. My limbs were too weak to hold me, but I was gripped about the waist in a hard-boned, painful hold, and always there were those thickened lips at my throat. The dazzling prism lights dulled before my eyes and blurred, too, the single stab of pain where my throat was pierced by this terrible being who had made himself my master. The loss of my own will was perhaps the worst thing of all. My fingers were still frozen about the shaft of the carving knife and yet my will to use it was gone. A part of my consciousness remembered that I must scream, that possibly the sounds would reverberate through these echo-haunted passages.

From far away I heard someone moan and wondered if it was I. By exerting all the reserves I possessed, I tried to draw away, to free myself of this frightful nightmare, but I was still subdued by the blinding aura of crystal prisms, and the singular power of this creature who seemed composed of many terrors.

Voices shimmered as if under water, and in a language uncomprehensible. Gradually, with the draining of strength and will and blood, came a ghastly peace, as a sense of weakness that must be like dying.

I shall not intrude on your imaginative indulgences so far as to analyze this passage; nor will I look around for the source of that heavy breathing I hear. I will only mention that Istvan Stavko, in his power relations with the heroine, in his authority over the household, in his stern and forbidding but erotic aspect, in his beaky nose and deep-set eyes, is to the heroine as Papa is to a young girl looking up at him.

I shall conclude not with another piece of schlock, but with a poem by Dylan Thomas. The poem is "The Hunchback in the Park," and its subject is what it is about writers that make them write:

> The hunchback in the park
> A solitary mister
> Propped between trees and water
> From the opening of the garden lock
> That lets the trees and water enter
> Until the Sunday sombre bell at dark
>
> Eating bread from a newspaper
> Drinking water from the chained cup
> That the children filled with gravel
> In the fountain basin where I sailed my ship
> Slept at night in a dog kennel
> But nobody chained him up.
>
> Like the park birds he came early
> Like the water he sat down
> And Mister they called Hey mister
> The truant boys from the town
> Running when he heard them clearly
> On out of sound

Past lake and rockery
Laughing when he shook his paper
Hunchbacked in mockery
Through the loud zoo of the willow groves
Dodging the park keeper
With his stick that picked up leaves.

And the old dog sleeper
Alone between nurses and swans
While the boys among willows
Made the tigers jump out of their eyes
To roar on the rockery stones

And the groves were blue with sailors

Made all day until bell time
A woman figure without fault
Straight as a young elm
Straight and tall from his crooked bones
That she might stand in the night
After the locks and chains

All night in the unmade park
After the railings and shrubberies
The birds the grass the trees the lake
And the wild boys innocent as strawberries
Had followed the hunchback
To his kennel in the dark.

From his crooked bones the hunchback makes a woman figure without fault, an object of desire straight as a young elm. So out of deficiency, deprivation, a sense of exclusion, and impossible longings writers write these shapely and compensatory poems, plays, and novels. So out of their own crooked bones readers read.

To sum up: Telling and taking in stories is a species-specific behavioral trait. It is adaptive. It helps us to get by long enough for our genes to become fruitful and multiply—or until we can become grandparents and baby-sit with the youngest custodians of those genes while our lazy, loafing sons and daughters go out on the town. The function of a professor of literature is to outfit his students with adaptive literature and to teach them how to recognize the maladaptive kind. From this admittedly self-serving demonstration I conclude that what I have been doing these last forty years at Columbia was worth doing.

THE LIBERAL EDUCATION FRONT

Remarks in acceptance of a Great Teacher's Award from the Society of Columbia Graduates, 1997.

Alumni, colleagues, students, friends, fellow learners all, I very much appreciate your coming here tonight, when you could easily be doing something that doesn't require a necktie or tight shoes. I especially want to thank the Society of Columbia Graduates for justifying my existence, for those of us whose work produces no tangible social good often feel a need to be justified. In that respect we are unlike people whose work it is to mislead juries or manufacture navel rings or think up new recipes for tofu. The fact is, I'd rather have this award than the Nobel Prize…except for the money. But then anyone who becomes a professor for the money is like the guy who studied ornithology in the hopes of learning how to lay a golden egg.

The fear of laying a different kind of egg is the one shadow hanging over my gratitude. After all, you have the right to expect that someone you have just certified as a great teacher will reciprocate with great words about what makes a great teacher great. As luck would have it, I have long pondered that question. Twenty years ago, for example, I asked a distinguished behaviorist from a teachers' college—his name was Raskolnikov, as I recall—what of all that goes on in teachers' colleges is convertible to the classroom, what of all he did was of practical use to the practicing teacher. He looked around to make sure no one was listening in, leaned forward, his fevered brow to my fevered brow, and began to jab me in the chest with his forefinger by way of emphasizing every word: "When the room is hot," he said, "open the window; when the room is cold, close the window." Then he abruptly turned and went for another vodka. That is the extent, so far, of my certain knowledge about teaching, although even I realize there must be more to it than that.

It probably helps, for instance, if the teacher knows what he is talking about, if he comes to class primed with out-of-the-way information, dagger definitions, and telling instances. But you can't be sure. Every experienced teacher can remember days when he came to class hungover, bleary-eyed, grumpy, and totally unprepared. Out of desperation, out of left field, he croaks some sonorous banality: "A human is not a bird," he might say; "the human is not born with all the knowledge he needs to get by. Therefore he needs literature, which is equipment for living." Before you are finished, if you are lucky enough to be teaching at Columbia, some wiseacre looking to straighten you out, will already have raised his hand. Then a second student will raise his hand looking to straighten out the first. Another will point out that Aristotle defined the human as a featherless biped. Still another will point out that animals are human too.

And so it goes, until out of the collision of partial truths from personal points of view at all angles to each other something relatively impartial and impersonal emerges, a truth about the relations between literature and life that for the moment we can all abide. In the process the students will give the teacher a class for which he can only be grateful—but only because he was too out of it to get in their way.

The funforall I have just described was called dialectic by Socrates, the patron saint of liberal educators. I do not mean that Socrates was that figure of fun, that recent object of derision and scorn, a liberal, nor necessarily are his successors. I mean that our goal is liberation. Our goal is to free the student from provincial bias, the historical fix, otherwise known as ideology, and private obsession. The method is to pound his bent against others until it begins to straighten out, to expose his point of view to as many others as apply. Truth is a hole, but you can only begin to see what is at the bottom of it from the near truths that approach it at a tangent.

And dialectical liberalism, when it works, can also purge the student of that undigested bolus of experience, observation, and learning that lies sodden and unmoving at the bottom of his mind, as that dinner you had at a German restaurant lies in your stomach. Whatever of this bolus the teacher gets the student to release into words becomes conscious and therefore manageable, becomes susceptible to criticism and self-analysis. The student can select from what he is what he wants to be. His belief system, his character even, becomes not a fate, but a choice.

What ignites this process is a mystery. My guess is that it goes off most naturally and frequently when the teacher has a feeling for his students, when he establishes what for want of better words we might call an erotic bond. I don't mean anything sexual: There are times when using a student's first name or shaking a student's hand is going far too far. But I do mean that the teacher wants to seduce his students into requiting his designs on them. I do mean that he wants to caress their minds with ideas that will arouse them to respond with ideas as stimulating as his own. I do mean that he will preen, strut, do cartwheels to get at them, in the hopes that they will show off their own stuff on exams and papers. I mean that he will look for the best in them, so that the reflections of themselves they see in his eyes will be something they want to live up to—as the dummy whose wife thinks he is all-knowing because he resembles her father will sometimes smarten up in response.

The problem, as someone who taught at four other institutions before he came to Columbia can tell you, is that not all students are equally loveable—or responsive. And having said that, I realize that by a roundabout way I have come to a conclusion about what makes for great teaching. Great teachers are made by great students. And great students are what have made these thirty-four years of teaching at Columbia such great fun. To those of you out there who are students and former students I therefore owe you double thanks. Thank you, thank YOU.

A PARABLE OF THE PEOPLE

From *Sex and Violence: A Love Story* by George Stade, (New York: Turtle Point Press, 2005).

Settle down chillen, while I tell you a story, a free improvisation on changes recorded by the anthropologist Lauriston Sharp. There once lived in western Australia a tribe that called itself "The People," so as to distinguish themselves from other people, whom they called "The Others." The People were divided into three, the Flaker clan in the north, the Staker clan in the south, the Maker clan in between. Before they collided with Europeans, as with a wrecking ball, the People had lived the same way for thousands of years, far as we can tell, for the People preferred to reinvent their past as needed, which is harder to do (unless you are a New Historicist) when it is written down.

Sure it is, in any case, that they had side-stepped the tedium of farming, the bother of domestic animals, the crowded and craven despotism of Neolithic culture. The People hunted and fished and gathered and raided The Others, and a very good time it was.

For the People, as you can well imagine, did not suffer from ontological insecurity, nor from anomie, accidie, abulia, bulimia, acid reflux, or gender role confusion. Serial killers were unknown. The People knew who they were and what to do and how to do it, there being no other way but theirs, for they were the People. But just to make sure, the social space was thick with instruction, with precept and example, with parable and saying, with cautionary tale and taboo, all of it dramatized in ritual, mimed in dance, chanted in hymns, and painted on pots, while the exacting eyes of the totemic powers, of tutelary ghosts and ancestral spirits, the wakeful dead, looked on, looked on, and the wakeful dead looked on. Fables of origin and myths of law-dropping heroes were devised, the present casting a shadow over the past, to show that as it was in the beginning is now and ever shall be, world without end, man. Barring ecological disaster, and the People had no memory of one, change, if it occurred at all, was gradual, unnoticed, untraumatic, a breeze.

The People had no chiefs: quotidian problems, the only kind they had, were calmly debated by a council of drunken elders, not because old men are wise, but because they are no good for anything else. The elders would talk and talk, for however long it took, until they all agreed upon a solution, the rare holdout thereby exposing himself as infested by a demon and therefore in for an exorcism, a particularly painful type of purge, the idea being that evil spirits entered you from below, but enough of that. *Enough of that.* There were no malcontents, or if there were, they learned to grin and bear it or how to act out their malcontent through one of the traditional roles designed to turn malcontent into spectacle.

Shamans, for example, were deferred to in person, as capable of infesting you with a demon, but derided behind their backs, as hysterics and sissies. Berserkers, however, were spoken of in tones of affrighted respect, as making manifest the awful power of the dingo-demon that possessed them.

The People, in short, were altogether all together. Every component of their culture was to every other, to paraphrase

William Coleridge, as form is to content in a poem. (He meant, of course, a pre-Modernist poem, not knowing any other kind.) Whatever was religious was also political; whatever was political was also economic; whatever was economic was also domestic; whatever was domestic was also educational; whatever was educational was also medical; whatever was medical was also magical; whatever was magical was also artful; whatever was artful was also practical; whatever was practical was also religious, down to the way you killed your enemy or dressed out a kangaroo or scarred your cheeks or cuddled with your spouse. *Coitus a tergo*, for instance, and any other kind was considered perverse, was religious in that it imitated the demiurge (a large bat), who in that position quickened Mother Earth (an immense kangaroo) into life; it was military in that the People's word for lovemaking derived from an archaic stem that meant "to cleave your enemy with an axe"; it was political in that it recapitulated the relations between the sexes, the man up, the woman down, as God intended; it was economic in that it was thought to ensure conception, and in those halcyon days children were considered an asset; it was a form of art in that it had to be enacted with a certain style and between ritual preliminaries and sequelae, which I will not go into here. What above all held the people together, believe it or not, was a short-handled axe called the Kilakang.

Heads for the Kilakang were made by the Flaker clan up north, whose turf was flinty. The Flakers were skilled at picking out likely chunks of flint, at polishing them, at chipping off flakes until the finished product was sharp and shapely, like an intelligent dancer. Handles for the Kilakang were gathered by the Staker clan down south, whose turf was swampy. The Stakers were skilled at searching out a kind of swamp ash, the wood of which is tough and straight-grained, in harvesting, peeling, curing, and storing the ash stakes, turning woods into goods. Heads and handles for the Kilakang were brought together by the Maker clan in the industrious midlands, whose turf was coniferous. The Makers were skilled at extracting and heating spruce gum, at cutting and treating strips of pine bark, for the bond, one capable of withstanding the most exuberant of chops. But that was not the end of it, not by a long shot, for the owner of a new Kilakang, his most valuable possession, unless he already had others, would color and carve designs all over it, some common to the People, some restricted to his clan, some special to his totem, some contrived by his family, some peculiar to himself. The finished Kilakang, you might say, was synecdoche for the People as a whole: it summed them up in shorthand. The finished Kilakang was also a thing of beauty, let me tell you, to which museums throughout Australia will testify.

Just the same, a strict morality governed their use, for the People had not reached that stage at which the good and the beautiful become incompatible, never to be reconciled, never, never to be together again. Only an initiated male could own a Kilakang; only an initiated male could make one, or any part of one; only a Kilakang could be used as a tool to make a Kilakang, for the People lacked the knack of making sacred wine out of secular water. A man's prestige and status were determined by the quantity and quality of his Kilakangs, even more than by the quantity and quality of his wives, although the two were related: no self-respecting woman would marry a Kilakangless man; but her self-respect depended upon her dad being able to spring two or three of them for a dowry. Women, who did all the work, had to borrow Kilakangs from their husbands; and they had to return them at night, as issued, or receive a drubbing, administered, we are told, more for the sake of appearances than to give pain or receive pleasure. Any boy wanting to practice the manly arts had to borrow a Kilakang from an initiated male relative; and he had to return it too, or receive a ragging, more painful than any drubbing, so we are told.

At his initiation ceremony, the post-pubertal male was stripped naked, made woozy with fermented honey, scarred (lines radiating from the mouth, like cat's whiskers), dragged through a tunnel representing the earth-kangaroo's womb, wrapped in swaddling clouts, given his first Kilakang, and told how at the beginning of things the bat demiurge slit open the earth-kangaroo's belly with a Kilakang. He then extracted the first man, told him to go up north and gather flints; extracted the second man and told him to go south and gather stakes; extracted the third man and told him to stay put, dammit. All the while drunken elders whirled Kilakangs tied to lengths of braided bark overhead. The resulting noise was described to the women, who were barred from the ceremony, but who braided the bark, as that of tutelary ghosts moaning mysteries. We are told that the women did not laugh at this pious fraud in the presence of the men.

After nine months, the initiate, now a man, could carry a Kilakang on the raid or hunt; he could use it to gather wild honey or scar a cheek or perform a rite of exorcism, for which activities the heads and handles of Kilakangs were the only permitted instruments. He could go on business trips to other clans, find himself some trading partners, who would become closer to him than parent or sibling or wife or child, closer than wife or child, wife or child. He could wheel and deal during the four great yearly festivals at which the clans gathered, to drink fermented honey, to arrange marriages, above all to trade heads, handles and whole Kilakangs. These partnerships, these exogamous marriages, these festivals, all dependent on the Kilakang, are what kept the clans from trying to exterminate each other. And so the uniform centuries accumulated, like rain in a roadside bottle—

Until missionaries from England arrived. They set up camp, three huts with tin roofs, in Maker turf, right next to the sacred grove, the bosky cleft in the earth-kangaroo's belly from which all living things were expelled, mewling, gasping, chirping, blinking at the light, finding their legs, swimming downstream to the ocean, flapping their fledging wings. These missionaries, who were as shrewd as they were naïve, saw immediately what the Kilakang was to the People. They ordered crates of mass-produced hatchets from Manchester. They then gave these hatchets to the People as bribes to attend services. The old men held out, but the young men, who at first derided Jesus as an hysteric and a sissy, wanted those hatchets. But even the young men were horrified when the missionaries, beaming with righteousness behind their wire-rimmed glasses, handed out hatchets directly to women and children. Soon these earnest innocents were traveling north and south, accompanied by troops with repeating rifles, to bribe the Flakers and Stakers. What was the result of all this benevolence? Things fell apart entirely.

Hatchets and Jesus and repeating rifles were just too much evidence that the People's way of being human was not the only way, nor even the most auspicious. The myths and beliefs of the People, balanced on the edge of a Kilakang, devolved into mere fictions, suspended over the void. Those precepts and parables and sayings, that elaborate morality of the Kilakang, received wisdom of any kind, what does it all amount to, anyway? A swindle perpetrated and perpetuated by the old boys to keep themselves in fermented honey and the rest of us in line. The dances and hymns and paintings on pots demystified themselves into mere décor. The components of the People's culture became not only distinguishable, but separable, a jumble of juxtapositions, like the shore after a storm. The past no longer justified the present; the present no longer stabilized the past; both became unknowable. They changed from day to day, like everything else. The totemic powers and tutelary ghosts and ancestral spirits turned into vampires. Women no longer laughed only behind their husbands' backs. Nor was any woman cowed by cautionary tales of how vampires kissed erring women into monsters of appetite who sucked the life out of husbands and children. She rather hoped she'd meet one. Parricide became a problem.

The People forgot how to carve and color Kilakangs or where to look for raw materials. Trading partners became cutthroat rivals. Trading festivals became drunken brawls. Initiation rites went out of style. So did exogamy. But the fashionable set began to scar both sets of cheeks. The demimonde underwent exorcisms just for the fun of it. Even respectable couples experimented with the missionary position and other perversions. For the first time ever, some of the People got fat. Malcontents began to pop up all over. Many people no longer deferred to shamans; worse, others began to take them seriously. The elders no longer could agree. Strongmen rose to replace them. They led their followers in raids not against The Others, but against their fraternal clans, as the missionaries wrung their hands. To the extent that reality is a social construct, it collapsed. To the extent that the self is a social product, it dissolved. The People had become modernists. . .like us.

And there you have my story. I hope it got to you, for that is above all what a storyteller wants, to get it on with his listeners, if you know what I mean. The next thing he wants is that his listeners apply his stories to their lives, for that is why we have stories, to apply them. He does not want interpreters, for to appropriate is not to apply. My claim is the storyteller's claim, that his story applies. The Parable of the People, so I claim, applies to that modernism with a small "m" that has overtaken many people at many times, in many places, ever since the shy Neanderthal was overtaken by the berserker Cro-Magnon. But it also applies to that big-bang Modernism, with a capital "M," that began going off in *fin de siècle* Europe, Britain, and North America. That Modernism, my friends, the Modernism that knows itself for what it is, the modernism that swallows up all the others, has yet to reach its boundaries in time or space. It is still happening here, there, everywhere, to you and to me, which is why the best of us lack conviction and the worst are full of passionate intensity.

SNOT, NAVEL-FLUFF, TOE-JAM, AND THE UNCENSORED BODY OF *ULYSSES*

First published as "Trilling and *Ulysses*" in the *Partisan Review*, Vol. LIX, No. 2.

Forty-five years ago, shortly after I began teaching at Columbia, Lionel Trilling, with his exacting sense of the obligations that rode on his fame, walked into the office in Hamilton Hall that I shared with three other instructors, introduced himself, and sat down, thus throwing me into that condition of frozen panic with which the wildebeest faces a lion, for that's what we juniors called Lionel Trilling, "the lion." And where my office-mates were, now that I needed them to absorb some of Trilling's armor-piercing, blue-eyed gaze, I can't remember. In a fruitless attempt to put me at my ease, Trilling offered me a cigarette, for in those days even smart people smoked, and asked me how I liked teaching Humanities A.

We agreed that Thucydides was a very smart man; and then, desperately rummaging around in my forebrain for something, anything, worth saying, I added that the course ought properly to conclude with Joyce's *Ulysses*, a book that both disestablished and salvaged everything that went before. I gather that you think *Ulysses* is a good novel, said Trilling. His tone was dry. The best ever written, I said, although I had by no means read them all.

What's good about it? asked Trilling. Now that was a stumper, for like Joyce, and maybe Trilling, I believed two things about value judgments: 1) that you couldn't help making them, and 2) that you couldn't in the end support them, for value judgments, to quote Joyce, were irremovably "founded, like the world, macro and microcosm, upon the void." So I opened my word-hoard to some commonplaces about the novel's stylistic innovations. Maybe, said Trilling, getting up, grinding out his cigarette. You'll remember, he said, moving toward the door, that at the end of his day, Leopold Bloom removes his shoe, sees his big toe poking through a hole in his sock, breaks off a piece of the nail, brings it to his nose, and smells it—"with satisfaction." That's what's really new—and good—about *Ulysses*, said Trilling, and he walked out the door.

Squelched as I was, I could still see that Trilling, like Leopold Bloom, had put his finger on something. For starters, he was right at least in the trivial sense that Bloom was the first character in fiction to sniff his toe-jam. I say this with confidence, although I still have not read all the novels. It is true, of course, that many of the body's waste and by-products had appeared in earlier literature, usually in sermons and satires, usually for the purpose of shaming us out of our congenital narcissism and self-regard. But the remarkable, and original, quality of the passage in *Ulysses* is its lack of emphasis, the absence of either sermonizing heat or satirical exaggeration, of either shame or shamelessness. There's a smile, but it is tolerant. Bloom does what he does because had he lived in the world rather than in Joyce's words that is what he would have done, because although no one had done it before in fiction, many of us have done something like it in life.

And Bloom does it as he does other things, as he loves his daughter, sorrows over his dead son, performs acts of charity, writes doggerel, ponders the structure of the cosmos. He does it, that is to say, naturally, because it is in his nature, because it is as natural for humans to produce toe-jam and smell it as it is to produce children and love them, produce poems and admire them, produce cosmologies and crouch under them. And Joyce has Bloom do it because to deny toe-jam is to move toward a denial of the source of love, poetry, and grand ideas—the human body. That denial would make love, poetry, and thought unnatural or supernatural, which amounts to the same thing, would make them the products of extraordinary efforts of the spirit, rather than of ordinary flesh. The censored body, in sum, is as alienated from its products as in the Marxist scheme a worker is alienated from the products of his labor.

Such, I take it, was part of Trilling's meaning, for any concrete instance has more potential meaning in it than is actual in the commentaries that bury it. Trilling, let's say, cited Bloom's toe-jam as a kind of synecdoche, a part for the whole. As there, so elsewhere in the novel, so in all. those passages in which characters pick their noses, probe their navels, pass menstrual blood, vomit, urinate, defecate, expectorate, eructate, ejaculate, and flatulate. Take, for example, the first of them, the episode in which Stephen Dedalus, Joyce's portrait of himself as a young man, walks along Sandymount Strand.

After trying to fix the watery flux of experience in words, Stephen watches a dog lift his leg. "The simple pleasures of the poor" he thinks. And then, out of his old obsessions and immediate sensations a poem comes to him, a vampirish love poem "Here. Put a pin in the chap, will you?" he thinks, and he leans out over a table of rock to write it down. But soon the "greengoldenly" flow of the seawater moves his "poor dogsbody," as Buck Mulligan calls it, to the simple pleasures of the poor. In the following passage from Stephen's stream of consciousness, sea water, water of another kidney, and watery words flow together:

> Better get this job over quick. Listen: a fourworded wavespeech: seesoo, hrss, rsseiss, oos.... In cups of rock it slops: flop, clap, slop; bounded in barrels. And, spent, its speech ceases. It flows purling, widely flowing, floating foampool, flower unfurling.

But Stephen's fit of creativity has not yet run its course. He searches in his pockets for a handkerchief as a minute before he had searched them for paper on which to write his poem—only to remember that earlier in that day, Buck Mulligan had taken it to wipe his razor. "That bard's noserag!" Mulligan had said: "A new colour for our Irish poets: snotgreen." And turning to Dublin bay, he describes the sea as "a great sweet mother" "the snotgreen, the scrotumtightening sea," his improvement on Homer's epithet, "the winedark sea." So now, Stephen Dedalus, Irish poet, all at sea, produces Irish art: "He laid the dry snot picked from his nostril on a ledge of rock, carefully," Joyce writes, and we can hope that the ledge is the same one on which Stephen wrote his poem, another bodily product, and like the urine, another emission of his substance.

The effect of such passages, as they accumulate, is multiple. On the one hand, Irish culture is naturalized: it's the color of the sea and Stephen's snot. On the other hand, the sea is acculturated: it's the color of Irish art, and it stands to Ireland as the Mediterranean stood to ancient Greece. Likewise, Stephen's snot is at once acculturated and naturalized: it's the color of Irish art and the sea. But for Joyce, the body comes first: art, words, culture, and our conception of the sea come out of the body.

In this respect, Joyce is unlike our hegemonic Foucaultistical, Lacanite, and Derridadist culture critics, for whom the body is constructed by culture and its discourses. When Frank Budgeon protested against Joyce's corporeal emphasis—"But the minds, the thoughts of the characters," he said—Joyce replied "if they had no body they would have no mind." To uncensor the body, therefore, is to demystify culture, a job that more than ever needs doing.

The equation between words and Irish culture, on the one hand, and the body's by-products, on the other, is developed throughout the novel—in the next episode, for example, the first given over to Leopold Bloom. As Bloom sits at stool, he reads a story entitled "Matcham's Masterstroke," the "prize tidbit" of this issue of *Tidbits* magazine. Finishing both with satisfaction, Bloom wipes himself with "Matcham's Masterstroke." And later in the day, Bloom walks out of the Ormond Bar, inside which Dublin layabouts are singing lugubriously, and feels gas burbling inside him, generated, he supposes, from a glass of burgundy he had drunk. He passes a shop window on display in which is a portrait of the Irish hero Robert Emmet and his famous last words: "When my country takes her place among the nations of the earth then and not till then, let my epitaph be written. I have done." As Bloom reads the words, he makes some music of his own:

> *When my country takes her place among.*
> Prrprr.
> Must be the bur
> Eff! Oo. Rrpr.
> *Nations of the earth.* No-one behind... *Then and not till then.* Tram kran kran kran. Good oppor. Coming.

> Krandlkrankran. I'm sure its the burgund.Yes. One,
> two. *Let my epitaph be.* Kraaaaaa.
> *Written. I have*
> Pprrpffrrppff.
> *Don*e.

And the chapter ends.

Leopold Bloom, we might, say, belongs to the logo-cloacal school of literary criticism, of which Stephen Dedalus is the most subtle theorist. In the library scene, you will remember, Stephen argues that Shakespeare's plays flow from and refer back to his bodily experience. "As we, or mother Dana, weave and unweave our bodies, Stephen said, from day to day, their molecules shuttled to and fro, so does the artist weave and unweave his image." His listeners are unsympathetic. They want to believe that the great poets, in the words of A.E., "Bring our minds into contact with the eternal wisdom, Plato's world of ideas." But Stephen holds to the here and now, and in the process is forced to recognize another equivalence: As Shakespeare's plays are to Shakespeare, so Stephen's theories are to Stephen. At one point Stephen says to himself "I think you're getting on very nicely. Just mix up a mixture of theolologicalphilolological. *Mingo, minxi, mictum, mingere,*" thus conjugating the Latin verb for "to urinate," thus conjoining the processes by which we make water, plays, philology, theology, and novels *like Ulysses.*

At first glance, such passages, and there are many of them, devalue art: it's just another secretion. At second glance, such passages revalue excretions: They are equated with art. But in a third glance, such passages normalize or naturalize both, for to Joyce the natural was the norm. Above all, such passages restore, or even resurrect, the body to consciousness. When Stephen

Dedalus, at the end of *Portrait,* announced that he was setting out to forge the uncreated conscience of his race, he spoke for Joyce; and that conscience, as created in *Ulysses* included the uncensored body.

Not everyone was grateful to Joyce for bringing snot, naval fluff, toe-jam, and the like to consciousness. The reaction to *Ulysses* of Francis Talbot, S.J. was typical of many:

> Many of the words were scummy, scrofulous, putrid, like excrement of the mind. The words are listed in the dictionary, but never in the writings or on the tongue of anyone except the insane, or the lowest human dregs. The critics said how brave. The sexual neurotics said how lovely. The normal person said I'm sick.

Virginia Woolf, reading *Ulysses* while she was writing *Mrs. Dalloway,* which borrows liberally from *Ulysses,* noted in her *Diary* that Joyce's novel was "brackish," that she was as "disillusioned by it as by a queasy undergraduate scratching his pimples." "An illiterate, underbred book it seems to me [she wrote]: the book of a selftaught working man, and we all know how distressing they are, how egotistical, insistent, raw, striking, and ultimately nauseating. " And Virginia Woolf's pal, E.M. Forster, described *Ulysses* as "a dogged attempt to cover the universe with mud," "an epic of grubbiness and disillusion," its aim "to degrade all things and more particularly civilization and art."

But an attempt to cover art with mud is precisely what *Ulysses* is not. It is an achievement, rather—and here I quote Stephen Dedalus—"of an artist forging anew in his workshop out of the sluggish matter of earth a new soaring impalpable imperishable being." We note that Stephen thinks of a work of art as "being," or as he says elsewhere, "a radiant body of everliving life." And we get a hint of what Stephen meant by "forging" from something that occurs just before Bloom's momentous sniff of toe-jam. The "Ithaca" episode, you will remember, is written in the form of questions and answers. As Bloom looks in the mirror, the questioner asks "what composite asymmetrical image in the mirror then attracted his attention?" The answer is "the image of a solitary (ipsorelative) mutable (aliorelative) man."

"Aliorelative" means "externally referential," and Bloom is aliorelative to the extent that he reflects and comments on a reality external to the novel, to the extent that he is realistic, mimetic, or better, naturalistic. The same goes for the novel as a whole. "Ipsorelative" means "a reflexive, self-contained organization of cross-references," and *Ulysses* is ipsorelative so far as it is an organization of actions, motifs, and episodes that reflect and comment on each other. And it is precisely such forged and reflexive relations between part and part and between part and whole that distinguished a work of art, as Joyce saw it, from other things. It is the forged relations among snot, navel-fluff, toe-jam and the other parts of the novel that transmute them into the "radiant body," "the impalpable, imperishable being," that is *Ulysses*.

Think back to the beginning of the novel, for example, to Buck Mulligan's snotgreen sea, our great sweet mother. Stephen moodily turns from Mulligan and his bowl of shaving lather to Dublin Bay, which he sees as a "dull green mass of liquid" held as in a bowl by a bayshore and skyline. Then, through a tangle of associations, and in the very next sentence, he thinks of his dead mother, how "a bowl of white china had stood beside her deathbed holding the green sluggish bile which she had torn up form her rotting liver by fits of loud groaning vomiting." Stephen thereby sets in motion a sequence of associations that exfoliates throughout the novel. Snot, urine, vomit; nature, art, the human body; the Irish Sea and the Mediterranean; Ireland and Ancient Greece; England and Ancient Rome; Bloom and Odysseus; Bloom's navel-fluff and the *omphalos*; Stephen's mother, other ghosts, his vocation, his need to cut the apron-strings; a thousand particulars, all become part of the reflexive, self-contained organization of cross-references that in *Ulysses* transmute the detritus of experience and the human body into art.

These cross-references, episode by episode, finally constitute the whole uncensored human body that the novel, in effect, becomes. Each episode, after the first three, is associated with a different part of the body, the Calypso episode with the kidney, the Lestrygonian with the esophagus, the Eumaeus with the nerves, and so on. "Among other things," Joyce told Frank Budgeon, "my book is an epic of the human body." And to Carlo Linati Joyce wrote that his intention was "to allow each adventure (that is, every hour, every organ, every art being interconnected and interrelated in the somatic scheme of the whole) to condition and even create its own technique." Those stylistic innovations, then, through a recital of which I had tried to impress Lionel Trilling, those too were conditioned, or even created, by the human body.

By the last episode, which Joyce called the *clou* of the novel, Molly Bloom's notorious soliloquy, the somatic scheme has been fleshed out entirely. "Though probably more obscene than any preceding episode it seems to me perfectly sane," Joyce wrote to Frank Budgeon; "*Ich bin der Fleisch der stets bejaht*," I am the flesh that always affirms. The phrase in German is Joyce's revision of Mephistopheles' self-defining announcement in *Faust*: "I am the spirit that denies." Joyce, characteristically, aligns himself with the flesh, which affirms, rather than the spirit, which denies. No reader of *Ulysses* will forget the fleshly rhythms and panting yeses of Molly's last words: "I put my arms around him yes and drew him down to me so he could feel my breasts all perfume yes and his heart was going like mad and yes I said yes I will Yes." To his French translator Joyce wrote "the book must end with the word yes. It must end with the most positive word in the human language." In another letter Joyce explicitly associated Molly's yeses with that part of the female body out of which all human bodies, and within which male human bodies, come.

Molly's "yes" is the novel's last word, but Molly's climax is not the novel's. The novel's climax, I believe, occurs earlier, not long after Bloom communes with his toe-jam, and Joyce had a tough time writing it. He could not at first figure out an appropriate parallel to the ferocious climax of the *Odyssey*, in which Odysseus and his mates kill over one hundred suitors and two dozen or so servants. Joyce disliked violence as he disliked other megalomaniacal displays of militant heroism. His solution was to have Bloom run his mind over Molly's suitors and then to accept them, and her adultery, with "equanimity," that shining word. "Equanimity?" asks the questioner. And the answer comes:

> As natural as any and every natural act of a nature expressed or understood executed in natured natures by natural creatures in accordance with his, her and their natured natures, or dissimilar similarity.

In that acceptance, in that equanimity, Joyce tells us, Bloom was "a conscious reactor against the void of incertitude."

The human body, that is, like everything else, is founded

on the void. To endorse it as a standard of value is to make an ultimately absurd leap into faith. But at least that standard provides you with a philosophic equanimity, an acceptance of life, the ability to enjoy it. It provides you with a ground, a shaky ground, but a ground, from which to judge the denials of spirit, the oppressions of an alienating culture, the insane distortions of disembodied intellect, all of which are mercilessly exploded in *Ulysses*. And that is why I honor James Joyce and Lionel Trilling: they made the absurd leap into a faith that value, sanity, a sense of proportion, renewal, in literature and life, emerge from and return to the uncensored human body, including its snot, navel-fluff, and toe-jam.

FICTION IN THE MODERNIST MODE

Review of *Da Vinci's Bicycle* by Guy Davenport. The *New York Times Book Review,* June 17, 1979.

Guy Davenport, whose accomplishments as a classicist, translator and poet are everywhere respected, has published one previous volume of stories, *Tatlin!* (1974). It was both extravagantly praised and emphatically dismissed, in one case, at least, by the same critic. The contention, in the main, was not over the matter but over the method. Let us see why.

In the first of these new stories, "The Richard Nixon Freischütz Rag," three things happen: (1) Richard Nixon visits China. He leans forward with attention, grinning, while a poem by Chairman Mao is read to him: The pass is frozen underfoot; over the hills a red sun rises. "He wrote that?" Nixon says. "Made it up? . . . My! but that's interesting."

(2) Leonardo thinks of how Columbus had completed the journey of the Magi. He contemplates the bicycle he has just invented, complete but for the chain. He thinks of another chain, the chain of existents, light from the farthest star flowing through leaves, down bole and roots, into rocks imprinted with fossil leaves: the world is knit by prophecy, by light. He capers with his beautiful and depraved apprentice, Salai Jacopo dei Caprotti, whose drawing of Leonardo's bicycle was discovered

only the other day.

(3) Gertrude Stein tells us how at Assisi she and Alice B. Toklas took off their shoes, sat in the grass, drank wine, touched feet, talked as lovers will, looked around at the hills, the pines, the rocks, the red roof tiles, the chickens. "I see all that, she says. And having seen it, Alice? I ask. It is there to see, she says. That is the answer, I say. It is also the question."

There's the method, then: one thing next to the other. Different styles, times, places, characters are juxtaposed sans connective or commentary, except that they comment on one another. They reflect on one another in ways too complex and numerous for commentary to fix in words. Less is more. The gaps fill up with meaning. But there is more to it than that. For one thing, the stories reflect on one another with the kind of variable light that the parts within the stories also shed on one another.

In the second story, C. Musonius Rufus, known to classicists as a first-century stoic philosopher always in trouble with the authorities, tells us things about himself hitherto unknown. His ashes speak to us from an urn, as though he were a character in Samuel Beckett (who is a character in another story). But unlike Beckett's potted raconteurs, Musonius can flow out of his jug, can seep into leaves, trickle down through bole and root, to iron ore imprinted with thunder. He re-experiences his imprisonment, his exile to an island without water, his servitude on a chain gang. He brings before us the imbecility of bureaucrats, the infatuate bestiality of the great, the debauchery of the rich, the blood lust of the crowd, the horrors of a crucifixion, the memorable day on which he was both crowned emperor and assassinated.

Suddenly Mussolini arrives at Rapallo in pomp. He makes a speech about the glories of Italy's military spirit. He visits Ezra Pound. This conversation ensues:

"— Why do you write poetry? he asked.
"—To put my ideas in order, Ezra Pound said.
"—Will you read us one of your poems?
"Ezra Pound read two pages from his *Cantos*.
"—*Ma quest'*, said Mussolini, *è divertente!*"

This version of the incident differs from Ezra Pound's, in Canto XLI, where Mussolini ("the Boss") is praised for being first to notice that the Cantos are amusing. In Mr. Davenport's version, Mussolini, like Nixon, Mao, Nero and numerous others in the stories to follow, is one of a series of farcical and ferocious despots. Pound, like Leonardo, Gertrude Stein and many others, is one of a series of artists whose concern is to discover or create order. But then we remember that Mao, in the first story, is also a poet. Then we remember that Gertrude Stein, in the first story, plays Napoleon and that Alice B. Toklas calls her "Augustus Caesar." In the fifth story we will read that Stein "has cut her hair short to look like a Roman emperor and to be modern."

But by this time, halfway through the book, the motifs have become so numerous, so complex in their combinations, that the mind cannot hold them together. One can only enjoy them as they occur and recur and intertwine. In that same fifth story, "Au Tombeau de Charles Fourier," we read this on Fourier's tomb: "*La série distribue les harmonies. Les attractions sont proportionelles aux destinées.*" ("The series distributes the harmonies. The attractions are proportionate to the destinies.") So it is with these stories: Behind the appearance of fragmentation and inconsequence, the various series distribute harmonies. And so it is with the world: Fourier, like his immediate predecessors, Cuvier, Linnaeus, Buffon and Swedenborg, "all searched out the harmonies, the affinities, the kinship of the orders of nature." Mr. Davenport, like the artists in these stories, searches out the attractions, proportions and destinies among the orders of history, literature and human nature. "All of nature is series and pivot," says Fourier, and so are all of Mr. Davenport's stories.

His series are of many different kinds: of historical characters (William James, Wilbur Wright, "randy old Socrates," Nijinsky, Apollinaire, Impressionist painters, Pythagoreans, James Joyce, "that charming rascal Picasso"); of structures (triumphal arches, phalanxes, wasps' nests, herms or stone phalluses); of flora (especially roses and seeds); of fauna (especially cats, goats, elk); of actions (especially spinning and dancing); of sentiments ("There is nothing more worthy of admiration to the philosopher's eye, Dr. Johnson said, says Gertrude, than the structure of animals"; "Great God! beside the anatomy of a grasshopper Chartres is a kind of mudpie," says James Joyce in another story); and of things that fly (bees, wasps, moths, doves—emblems of the soul—chickens, owls, airplanes, and pteroi or winged phalluses, for "it takes the animal in us to lead the spirit a dance").

Above all, holding all the other series together, is a series of figure eights. Leonardo's bicycle forms a figure eight. Wasps fly in figure eights, as did Wilbur Wright's airplane at Le Mans. The mischief-making demiurge of the Dogon, an African tribe, fell to earth in figure eights. The impulses of the bicameral brain, as they move from left lobe to right hand and from right lobe to left hand, and back, form figure eights. The pushes and pulls between discontinuity and order, between chance and law, form a figure eight. As one character says, "the universe runs by strict laws which are the mercy of chance."

The last words in this volume are spoken to us by Robert Walser, who for twenty-seven years has been confined to an insane asylum in which Nijinsky is also an inmate. In apparently insequential vignettes, he recounts to us the pratfalls, gripes, reflections, moral victories, and material failures that have made up his career. His very last words are these: "But let us desist, lest quite by accident we be so unlucky as to put these things in order." But his disorders have already taken their places within the serial orders running through the volume. "Accident is design," we are told. Amen.

A LUMINOUS PARABLE

Review of *Man in the Holocene* by Max Frisch. The *New York Times Book Review,* June 22, 1980.

The Swiss writer Max Frisch, I am told (and not just by his publisher), is a leading contender for the Nobel Prize. Certainly his published work, written over a 45-year period, has the variousness and originality of style, the weight and humanity of substance that we expect, and occasionally get, from Nobel laureates.

This work, the essays, plays and novels, the two remarkable sets of journals, *Sketchbook 1946-1949* and *Sketchbook 1969-1971*, is hard to characterize—largely because of its variousness and individuality, but also because of the elusiveness of the personality we feel but can't quite find behind the work. "I have been serving up stories to some sort of public, and in these stories I have, I know, laid myself bare—to the point of non-recognition."

So Frisch writes in *Montauk* (1975), a novel-like account of a weekend spent among the sand dunes with an American girlfriend and a golden opportunity for some confessional writing, which, however, never comes. Frisch is always impersonal, never more so than when he writes about himself. That his novels and his plays often seem the work of two different men makes him all the harder to get hold of.

His plays (such as the frequently produced *Andorra*, 1961,

and *The Firebugs*, 1958), although various in subject matter all have about them something of the political parable in the Brechtian manner. Each has its moral, in the sense that the problem it poses, in theory at least, is capable of solution. The problem is some sort of political or social aberration; the moral is that we better do something about it. (Frisch is a socialist of the democratic variety.)

His novels, on the other hand, are each different in form, though similar in subject. Each has as its central character either someone who tries to escape from himself (*I'm Not Stiller*, 1954) or who writhes in the nets of definition others cast over him (*A Wilderness of Mirrors*, 1964) or who finds out, too late, that he is not what he took himself to be (*Homo Faber*, 1957). These novels, like Frisch, are elusive. Their ironies are reflexive, à la Svevo, rather than aggressive à la Brecht. Each has not a moral, but meanings of indeterminable purport. The problems they pose are not solvable, but built into the human condition. Remove the problem, and you remove the humanity, which the novels, including *Man in the Holocene*, have in plenty.

This new novel is akin to the plays in moving like a parable, and akin to the other novels in its absence of a moral. Above all, it has about it the aspect of a classic, not because it imitates an ancient author, but because of its lucidity and elegance of form, its severe impersonality, its restraint, its universality. You don't say to yourself, as you read it, "this might have happened"; you say, "this happens, inevitably, wherever there are humans."

Here is what happens: Herr Geiser, 74 years old, retired engineer and widower, lives in the canton of Ticino in the western Alps, on the slope of a mountain. It has been raining for a week. Hail has destroyed the roses. The collapse of a retaining wall built by Geiser himself has flattened his lettuce. The picture on his television set slips off the screen. The hot plate goes off, then on, then off. A mud slide must have cut the highway, because one no longer hears the horn of the mailbus. Geiser tells himself how unlikely it is that a slide will bury his house and the village below, but cannot help imagining an avalanche of rocks filling the valley, a cataclysmic flood turning the Alps into an archipelago. When he looks around for evidence of his apocalyptic fears (and longings), a fog limits the world to a few feet.

Geiser passes the time by trying to build a pagoda out of crispbread, by cataloguing the kinds of thunder (he gets up to sixteen), the kinds of rain (twelve), but mostly by trying to remember: "No knowledge without memory." He can remember the Pythagorean Theorem, but not the Golden Section, which he has to look up. He copies it out on a slip of paper and tacks the slip on the wall: Knowledge is reassuring. He writes out and tacks to the wall other bits of information it seems important to remember: "Always be prepared"; "Fish do not sleep." He then begins to underline and then copy out passages from this book and that, from the Bible ("The earth was without form and void"; "And the waters prevailed"); from pamphlets on local history ("In the far distant epochs of geological history, the present canton Ticino, like all else, lay for long periods beneath the deep sea"); from articles in a 12-volume encyclopedia ("Man emerged in the Holocene"), on natural disasters, human evolution, the age of dinosaurs, metamorphosis ("man into animal"), loss of memory.

To save time and because his handwriting is shaky, Geiser begins to cut rather than copy out the passages he wants to retain. He loses his scissors, but makes do with a nail clipper. He runs out of paneled wall space, so he has to tack his slips onto plaster, where they do not hold very well. He runs out of tacks, so he resorts to magic tape, which is even less reliable. The slips curl in the damp; drafts blow them off the wall. Those high up are difficult to read, particularly after Geiser breaks his reading glasses. For those slips high on the wall, the magnifying glass is of no more use than his binoculars in the fog.

A salamander appears in Geiser's bathroom. He walks to the village to ask what day it is, but forgets to ask. The salamander is in the living room. Geiser throws it out with a shovel. At various times he notices that the television, the telephone, the hot plate, the boiler, the freezer, the doorbell, have all ceased to function. He forgets to eat. Power must have failed throughout the village, for Geiser can no longer hear the church clock strike the hours. The salamander reappears in the bathroom. Were there one, two or three salamanders? Did Geiser actually throw one out? In the mirror he himself begins to look like a newt. The rains continue to fall.

Geiser decides to make his escape. He slogs heroically up the mountain through devastated scenery, over the pass, down toward an Italian village. A few hundred yards from his destination, he turns and sloshes home through the night, losing his umbrella. He comes to, one time, at the foot of the stairs, down which, apparently, he has fallen, perhaps because he had removed the banister in his search for something with which to brush away the cobwebs high on the ceiling of the stairwell. He comes to in front of the fireplace, where he is roasting his cat.

He locks the door from the inside, latches the shutters. When friendly villagers rap for entry, he chases them off with a well-flung cup. The power comes on and the sun comes out; the phone and doorbell ring and ring, but Geiser refuses to answer. Finally his daughter arrives from Basel. When she serves him tea, her eyes are moist. "She smiles like a hospital nurse and talks to her father as if he were a child." Geiser has a headache. His left eyelid and the corner of his mouth are numb. We are then presented with a series of short encyclopedia entries, on erosion, on the chestnut canker, on eschatology, on coherence, on the apoplectic stroke.

These articles, like the other passages Geiser hangs on his walls, are from actual books, which are named. But they are so sinister in context, so grimly comic, so ironically appropriate, that they feel as though Frisch had written them. They comprise about one-quarter of the text, but they lend their objective quality to the rest. At the same time they are as much a part of Geiser's subjectivity as are his memories, perceptions and thoughts, which lend their subjective quality to the passages from the encyclopedia, that repository of collective human knowledge through which Geiser tries to prove to himself that he is not a newt.

The life of this book lies in its many concrete details, in their sequence, recurrences and combinations. They are engrossing enough in their own right so that you are not likely to pull back, while taking them in, to ask what they all amount to. But once you have finished and the novel begins to turn over and over in your mind, as it will, you might want to tack or tape a moral or two on it, thus: 1) Humans subjectify objective reality; novels objectify human subjectivities. 2) Our humanity depends on our knowledge. Knowledge depends on memory. Without memories we are newts. 3) Old age is sad. 4) Knowledge is a kind of character armor, a defense system against the natural disasters, the emotional floods, within us. 5) Knowledge is no more solid than the minds that contain it. 6) Crumbling minds, like decaying civilizations, fear and long for apocalypse. 7) Isolation makes you crazy. 8) The human age, the Holocene, is just one in a series, transitory as the age of dinosaurs. 9) Your mind is you. Whatever from outside your mind seeps into it is also you. It can seep out again, taking you with it. 10) Always be prepared. 11) This is how things go—with individuals, with civilizations, with us.

I should also mention that, as far as I can tell, this luminous parable of indeterminable purport is also a masterpiece.

AFTERWORD TO TWO NOVELS BY FRIEDRICH DÜRRENMATT

Afterword to *The Judge and His Hangman* and *The Quarry* by Friedrich Dürrenmatt, (Boston: Godine, 1983).

Friedrich Dürrenmatt was born on January 5, 1921, in the village of Konolfingen, in the canton of Berne, in Switzerland. But then Switzerland is itself a kind of village in the back hills of Europe—if you can believe some of its writers. Dürrenmatt, at least, seems to think of himself as listening in or looking down on European civilization from a prospect on its rim. What he sees, he writes out in cool and impeccable German. Yet he also thinks of himself as very much a European. He finds himself, then, in the interesting (and modern) position of seeing his own culture—his own consciousness, in fact—as from a distance, as though it were both inside and outside; he sees it as familiar and alien, intimate and estranged. He sees his own culture and consciousness, that is, as though they were demonic.

"I am not a small-town writer," Dürrenmatt once wrote. And indeed he is not: his plays have been translated into a couple of dozen languages and produced on five continents (at least); his radio plays and the films based on his novels, dramas, and original scripts have been heard or watched by millions of people;

he is a recurrent candidate for the Nobel Prize. And his style, for all its swiftness and clarity, has a European-humanist heft to it, a felt weight of his predecessors. I am thinking of those writers in German—dramatists like Reinhold Lenz, Georg Büchner, and Berthold Brecht, tellers of tales like Keller, Teick, Hoffmann, Kleist, and Kafka—who over a century and one-half developed a kind of writing for which there is no one name, although it has been called many things. It is a kind of writing that is at once sinister and comic, matter-of-fact and grotesque, lucid and ambiguous; a style that comes naturally to those squint and bifocal observers who look at reality both through and around our conventional accounts of it.

"But the village produced me." For all that is pan-European and modernist about Dürrenmatt, there is also something provincial, something at once wide-eyed and dead-pan, something sly, wry, and country-cunning, something of the New England rustic giving misdirections to the New York City slicker. "I am still a slow-talking villager," he says. "Though I probably couldn't live in a village any more."

Dürrenmatt's grandfather, Ulrich Dürrenmatt (1849-1908), was the son of a farmer, but seems never to have been slow-talking. He started out as a hometown schoolmaster; moved on to other and bigger towns; took on the editorship of a newspaper; won election first to the district legislature and then to the national assembly. By this time he was as enthusiastic a conservative as he had once been a radical. The editorials he wrote for his newspaper were outspoken and influential. They were also written in verse, believe it or not. Some 2,500 of his poems, not all of them editorials, survive. A two-volume critical appreciation of his life and work, published in 1926, eighteen years after his death (when his grandson was five), has this imposing subtitle: *A Chapter in the History of Literature and the History of Switzerland.*

Friedrich Dürrenmatt has often expressed his admiration for this grandfather, whose poems he can quote. There is something quaint, tough, invigorating, and extinct about Ulrich, like country breakfasts of beer soup and blood pudding. He is a constant reminder to his writer-grandson of what is no longer possible. Dürrenmatt has had much less to say about his father, Reinhold, a Protestant minister. But then it's easier to admire a grandfather you have never met than a father you have to live with.

Dürrenmatt's male progenitors strike me as just the kind a writer needs. A farmer great-grandfather is evidence that your roots are deeper than industrial civilization, that your family was once intimate with Mother Earth. Such an ancestor adds poignancy and point to your current status as rootless intellectual. A grandfather who was a representative man, a heroical self-made Victorian striver, a sage, a poet, a public figure, a man who knew what was what, what was right and what wrong (even when he changed his mind), is more useful still. Such an ancestor allows you to feel, as though in your germ plasm, the irrevocable pastness of the past. He personalizes your myth of decline, without which no modern writer would be modern, as he allows you to treat it ironically, on the grounds of your greater sophistication and self-consciousness. And as for something concrete to rebel against, a private motive for an art that is iconoclastic and parricidal, nothing beats having a Protestant minister for a father.

But what we rebel against, like what we repress, slowly returns. The professional utterances of Protestant ministers aspire to the condition of the parable. So do the plays and stories of Friedrich Dürrenmatt. His fictions, like parables, have an austerity about them, a relative absence of ornament and merely realistic detail, as though all the components were shaped and pressed into place by the moral they add up to. But if Dürrenmatt is a preacher, he is the kind who has no moral; and if he is a teacher, it's not because he has a lesson.

> Misunderstandings creep in, because people desperately search the henyard of my dramas for the egg of explanation that I stubbornly reuse to lay.

Those words come from Dürrenmatt's closest approach to a full-fledged manifesto. They come from a lecture, entitled "Problems of the Theatre," that he delivered before a number of Swiss and German audiences in the fall of 1954 and the spring of 1955. Although explicitly about the henyard of modern drama, it tells us as much about the bullpen of his detective novels, all of which were written from 1950 to 1958, just before and just after the lecture.

He begins by asking his audience not to think of him as spokesman for any movement or technique, nor as a traveling salesman of Marxism or Christianity, of expressionism or nihilism or existentialism, trying to get a foot in the door. His characters have a lot to say, but that is because picking up, mulling over, and speaking out ideas is something people do—and in any case, he is not interested in mime. But his works were not written, nor should they be read, for any doctrine. "I refuse to find the universal in a doctrine. The universal for me is chaos. The world (hence the stage, which represents this world), is for me something monstrous, a riddle of misfortunes, something you must accept but must not give in to." His audience, therefore, will have to take him as he is, someone who speaks "only to those who fall asleep while listening to Heidegger."

Given the universal chaos, there is no uniform style of writing—nor of painting or composing music, for that matter—nor can there be. "Contemporary art is a series of experiments, nothing more or less, just like all of our modern world." No writer's experiments or solutions are of much use to any other writer; each must exploit the chances offered to him by his time in whatever way his temperament allows him. But if writers can't find communal solutions, they still face common problems. One of those is how to imagine a hero, a serious matter: "The hero of a play not only propels an action on, he not only suffers a certain fate, but he also represents a world. Therefore we have to ask ourselves how we should present our own questionable world and with what sort of heroes." Clearly, neither the noble heroes of Shakespeare and Racine nor the bourgeois heroes of Lessing and Schiller will serve to "catch and reflect" the world as it now is.

For one thing, we no longer have representative men. Our heroes are anonymous. "Any small-time crook, petty bureaucrat, or policeman better represents our world than a senator or president. . . . Creon's secretaries close Antigone's case." The last hero in the old sense was probably Napoleon. Instead of tragic heroes, we have "only vast tragedies staged by world butchers and produced by slaughtering machines." And it is no use trying to turn, say, Hitler and Stalin into, say, MacBeth and Wallenstein. "Their power was so enormous that they themselves were no more than incidental, corporeal, and easily replaceable expressions of this power." The state as something the inner eye can take in, as something that can be represented by a hero, is gone, "has lost its physical reality, and just as physics can now only cope with the world in mathematical formulae, so the state can only be expressed in statistics." No tragedy for us, and therefore no large-gestured heroes. For us there is that subspecies of comedy called the grotesque:

> Tragedy presupposes guilt, distress, measure, insight, responsibility. The confusion of our age, the sellout of the white race, leaves no room for guilt, nor for responsibility. Nobody is to blame or can be charged with complicity. Things just happen. Everybody is swept away and stuck somewhere. We are all collectively guilty, collectively bogged down in the sins of our fathers and forefathers. We are the offspring of children. That is our misfortune, not our guilt. Guilt can only exist in the form of a personal achievement, as a religious deed. Comedy alone is suited for us. Our world led as inevitably to the grotesque as it did to the atom bomb, just as Hieronymous Bosch's apocalyptic paintings are grotesque in nature. The grotesque, however, is only a sensuous expression, a sensuous paradox, the shape of a shapelessness, the face of a faceless world...
>
> But the tragic is still possible, even if pure tragedy is not. We can achieve the tragic out of comedy. We can bring it forth as a frightening moment, as an abyss that suddenly opens...
>
> It is still possible to depict humankind as courageous...
>
> In laughter man's freedom becomes manifest, in crying his necessity. Our task today is to demonstrate freedom.

But how? Our cultural conditions are such that high literature can be studied but not made. Universal literacy, scholarly demythifications, are by no means the dramatist's friends. How can the artist even exist in a world of educated and literate people? "This question oppresses me, and I know no answer."

> Perhaps the writer can best exist by writing detective stories, by creating art where it is least expected. Literature must become so light that it will weigh nothing on the scale of today's literary criticism: only in this way will it regain its true worth.

So ends "Problems of the Theatre"—with a conclusion that expresses an intention Dürrenmatt had already carried out. Three years earlier, in 1950, *The Judge and His Hangman* had been published serially in the *Beobachter*. *The Quarry* followed in 1951. These are the interconnected detective stories reprinted in this volume. They make for light reading, but will bear the weight of as much commentary as you care to put on them.

In 1956, three years after he wrote the lecture, Dürrenmatt completed *Traps*, novel and radio play, which contains neither a detective nor a crime, in any usual sense. Its characters are a traveling salesman and the four codgers who offer him lodging: a retired judge, a former trial lawyer, a onetime prosecuting attorney, an ex-executioner. Together these five do the detecting: during a regular orgy of food and drink, they decide to play a game, to conduct a mock trial, with the traveling salesman, whose punning name is Traps, as the defendant. The oldsters are shrewd, tipsy, fantastic, and sporadically senile; they have a theory that everyone is guilty of something: it's guilt that makes you what you are. Traps finally accepts the logic of the evidence that he himself provides: he finally admits, then insists, that he is guilty of the death of his boss (and rival). His defense attorney argues that Traps is only "a victim of the age." But Traps has felt the pangs of rebirth, the sharp tang of an awakened identity, a sense of achievement, an inkling of how meaning is created by human action. That night, in a state of something like exaltation, he hangs himself. "For God's sake, what were you thinking of?" says the prosecutor when he discovers the body. "You've ruined the most wonderful evening we've ever had."

In 1958 Dürrenmatt completed his last detective novel, *The Pledge*, and its film version, *It Happened in Broad Daylight*. The pledge in question is one made by detective Matthäi, a promise to catch the killer of a young girl. In spite of knockdown evidence pointing to a peddler, evidence that satisfies everyone else, Matthäi is sure that the murderer has to be a salesman, that he will travel along the road from Chur to Zurich. He sets a trap: he takes over a garage, moves in with a woman who has a daughter resembling the murdered girl. But the murderer never shows up; Matthäi waits for years; his formerly admiring colleagues begin to snicker; he takes to drink; he begins to come apart at all his seams. His premises had been like rock; his logic impeccable; his conclusions irrefutable. Why, then, had the psychopath not fallen into his trap? Well, because, unknown to Matthäi, he had been killed in a car accident before he could get there. Reason, dedication, method, justice have no chance against chance. But Matthäi is a man with a fixed idea, "a fanatic of justice," as one critic calls him, a monomaniacal ratiocinator, as though the quality that makes a great detective great had been isolated in Matthäi from everything else that would have made him human. The subtitle of his story is *A Requiem for the Detective Story*.

The Judge and His Hangman and *The Quarry* are something else. They are instances of the thing itself, rather than long goodbyes to it. They do not violate our expectations—they give us what we expect from detective stories, and something more, and in unexpected ways, as the best ones always do. Take, for instance, the hero of these two novels, Commissioner Hans Barlach, in whom the qualities that make for a great detective are mixed with the all-too-human. He has the eccentricities of a Dupin, a Holmes, a Poirot; the humanity of a Maigret; and the absurdist and solitary professionalism of a Sam Spade. Like the other great detectives of fiction he is no more a solid citizen than are the criminals against whom he is our champion. The great fictional detectives have an imaginative sympathy for lawlessness that allows them to sniff out criminals where the noses of the official custodians of law and order get stuffed. That's why we need these decadent aristocrats, these cocaine addicts, these dandified outsiders, these near-hoods: they stand between us solid citizens and criminals in more ways than one. If we had to rely on the official custodians of law and order—as in real life we do—the innocent would often go to jail and the guilty go free—as in real life they do. Commissioner Hans Barlach, who is suffering from cancer, has at most a year to live—the point being that what he represents is not long for this world.

The solid citizen in power is a bureaucrat; such is Dr. Lucius Lutz, Hans Barlach's superior in office, if in nothing else. Lutz has studied with the police in Chicago and New York in order to learn at first hand "the up-to-date criminological methods" he is always trying to force on Barlach, whose own methods are lamentably unscientific and singular. Lucius Lutz, of course, is politically ambitious. His immediate goal is a seat on the executive committee of "the conservative-liberal-socialist wing of the Independent Party." A popular prejudice against his first name has so far blocked his just expectations. There is at least one character like Lutz in most detective stories. His role is to reflect the inevitable friction between institutional authority and individual ability, the friction between Agamemnon and Achilles. He hampers the detective from one side, while the criminal threatens him from the other. He is the mediocre norm against which the extraordinary becomes visible. He is also a pointsman for society, for any society with solid citizens, who by definition need, fear, and resent the anti-social powers of their heroes. Near the beginning of *The Quarry*, Lutz forces Barlach into retirement.

But you can't retire from your instincts. Barlach, "a big black old Tomcat that likes to catch mice," has already smelled a rat. He is already stalking a murderer, a master criminal, a man as extraordinary as he is—his negative image, in fact, as the number of pointed connections between them makes clear. In that respect he is like Barlach's adversary in *The Judge and His Hangman*. In that novel, a character called simply (and coyly) "the novelist" describes Barlach's adversary for him. This phenomenon is that rare thing, "a human being who is truly a nihilist," a man for whom good and evil do not exist, who may do either, but always out of sheer caprice, and always as "the expression of his unique brand of freedom: the freedom of nothingness, and that is the freedom of the true nihilist." Barlach's contest with this nihilist is a kind of joust between a "quixotic" and skeptical knight of faith and the dragon of denial. These well-matched opposites have been after each other for forty years. Barlach's task is to assert that meaning exists—or, at least, that it can be created.

The novelist goes on to argue that from this nihilist you could construct another, as from one geometrical proposition you could construct its symmetrical reflection. The second kind of nihilist does evil not out of caprice, but with a purpose; he "has become a criminal because the evil element represents his ethics, his philosophy, if you like. Therefore, this type of man is just as fanatical in his pursuit of evil as another man would be in his pursuit of the good." The novelist is sure that this kind of nihilist exists somewhere. "Perhaps someday you will meet him," he says to Barlach; "if you meet the one, you will invariably meet the other." Barlach does meet him, in *The Quarry*.

In one memorable scene of that novel the nihilist has Barlach at his mercy but offers to set him free if the detective can declare a faith equal to his own. In a long and eloquent speech he states his credo—along the way using phrases and ideas that elsewhere Dürrenmatt had called his own. Periodically, he interrupts himself to ask Barlach what *he* believes in. God? The old man is silent. Christianity? No response. Socialism? Barlach says nothing. Humanism? Silence. Justice? Tolerance? The Golden Rule? Living decently, according to one's own conscience? Making money? Barlach remains silent. The nihilist is shouting by now. He offers Barlach one last chance to escape agonizing torture unto death. All he has to do is to declare a minimum faith in the mere possibility that goodness just might exist. But the detective says nothing.

As for the nihilist, he compares himself to the Christian who believes in three things that are also one—the Trinity. "I believe in two things which are one and the same, namely that something is and that I am. I believe in matter." There is only matter, which is what he is; there is nothing else. There is no justice, for example. "How could matter be just?" Because there is nothing else, he is free. But his freedom is one that exists only in its demonstration. "Freedom is the courage to commit crime; for freedom itself is a crime." Crime places him outside "all the order of this world, created by our weakness." Therefore he is a torturer and mass murderer. "The screams and the pain which flood toward me from glassy eyes and open mouths, the convulsing, impotent white flesh under my knife, reflect my triumph and my freedom and nothing else."

But our nihilist is not serene in the possession of his faith. His excited emphasis suggests that he has an inkling of what's wrong with his credo. He senses, maybe, that he tortures people not out of choice, but from a compulsion, from doubt, rather than conviction. Only in the agonized gaze of his victims can he find evidence of his existence—which deep down he doubts. "Say something!" he finally screams at the old man. "Your faith! *Show me your faith!*"—as though his life depended on it. If someone like Barlach can believe in something, there might, after all, be an alternative to nihilism. But Barlach remains silent. Just the same, Barlach needs help from a fabulous intercessor to defeat his titanic adversary.

For the sake of people like me, who read afterwords before what comes before them, I had better not say any more. I will just mention that *The Judge and His Hangman* begins in the classic manner, begins, as do *The Maltese Falcon* and *I, the Jury*, for instance, with the murder of a detective, a colleague of the hero. To Lucius Lutz this murder of a policeman is "a sure sign that something is beginning to crack in the structure of our public safety." In *The Quarry*, Barlach, looking around him, notes that "something was wrong with the nice, simple, homely order of the world." His job, the task of all the great fictional detectives, is to seal that crack and restore order. In these two parable-like entertainments Barlach succeeds—just barely. His opponents are mighty and he is dying of cancer. In Dürrenmatt's subsequent writings there is no one like Barlach.

WILLIAM GADDIS'S FRIGICOM

Review of *JR* by William Gaddis.
The *New York Times Book Review*, November 9, 1975.

One of the hundred or so characters in this novel, a failed teacher and aspiring lecher named Vogel is working on a process to convert noise pollution into frozen shards, which when collected and dumped into the sea will defrost out of hearing and out of harm. Environmentalists, naturally, are interested; but the promotional literature on Frigicom stresses its applicability to the arts. Whole concerts, operas, books read aloud will be frozen and preserved; in particular, Frigicom will make widely available "longer works of fiction now dismissed as classics and remaining largely unread due to the effort involved in reading and turning more than two hundred pages."

A longer work of fiction sometimes dismissed as a classic, but in any case largely unread, is *The Recognitions*, Gaddis's first novel, published in 1955. It seems twice as long as its thousand pages, not because it is ever dull, for it isn't, but because so much more happens per word than is usual. A number of critics have described it as one of the most important novels written by an American since World War II. It is certainly that. It is also a permanent contribution to world literature, more specific to the literature of modernism, the restless ghosts of which *The*

Recognitions incorporates so that we can see what it is that had obsessed us all those years. Even now, twenty years later, the modernist presences in *The Recognitions* look less like memories or like fading images seen in a mirror than like what those images must see when they look out at us. The book seems still to read us as we read it.

Briefly stated, its theme is the multiple and paradoxical relations between recognition and forgery (of every kind: of paintings, money, ideas, social status, and sexual roles). Its embodied question is whether there is any real gold to forge, any true coin to counterfeit, or whether all human products and activities are each no more than items in a series of copies for which there is no original. Its tentative conclusion is that a faithful copy, one produced by an exacting regard for the spirit and letter of the original in life or art and by a total submission of self-regard to what you are copying, will take you beyond words, paint, or notes to reality, the only gold that is there to be forged. And you come through to reality, as it turns out, with a sense of recognition, rather than discovery. One of the novel's plagiarists, Otto, the two halves of whose name mirror each other, jots down in shorthand an observation made by a master copyist: "Orignlty not inventn but snse of recall, recgntion, pattrns alrdy thr, q." The surprise in store for the faithful copyist is that his forgeries are both restorations and originals.

The Recognitions is a demonstration of its own thesis. Its year of nativity is 1922, the year in which Gaddis was born and the year of *Ulysses* and *The Waste Land*, the methods and themes of which are faithfully restored and alluded to in *The Recognitions*. And yet it is a profoundly original rendering of the reality contemporary to it. As much, and more, can be said about Gaddis's new novel, *JR*. Contemporary reality as represented in *JR* is a chaos of disconnections, a blizzard of noise. All the passages of narrative and description together would not add up to fifty of the book's over seven hundred pages. The rest is talk: conversation, monologue, harangue; voices on telephones, intercoms, radios, TV, sound tracks; the slang of schoolchildren and hipsters; the doublequackduckspeak of commissars, of law, science, business, PR, and education; the broken poetry of drunkenness and nervous breakdown—all interrupting each other. Gaddis's ear for the various tics and jargons, the pitch, stress, and clangor of current American speech is so precise that its effects are uncanny. So is the sense we get of people ridden by some malign and centrifugal force of cosmic disruption at work scattering everything in their heads, homes, and work apart from whatever they were parts of.

Both ridden by and riding this force is JR, an ingenious and ingenuous sixth-grader, who puts into practice the lessons on free enterprise he has learned in his social studies classes. Huddled in phone booths, sneakers burst, nose running, a handkerchief stuffed in the mouthpiece to make his voice sound deeper, JR begins small, with free samples and penny stock. Then, without quite understanding how it happens, he parlays a sale of Army-surplus picnic forks (the Navy buys them) into a juggernaut conglomerate "family of companies" involving, among many others, a brewery (cobalt in the water makes an exceptional head on the beer), a publishing house (specializing in school books with interleaved pages of advertising), a shipping line (one capsized ship), pork bellies (they are bearish), sheep membranes, pharmaceuticals (the aspirin keep coming out green), nursing homes (markets for the pharmaceuticals), funeral parlors (to service the nursing homes), cemeteries, "Mary Jane" (legalized) cigarettes, and a company that specializes in pornographic films. Caught in the wheels and deals of the JR Corp. are bankers, brokers, lawyers, teachers, businessmen large and small, local and national politicians, PR men, lobbyists, two-star generals, Indians (who are dispossessed of their lands), an African nation (manipulated into civil war), writers, artists, composers, and the lovers, spouses, and children of these. Most of the characters are accomplices of JR's designs, and their own fates, whether appalling, hilarious, or both—but not because they planned it that way.

Nothing much happens as people plan it, according to a law formulated by Jack Gibbs: "life is what happens to us while we are making other plans." And while we listen to the voices of the dozen or so main characters talk about something else, we pick up bits of the life that is happening around the edges of their plans. It is a life of ruined careers and marriages, of children neglected, lost, or abandoned, of obsession, madness, murder, and suicide, of casual slaughter and continuous betrayal, of artists who can't work, teachers who won't teach, men of affairs who mismanage them, of collisions, interruptions, malfunctions, and breakdowns, of, above all, an accelerating entropy that no one can escape, let alone control.

One of the epicenters from which the entropy spreads is a dingy apartment on east Ninety-Sixth Street in Manhattan. Through a series of misunderstandings it becomes uptown headquarters of the JR Corp. It was originally rented in the name of Grynszpan, a mythical figure invented and put through Harvard by two writers who now use the apartment as a kind of storeroom. It is piled to the ceiling with stacks of newspapers and paper bags (which Jack Gibb, one of the writers, collects), with cartons of books, notes, MSS, cans of film. The door is on one hinge. Hot water pours at the rate of two and three gallons per second from broken faucets on the sink and old-fashioned sink-tub. The single lamp with its perforated shade goes on and off unpredictably and usually inconveniently. Buried beyond reach under boxes where no one can turn it off is a radio; it only becomes audible, however, when you stand at the particular angle to it that turns you into an aerial. Under the broken-down couch is a clock that runs backward. The window shade has footsteps running up it. Outside the window a piece of bubble gum on a string bobs up and down trying to pick up a quarter that Gibbs has glued to the sill.

Rhoda, who moved in from next door after her consort committed suicide, spends her time taking bubble baths and offering her favors to anyone who seems as though he might like her enough to talk with her after accepting them. The melting pizzas and opened cans of oily delicacies she lifts from the supermarket get lost among the sacks of mail, piles of reference works, and reams of documents delivered for the JR Corp. To dress up the office he never sees, JR sends an electric mail opener (which cuts letters neatly in half). He also sends a *picturephone, through which businessmen callers can see Rhoda in the tub or hear her tell them to bleep off. Or they can listen to the amazing advice (usually taken) given by whoever happens to pick up the phone as to what should be done about this merger, that tax shelter, and all these bankruptcies. One of Rhoda's boyfriends drops in to practice on his out-of-tune guitar. Reporters, health, fire, and postal inspectors, Treasury Agents, U.S. Marshals, and bill collectors arrive looking for officers of the JR Corp. and for Grynszpan, who has never yet paid a bill. A trucker insists on delivering a thousand gross of plastic flowers from Hong Kong. Rhoda's cat drowns in the tub-sink. Tom Eigen, the other writer, brings in a simple-minded former classmate who seems perfectly harmless until he shoots the radio when a piece of serious music is interrupted by an ad for one of the JR products. Amid all this sits Edward Bast trying to write out the score of an original composition for ninety instruments. The music is to serve as background to a promotional film concocted by a stockbroker who wants public support (and funds) for a pet project. His idea is to transport zebras and wildebeest to the western plains and elephants and hippos to the Everglades, where he can hunt them on weekends. And amid all this sits Jack Gibbs trying to finish a "book he hadn't worked on for the previous sixteen years." Its title is *Agape Agape*—"a social history of mechanization and the arts, the destructive element." And that ain't half of it. There has been nothing like Grynszpan's apartment since the stateroom scene in *A Night at the Opera*, of which the former is the epical version.

And there are other epicenters of disorder—a Long Island school, bedrooms, the offices of brokers and boards of directors—equally spectacular. But if you stand back from the wild and whirling words to where you can see the novel as a structure, as a system of relations among its parts, rather than as an assemblage of referents to what is outside it, you see something other than the centrifugal forces of disruption at work. You see the equal if opposite centripetal forces of recurrence, reflection and, analogy, of interlocking motifs and linked images, of buried puns and covert allusion, connecting the fragments. The aesthetic order within the work is experienced as a compensation of sorts for the disorder without to which it refers. In this respect, *JR* is like The *Recognitions* and like the classic texts of modernism.

In *JR*, however; the material for the motifs, images, and allusions has not been quarried from past literature, from the cultural detritus of 3000 years that clogged the minds of Eliot's Tieresias and Joyce's Dedalus, but from the instant Kitsch midden of contemporary technology, politics, and big business. In this respect *JR* is like Pynchon's *Gravity's Rainbow*, McElroy's *Lookout Cartridge*, and Heller's *Something Happened* (the publication of which four books, by the way, has already made the seventies an auspicious decade for American fiction). One more comparison: whereas *The Recognitions* was like *The Waste Land* for its apocalyptic fears and longings ("we have entered the period of final woe at last," says one character), *JR* is like *Ulysses* for its sustained comedy and clear-eyed regard for the homely virtues.

The comedy, then, is wild, and the pace is frantic, but the satire is precise. On every page the images looking out are recognitions of the life that is happening to us while we make other plans. No other novel I know of catches up so much of contemporary reality, or renders it so exactly, and with such telling detail. And no recent novel I know of with anything like the fullness or accuracy of *JR* is at once so inventive and subtle in the structure of relations among its parts. Certainly no recent satire or black comedy is so entirely devoid of the satirist's congenital vice, which is heartlessness. The appalling and hilarious fates of this novel's characters are also moving, partially because in them we see our own possibilities, but mostly because Gaddis is aware that suffering is real, because his imagination has reach enough to participate and make us participate in the suffering of the real people of whom his characters are images. Behind the wild comedy, the frantic pace, the precise satire, the rigorous art, there is the somber mood of something that for want of a better word we might just as well call tragedy.

A FICTION MADE OF HISTORY, WHICH IN TURN WAS MADE OF FICTIONS

Review of *Ragtime* by E.L. Doctorow. The *New York Times Book Review*, July 6, 1975.

The problem is not so much *what* as *how*. Since the time of Henry James, at least, serious novelists have had more trouble deciding how to write than what to write about. Most have felt that the traditional methods of narration had exhausted their possibilities, that they were bound up with conceptions of exterior and interior reality we no longer share, that they were the product of vicious or extinct social conditions; and many novelists also felt that a work of art should be an object in its own right, rather than a report or illustration, that a work of art should explore, not represent, that aesthetic like scientific truths can be proved only by experimentation, that, in short, new realities call for new fictions, or that new fictions remake reality.

The greatest and most experimental of experimental novelists is still James Joyce. Writing to a friend about *Ulysses* Joyce explained that "each adventure (that is, every hour, every organ, every art being interconnected and interrelated in the structural scheme of the whole) should not only condition but even create its own technique." Joyce chose to let his subjects dictate his methods rather than to impose a method upon his subjects. And that is in part why his experiments remain significant, unlike most of those conducted less out of solicitude toward a subject than out of an aptitude for self-absorption. The special significance of E. L. Doctorow's new novel is that the *what* for which he has found a *how* is an historical moment, as opposed, say, to a single adventure or a theory about the self.

A method for giving us the *feel* of a historical moment—as distinct from information about it—is something that more and more of our novelists may soon be after, now that Thomas Pynchon and Doctorow have shown us how it is done, now that the millennial sixties are over and we are looking back to see what happened rather than forward to see what next. Such a method is something that Doctorow did not himself have in three previous novels, including *The Book of Daniel*, an otherwise successful book about the life and times of a man whose parents were very like Ethel and Julius Rosenberg. The method of his new novel is dictated by the lives and times of Americans during that moment between the turn of the century and World War I, the moment of arrival for the Model T, the assembly line, the moving picture, and Scott Joplin's rags. *Ragtime* succeeds entirely—as his three earlier books did not—in absorbing, rather than annotating, the images and rhythms of its subject, in measuring the shadows of myth cast by naturalistic detail, in rousing our senses and in treating us to some serious fun. Let us see how.

Mameh, Tateh and the Little Girl in the pinafore live in one room and everybody works. Mameh and the Little Girl sew knee pants and get seventy cents a dozen. Tateh is a peddler, but has the wrong temperament for his work. One day when two week's rent is due, Mameh lets her employer have his way with her on a cutting table. Tateh drives her from the house and mourns her as though she were dead. Tateh is a socialist.

He is also an artist, president, in fact, of the Socialist Artists' Alliance of the Lower East Side. On a hot June just this side of 1900, he stands on the sidewalk before a display cart of framed silhouette portraits. One end of a clothesline is tied around his waist, the other around the wrist of his beautiful Little Girl. White slavers lurk everywhere. For fifteen cents, he will cut your image on a piece of white paper and mount it on a black background. "With his scissors he suggested not merely outlines, but textures, moods, character, despair."

To amuse his daughter he puts 120 silhouettes on pages no bigger than your hand. He binds them with a piece of string. She flips the pages with her thumb and watches herself skating away and skating back, gliding into a figure eight, returning, pirouetting and making a lovely bow to her audience. Now catch the movement of images in this bit of prose describing the sidewalk artist's world: "...by the end of the month a serious heat wave had begun to kill infants all over the slums. The tenements glowed like furnaces and the tenants had no water to drink. The sink at the bottom of the stairs was dry. Fathers raced through the streets looking for ice. Tammany Hall had been destroyed by reformers but the hustlers on the ward still cornered the ice supply and sold little chips of it at exorbitant prices. Pillows were placed on the sidewalks. Families slept on stoops and in doorways. Horses collapsed and died in the streets. The Department of Sanitation sent drays around the city to drag away horses that had died. But it was not an efficient service. Horses exploded in the heat. Their exposed intestines heaved with rats. And up through the slum alleys, through the grey clothes hanging listlessly on lines strung across air shafts, rose the smell of fried fish."

Such sentences are the verbal equivalents of riffling silhouettes. They are all plane and outline, nothing filled in.

They do not caricature; even less do they travesty; nor do they simplify, exactly; their effect is to clarify what would otherwise be lost in featureless detail. Yet they suggest every depth and quality of texture, mood, character and despair. But wait.

Living in New Rochelle, rather than New York, is another anonymous family, another family in silhouette. There is Father, manufacturer of flags, buntings, fireworks and other accouterments of patriotism, president of the New York Explorers Club, companion of Peary during his third expedition to the Pole. There is Mother, blonde, beautiful, full-bodied, whose golden gestures are outlined as by the rays of the late-afternoon sun: "Mother lifted the back of her wrist to her forehead and pushed aside a strand of hair." There is Grandfather, retired professor of classics. There is the Little Boy, who learns from Grandfather's stories out of Ovid that the forms of life are volatile and that everything in the world has been and will be something else. There is Mother's Younger Brother, who is thought to be having difficulty finding himself and who is in love with the notorious Evelyn Nesbit, over whom the infamous Harry K. Thaw shot the famous architect Stanford White. The murder occurs during the opening night of *Mamzelle Champagne* on the roof garden at Madison Square at the beginning of the June heat wave that kills infants all over the slums.

One day Mother nearly steps on an infant buried, but not very deep, in her flower garden. The baby is still alive and has a brown skin. Mother takes in not only the child, but also its mother, Sarah, whose last name no one ever discovers. Father is dubious. He becomes more dubious still when Coalhouse Walker Jr. appears one Sunday to court Sarah. Correct, fastidious and resolute, Walker arrives in his gleaming Model T Ford every Sunday for over a year until the equally proud Sarah relents and agrees to marry him.

Formerly a traveling man, Coalhouse Walker is now permanently located in Harlem, where he works as pianist for the Jim Europe Clef Club Orchestra. "The clusters of syncopating chords and the thumping octaves" of Scott Joplin's "Maple Leaf Rag" are like a revelation to the family. "This was a most robust composition, a vigorous music that roused the senses and never stood still a moment." But the Boy perceives it visually—"as light touching various places in space, accumulating in intricate patterns until the entire room was made to glow with its own being." Now catch the rhythm in this bit of prose describing the world of New Rochelle before the arrival of Coalhouse Walker: "Women were stouter then. They visited the fleet carrying white parasols. Everyone wore white in summer. Tennis racquets were hefty and the racquet faces elliptical. There was a lot of sexual fainting. There were no Negroes. There were no immigrants. On Sunday afternoon, after dinner, Father and Mother went upstairs and closed the bedroom door."

Plink-a-plink, a-plink-plink, a-plink plink. The rhythm of the sentences and events in this novel is the verbal equivalent of ragtime. The left hand pounds out the beat of historical change. It modulates from the WASP to the immigrant to the black families as through the tonic, dominant and subdominant chords upon which the right hand builds its syncopating improvisations. These are variations on themes provided by representative figures and events of the time.

Harry Houdini, the famous escape artist, appears and reappears like a refrain of restless, driven, immigrant ambition. The indomitable anarchist Emma Goldman is a rich and recurrent chord of experienced wisdom. She takes in Evelyn Nesbit as Mother takes in Sarah as Evelyn Nesbit takes in the

Little Girl, as one musical phrase may combine with others, and as one theme may echo another. Sigmund Freud is escorted around New York City and to Niagara Falls by Jung, Ferenczi, Jones and Brill. "America is a mistake," he concludes, "a gigantic mistake." Henry Ford and J. P. Morgan meet privately to discuss reincarnation. The Archduke Franz Ferdinand congratulates Houdini for having invented the airplane and bumbles into an assassin's bullet. Jacob Riis, Theodore Dreiser, Mrs. Stuyvesant Fish, "the eminent Lavinia Warren, the widow of [the midget] Tom Thumb," John J. McGraw, and Booker T. Washington all flicker before our eyes like interleaved silhouettes. They fill our ears with their harmonious or dissonant relations to each other and to the three families, while the implacable left hand takes them through its changes.

By the end of the novel Grandfather is dead, having slipped while doing a jig to welcome in spring. Father is dead, blown up with his own munitions and the "Lusitania." Mameh is dead, swallowed up by the slum. J. P. Morgan is dead, after having spent a night in the Great Pyramid of Giza awaiting a vision. Sarah is dead, mistaken for a terrorist. Coalhouse Walker Jr. is dead, after a career of terrorism that begins when fire-house rowdies vandalize his car and ends with his hand on a detonator inside the J. P. Morgan Library. Mother's Younger Brother is dead, fallen by the side of Emiliano Zapata.

But Mother has been rejuvenated by her marriage to Tateh, now the Baron Ashkenazy, a film-maker. The Baron, looking at his beautiful olive-skinned Little Girl, at his handsome blond stepson, and at Coalhouse Walker III, his ward, gets an idea for a movie. He has a vision of a gang of kids of different colors, classes, kinds, like all of us, getting into scrapes and getting out of them. "And by that time the era of Ragtime had run out, with the heavy breath of the machine, as if history were no more than a tune on a player piano."

And so it is in this excellent novel, whose silhouettes and rags not only make fiction out of history but also reveal the fictions out of which history is made. It incorporates the fictions and realities of the era of ragtime while it rags our fictions about it. It is an anti-nostalgic novel that incorporates our nostalgia about its subject. It is cool, hard, controlled, utterly unsentimental, an art of sharp outlines and clipped phrases. Yet it implies all we could ask for in the way of texture, mood, character, and despair.

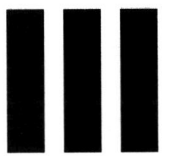

HORROR AND DISSOCIATION

"Horror and Dissociation, with Examples from E. A. Poe," in *Split Minds/Split Brains*, ed. Jacques M. Quen (New York and London: New York University Press, 1986).

The first whodunnit ever written, "The Murders in the Rue Morgue," begins as though it were an essay—or more accurately, as though it were a paper to be read before a gathering of psychical researchers. A peculiarly emphatic speaker, who never identifies himself, is going on about something he calls *analysis*. "The mental features discoursed of as the analytical," he says, "are, in themselves, but little susceptible of analysis. We appreciate them only in their effects." We do know, our speaker continues, that the possessor of analytic powers derives from them "the liveliest enjoyment." He therefore searches out enigmas of all kinds—and solves them, too. His solutions seem "preternatural" to the layman; they have about them "the whole air of intuition," or worse, improvisation; but in fact they are achieved "by the very soul and essence of method." His method, however, is not that of the master chess player or mathematician, mere calculators whose reputations for analytic prowess are very much exaggerated. No, the true analyst is imaginative rather than ingenious—and that is why he alone excels in "these more important undertakings where mind struggles with mind." His method is nothing less than identification: "Deprived of ordinary resources, the analyst throws himself into the spirit" of the mind he is trying to master "and identifies himself therewith."

Just as we are beginning to wonder whether Edgar Allan Poe, in 1841, wrote an anticipatory apology for psychoanalysis, the essay turns into a story. Abruptly, we are introduced to an extraordinary friend of the narrator's, a certain C. Auguste Dupin. They met, characteristically enough, in an obscure library, both of them "in search of the same very rare and remarkable volume," for they are alike in valuing only those things that the world despises. Dupin, we read, is a ruined aristocrat who has "ceased to bestir himself in the world, or to care for the retrieval of his fortunes"—he is the very antithesis of the bustling burgher, the Western world's new exemplary man, his tastes the latest thing, his standards the grounds for invidious comparisons with everything else. Dupin's aesthetic withdrawal and aristocratic disdain attract him to the narrator, as does "the wild fervor, and the vivid freshness of his imagination." At the narrator's expense they set up housekeeping together in a "time-eaten and grotesque mansion, long deserted through superstitions… in a retired and desolate portion of the Faubourg St. Germain." They furnish this atmospheric pile, according to the narrator, in a style that "suited the fantastic gloom of our common temper."

Each morning at first dawn, they shut out the daylight with "mossy shutters," ignite a couple of feeble and perfumed candles, and mope around dreaming, reading, writing, and talking. "We existed within ourselves alone," says the narrator. At night they wander arm in arm through "the wild lights and shadows of the populous city." Had their routine become known, our narrator boasts, "we should have been regarded as madmen." During one of their nocturnal excursions, Dupin demonstrates his uncanny powers as an analyst. He uncoils the chain of associations, of many tangled links, that flitted through the narrator's mind from the time a fruiterer bumped into him until, minutes later, he glanced up at the constellation of Orion. And the whole passage reads like something that Freud, perhaps wisely, cut out of *The Interpretation of Dreams*. The narrator, acting for the first time like his descendant, Dr. Watson, is astounded. With respect to himself, observes Dupin, most men "wore windows in their bosoms." Here is how Dupin, when taken by a fit of analysis, looks to his sidekick:

> His manner at these moments was frigid and abstract; his eyes were vacant in expression; while his voice, usually a rich tenor, rose into a treble which would have sounded petulantly but for the deliberateness and entire distinction of the enunciation. Observing him in these moods, I often dwelt meditatively upon the old philosophy of the Bi-Part Soul, and amused myself with the fancy of a double Dupin—the creative and the resolvent.

Just as we might expect, the first (psycho-) analyst had an unstable personality. And as we might have guessed, it is precisely when he undertakes an analysis that he dissociates, that an otherwise hidden self takes over, one whose manner is frigid and abstract, the eyes vacant, the voice pedantic. A marginal type to begin with, at odds with his time and place, out of touch with common humanity, an *artiste manqué* with scientific pretensions, gloomy, eccentric, fantastical, irresistibly drawn to the dark undersides of things, a kind of secular necromancer, Poe's analyst is good at sniffing out crime and madness because he has an affinity for them. In that respect nothing has changed. At least,

I hope not. Poe's narrator, in any case, assures us that Dupin's strange manner when in an analytic mood is not some fantasy out of a romance, but "merely the result of an excited, or perhaps of a diseased intelligence."

What Poe depicted in Dupin's fit of analysis, of course, we now call "dissociation"; but what Poe himself thought he meant by "the old philosophy of the Bi-Part Soul"[1] is another matter. His annotators are not of much help. Two of the most recent, summing up over a century of commentary, note that "no one seems able to explain exactly what Poe means by 'the old philosophy of the Bi-Part Soul.'" Poe's own essays, letters, and marginalia are also of little help. None of them discuss the Bi-Part Soul. Neither do Poe's stories, although one of them besides "The Murders in the Rue Morgue" mentions it. What his stories do, rather, is depict bi-, tri-, and poly-part souls at all angles of attraction and repulsion to each other.

The other story that mentions the Bi-Part Soul is one of Poe's first, a spoof called "Lionizing." There we are introduced to a character called Aestheticus Ethix. "He spoke of fire, unity, and atoms; bi-part and pre-existent soul; affinity and discord; primitive intelligence and homoomaria." That's all we hear about him, but what we do hear is enough to tell us that he is both ethical and aesthetical, traits normally opposed to each other, except in works of art; that in him discords have an affinity for each other; and that he is familiar with both primitive intelligence and homoomaria, which may be defined as "the doctrine that elementary substances are composed of parts each similar to

---

[1] Stuart and Susan Levine, eds., *The Short Fiction of Edgar Allan Poe.* (Indianapolis: Bobbs-Merrill, 1976), p. 153.

the whole"² —a doctrine that applies both to works of art (in romantic theory) and selves composed of harmonious subselves.

In an ideally integrated self, that is, each subself is synecdochically related to the whole: each is identical to the whole, yet distinguishable from it, as in that other brainteaser, the dogma of the Trinity. But in Poe's horror stories, the self is full of flaws; along these it splits, fractures, and falls apart into independent agents that haunt, menace, and possess each other, unto madness or death. All that is what makes them horror stories. It is to them that I shall now detour in the hopes that we can return to "The Murders in the Rue Morgue" with a better sense of just what horror, what primitive intelligence it is that Dupin alone is able to identify, identify with, and exorcise through analysis.

The Poe story most discussed by students of dissociation and *Doppelgänger* is, of course, "William Wilson." William Wilson, who tells his own story, tells us early on that William Wilson is not his real name, which, however, is equally plebian, redundant, and detestable. He is a rich English commoner with aristocratic yearnings. He is also the product of an inherited hyperactive imagination and indulgent parents, who spoil him. By the time he is sent away to school, he is excitable, capricious, imperious, self-willed, malicious, and "prey to the most ungovernable passions"—in short, a brat. You would think, then, that he would blame his upbringing or himself for his grownup years of what

---

² *The definition is by Thomas Ollive Mabbott, ed., in The Collected Works of Edgar Allan Poe, Tales and Sketches, 1831-1842. (Cambridge: Harvard University Press, 1978), p. 185. All E. A. Poe quotations in the text come from this edition.*

he calls "unparalleled infamy" and "unpardonable crime." But he does not. Instead, he pleads with the reader to believe that in all his many crimes he has been "the slave of circumstances beyond human control." He does not, as would his modern equivalent, say that society made him do it, whatever the *it* might be. The something that made him do it, although outside his control, bears his name, was born on the same day, looks and dresses like him, and speaks with his voice, if only and always in " *a very low whisper.*"

William Wilson first meets this "fatality," this other William Wilson, at school, at an academy that quickly becomes a metaphor for the mind, for the mind as Poe understands it, which is pretty much how the more pessimistic and skeptical among us still understand it. The grounds of the academy are entirely enclosed by a high, wide brick wall, its top embedded with broken glass. The enclosed grounds are extensive—impossible to say how extensive, for they are irregular and full of out-of-the-way recesses. Even more impossible to survey is the gothic house in which the boys study and sleep:

> There was really no end to its windings—to its incomprehensible subdivisions [says William Wilson]. It was difficult, at any given time, to say with certainty upon which of the two stories one happened to be. From each room to every other there were sure to be found three or four steps either in ascent or descent. Then the lateral branches were innumerable—inconceivable—and so returning in upon themselves, that our most exact ideas in regards to the whole mansion were not very far different from those with which we pondered upon infinity.

There are two stories, that's clear, a higher level and a

lower, one resolvent and one creative perhaps, or one devoted to consciousness and rule and one given over to dreams and impulse. But from the inside you cannot tell which is which, and there is no other place but inside—a discouraging picture of the mind for anybody who hopes to learn about it through introspection or observation. The large schoolroom, magazine and dispensary of our culture's accrued learning, is equally a maze:

> Interspersed about the room, crossing and recrossing in endless irregularity, were innumerable benches and desks, black, ancient, and time-worn, piled desperately with much bethumbed books, and so beseamed with initial letters, names at full length, grotesque figures, and other multiplied efforts of the knife, as to have entirely lost what little of original form might have been their portion in days long departed.

Amid the mind's cultural clutter, amid this imagery of the desperately piled and half-effaced detritus of humanity's attempts to understand or make its mark on the world, there is only one nook of order and certainty. "In a remote and terror-inspiring angle was a square enclosure of eight or ten feet, comprising the *sanctum* of the school's principal"—and a very neat image of what we now call the superego is this principal, who is also the school's pastor. Here is how he looks to William Wilson as he presides over the services to which the students are marched twice each Sunday:

> With how deep a spirit of wonder and perplexity was I wont to regard him from our remote pew in the gallery, as, with a step solemn and slow, he ascended the pulpit! This reverent man, with countenance so demurely benign, with robes so

glossy and so clerically flowing, with wig so minutely powdered, so rigid and so vast,—would this be he who, of late, with sour visage, and in snuffy habiliments, administered, ferule in hand, the Draconian laws of the academy? Oh, gigantic paradox, too utterly monstrous for solution!

Principal and pastor, benign and forbidding, enforcer of the tribe's secular precepts and religious values, the Reverend Dr. Bransby is the story's one distinct character. His indistinct proxy among the boys arrives on the same day as William Wilson. This second William Wilson becomes the first William Wilson's only rival for supremacy among the boys. He is the only boy, says the first William Wilson, "to refuse implicit belief in my assertions, and submission to my will— indeed to interfere with my arbitrary dictation in any respect whatsoever." The second William Wilson seems to exist only to "thwart, astonish, or mortify" his namesake; and what is particularly galling, he does it all with a "most unwelcome *affectionateness* of manner."

At the beginning, William Wilson cannot bring himself to hate his rival altogether. After all, imitation is a form of flattery. And there were "many strong points of congeniality" in their tempers. Further, the admonitions of his rival, says William Wilson, were always ethically sound—"his moral sense, at least, if not his general talents and worldly wisdom, was far keener than my own." The two become "the most inseparable of companions." But only for a while. Soon, the second William Wilson's "intolerable spirit of contradiction," his "distasteful supervision," his "disgusting air of patronage," turns the first William Wilson's tolerance into "positive hatred." Above all, he cannot bear the thought that someone might allude to a similarity between them, although no one does. He makes his feelings known. The second

William Wilson shies away. With neurotic logic, the first William becomes all the more enraged.

One night, an unspecified mean trick in mind, he steals through "a wilderness of narrow passages," through "many little nooks or recesses, the odds and ends of the structure," in which the boys have their separate rooms, to his rival's chamber. He draws back the bed curtains and shines his lamp on the sleeper's face, which he seems now to see clearly for the first time. What follows is a classical description of someone in the throes of horror:

> I looked;—and a numbness, an iciness of feeling instantly pervaded my frame. My breast heaved, my knees tottered, my whole spirit became possessed with an objectless yet intolerable horror. Gasping for breath, I lowered the lamp in still nearer proximity to the face. Were these—*these* the lineaments of William Wilson? I saw, indeed, that they were his, but I shook as if with a fit of ague in fancying they were not.

That's all we are told: the horror is intolerable, but objectless; the sleeper's face is familiar, yet strange—*heimlich* and *unheimlich*, we might say. That's all, but it is enough to make William Wilson flee the academy at once.

At Eton, William Wilson plunges into a "vortex of thoughtless folly," of "soulless dissipation" and novel "debaucheries." Once, at the climax of an all-night bash, "while our delirious extravagance was at its height," just as William Wilson is about to propose an especially profane toast, a visitor arrives. William Wilson meets him in the vestibule, in the dim light of which the stranger's features are obscured. The stranger merely seizes William Wilson by the arm, and in a familiar voice whispers their name in his ear. It's enough to send William Wilson packing—to Oxford, where he throws off all restraints "in the mad infatuation of his revels," as he puts it. Though already too rich for anybody's good, he stoops to cheating at cards. He can't say why, exactly—because of the enormity of the offense maybe, because it's the lowest crime he can think of, to vex himself, to thwart his namesake. But William Wilson's namesake is the kind of entity that thwarts you precisely and only when you try to evade him. One night, when William Wilson is on the verge of ruining a young *parvenu* nobleman," all the doors of the gaming room suddenly fly open; the candles "as if by magic" go out; a figure whose presence can be felt but not seen tells everybody present how William Wilson has been playing with a marked deck; he then disappears. William Wilson, as you can well imagine, flees Oxford "in a perfect agony of horror and shame."

But he flees in vain. His "spectral" pursuer thwarts his ambition at Rome, his revenge at Paris, his passionate love at Naples, his schemes in Egypt, Vienna, Berlin, and Moscow. The climax is vintage Poe. It is carnival time in Rome. The Duke Di Broglio throws a masquerade ball in his mazy palazzo. The wine flows, especially into William Wilson, who has become something of a lush. The setting, recurrent in Poe's stories, is one of disinhibition: the costumes, the masks, the wine, the dancing and music melt character armor. William Wilson is looking for "the young, the gay, the beautiful wife of the aged and doting Di Broglio." He is arrested by a hand on his shoulder, a whisper in his ear, by a figure in a costume exactly like his own. He drags the figure into an antechamber, challenges him, draws, and as he says, "plunged my sword, with brute ferocity, repeatedly through and through his bosom."

Someone tries the latch on the door; William Wilson hurries off to prevent any intrusion—outside reality beckons, that is, but is sealed off. He returns: "what human language," he asks, "can adequately portray *that* astonishment, *that* horror which possessed me at the spectacle then presented to view?" The horror that possesses William Wilson is this: the whole further end of the room has turned into a mirror in which he sees himself, all over bloody, advancing to meet himself. But no, integration never occurs; the mirror image resolves itself into the other William Wilson, who speaks the story's final words:

> *'You have conquered, and I yield. Yet, henceforward art thou also dead—dead to the World, to Heaven, and to Hope! In me didst thou exist—and in my death, see by this image, which is thy own, how utterly thou has murdered thyself.'*

These last words are spoken not in a whisper, but in a voice that William Wilson finally recognizes as his own. For the sake of the story, I wish that the two of them had for once kept their single mouth shut. What I mean is that those portentous last words nearly succeed in reducing the tale to an allegory. Taken allegorically, William Wilson becomes that portion of the self that is aware of itself, that wills and reflects, the ego, if you will. The Reverend Dr. Bransby, principal and pastor, then becomes the rules and values of William Wilson's culture so far as they have been internalized. The school and its grounds would represent the rest of the mind and its contents; the other characters would represent internalized public opinion. And the whole story becomes a cautionary tale in the usual tautological manner: if you kill your conscience, it will die; crime and vice are their own punishment, as all sinners, to their sorrow, will ultimately learn.

But somehow "William Wilson" does not feel like a cautionary tale; it feels like a horror story. After any allegorical reading of it, something is left over, and that something is horror, the subject to which I shall now turn. Having detoured from my account of "The Murders in the Rue Morgue" to discuss Poe's horror stories, I will now detour from my account of his horror stories to talk about horror in general—for my model for this discussion is not a theorem in mathematics or the 100-yard dash, but Freud's *Moses and Monotheism*, in which a thread is unraveled, then dropped, another picked up, unraveled, then dropped, a third picked up, unraveled, and then tied to the others into a neat knot, right around our necks. This digression is in the mood of Halloween, a time when the sleep of reason leads to every sort of divagation from the straight and narrow.

"Halloween is the carnival-time of disembodied spirits," said Nathaniel Hawthorne, who knew what he was talking about. A proper carnival is a rite of disinhibition, a riot of release, a good time for letting go, for letting out what you normally keep in. That is what makes Halloween fun. What makes Halloween scary is the nature of the spirits that are let out. They are re-embodiments of our secret fears and desires, of monstrous hungers and frightful lusts. Ghosts, ghouls, witches, incubi, succubi, vampires, werewolves, possessive demons and demonic children are figures combining fascination, repulsion, and threat. They are fascinating because they are representatives of a suppressed wish; repulsive because we consider the wish shameful or disgusting; and threatening because we expect to be punished for the wish. Halloween threatens with what it promises, like a vampire puckering up for a kiss.

The literary equivalent of Halloween is horror fiction, in which re-embodied spirits solicit and scare us with a sinister and insinuating allure. In honor of Halloween, I should like to celebrate these spirits, not by abandoning myself to them, but—and this is how it goes with those of us who live by (or through) the word—by talking about them.

Among the many oddities of our emotional life, the *frisson* of horror is one of the oddest. In the first place, it is usually a response to something that is not there. Under normal circumstances, that is, it attends only such things as nightmares, hallucinations, phobias, and literature. In that respect it is unlike *terror*, for instance, which is extreme and sudden fear in the face of a material threat. If coming around a corner on a path in Central Park, you find yourself face to face with a lion snarling and crouched for a spring, you feel terror. The terror can be dissipated by a SWAT team with flamethrowers or by a scramble up a tree. *Horror*, on the other hand, is extreme and sudden fear in the face of an immaterial cause. The frights of nightmares, daymares, and nightmarish literature cannot be dissipated by a SWAT team; to flee them is to run into them at every new turn.

Phobias, sure enough, seem to have material causes. But if you have a phobia of earmuffs or peaches, say, of toadstools or dripping faucets, it is because they are convenient retainers for some meaning you have invested in them. It is what they remind you of that horrifies you, not what they are materially. A person in the grip of a phobia is hallucinating a memory he has forced himself to forget.

There are indeed times when a sinister conspiracy of coincidences seems to echo or expose our thoughts, or worse, seems produced by them—when, that is, the effect of horror is caused by something actually there. We all have our bouts of paranoia, when our most abysmal fears and fantasies seem to become flesh. I gather from the accounts of those who have recovered, or from the recorded speech of those who have not, that paranoid schizophrenia is a condition of sustained horror; the whole world becomes your phobia, as though you were a character in a story by Poe or Kafka, as though you were Leopold Bloom in the Circe episode of *Ulysses*. Madness, in spite of those who champion it as the higher sanity, is always horrifying, in literature and in life. It is a horror to the sane because it is a temptation to let it all hang out; it is a horror to the insane because it feels like a punishment for letting it all hang out. Before the twentieth century, at least, we hid madmen away, I suggest, largely because of what they revealed to us about ourselves.

We have come far enough for an attempt at a preliminary definition. Horror resides in an image, or object, or situation that evokes for a perceiver the substance of his nightmares, or repressed wishes made fearful by repression. Different people, of course, are bedeviled by different nightmares. Some people claim not to have nightmares at all (but my guess is that they are kidding either us or themselves). It follows that different objects and situations are nightmarish to different people. *The Exorcist* got to Mary, but not to John, who had palpitations while watching *Psycho*. And some people, the aliens among us no doubt, seem entirely immune to the infectious chills of all horror fiction. Just the same, I believe that of the popular genres horror fiction cuts widest along the lines of class, occupation, sex, and educational level. Fans of westerns may be turned off by romances, and readers of Harlequins may wonder what anyone sees in science fiction, but the traits that keep these groups of readers apart will not seal off a susceptibility to horror, which is not affected by social barriers.

In any case, we immediately recognize scenes that are supposed to provoke horror, no matter how we feel about them.

A child watching his first horror movie does not have to be told when to hide under his seat. The conventions of horror fiction and films, I conclude, are metaphors for very common fantasies of mixed fear and desire that we already know from the inside. These conventions are few in number, although infinitely variable.

Here are a few actual or synthetic instances: (1) A timid and lovelorn ventriloquist gradually succumbs to the will of his raunchy, wisecracking, and immortal dummy. (2) The benevolent, philanthropic, and very proper Dr. Jekyll decides to try a new potion on himself. (3) Mr. Griffen, who gives up medicine to study physics, learns how to make himself invisible; the drugs involved, however, bring out what is worst in his character. (4) There is a pair of twins, both beautiful, one good, one evil; but who knows which is which? Even they are not sure. (5) Under a harvest moon, shy and mild-mannered Larry Talbot hates what is happening to him, but cannot prevent his canines and a pelt from sprouting; he howls at the moon.

These are all metaphors of dissociation: what is sane, tame, and daylit in us gives in, loses control, to what in us we consider evil and monstrous, to appetites we have good reason for keeping out of sight and out of mind. The wages of this sin are madness and death.

Or take another convention with its variants: (1) A pubescent girl is inhabited by Satan; she curses, blasphemes, and stabs herself in the privates with a crucifix. (2) Carrie, after her first menses, develops magical powers; she uses them to destroy her enemies and the town they live in. (3) A nubile woman is taken over by (a) a computer, (b) a demonic or dead lover, (c) the fetus she is carrying, begot in a nightmare by Satan, or (d) a spirit long resident in a picturesque old house the woman just moved into. She thereupon begins to misbehave. (4) Aliens from outer space scoop out the minds and souls of human beings; they occupy the space left vacant. You can always spot an alien, for it lacks the ordinary human emotions. All it wants is power, control—it is an unfeeling and immoral appetite we cannot master. All the reason, morality, and fine feelings we are so proud of cannot deter its implacable progress. These instances suggest something we already know from other sources: whatever possesses you comes from within; it seems to come from without because we can't or won't acknowledge it. A person trying to fight off an attack of dissociation must feel as though he were possessed.

In real life, hunchbacks, dwarfs, midgets, fat ladies, and the skeletal man are just folks like the rest of us. In horror fiction and in the recesses of our minds they are reminders of our freakish inner lives. Similarly, homosexuals, hermaphrodites, and transvestites bear the burden of desires we fear in ourselves. All sexual perversions are horrifying to those who do not have them, and perhaps to those who do, if we are to judge from recent homosexual novels. Since all human sex is tinged with perversion, all human sex can be depicted as horrifying. He: "Do you think sex is dirty?" She: "When it's done right." The Reverend Davidson was horrified by what he did with Sadie Tomkins, although it was nothing out of the ordinary.

Haunted houses are phobias writ large. They reflect the condition of childhood, when whatever house we lived in was haunted. The two most famous haunted houses of fiction, Rochester's fire trap in *Jane Eyre* and the equally combustible chateau in *Rebecca*, are the scenes of fantasies in which girls supplant their mad, bad, and sexy mothers in the affections of their fathers.

Horror story plots revolving around the demonic potential of children would be: (1) A pretty little girl lives in a neat little house with her beautiful mommy and her handsome daddy. She's a cute little devil. It is a shame that someone killed her snoopy little brother and her rival at school. (2) In the sewer system of a great city, in an abandoned tenement, or in a cave in Central Park, a pack of children munch on the bones of their latest victim. (3) During a night of inexplicable electrical disturbances all the women of childbearing age become pregnant; nine months later they deliver whiz kids who show no affection, no feeling of any kind, for their parents or anyone else. They aspire to nothing but complete control over everything on earth. (4) Little Damien has a ferocious black dog as playmate and protector: with his tricycle he knocks his mother over a balustrade; hidden under his neat black hair is a birthmark shaped like the number 666.

Children become demonic during those moments when we can't help seeing that they are less innocent than we officially pretend. One critic observed that horror fiction is strictly for the kids—but only because he could imagine nothing more dreadful than the fantasy life of an adolescent boy. More often, children become demonic when we attribute to them the evil wishes, of various kinds, that they inspire in us. It is no longer news that children are frequently molested, nor that even the best of parents secretly feel that their little vampires are draining them dry. Tales of demonic children are written mostly by women; tales of demonic women are written mostly by men.

Other horror fiction concentrates on the theme of the living dead: (1) On London's lamplit streets King Tut's mummy walks. That girl he is carrying, the one in the diaphanous dress, has fainted. (2) On a Carribbean island zombies stalk the living. (3) A tombstone tilts; the earth crumbles open; a bony arm reaches out to grab you. (4) Atomic testing rouses the dead, who have a taste for human flesh, particularly the liver. We fear the living dead as we fear corpses and skeletons, because we fear death. We fear death for a number of reasons, some reasonable, such as that we like life, some irrational, such as the superstition that death is a punishment for sin. We fear the dead simply because we are living, because we assume that the dead have a grudge against us. We have all wished someone dead, or at least thought "better you than me." We fear the living dead because they are like aliens—apparitions of appetite without feelings or conscience or restraint. The living dead are mixed figures of our ghastly longings and the punishment for them. We fear dissociation because it involves the death of the ego. But then for a religious person death is only a variety of dissociations.

The dolls, mannikins, wax works, and dummies of horror fiction are like the living dead, in that they are normally insentient things that have become animate, all the better to act out their designs upon us, which are our own. They are like masks and magic mirrors, in that they reveal to us what we otherwise don't see, the *risus sardonicus* we can't turn our faces around to face. The melting faces of *Westworld* and *Alien* are related—mobile human features dissolving to reveal the rigid and malevolent automaton within. These dolls, mirrors, and melting faces are like the attendant animals in horror fiction in that they are estranged and uncanny versions of familiar things. A wolf is an uncanny dog, man's best friend become nocturnal and predatory. Bats are eerie parodies of birds, as are owls, both predatory creatures of the night. Rats and mice are wild animals that act as though they belong in our houses, in which at night they romp like bad dreams.

Like Freud's uncanny, these animals are all both familiar and alien, domestic and wild, *heimlich* and *unheimlich*. And like all the other literary horrors I have surveyed, they are representations of either dissociation or projection, or both at once, when they appear in fiction or in the life of our imagination, as distinct from the life outside our imaginations, assuming there is any.

Fine. But all that still does not explain what horror is good for, or why certain classes of images and situations stimulate it. Since as well as being a half-baked Freudian, I am a half-baked Darwinian, I shall give an evolutionary answer. Once again, a comparison with terror will help us out. Terror I would guess is the emotional concomitant to the body's getting ready for flight in the face of a sudden and unconquerable threat. It is what we feel when those secretions flow, the bowels loosen, and muscles tense. It helped us to survive in a natural environment that at one time was more dangerous than we are—it evolved, that is, in response to extraspecific selective pressures. But some of every animal's physical traits, behavior patterns, and emotions evolved in response to conspecific selective pressures, to pressures exerted on an animal by the other members of its species. Take, for example, the tails of peacocks and the equally gorgeous behinds of baboons. Neither attraction is of much use to peacocks and baboons in their struggle with nature; their function, rather, is to stimulate meaningful interpersonal relations. Whether female peacocks and baboons experience the emotion of love when they spot these come-ons we don't know, but they act as though they do. In any case, when human males are stimulated by the homologous portions of their female conspecifics they feel an emotion we might as well call love, while their bodies get ready for it. Similarly, *horror* evolved intraspecifically as the emotional concomitant to the breaking of a taboo. The feeling of horror is a signal that we are indulging actually or imaginatively in something we have forbidden ourselves, usually for the sake of the group. The bodily weakness, numbness, feeling of suffocation, and inability to move prevents us from indulging ourselves further. A phobia, by the way, is close to being a personalized taboo.

Having thus in seven sentences established my lack of credentials as a scientist, I shall detour back to literature, to Poe's horror stories. We are now in a position to see that "William Wilson" is in one crucial respect the opposite of all the other stories alluded to in my catalogue of horrors. In tales of ventriloquists, Jekylls and Hydes, Dorian Grays, werewolves, demonic possession, aliens, the walking dead, and creeping whatnot, the portion of the self that is split off or projected is evil, appetitive, monstrous, somehow *lower*. In Poe's story, the self that is split off, the second William Wilson, is ethical, self-effacing, a counsel of restraint, intelligent, somehow *higher*. It is the conscious ego, the portion of the self that thinks of itself as the entire self, that is evil and criminal. But it is the conscience that is horrifying. Poe's positioning of us, however, his giving over of the narrative to the criminal ego, forces us to sympathize, perhaps even to identify with it—and with its evil projects. Such is the moral topography of all of Poe's best horror stories.

Consider "The Imp of the Perverse," which also begins as though it were an essay. An agitated speaker seems to be delivering a treatise on some previously unknown propensity of the human soul. "In the pure arrogance of the reason," he says, "we have all overlooked it." We have overlooked it "simply because of its supererogation," because it is gratuitous, absurd, because we could see no need for it. Yet the speaker is sure that this impulse or propensity is "radical, primitive, irreducible," a *primum mobile* that is not *motivirt*, a motive without a motive, a first cause without a cause, a refutation in itself of the argument from design. For want of a better term, our speaker calls this irresistible drive to perverseness, the Imp of the Perverse. "I am not more certain that I breathe," he says "than that the assurance of the wrong or error of any action is often the one unconquerable *force* which impels us, and alone impels us to its prosecution. Nor will this overwhelming tendency to do wrong for the wrong's sake, admit of analysis, of resolution into ulterior elements."

Among a number of illustrations, this is the most striking:

> We stand upon the brink of a precipice. We peer into the abyss—we grow sick and dizzy. Our first impulse is to shrink from the danger. Unaccountably we remain. By slow degrees our sickness, and dizziness, and horror, become merged in a cloud of unnameable feeling. By gradations, still more imperceptible, this cloud assumes shape, as did the vapor from the bottle out of which arose the genius of the Arabian Nights. But out of this *our* cloud upon the precipice's edge, there grows into palpability, a shape, far more terrible than any genius, or any demon of a tale, and yet it is but a thought, although a fearful one, and one which chills the very marrow of our bones with the fierceness of the delight of its horror. It is merely the idea of what would be our sensations during the sweeping precipitancy of a fall from such a height. And this fall—this rushing annihilation—for the very reason that it involves that one most ghastly and loathsome of all the most ghastly and loathsome images of death and suffering which have ever presented themselves to our imagination—for this very cause we now most vividly desire it. And because our reason violently deters us from the brink, *therefore*, do we the most impetuously approach it. There is no passion in nature so demonically impatient, as that of him, who shuddering upon the edge of precipice, thus meditates a plunge. To indulge for a moment, in any attempt at *thought*, is to be inevitably lost; for reflection but urges us to forbear, and *therefore* it is, I say, that we *cannot*. If there be no friendly arm to check us, or if we fail in a sudden effort to prostrate ourselves backward from the abyss,

we plunge, and are destroyed.

Abruptly, the dissertation breaks off, and we are plunged into a narrative. The speaker confesses to us that he has committed a crime, a perfect crime in fact, a murder. His means was a poisoned candle; for years now he has been living high in perfect security on the fortune he inherited from his victim. It is impossible that anyone should ever find him out. It is just that of late he has been harassed and haunted by a phrase that he can't stop repeating under his breath, the phrase "I am safe." Here is how the story ends:

> One day, while sauntering along the streets, I arrested myself in the act of murmuring, half aloud, these customary syllables. In a fit of petulance, I remodelled them thus:—"I am safe—I am safe—yes—if I be not fool enough to make open confession!"
> No sooner had I spoken these words, than I felt an icy chill creep to my heart. I had had some experience in these fits of perversity, (whose nature I have been at some trouble to explain,) and I remembered well, that in no instance, I had successfully resisted their attacks. And now my own casual self-suggestion, that I might possibly be fool enough to confess the murder of which I had been guilty, confronted me, as if the very ghost of him whom I had murdered—and beckoned me on to death.
> At first, I made an effort to shake off this nightmare of the soul. I walked vigorously—faster—still faster—at length I ran. I felt a maddening desire to shriek aloud. Every succeeding wave of thought overwhelmed me with new terror, for alas! I well, too well, understood that to *think* in my situation, was to be lost. I still quickened my pace. I bounded like a madman through the crowded thoroughfares. At length, the populace took the alarm, and pursued

me. I felt then the consummation of my fate. Could I have torn out my tongue, I would have done it—but a rough voice resounded in my ears—a rougher grasp seized me by the shoulder. I turned—I gasped for breath. For a moment, I experienced all the pangs of suffocation; I became blind, and deaf, and giddy; and then, some invisible fiend, I thought, struck me with his broad palm upon the back. The long-imprisoned secret burst forth from my soul.

They say that I spoke with a distinct enunciation, but with marked emphasis and passionate hurry, as if in dread of interruption before concluding the brief but pregnant sentences that consigned me to the hangman and to hell.

Having related all that was necessary for the fullest judicial conviction, I fell prostrate in a swoon.

But why shall I say more? To-day I wear these chains, and am *here*. Tomorrow I shall be fetterless!—*but where?*

Poe's Imp of the Perverse is once again equivalent to the conscience, although this time it becomes manifest not in a double, but in a compulsion to confess. Just the same, its victim experiences it first as a possessing demon or imp and then as a projected "invisible hand," a dissociated ghost of his repressed guilt that grabs him by the shoulder, whispers in his ear, and slaps him on the back, thus making him cough up his secret. Once again the conscious persona is criminal, and the conscience is alien and horrifying. Similar stories are "The Black Cat," in which the narrator's conscience is projected onto first one black cat, and then onto another, and "The Tell-Tale Heart," in which the narrator's guilt is projected onto an old man's "eye of a vulture—a pale blue eye, with a film over it." In both stories the narrator literally gets away with murder until the Imp of the Perverse forces him to reveal to the police his victim's corpse. But the most celebrated and most complex of Poe's tales of dissociation is "The

Fall of the House of Usher," in which all the characters are aspects of each other.

As usual, the narrator is anonymous, but the most self-aware portion of that single mind within which the story occurs goes by the name Roderick Usher. Critics have long observed that Roderick Usher looks exactly like Edgar Allan Poe. Here is how the narrator describes him:

> A cadaverousness of complexion; an eye large, liquid, and luminous beyond comparison; lips somewhat thin and very pallid, but of a surpassingly beautiful curve; a nose of delicate Hebrew model, but with a breadth of nostril unusual in similar formations; a finely moulded chin, speaking, in its want of prominence, of a want of moral energy; hair of a more than web-like softness and tenuity; these features, with an inordinate expansion above the regions of the temple, made up altogether a countenance not easily to be forgotten.

Usher has summoned the narrator to sit with him through a bout with an indefinable "mental disorder." He is nearly out of his mind with depression and dread, with unassigned horror. Nothing in particular aroused Usher's dread, but everything increases it, as unconsciously he arranges his own dissolution. Usher fears no particular danger; he fears only fear itself. "The period will sooner or later arrive," he tells the narrator, "when I must abandon life and reason together, in some struggle with the grim phantasm, FEAR." Usher's fear is contagious; his mind, says the narrator, is one "from which darkness, as of an inherent positive quality, poured forth upon all objects of the moral and physical universe in one unceasing radiation of gloom."

Usher's horror of horror infects the narrator, who begins to share Usher's hallucinations. It infects Usher's twin sister, who falls into catalepsy and is buried alive by Usher. It infects all of the "House of Usher," the name given by local people to both the family and the building they have lived in for generations. The house, looking with its "vacant and eye-like windows" like a human face from the outside, is reflected in a lurid and lustrous tarn that lies beside it, and resembles Usher in that a crack runs through it from top to bottom. Aware of the connection, Usher has constructed a theory of the sentience of all matter, especially the house. At the end, Usher dies of horror as his sister in her final death agonies falls upon him and bears them both to the floor as corpses. The house then splits along its crack and crumbles into the tarn.

I think it is fair to say that what Usher fears and dies of is dissociation—although his death may be taken as a metaphor for the conscious self's submergence into another self that then comes to the surface. And what makes Usher so polymorphously susceptible to dissociation is his artistic genius. We get a close look at one of his paintings—of the interior of a funeral vault, like the one in which he inters his sister. We hear of his prodigious musical virtuosity, especially of his long improvised dirges. We read one of his poems, "The Haunted Palace," in which the palace figures as an extended simile for a mind that moves from a sane and harmonious happiness to a discordant and desolate madness. To Poe, an artist was above all someone with an imagination. And for him an artistic imagination was not just a capacity for forming images, but a capacity for projection. Poe's artists, like Keats's Shakespeare, has "negative capability"; he distributes himself among the subject of his art. He breaks off so much of himself into all he renders, into all he imagines, that a point comes at which he cannot pull himself together again. Poe's version of the old notion of a connection between madness and genius thus has a certain specificity. To have genius is to have an imagination. To have an imagination is to have a personality without boundaries, to see yourself or put yourself into whatever your imagination seizes on. To have an imagination is to dissociate. To dissociate is to go mad. There is no way of getting out of your mind; there is no way of resisting its processes. In the artist's attempt to get out of his mind, he goes out of it—he falls apart.

We are now ready for our last detour, back to our point of origin, "The Murders in the Rue Morgue," to the horror that Dupin subdues by analysis. He and his companion first learn of this horror through newspaper reports of the murder of Madame L'Espanaye and her daughter in a fourth-floor apartment on the Rue Morgue:

> The apartment was in the wildest disorder—the furniture broken and thrown about in all directions. There was only one bedstead; and from this the bed had been removed, and thrown into the middle of the floor. On a chair lay a razor, besmeared with blood. On the hearth were two or three long and thick tresses of grey human hair, also dabbled in blood, and seeming to have been pulled out by the roots. Upon the floor were found four Napoleons, an ear-ring of topaz, three large silver spoons, three smaller of *metal d'Alger*, and two bags, containing nearly four thousand francs in gold. The drawers of a bureau, which stood in one corner, were open, and had been, apparently, rifled, although many articles still remained in them. A small iron safe was discovered under the bed (not under the bedstead). It was open with the key still in the door. It had no contents beyond a few old letters, and other paper of little consequence.
>
> Of Madame L'Espanaye no traces were here seen; but an unusual quantity of soot being observed in the fire-place, a search was made in the chimney, and (horrible to relate!) the

corpse of the daughter, head downward, was dragged therefrom; it having been thus forced up the narrow aperture for a considerable distance. The body was quite warm. Upon examining it, many excoriations were perceived, no doubt occasioned by the violence with which it had been thrust up and disengaged. Upon the face were many severe scratches, and, upon the throat, dark bruises, and deep indentations of finger nails, as if the deceased had been throttled to death.

After a thorough investigation of every portion of the house, without farther discovery, the party made its way into a small paved yard in the rear of the building, where lay the corpse of the old lady, with her throat so entirely cut that, upon an attempt to raise her, the head fell off. The body, as well as the head, was fearfully mutilated—the former so much so as scarcely to retain any semblance of humanity.

To this horrible mystery there is not as yet, we believe, the slightest clew.

The police are baffled: so far as they can tell there was no way for the murderer either to get in or get out, for the doors and windows were all locked from the inside. Was some demon at work? But Dupin is resolutely secular—"It is not too much to say that neither of us believe in præternatural events," he observes to his companion. He determines the means of ingress and egress by observation and logic. But he determines the identity of the murderer by the analytic method, which, as you recall, involves identifying himself with the mind he is trying to master. After a long exposition, he sums things up for the narrator:

> we have gone so far as to combine the ideas of an agility astounding, a strength superhuman, a ferocity brutal, a butchery without motive, a *grotesquerie* in horror absolutely alien from humanity, and a voice foreign in tone to the ears of men of many nations.... What impression have I made upon your fancy?

The narrator feels his flesh creep. "A madman," he says, "has done this deed—some raving maniac, escaped from a neighboring Maison *de Santé*." "In some respects," responds Dupin, "your idea is not irrelevant." He shows the narrator some long red hairs found at the scene of the crime and then points out to him a passage from Cuvier:

> It was a minute anatomical and generally descriptive account of the large fulvous Ourang-Outang of the East Indian Islands. The gigantic stature, the prodigious strength and activity, the wild ferocity, and the imitative propensities of these mammalia are sufficiently well known to all.

Reading this passage, says the narrator, "I understood the full horrors of the murder at once."

But I am not sure that our unimaginative narrator understands half of it. The wild ferocity and imitative propensities of orangutans may have been well known to all, but not from observation. Poe is far from the only nineteenth-century writer to use one of the great apes as a stand-in for what is still primitive, ferocious, and insane in the most exalted of creatures, the one made in God's image. Poe's orangutan is one with horrors I discussed earlier, another product of dissociation and projection. Dupin, the highest of men, recognizes himself in the subhuman orangutan; the police do not; they are above all unimaginative—which in this case means out of touch with themselves.

We later learn from the beast's owner, a sailor, what happened on the night of the murders. Coming home one night from a carouse, he found the beast broken out of his closet, razor in hand, fully lathered, trying to shave, in imitation of its master. The sailor reaches for his whip; the ape flees; the sailor pursues;

the ape clambers up a lightening rod and into the room of the two women; the sailor follows it up the rod, looks in the window, and "nearly fell from his hold through excess of horror," Here's what he sees:

> the gigantic animal had seized Madame L'Espanaye by the hair, (which was loose, as she had been combing it,) and was flourishing the razor about her face, in imitation of the motions of a barber. The daughter lay prostrate and motionless; she had swooned. The screams and struggles of the old lady (during which the hair was torn from her head) had the effect of changing the probably pacific purposes of the Ourang-Outang into those of wrath. With one determined sweep of its muscular arm it nearly severed her head from her body. The sight of blood inflamed its anger into phrenzy. Gnashing its teeth, and flashing fire from its eyes, it flew upon the body of the girl, and imbedded its fearful talons in her throat, retaining its grasp until she expired. Its wandering and wild glances fell at this moment upon the head of the bed, over which the face of its master, rigid with horror, was just discernible. The fury of the beast, who no doubt bore still in mind the dreaded whip, was instantly converted into fear. Conscious of having deserved punishment, it seemed desirous of concealing its bloody deeds, and skipped about the chamber in an agony of nervous agitation; throwing down and breaking the furniture as it moved, and dragging the bed from the bedstead. In conclusion, it seized first the corpse of the daughter, and thrust it up the chimney, as it was found; then that of the old lady, which it immediately hurled through the window headlong.

The ape in this passage is not ferocious by nature, but by nurture, or rather by the lack of it. His original intentions, we read, were "probably pacific." He is made ferocious by confinement and the whip, by fear and guilt, by horror in the gaze of the humans he emulates. But at the outset, the orangutan wanted no more than to ape its master, to become human. In all these respects Poe's orangutan is different from the figures in my earlier catalog of horrors, all of which were implacable in their malevolence from the outset. Although the ape is a representation of something abysmal and inhuman in humanity, some system of primitive appetites split off and projected onto a figure of horror, Poe seems to recognize that it was made into a horror by oppression. Poe does not, as would most writers of horror fiction, destroy his monster, but finds a home for it in a botanical garden. There's a moral here, but I refuse to draw it.

Instead, I should like to point to a kind of logic in the fact that the world's greatest writer of horror fiction also invented the detective story. Poe's horror stories, although fantastic in method, are informed by the reality principle: this is how it goes with us. His detective stories, although realistic in method, are informed by the pleasure principle: this is how I wish things went with us. Dupin is imaginative; he dissociates at will; he is sympathetically attuned to the horrors he exorcises and the criminals he exposes. Without Dupin, the horrors within would destroy us. Without Dupin, since God no longer enters the picture, the wicked would go free and the good would be punished. In "The Murders in the Rue Morgue," the police arrest a man named Adolphe Le Bon for the murders of the two women. This innocent's name not only sounds like "Auguste Dupin"; it also means "Adolph the good." Dupin is our savior; in his sight, we wear windows in our bosoms, as we did in the sight of the original Savior, recently absconded. It is precisely because Poe knew how much we need to be saved, how little we are able to save ourselves, that he invented detective stories in which the horrors that otherwise destroy us are analyzed out of existence. For similar reasons, no doubt, Freud invented himself.

But my charge in these remarks, as I understand it, is not to reach conclusions, but to provoke discussion. I shall therefore conclude not with an assertion, but with a question: Why is the idea of drowning in water terrifying, while the idea of sinking into quicksand is horrifying?

DRACULA'S WOMEN, AND WHY MEN LOVE TO HATE THEM

"Dracula's Women, and Why Men Love to Hate Them," in *The Psychology of Men, Psychoanalytical Perspectives*, eds. Gerald I. Fogel, Frederick M. Lane, and Robert S. Liebert, Yale University Press. First read to the Postgraduate Psychoanalytical Society, Nov 15, 1985.

I think I can claim one distinction from the other contributors to this volume. Unlike them I have no expert knowledge of male psychology—nor do I want any. Expert knowledge has a way of exploding myths, and at this late stage of the game I am in no condition to get by without the *mythos* of masculinity. We men, nowadays, have all the ontological insecurity we can handle. I don't see why we should go around looking for more of it, even for the sake of the truth.

For the sake of the truth, however, I will confess to more anxious reading in the psychology of men than can possibly be good for me. And certainly there must have been a time when I half-consciously studied other males for cues as to how men are supposed to perform. I know for sure that there was a later time when I obsessively read whatever narratives came my way, from the *Iliad* to *The Idiot*, from *Tropic of Cancer* to *Tarzan of the Apes* for similar cues—and found them, too. For the sake of the truth,

I will even confess to thirty-five years of queasy introspection. I am happy to report, however, that all this reading, observation, and introspection has not resulted in anything that you could dignify by the word "knowledge." The sole fruit of my wild-eyed glancing about, a fruit that was already worm-eaten in 3,000 B.C. when the Sumerians pressed their yarns about Gilgamesh into clay, is this sour gripe: when it comes to women, all men are fools.

The father of psychoanalysis, in this respect no different from other men, notoriously asked "What do they want?"—it being understood that (as usual) by "they" we mean women. For our purposes the more appropriate question is "What do we want from them?"—it being understood that (as usual) by "we" we mean men. That question leads inevitably to another, which is "Why do we want it?" Thus we move, question by question, from the psychology of rumor to the psychology of men.

I base this large claim on a suspicion that in the equations of both academic and folk psychology women still occupy the position of an unknown. Any confident assertion about an unknown reflects the speaker more than what he is talking about. Such assertions have the logical force more of exclamations than of testable propositions. For the diagnostician of male psyches, then, women are inkblots, the Rorschachs of everyday life. The maleness of a man, as distinct from his humanity, is never more exposed than in his attitudes toward women. More specifically, what men say about women reveals what ails men (see Wolff 1972). To the practitioners among you I offer free of charge this infallible diagnostic instrument: just ask your male patients what they think about women.

So far I have been pretending to write about life, but that was just to get the ball rolling. From the mere fact that the organizers of this conference asked me to contribute I assume that psychoanalysts, too, have had it up to here with life. The equivalent in literature to male discourse about women in life is not what male characters say about women, but how male writers depict them. How male writers depict women exposes what ails the male, as distinct from his humanity. To pile assumption upon assumption, as you might pile ice cube upon ice cube in a 500-degree oven, I assume that any literary work written by a male, of enduring interest to male readers, and in which women are lovingly or loathingly lingered over, will expose what ails men in general.

For evidence and instance I might have chosen many works, from the *Odyssey*, in which dangerous and nubile mother-goddesses preside, to *Ulysses*, in which before going to bed Leopold Bloom worries over the problem of "what to do with our wives," and then gives it up as unsolvable. But I wanted a work that (1) readers have long chosen to read for fun, rather than because it was alleged to be improving or assigned in a course; (2) was naïve rather than sophisticated, its symptoms neither undercut by irony nor displaced by self-consciousness; (3) was modern, just in case it is really true that human nature changes; but (4) was pre-Freudian, to avoid putting myself in the position of the man who tried to hold himself at arms' length by his own hair; (5) appealed neither to the specific prejudices of highbrows or lowbrows, but to the prejudices they have in common; (6) subjected stock female characters to extreme situations, because stock female characters are refractions of a group's professed ideal woman, whereas extreme situations reveal what we would really like to do to her; and (7) was polymorphously sexy, because that's wherein lies the fun—and because to talk about what ails men without mentioning their baffled and raging lusts is like talking about the last days of Pompeii without mentioning the volcano.

The book that most conveniently fits my case is Bram Stoker's *Dracula*. Unlike many greater works, it has never been out of print, although it was published way back in the dark ages, in 1897. Its avid readers have ranged from people like T.S. Eliot and Dylan Thomas to the kind of guy you couldn't flog into reading more than one book every other year. The British stage version of 1923 broke record after record for performances, attendance, and take. So did the American stage version of 1927 (Ludlum 1962). During these performances, according to an actor of the time, it was mostly men who fainted. Nurses and ambulances attended every performance to cart them away. The film version of 1931 bailed out a sinking Universal Studios (McNally and Florescu 1982). The one hundred or so other *Dracula*-derived movies puffed the sales of lesser craft; there are as many *Dracula*-derived novels. And *The Night Stalker*, in which an immigrant Dracula romps through Las Vegas, was, last time I looked, the most popular made-for-TV movie ever shown. Dracula, along with his near contemporaries Sherlock Holmes, Wister's Virginian, and Tarzan, was invented by an individual but co-opted by the group mind. If figures like this can be taken, at least half-seriously, as aspects of a single personality, Dracula's position among them is that of a repressed wish.

And just as we can study the unconscious only through its effects, so the shaky focus of Stoker's novel is not on the vampire, but on his victims. These are all women, except for Renfield, who is a madman; but his madness, in this novel's system of equivalences, makes him very like a woman. What Dracula does to and for women we never see directly; the novel has no omniscient narrator; its action comes to us through letters, diaries, newspaper clippings, a ship's log, bills of lading, and other such documents, only one of which describes (in an emotional haze) an attack by Dracula on one of his victims. He casts no shadow because he is one, a darkness round the periphery of the mind's inner eye. He is at best a reflection, not in mirrors but in the reactions to him of the other characters. We can sum it up by saying that women react to him by becoming sexy; men, by going or getting mad. Our first job is to put together what we know of Dracula's attributes; these ought to tell us what it is about him that appeals to women.

Dracula's attributes, as we fit together the scattered bits and pieces, amount to those of a negative Eros, not the plump, dimpled, and cuddly babe of love, but an ancient, lean, mean demon of lust made kinky by repression. He is rank of breath, hairy of palm, livid of lip, and anaemic, all of which, according to cautionary old wives' tales, are what you get and deserve for self-abuse and sexual excess. His brows meet over his nose; his teeth are sharp, his ears pointed—all signs of his animal nature. He has a "grip of steel," which means that once he gets a hold on you, he doesn't let go. On the other hand, he does not embrace you without an invitation: he will not cross your threshold or sill unless you ask him in. When early in the novel Jonathan Harker visits Dracula's castle, he is at first left standing outside the door. The count, from inside, greets him like this:

> "Welcome to my house! Enter freely and of your own will!" He made no motion of stepping to meet me, but stood like a statue, as though his gesture of welcome had fixed him into stone. The instant, however, that I had stepped over the threshold, he moved impulsively forward, and holding out his hand grasped mine with a strength which made me wince. ... .

Once you have entered his house or he has entered yours, he will hypnotize you. Under his penetrating glare you will become passive, submissive, or, as we used to say, feminine; your will and intelligence, all your inhibitory faculties, become subservient to what they normally inhibit. "I know that when the Count wills me I must go," says Mina Harker after Dracula has had his way with her. "I know that if he tells me to come in secret, I must come by wile; by any device to hoodwink—even Jonathan," who is her husband. Mina sounds like a philandering wife, but Jonathan ought to be understanding. He had nearly come under Dracula's spell himself. Renfield, who succumbs entirely, explains how it feels: "His eyes, they burned into me and my strength became like water." Dracula has the evil eye—which means that his gaze is a projection of your guilt; you see him seeing in you what you have tried to hide from yourself.

Most often he visits his victims when they are asleep, when hypnosis would be redundant, for to sleep is to dream, and to dream is to become passive before those fantasies we normally inhibit. Dracula's victims, when they awake, remember him, if at all, as a dream of suffocation and blood. After he has visited her a few times, Lucy Westenra, for example, begins to think of sleep, in her words, as "a presage of horror." "What do you mean?" asks her doctor. "I don't know," she answers; "oh, I don't know. And that is what is so terrible. All this weakness comes to me in sleep; until I dread the very thought." But after a while her dread turns to something else, and she sleeps as much as her interfering friends will allow. Though finally on her deathbed, Dr. Van Helsing tries to keep her awake: "It will be much difference [*sic*], mark me, whether she dies conscious or in sleep"—for if she dies in her sleep, she will awake as a vampire; if she dies conscious, she will simply die. Much later, Mina Harker, after a few nocturnal visits from Dracula ("tainted as she is with that vampire baptism"), keeps in touch with him telepathically while she sleeps. To find out where he is, Dr. Van Helsing, Dracula's opposite and opponent and alter ego, puts her into a hypnotic trance. "Where are you?" he asks. "Sleep has no place it can call its own," she answers, thus letting in the chill of interstellar space.

The night, starlit or moonlit, is a chiller in itself, and not just because that is when we sleep and dream. "No man knows till he suffers from the night how sweet and how dear to his heart and his eye the morning can be," writes Jonathan Harker in his diary. One of Dracula's many advantages over us is his ability to see in the dark, his native element. "I love the shade and the shadow," he says. Dr. Van Helsing provides a partial explanation: "His power ceases, as does that of all evil things, at the coming of the day." But during the night he can materialize out of mists, dust motes, and moonbeams, things there and not there, but there enough to prod an agitated imagination into connecting the dots. And at night he can transform himself into a wolf or a bat; he can call up or command legions of animals such as these, animals that fit Freud's definition of the uncanny, animals that are nocturnal, familiar, and alien. A wolf is an uncanny dog; a bat is an uncanny bird; a rat is domestic and wild, *heimlich* and *unheimlich*. Dracula's bite is equally uncanny. Although his canines are wolfish, the holes he leaves in Lucy's neck look to Mina "like pin-pricks," as though made by the pin of a brooch pushed accidentally through a tiny fold of skin. Dracula's bite, in short, is that of a serpent, author of all our woes.

Like Satan, Dracula is a dark parody of Christ, whom he quotes: "The blood is the life!" he says, reminding us that he, too, participates in a kind of Eucharist—for Dracula not only drinks his victim's blood, but he also makes Mina, at least, drink some of his, from a vein he opens in his breast. And as Dracula recapitulates Satan, so do his victims recapitulate Eve. Late in the novel, after Jonathan Harker discovers that Dracula has begun to visit his wife, Mina, he comes to a resolution:

> To one thing I have made up my mind: if we find out that Mina must be a vampire in the end, then she shall not go into that unknown and terrible land alone. I suppose it is thus that in old times one vampire meant many; just as their hideous bodies could only rest in sacred earth, so the holiest love was the recruiting sergeant for their ghastly ranks.

If Mina is going to play Eve, he will play Adam as, bite for bite, the repressed slowly returns.

In Harker's mention of sacred earth there is even a sign of some dim awareness on Stoker's part (and their names rhyme for a reason) that puritanical Christianity produces prurient fantasies, of which Dracula is an instance. In the movies, Dracula must sleep in his own coffin; in the novel, it is enough that he sleep in consecrated ground. "This evil thing," says Van Helsing, "is rooted deep in all good; in soil barren of holy memories it cannot rest." When Dracula travels from Transylvania to London, he brings with him fifty crates of consecrated earth, to make sure he isn't caught short. Van Helsing and his comrades render these coffin-crates, one by one, unfit for Dracula's repose through a kind of homeopathic magic, by sprinkling them with holy water and bits of consecrated wafer. Van Helsing's explanation is not impressive for its logic:

> And now, my friends, we have a duty here to do. We must sterilise this earth, so sacred of holy memories, that he has

brought from a far distant land for such fell use. He has chosen this earth because it has been holy. Thus we defeat him with his own weapon, for we make it more holy still. It was sanctified to such use of man, now we sanctify it to God.

I must outline one more of Dracula's attributes, one that explains why women can't resist him. That attribute is Dracula's multiplex relation to madness, especially in men. Nearly all the male characters, as they watch Dracula's effect on women, wonder whether they are going or have gone mad. Jonathan Harker actually comes down with brain fever and has to do time in an asylum. Dr. Seward has to take chloral hydrate to sleep: "I sometimes think we must all be mad and that we shall wake to sanity in straitjackets," he says. Even the stalwart Van Helsing gives way to what Dr. Seward calls "a regular fit of hysterics," during which he "laughed and cried together, just as a woman does," babbling all the while how he and his three male comrades are all Lucy's husbands because they have given her transfusions of blood and how "this so sweet maid is a polyandrist," thus implying what we had already guessed, that the exchange of blood is a metaphor for sexual intercourse.

When Dracula comes to England he selects for his first base of operations the grave of a young man who killed himself to spite his mother. A local gaffer tells Lucy and Mina the story:

> He hated her so that he committed suicide in order that she mightn't get an insurance she put on his life. He blew nigh the top of his head off with an old musket that they had for scarin' the crows with. I've often heard him say masel' that he hoped he'd go to hell, for his mother was so pious that she'd be sure to go to heaven, an' he didn't want to addle where she was.

The grave of this young mother-hater (to whom Stoker has given a number of his own feelings)[1] looks over the harbor; Lucy and Mina often sit on a slab that covers it for the breeze and the view. That's how Dracula gets his teeth into Lucy. One night, under his influence, she sleepwalks to the grave, where Dracula is waiting for her. Her habit of sleepwalking is given in the novel as evidence of her lack of character and will. ("Lucy is so sweet and sensitive that she feels influence more acutely than other people do.") It is also evidence of an impulse she doesn't know she has.

But the novel's prize madman is of course Renfield, an inmate of Dr. Seward's asylum, located next door to Dracula's main London address. According to Dr. Seward's unconventional diagnosis, Renfield is "a zoöphagus (life-eating) maniac; what he desires is to absorb as many lives as he can." He first spreads sugar on the windowsill of his cell to attract flies, which he eats. He then feeds his flies to spiders, a more concentrated form of nourishment, in that they each contain the lives of numerous flies. From spiders he advances to sparrows. But Dr. Seward, unlike our more advanced medical experimenters, knows when to stop: he turns down Renfield's wheedling request for a pet cat. Like Mina later on, Renfield is in telepathic communication with Dracula; he sees his "Master" in visions and knows what he wants. He opens his window sash a crack so that Dracula can pour in, solidify, and find his way to Mina, who with her husband is visiting Dr. Seward. Thus in each case Dracula gains

---

[1] *"Central to the structure and unconscious theme of* Dracula *is, then primarily, the desire to destroy the threatening mother, she who threatens by being desirable." So argues Roth (1982, p. 123). See also Farson (1975, chap. 19, "The Sexual Impulse") for Stoker's relation to his wife.*

access to his two female victims through the intermediary of a madman.

The nature of Dracula's affinity for madness is explained in an impromptu lecture that Van Helsing bestows on Mina and Dr. Seward (and here his accent, which is supposed to be Dutch, becomes a trial):

> To begin, have you ever study the philosophy of crime? "Yes" and "No." You, John [Seward], yes; for it is a study of insanity. You, no, Madame Mina; for crime touch you not—not but once [when Dracula attacked her]...The criminal has not full man-brain. He is clever and cunning and resourceful; but he be not of man-stature as to brain. He be of child-brain in much. Now this criminal of ours is predestinate to crime also; he, too, have child-brain, and it is of the child to do what he have done...

This passage, and others like it, sets up a series of equivalences: to be insane is to be criminal is to be childlike is to be a monster of appetite is to be piggy about sex is to have an undeveloped brain.

In setting up these equivalences, the distinguished Dr. Van Helsing is not shooting from the hip: he is internationally renowned for having "revolutionized therapeutics by his discovery of the continuous evolution of brain-matter." He is qualified, therefore, to recognize in Dracula the paradox of the primitive: Dracula is both older and younger than we are, younger because older, a centuries-old case of arrested development, of incomplete moral evolution, victim of a culturally undernourished environment, namely Transylvania, where nothing is up to date. He is where we once were, but he has come to London expressly to feed his brain, to grow up: "With the child-brain that was to him he have long since conceive the idea of coming to a great city. What does he do? He find out the place of all the world most of promise for him... It help him to grow as to his brain... What more may he not do when the greater world of thought is open to him."

He will then be pretty near invincible, although he is hard to resist as it is. We are susceptible to him because he is already in us, which is why, as Dr. Van Helsing puts it, "all men are mad in some way or the other." In the continuous evolution of brain-matter, that is, nothing is discarded. The old is merely overlaid with the new, one function of which is to keep the old in its place. The primitive brain that makes Dracula what he is lies dormant even in cultured British gentlemen, but in them it is entombed in an overlay of new brain-matter generated by progressive Victorian culture. The overlay manifests itself as a kind of self-control or self-denial, a resistance to temptation, what in the novel is called "bravery." It is what distinguishes Victorian gentlemen from Victorian ladies, in whom the overlay is thin.

Women are so much more susceptible to Dracula because very little stands between them. Their beauty is skin deep: right beneath it, they are crazy, criminal, selfish, and sexy, half-evolved monsters of appetite. Dracula merely releases something in them that is already raging to get out—and they know it. "Why are men so noble," Lucy writes to Mina, "when we women are so little worthy of them?" And women fear what they know about themselves—which fear sends good women looking for husbands. "I suppose we women are such cowards," Lucy writes, "that we think a man will save us from our fears, and we marry him." A woman needs a husband to keep her in line; she has nothing in her of her own with which to resist Dracula. And to be bitten by Dracula is to become abandoned to lust, a kind of moral rabies. And that is what it is about Dracula that appeals to women.

Take the three lovelies Jonathan Harker meets early in the

novel. He has come to Dracula's castle on business. Soon he finds himself a prisoner, of whom or what he can't quite figure out. One night, looking for a means of escape, he wanders into a ladies' boudoir, "where in old times possibly some fair lady sat to pen, with much thought and many blushes, her ill-spelt love-letter." He decides to sleep there, rather than in his own spartan chamber. He dozes off on a couch, then awakes to find that he is not alone. Under his lashes he sees three beautiful young ladies, two dark, with aquiline noses and red eyes. "The other was fair, as fair as can be, with great wavy masses of golden hair and eyes like pale sapphires. "I seemed somehow to know her face, and to know it in connection with some dreamy fear, but I could not recollect at the moment how or where." The women have prominent teeth and "voluptuous lips." "I felt in my heart a wicked, burning desire that they would kiss me with those red lips," Harker confesses. The women seem ready to oblige. "Go on! You are first, and we shall follow,' says one of the brunettes. "He is young and strong; there are kisses for us all," answers the blonde. Here's what happens next:

> I lay quiet, looking out under my eyelashes in an agony of delightful anticipation. The fair girl advanced and bent over me till I could feel the movement of her breath upon me. Sweet it was in one sense, honey-sweet, and sent the same tingling through the nerves as her voice, but with a bitter underlying the sweet, a bitter offensiveness, as one smells in blood.
> I was afraid to raise my eyelids, but looked out and saw perfectly under the lashes. The girl went on her knees, and bent over me, simply gloating. There was a deliberate voluptuousness which was both thrilling and repulsive, and as she arched her neck she actually licked her lips like an animal, till I could see in the moonlight the moisture shining on

the scarlet lips and on the red tongue as it lapped the white sharp teeth. Lower and lower went her head as the lips went below the range of my mouth and chin and seemed about to fasten on my throat. Then she paused, and I could hear the churning sound of her tongue as it licked her teeth and lips, and could feel the hot breath on my neck. Then the skin of my throat began to tingle as one's flesh does when the hand that is to tickle it approaches nearer—nearer. I could feel the soft, shivering touch of the lips on the super-sensitive skin of my throat, and the hard dents of two sharp teeth, just touching and pausing there. I closed my eyes in a languorous ecstasy and waited—waited with beating heart.

But at that instant, another sensation swept through me as quick as lightning. I was conscious of the presence of the Count and of his being as if lapped in a storm of fury.

In a tremendous rage, the count hurls the fair lady behind him. "How dare you?" he says; "this man belongs to me." But "with a laugh of ribald coquetry," she sasses him back: "You yourself never loved; you never love!" They both know better: "Yes, I too can love; you yourselves can tell it from the past. Is it not so?" In a conciliatory spirit he promises the women that when he finishes his business with Harker, they can kiss him at will. Meanwhile he throws them a bone, or rather a sack containing a child he kidnapped from a nearby village. Writing in his diary the next morning, Harker notes "that of all the foul things that lurk in this hateful place the Count is the least dreadful to me; that to him alone I can look for safety." In general, "nothing can be more dreadful than those awful women," but just the same, they make him think of his angelic fiancé, later his wife. "I am alone in the castle with those awful women. Faugh! Mina is a woman, and there is nought in common. They are devils of the pit." At this point we might allow ourselves the venerable psychoanalytic stunt of reading denial as affirmation; certainly later events would bear us out.

There is much to mull over in this episode, in particular the equal and opposite emotions of attraction and revulsion, one revolving around the other; the familiar look of the blonde; and the implication that you have to be strong to hold up to a kiss, that for a woman to kiss a man is to drain his strength, although the blonde seems to be getting herself ready more for one of the common oral perversions than for a kiss. But what in retrospect seems most curious is that Stoker never allows us to enjoy through Harker the dangerous caresses of these *femmes fatales*. Perhaps the idea was too horrible to contemplate. In any case, such scenes of *interruptus* must have occupied a good portion of Stoker's fantasy life, for they occur throughout the novel.

Lucy, for example, a few minutes before she is to expire (for the first time), lies in a coma watched over by Dr. Van Helsing, Dr. Seward, and her fiancé, Arthur Holmwood. Then suddenly she awakes:

> Her breathing grew stertorous, the mouth opened, and the pale gums, drawn back, made the teeth look longer and sharper than ever. In a sort of sleep-waking, vague, unconscious way she opened her eyes, which were now dull and hard at once, and said in a soft, voluptuous voice, such as I had never heard from her lips:—
>
> "Arthur! Oh, my love, I am so glad you have come! Kiss me!" Arthur bent eagerly over to kiss her; but at that instant Van Helsing... swooped upon him, and catching him by the neck with both hands, dragged him back with a fury of strength which I never thought he could have possessed, and actually hurled him almost across the room.
>
> "Not for your life!" he said; "not for your living soul and hers!" And he stood between them like a lion at bay.

The scenes are structurally akin, but in the second Van Helsing, rather than Dracula, does the interrupting. The two men, after all, have a lot in common: both are old, both foreigners who speak with an accent, and both sum up the advanced thinking of their respective times. Van Helsing, what is more, owes his life to benevolent vampirism—to the sucking (by Dr. Seward) of infected blood from his hand. Like Dracula, he lets out a sharp hiss when startled; his bushy eyebrows, like Dracula's, meet over his nose. Van Helsing is to Dracula as Victor Frankenstein is to his monster, as Holmes is to Moriarty, as Dr. Jekyll is to Mr. Hyde, as Freud's ego is to his id. "Oh, unconscious cerebration," exclaims Dr. Seward, who is Van Helsing's pupil, "you will have to give the wall to your conscious brother"—which amounts to saying where id was, there let ego be. I conclude from all this that as women need husbands to save them from Dracula or themselves, so men need a patriarch, whether in his aspect of good father or bad, to save them from women. Van Helsing, by the way, shares his first name, Abraham, with Stoker and with Stoker's father, a retiring man who failed to protect his son from his much younger and aggressive wife, a feminist with a vengeance and a good friend of Lady Wilde, Oscar's mother.

We meet Harker's three would-be paramours only once more, at the very end of the novel, when Dracula is already cornered. Van Helsing is looking for their crypts, so that he can cut off their heads and transfix them with stakes, thus forever ridding the world of their menace. But as he lingers over his task, he pins their menace on their charms:

> She lay in her Vampire sleep, so full of life and voluptuous beauty that I shudder as though I have come to do murder. Ah, I doubt not that in old time, when such things were,

> many a man who set forth to do such a task as mine, found at the last his heart fail him, and then his nerve. So he delay, and delay, and delay, till the mere beauty and the fascination of the wanton Un-Dead have hypnotise him; and he remain on and on, till sunset come, and the Vampire sleep be over. Then the beautiful eyes of the fair women open and look love, and the voluptuous mouth present to a kiss—and man is weak...
>
> ...Yes, I was moved—I, Van Helsing, with all my purpose and with my motive for hate—1 was moved to a yearning for delay which seemed to paralyze my faculties and to clog my very soul...
>
> ...She was so fair to look on, so radiantly beautiful, so exquisitely voluptuous, that the very instinct of man in me, which calls some of my sex to love and to protect one of hers, made my head whirl with new emotion.

But a despairing and distant wail from Mina breaks Van Helsing's spell. He steels himself to "the horrid screeching as the stake drove home; the plunging of writhing form, and lips of bloody foam," until his work is finished. Well, vampires are "undead" in the first place because the wages of sin is death. The vampire women are killed doubly dead for the same reason. The sin, in this case, is female sexuality. What is sinful about it is that it arouses men, who are weak. Why men should not be aroused, Stoker doesn't say, but one can guess.

These notions are easier to laugh at—in a nervous sort of way— when abstracted from the novel's events than when left latent in them. Stoker's terrific sincerity is the very opposite of camp. Especially the novel's main event, Lucy's transformation, which is stretched as on a rack over two hundred pages, pulls you in by the lapels. Her full name is Lucy Westenra, which, as a number of critics have remarked, means roughly "Light of the

West"; her decline into vampirism has about it the atmosphere of a world-historical catastrophe. Certainly she has the qualities of a daydream we can document in the writings of Western males straight back to Chaucer, at least. She is very fair, so gorgeous that three well-set-up males propose to her in a single day. She is virginal, innocent, inexperienced, sweet, defenseless, a damsel in distress, a stimulus to fantasies of sexual assault. And she has all the right attitudes: she regularly makes invidious comparisons between the sexes in favor of the male's greater nobility, bravery, generosity, fair-mindedness, competence, good sense, steadfastness of purpose, self-control, and all-around virtuousness. She has nothing but scorn for the "New Woman," the feminists of her day.

But this paragon, as she sleepwalks out to Dracula and thereafter night after night opens her window to him, proves that after all she is only a woman. One good effect of Lucy's assignations with Dracula is that it brings together the novel's main male characters, whose bonds of friendship to each other are made of better stuff than the love of a woman. When her fiancé, Arthur Holmwood, later Lord Godalming (a good name for a would-be savior), becomes alarmed over her lethargy and anaemia, he calls in his friend, Dr. Seward, one of Lucy's former suitors. Dr. Seward brings with him Quincey Morris, an outdoorsy but housebroken American, Lucy's third suitor. Stumped by Lucy's symptoms, Dr. Seward then calls in his old teacher, Dr. Van Helsing, for a consultation. Now that the patriarch is in place, this primal horde comes close to saving Lucy from herself, from her openness to Dracula. Their treatment, in the main, is to make Lucy eat a lot, to decorate her person and her bedchamber with the symbols of Christianity and with garlic plants, and, above all, to give her transfusions of blood. "A brave man's blood is the best thing on this earth when a woman is in trouble," says Van Helsing to Quincey Morris. "You're a man and no mistake. Well, the devil may work against us for all he's worth, but God sends us men when we want them."

That's what Lucy thinks, too. Flustered at having to turn down two of her three suitors, Lucy had prettily asked "Why can't they let a girl marry three men, or as many as want her, and save all this trouble?" She gets her wish, metaphorically speaking, as the men empty their vital fluid into her. Each time, the transfusion restores Lucy's rosy cheeks, but leaves the donor pale and limp. "No man knows, till he experiences it, what it is to feel his own life-blood drawn into the veins of the woman he loves," says Dr. Seward, with a sigh. And each time the sacrifices of the men are negated by women, as Lucy, her mother, or maidservants remove those smelly garlic plants or crucifixes, or sleep on the job of lookout while the depleted men try to revivify themselves with sleep, Death's brother. As Lucy inexorably sinks, all the parental figures die off—Lucy's mother, Arthur's father, Harker's foster father, even Gerald Swales, one hundred years old, who had taken Lucy and Mina under his wing. (Lucy had been fatherless and Mina had been motherless and fatherless to begin with.) Parental authority out of the way, Lucy dies into undeath.

Soon there are newspaper stories of a "Bloofer Lady," or beautiful lady, who kidnaps children and then leaves them where patrolling Bobbies find them dazed, weak, and with pinpricks on their necks. Dr. Van Helsing knows what is happening, but his comrades refuse to believe him. One night, at the stroke of twelve, he leads them to Lucy's grave, so that they can see for themselves.

Here, in Dr. Seward's words, is what they see:

a dark-haired woman, dressed in the cerements of the grave. We could not see the face, for it was bent down over what we saw to be a fair-haired child. There was a pause and a sharp little cry, such as a child gives in sleep....My own heart grew cold as ice, and I could hear the gasp of Arthur, as we recognized the features of Lucy Westenra, but yet how changed. The sweetness was turned to adamantine, heartless cruelty, and the purity to voluptuous wantonness....We could see that the lips were crimson with fresh blood, and that the stream had trickled over her chin and stained the purity of her lawn death-robe.

When Lucy—I call the thing that was before us Lucy because it bore her shape—saw us she drew back with an angry snarl, such as a cat gives when taken unawares; then her eyes ranged over us. Lucy's eyes in form and colour; but Lucy's eyes unclean and full of hell-fire, instead of the pure, gentle orbs we knew. At that moment the remnant of my love passed into hate and loathing; had she then to be killed, I could have done it with savage delight. As she looked, her eyes blazed with unholy light, and the face became wreathed with a voluptuous smile. Oh, God, how it made me shudder to see it! With a careless motion, she flung to the ground, callous as a devil, the child that up to now she had clutched strenuously to her breast, growling over it as a dog growls over a bone. The child gave a sharp cry, and lay there moaning. There was a cold-bloodness in the act which wrung a groan from Arthur; when she advanced to him with outstretched arms and a wanton smile he fell back and hid his face in his hands.

She still advanced, however, and with a languorous, voluptuous grace, said:—

"Come to me, Arthur. Leave these others and come to me. My arms are hungry for you. Come, and we can rest together. Come, my husband, come!"

There was something diabolically sweet in her tones—something of the tingling of glass when struck—which rang through the brains even of us who heard the words addressed to another. As for Arthur, he seemed under a spell; moving his hands from his face, he opened wide his arms. She was leaping for them, when Van Helsing sprang forward and held between them his little golden crucifix. She recoiled from it, and, with a suddenly distorted face, full of rage, dashed past him as if to enter the tomb....

Never did I see such baffled malice on a face; and never, I trust, shall such ever be seen again by mortal eyes. The beautiful colour became livid, the eyes seemed to throw out sparks of hell-fire, the brows were wrinkled as though the folds of the flesh were the coils of Medusa's snakes, and the lovely, blood-stained mouth grew to an open square, as in the passion masks of the Greeks and Japanese. If ever a face meant death—if looks could kill—we saw it at that moment.

Lucy's sweetness turns into heartless cruelty, her purity into voluptuous wantonness, her gentle orbs into unclean hell-fire, her beautiful color into a livid flush. And because of these changes, Dr. Seward's love turns into hate and loathing. "Had she then to be killed," he says, "I could have done it with savage delight." The single catalyst for these transformations is the element of sex. All that has been perceptibly added to Lucy is sexuality. "Come, my husband, come!" she says, like many an exasperated wife before her. But before Arthur can come, Van Helsing intervenes, as he had intervened once before, as Dracula had intervened between Jonathan Harker and the vampire ladies. And as though she were not already hateful enough, Lucy "with a careless motion" flings the child from her breast, where instead of nursing it, she had been feeding on it. An aroused female sexuality, that is, does not nurture children and husbands; it drains them dry and tosses them aside. Female sexuality is insatiable and selfish, indifferent to the decent self-restraint, the self-sacrifice and suppression of appetite upon which survival of the family depends. It is the very antithesis of Motherhood. Thus the Light of the West goes out. No wonder the men agree that the next day at noon they will put stop to the nonsense once and for all.

As they look down into Lucy's coffin, any qualms they may have felt are quenched by her debauched aspect, by "the bloodstained, voluptuous mouth—which it made one shudder to see— the whole carnal and unspiritual appearance, seeming like a devilish mockery of Lucy's sweet purity." As Lucy's fiancé, Arthur has best claim to do the honors—"the work of her destruction was yielded as a privilege to the one best entitled to it." He places the point of a sharpened stake over her heart, so that you can "see its dint in the white flesh," while Van Helsing reads a prayer for the dead. "Then he struck with all his might," and Dr. Seward's choice of words makes us see an even more primal scene behind the one he describes:

> The Thing in the coffin writhed; and a hideous, blood-curdling screech came from the opened red lips. The body shook and quivered and twisted in wild contortions; the sharp white teeth champed together till the lips were cut, and the mouth was smeared with a crimson foam. But Arthur never faltered. He looked like a figure of Thor as his untrembling arm rose and fell, driving deeper and deeper the mercy-bearing stake, whilst the blood from the pierced heart welled and spurted up around it. His face was set, and high duty seemed to shine through it; the sight of it gave us courage so that our voices seemed to ring through the little vault.
>
> And then the writhing and quivering of the body became less, and the teeth seemed to champ, and the face to quiver. Finally it lay still. The terrible task was over.
>
> The hammer fell from Arthur's hand. He reeled and

would have fallen had we not caught him. The great drops of sweat sprang from his forehead, and his breath came in broken gasps. It had indeed been an awful strain on him....

The sympathy, which has a narcissistic ring to it, is all for poor Arthur, maybe because Lucy seems to be having the best orgasm in recorded history. Either way you look at Arthur's mercy-bearing stake, Lucy is the sole beneficiary, either of a saved soul or a satiated body. No doubt that is why high duty shone on Arthur's face—which only shows how easy it is to do one thing while your mind is on another, a slight of mind not restricted to bedrooms of the Victorian era. That high duty, we gather, is to give Lucy in spades the punishment she was asking for, but the trick lies in not letting yourself know that you enjoy doing it. The knowledge would cancel out the enjoyment. One therefore does one's duty, but the strain is awful.

That Stoker is not the only one who felt this strain we can tell from a medical text first published in 1857 and then regularly brought out in new editions, translations, and reprints until 1894, around when Stoker began to write *Dracula*. This text is evidence that the fears behind Dr. Seward's hate and Arthur's retribution had their public and scientific equivalents. The author of the text was William Acton, a reform-minded doctor known for his enlightened views on the problem of prostitution. The full title of his book is *The Function and Disorders of the Reproductive Organs, in Childhood, Youth, Adult Age, and Advanced Life, Considered in their Physiological, Social, and Moral Relations*. That seems to say it all, but the book has important omissions: only two very brief passages mention women at all, as though they had no reproductive organs worth mentioning. The longer of these passages reveals why Acton was anxious to keep these organs out of sight and out of mind. Here is how he reassures young men hesitating on the brink of marriage for fear that their bedroom duties will be too much for them: [2]

> I should say that the majority of women (happily for them) are not very much troubled with sexual feeling of any kind. What men are habitually, women are only exceptionally. It is too true, I admit, as the divorce courts show, that there are some few women who have sexual desires so strong that they surpass those of men.... I admit, of course, the existence of sexual excitement terminating even in nymphomania, a form of insanity which those accustomed to visit lunatic asylums must be fully conversant with; but, with these sad exceptions, there can be no doubt that sexual feeling in the female is in the majority of cases in abeyance...and even if roused (which in many instances it never can be) is very moderate compared with that of the male. Many men, and particularly young men, form their ideas of women's feelings from what they notice early in life among loose or, at least, low and vulgar women.... Any susceptible boy is easily led to believe, whether he is altogether overcome by the syren or not, that she, and therefore all women, must have at least as strong passions as himself. Such women however give a very false idea of the condition of female sexual feeling in general. Association with the loose women of London streets, in casinos, and other immoral haunts (who, if they have not sexual feeling, counterfeit it so well that the novice does not suspect but that it is genuine), all seem to corroborate such an impression, and... it is from these erroneous notions that so many young men think that the marital duties they will have to undertake are beyond their exhausted strength, and from this reason dread and avoid marriage....

---

[2] *The substance of this paragraph and the quotation that follows it come from Steven Marcus (1966).*

> The best mothers, wives, and managers of households, know little or nothing of sexual indulgences. Love of home, children, and domestic duties, are the only passions they feel.
>
> As a general rule, a modest woman seldom desires any sexual gratification for herself. She submits to her husband, but only to please him; and, but for the desire of maternity, would far rather be relieved from his attentions. No nervous or feeble young man need, therefore, be deterred from marriage by any exaggerated notion of the duties required from him. The married woman has no wish to be treated on the footing of a mistress.

Having argued that in the equations of medical science women are an unknown, I am in no position to say whether this passage is true or false, so far as it regards women. So far as it regards men, I can say a little, on the presumption of an insider's knowledge. That men are in general fearful and weak, for example, any woman who has been married to a man can testify. But most men, I think, would find it hard to locate within themselves Acton's specific shrinking horror and resultant denial of female sexuality. For myself, all I have ever consciously wanted, since about age eleven, is for some woman to take me as a sex object entirely. No doubt the horror is buried very deep, which may be why Stoker had to disguise it as a fear of vampirism. Quite likely, it is in part an elaboration of a still deeper fear of castration. After all, who wants to be castrated? But all that is for those of you with expert knowledge to say. For me the symptoms are enough, more than enough. I am not yet so far gone as to want to know the first cause of anything. That's where the real horror lies.

If Lucy becomes an epitome of what is horrifying about women, Mina is an exemplar of what women must become to avoid the mercy-bearing stake. Oh, she is enough of a woman to fall some distance into vampirism. ("I suppose it is some of the taste of the original apple that remains still in our mouths," as she herself observes.) But she does not go all the way. The traits that enable her to hold back from going all the way are the traits that make her an exemplar of feminine virtue. For one thing, she knows enough to put her fate into the hands of men. When the men decide to keep her in the dark about their plans for destroying Dracula—"It is too great a strain for a woman to bear," says Dr. Van Helsing—she agrees that they know what is best for her: "I suppose it is one of the lessons that we poor women have to learn," she says.

For another thing, she understands that her gender-specific purpose in life is to be of service to men. While still only engaged to Jonathan she studied shorthand, timetables, and business law, so as to be "useful" to her future husband. "I must attend to my husband" is her constant refrain. But if she is wifely to Jonathan, she is daughterly to Van Helsing, sisterly to Quincey Morris, and motherly to Arthur in his bereavement. "We woman have something of the mother in us that makes us rise above smaller matters when the mother spirit is evoked," she says; "I felt this big sorrowing man's head resting on me, as if it were that of the baby that some day may lie on my bosom, and I stroked his hair as though he were my child"—thus showing that, unlike Lucy, she knows what a bosom is for.

Again unlike Lucy, she is fully conscious of her taint, which she properly abhors. By way of introduction to a plea that the men do away with her should she become a full-fledged vampire, she says this:

> I know that all that brave earnest men can do for a poor weak woman, whose soul perhaps is lost—no, no, not yet, but is at any rate at stake —you will do. But you must remember that I am not as you are. There is a poison in my blood, in my soul, which may destroy me; which must destroy me, unless some relief comes to us.

Better yet, and still unlike Lucy, she knows how dangerous her taint is to men, how vigilantly she must suppress her passion to infect Jonathan. "Unclean, unclean!" she exclaims. "I must touch him or kiss him no more. Oh, that it should be that it is I who I am now his worst enemy, and whom he may have most cause to fear."

It is not surprising, then, that prose poems in praise of Mina, that "pearl among women," flow from Van Helsing's lips: she is proof "that there are good women still left to make life happy." In fact, "she is one of God's women, fashioned by His own hand to show us men and other women that there is a heaven where we can enter, and that its light can be here on earth. So true, so sweet, so noble, so little an egoist—and that, let me tell you, is much in this age, so sceptical and selfish." Mina is a haven in a heartless world. That's much, but not everything. What above all enables her to resist Dracula, to conquer her own female nature, is that she is not entirely a woman. Morally speaking, that most important component in her makeup is masculine. She does not have the primitive and criminal brain of Dracula. She has the brain of a man. "Ah, that wonderful Madame Mina!" says Dr. Van Helsing. "She has a man's brain—a brain that a man should have were he much gifted—and a woman's heart," the perfect combination. It is through application of "her great brain which is trained like a man's brain" that she is able to organize a mass of documents so as to reveal to the men exactly what Dracula is, what his plans are, and how to track him down. Thus her better half helps to defeat her worser.

So there we have it: through Mina, we see what men want of women. Through Lucy we see what men both want and don't want. Men want women to be at once sexy and virginal, for example, and motherly to boot. They like their women to be womanly, but will kill them for it, at least in their imaginations. They also like their women to be manly. But it would take a far less easily fatigued pen than mine to itemize all that men want of women, for men are weak. I will skip the addition and guess at the sum: men say that women are this or that, rather than that or this, because they need women to be this or that—which has the sound of a tautology (like other statements about matters of importance). But between the first term and its return we pass through one explanation of misogyny. I would say that the size of a man's misogyny is equal to the distance between the compliant creatures of his daydreams and the women he actually meets, who are different, to put it mildly.

One final word, for the last thing I want to be confused with is a feminist. Although I know nothing about women, I believe that if you were to look at how women writers depict men, in, say, *Frankenstein* and *Jane Eyre*, you would find yourself in a separate but equal madhouse of fascination and dread, of displaced horror, misdirected violence, and abysmal longings. For although I know nothing about women, I am a firm believer in the equality of the sexes.

BIBLIOGRAPHY

Farson, D. 1975. *The Man who Wrote Dracula: A biography of Bram Stoker*. London: Michael Joseph.

Ludlam, H. 1962. *A Biography of Dracula: The life story of Bram Stoker*. London: W. Foulsham, see Chap. 24: "Dracula as Play."

McNally, R T., and Florescu, R 1972. *In Search of Dracula*. Greenwich, Conn.: New York Graphic Society.

Marcus, S. 1966. *The Other Victorians: A study of sexuality and pornography in mid-nineteenth century England*. New York: Basic Books.

Roth, P. A. 1982. *Bram Stoker*. Boston: Twayne Publishers.

Stoker, B. 1897. *Dracula*. With an introduction by George Stade. New York: Bantam Books, 1981.

Wolff, C G. 1972. "*A Mirror for Men: Stereotypes of women in literature.*" *Massachusetts Review* (Winter-Spring): 205-218.

FRANKENSTEIN'S MEN, AND WHY MARY HATED TO LOVE THEM

Response to a lecture on Frankenstein given to the English Institute. Previously unpublished.

The full title of Mary Shelley's novel is *Frankenstein, or the Modern Prometheus.* To the Romantics, among others, Prometheus was the Titanic form of mankind as rebel against the gods, as antagonist of Zeus, God of things as they are, as stealer of fire from heaven, as heroic striver. He was taken as both the creator of humanity and the type of its aspiring energies, as that in humanity out of which humanity creates itself. His name means Fore-Sight, the specifically human category of intelligence. Only ten years before the publication of *Frankenstein*, Goethe had published Part I of his masterpiece, in which the Prometheus that the Renaissance had resurrected as Faust was re-resurrected as mainly a victimizer of women. To Mary Shelley, the career of Prometheus-Faust was a cautionary tale of how the attempts of men to be more than human made them something worse and less—and how it made the lives of their women miserable.

For examples of Prometheanism around her she had, on the one hand, the French revolution, favorite topic of discussion in her father's circle, which included such Protheans as William

Blake and Tom Paine. And she had, on the other hand, the equally revolutionary transformation of the world by science, industry, and technology, a favorite subject of the Romantic poets. Her husband was a rebel, an atheist, an advocate of free love, an idealist, a Platonist, an occultist, a man who dabbled in alchemy and science and nearly blew himself up during an experiment. It is easy to think of him as someone who anticipated in himself the whole of the 1960s in America. Her mother was a passionate and impetuous feminist with one illegitimate child when she married Mary Shelley's father once again four months pregnant. She was author of A *Vindication of the Rights of Woman*, which can be looked at, not quite fairly, as an attempt to claim for women the Promethean fire men had stolen from Zeus. Her daughter became an anti-feminist champion of domestic regularity. Mary Shelley's father was a philosophic anarchist and theoretic revolutionary, another totally impractical idealist, author of a book entitled *Lives of the Necromancers*, a man who systematically put reason over feeling, which he mainly thought of as evidence of lamentable but curable human imperfection. He was always saying such things as this:

> Perfectibility is one of the most unequivocal characteristics of the human species, so that the political as well as the intellectual state of man may be presumed to be in a course of progressive improvement.

And:

> We talk familiarly indeed of the limits of our faculties, but nothing is more difficult than to point them out. Man, in a progressive view at least, is infinite.

And:

Reason may yet discover the secret of physical immortality and perpetual youth.

Dr. Frankenstein becomes a scientist in an attempt to discover the secrets of physical immortality and perpetual youth. He wants to banish sickness and death, to turn men into gods. He leaves his pining family, forgets them for years, labors in solitary demonic energy to recapitulate in himself the whole history of science, from ancient magic to some futuristic version of experimental biophysics. "I had retrod the steps of knowledge along the steps of time," he says, but he approaches his goal with ambivalent feelings, On the one hand he is euphoric:

No one can conceive the variety of feelings which bore me onward, like a hurricane, in the first enthusiasm of success. Life and death appeared to me ideal bounds, which should I first break through, and pour a torrent of light into our dark world. A new species would bless me as its creator and source; many happy and excellent natures would owe their being to me. No father could claim the gratitude of his child so completely as I should deserve theirs. Pursuing these reflections, I thought that if I could bestow animation upon lifeless matter, I might in process of time... renew life where death had apparently devoted the body to corruption.

On the other hand, he has the creeps:

Now I was led to examine the cause and progress of... decay and forced to spend nights in vaults and charnel houses. My attention was fixed upon every object the most insupportable to the delicacy of human feelings.

Often, there was a prurient curiosity, an atmosphere of the primal scene:

> After days and nights of incredible labor and fatigue, I succeeded in discovering the cause of generation and life; nay, more, I became myself capable of bestowing animation upon lifeless matter—

which sounds like something a boy might say upon finally masturbating to ejaculation. In any case, there is a pervasive sense of obscene violation:

> It was the secrets of heaven and earth that I desired to learn... the physical secrets of the world.
>
> He wanted to penetrate into the recesses of nature and show how she works in her hiding places.
>
> I will pioneer a new way, explore unknown powers, and unfold to the world the deepest mysteries of creation.
>
> He had a fervent desire to penetrate the secrets of nature, to unveil the face of nature, to enter the citadel of nature.

Well, he does, and then begets there what he describes as that "living monster of presumption and rash ignorance which I had let loose on the world." The victims of this presumption are first, William, the doctor's angelic and pre-adolescent brother, whose name, to the amazement of biographers, is that of Mary Shelley's infant son, but also of her father, and of her half-brother and rival, son of her father and step-mother. The second victim is Justine, an orphan, an instance of the girlish innocence that so excited the Marquis de Sade, about whom the Shelleys seem to have known. She is framed by the monster and hanged by a heartless all-male jury. Another victim is Henry Clerval, the doctor's friend, a poet, a representative of Shelley in his aspect of blithe spirit of nature. While Frankenstein studies science, Clerval studies Oriental literature and languages, which are described as "a garden house of the affectionate pleasures." A fourth victim is Elizabeth Lavinzer, Dr. Frankenstein's fiancée, "the living spirit of love," as she's described, whose own mother died in childbirth, whose father was a rash and daring Italian painter, dumped in a prison, fate unknown. Then there is Frankenstein's mother, Caroline, a type of maternal love and self-sacrifice, whose mother also died young, whose father was a self-absorbed and rashly speculative businessman. Finally there is the doctor's father, who after all this, dies of grief. These characters are all "hapless victims of my unhallowed arts," all victims of a universal conspiracy against domesticity, the maternal, the female, the natural, the familial, a conspiracy that turns such minor women characters such as Agatha de Lacey and Safie into fugitives—and that puts Safie's Christian mother into the harem of a randy Turk.

And these victims had their equivalents in Mary Shelley's experience. Her mother died giving birth to her, for which she never forgave herself or her mother, even though she spent many hours at her mother's grave, reading her works. Fanny Imlay, Mary's stepsister, her mother's other daughter, committed suicide four months after Mary began *Frankenstein*, perhaps out of despairing love of Shelley, perhaps after Godwin coldly informed her that he was not her father. Harriet Shelley, to whom Percy Bysshe was still married when Mary ran off with him, also committed suicide. In her drowned body was found a five-month-old fetus, father unknown. On a finger was Shelley's wedding ring. And Mary's first child died eleven days after its birth. Soon after, Mary had a dream "that my baby came to life again; that it had been cold, and that we rushed it before the fire, and it lived."

The outer rim of the novel's meaning, then, revolves between opposed energies. On the one side is masculine striving, aggressive attempts to subjugate the world by mind; pure reason and revolutionary enthusiasm; disembodied cerebration, intellection stifling the affections; science, technology—the project, in short, of making mother nature groan in a conceptual embrace. On the other side is a diffuse feminine Eros which laves people in the warm bath of domestic tranquility. It suffused Nature until men alienated us from her. The moral is pointed out by a chastened Dr. Frankenstein himself:

> A human being in perfection ought always to preserve a calm and peaceful mind and never to allow passion or a transitory desire to disturb his tranquility. I do not think that the pursuit of knowledge is an exception to this rule. If the study to which you apply yourself has a tendency to weaken your affections and to destroy your taste for those simple pleasures in which no alloy can possibly mix, then that study is certainly unlawful, that is, not befitting the human mind. If this rule were always observed; if no man allowed any pursuit whatsoever to interfere with the tranquility of his domestic affections, Greece had not been enslaved. Caesar would have spared his country. America would have been discovered more gradually, and the empires of Mexico and Peru had not been destroyed.

Concentric within this meaning is another. As everyone has noticed, the monster is the doctor's alter ego, his repressed unconscious, in fact. Says the doctor: "I considered the being whom I had cast among mankind, and endowed with the will and power to affect purposes of horror, nearly in the light of my own vampire, my own spirit let loose from the grave, and forced to destroy all that was dear to me." Says the monster, "my form is a filthy type of yours, more horrid even from the very resemblance."

The monster is both familiar and horridly alien, both *heimlich* and *unheimlich*, the domestic become wild and the wild domesticated, according to the principles announced by Freud in his essay on the uncanny. It is fascinating because it is the apparition of a wish and because the wish is ours; it is revolting because it is repressed, because the repressing agencies see it that way, because they made it that way. We are sympathetic to it because it represents something we desire; we hate it for the same reason, "I am malicious because I am miserable," says the monster, "I will avenge my injuries; if I cannot inspire love, I will inspire fear." Women faint at the sight of it; men become violent. It is utterly alone: it pleads for a mate: "I demand a creature of another sex, but as hideous as myself," it says. The doctor complies, but has second thoughts as he looks his handiwork over:

> She might become ten thousand times more malignant than her mate and delight for its own sake, in murder and wretchedness.... They might even hate each other; the creature who already lived loathed his own deformity, and might he not conceive a greater abhorrence for it when it came before his eyes in the female form?

In a fury of revulsion, the doctor rips the thing up, thereby adding to the list of female victims.

The monster, who is a stickler for symmetry, reciprocally kills Elizabeth on the night of her wedding to the doctor—the point being that repressed sex destroys all possibilities of the other kind, of love. Thereafter, the doctor pursues the monster, as he puts it, with "the mechanical impulse of some power of which I was unconscious." They switch positions of power as the repressed gains ascendancy: "You are my creator; but I am your master; obey!" says the monster.

Within this inner circle of meaning is still another. As the monster is to the doctor, so is the doctor to whatever created him. After a conversation with his progeny, the doctor ruminates: "For the first time, also, I felt what the duties of a creator towards his creature were, and that I ought to render him happy before I complained of his wickedness." In short, it is God's fault, whatever God is, that we are as we are, that we are like Dr. Frankenstein in one way, like his monster in another.

A long central portion of the novel is given over to the monster's autobiography. His career is a summary of the whole history of the evolution of human consciousness, culture, and civilization as Shelley's generation understood it. He moves from food-gathering, to fire-making, to tool-using, to speech, to a fallen knowledge of history, of the destruction of empires. His first library consists of *Werther*, Plutarch's *Lives*, and *Paradise Lost*, He moves from an innocent and benign love of nature, of other humans, and of all living creatures (the monster is a vegetarian—"My food is not that of man: I do not destroy the lamb and the kid to glut my appetite; acorns and berries afford me sufficient nourishment,") to ideals, to disenchantment, to wretchedness, to self-consciousness, to alienation from nature, to mad vengeful fury. In the beginning, he says, "my thoughts were once filled with sublime and transcendent visions of the beauty and majesty of goodness." But then: "Increase of knowledge only discovered to me more clearly what a wretched outcast I was." Finally: "From that moment I declared everlasting war against the species, and more than all, against him who had formed me and sent me forth to this insupportable misery."

The monster, that is, represents what Shelley feared mankind was coming to. Through a long inexorable historical process, we have increasingly repressed eros, associated with women, nature, domesticity, in behalf of knowledge and power, associated with men. But as the repressed slowly returns, Eros exacts its revenge in the monstrous form of a raging lust, dripping death. What was best in us becomes the worst thing in the world. In another of Shelley's novels, The *Last Man*, humankind finishes itself off.

But the hub of the novel's meaning, the circle within the circles, revolves on Mary Shelley's own fearful aspirations. The sad fact is that she wanted to be a man, and in the novel she acts out this fearful aspiration through three male personas: Walton, the frame narrator, Dr. Frankenstein, the main narrator, and the monster, who in a long central passage, narrates the central mystery. No one but Mary Shelley unleashed that monster; she herself, in fury, hate, and vengeance directed the monster to kill stand-ins for her father, her child, her half-brother, all named "William." She herself, again and again, had it kill stand-ins for her mother, who was responsible for Mary's being born a daughter. It was she, not men, who wanted to kill the woman in her, on the basis of the understandable sentiment that it is preferable to be a victimizer rather than a victim. Of course, she also hated her aspiration, feared it, felt guilt over it—that's why *Frankenstein* is a horror story.

HIS ALTER EGO IS A KILLER

Review of *The Dark Half* by Stephen King. The *New York Times Book Review*, October 29, 1989.

This is not the first time that Stephen King has written a dark allegory of the fiction writer's situation. *Misery* (1987) is a parable in chiller form of the popular writer's relation to his audience, which holds him prisoner and dictates what he writes, on pain of death. Mr. King's new novel, *The Dark Half*, is a parable in chiller form of the popular writer's relation to his creative genius, the vampire within him, the part of him that only awakes to raise Cain when he writes, the fratricidal twin who occupies "the womblike dungeon" of his imagination.

Thaddeus Beaumont is the writer in question. At age eleven he writes his first story. Around the same time he begins to get excruciating headaches, which culminate in a convulsion. Surgery reveals something startling—first an eye, then other small fragments of an incompletely absorbed twin that's lodged in his brain. This sort of "*in utero* cannibalism," according to his doctor, is not unusual, although rarely is anything left undigested, as it is in Thad Beaumont's case.

The operation is a success, and Thad grows up to be a mild-mannered professor of creative writing, a doting husband and the father of twins, a modestly successful writer of novels with titles like *Purple Haze*. But under the pen name of George Stark he is the bestselling author of ferocious thrillers like *Sharkmeat*

Pie, the protagonist of which is named Alexis Machine because he kills like one.

Circumstances force Thad to own up to his pseudonym, which in any case has become irksome. He has decided to go it on his own, to lay his fictional self to rest. He and his wife even hold a mock burial service for George Stark, papier-mâché tombstone and all. But one morning a man-sized cavity is discovered at the site. Footprints lead away. Very soon, people begin to die horribly, in particular everybody associated with Thad's decision to bury George Stark, whose prose style governs the graphic and gruesome descriptions of the murders. For George Stark has materialized. As Stark himself puts it, "The word became flesh, you might say."

But George Stark is not content to be merely undead. He wants to be alive entirely. He wants Thad to begin another novel under Stark's name. In fact, he wants to collaborate with Thad, to learn how to write, to become independent. Unless Thad complies, Stark will truly fade out of existence, for his flesh has begun to rot, decay, stink and ooze fluids, although no outside force seems capable of destroying him. Thad is forced to comply, for Stark has taken his wife and children hostage. As the collaboration gets going, Stark begins to heal; Thad develops running sores.

On the whole, Mr. King is tactful in teasing out the implications of his parable—never mind an author's note that acknowledges a debt to "the late Richard Bachman," Mr. King's own pseudonym, without whom "this novel could not have been written." No character in the novel comes right out and says, for example, that writers exist (at least to readers) only in their writing, that each person (at least to himself) is his own fiction, that the writer's imagination can feel alien to him, a possessing and possessive demon, a Dracula arisen to prey on the whole man and his family. Nor does anyone in the novel say outright that reality inevitably leaks fiction, which then floods reality, that reality and fiction feed on and feed each other, that they are at war yet they are twins—so identical that attempts to say which is which only lead to more fictions. Such things are better left unsaid, anyhow. Stephen King is not a post-modernist.

He is, however, a very good storyteller. *The Dark Half* mostly succeeds, as both parable and chiller, in spite of occasional clichés of thought and expression and bits of sophomoric humor (the F.B.I. is "the Effa Bee Eye," marijuana is "wacky tobaccy"). At the end, the decent family man wins out, but at a cost—which is how it should be. Most readers, I believe, will want decency and reality to triumph, but only with some reluctance, only after their most monstrous imaginings, like George Stark, have been unearthed and indulged. And few writers around are better than Stephen King at giving readers what they want.

MONSTERS HAVE NEEDS, TOO

Review of *Mr. Murder*, by Dean Koontz. The *New York Times Book Review*, October 31, 1993.

The plot of Dean Koontz's new novel, his twenty-second, is one that with variations he has used before (understandably enough)—but so have others, including Mary Shelley. And why not? The professional responsibility of a popular writer to good stories is precisely that he retell them (with variations), a good story being one that scratches you where you itch. The story in *Mr. Murder* is that of a misbegotten monster whose form is human, whose powers are demonic, whose motive is revenge, whose rage is implacable, whose nemesis is also an alter ego. The objects of his rage are Marty Stillwater, a mystery writer; his plucky wife, Paige, a therapist; and their lovable daughters, Charlotte and Emily, who are sometimes tough to take.

The monster, when we first meet him, is referred to simply as "the killer," although he gets other names later, like "the Other." He seems to be a professional assassin, but after one job well done, he is driven by an inexplicable and irresistible urge to travel cross-country (leaving corpses in his wake) toward California, where the Stillwaters live. He does not know who or what he is; he has no memories, no experience to guide him. But unlike Mary Shelley's monster, who learns how to live by reading Plutarch and *Paradise Lost*, Mr. Koontz's monster goes to the movies ("Movies had all the answers to life's problems," he thinks). And unlike Frankenstein's monster, who is a vegetarian, the killer is a prodigious consumer of junk food, a very modern monster. What is more, the killer, was manufactured not by a fevered genius but by a shadowy organization called the Network, run by experts in genetic engineering, among other things (in our times mad doctors tend to be corporate, rather than individual).

Just the same, there is something primitive about him, something of those energies that reason and civilization were invented to control. Like Frankenstein's monster and like the unconscious, he is a rampaging appetite, his slogan "I need." Early on he says, "I need to be someone"; near the end he says, "All I needed was to be loved," for like his original, he is full of self-pity. But he does not know exactly what it is he needs until he breaks into Marty Stillwater's house. There, from photos and other evidence, he decides that Marty, who looks exactly like him down to the smallest detail, is a "replicant" who has stolen his family from him—his loving wife and daughters, who he thinks will love him all the more for the iron discipline with which he means to rule his household. The thought of their gratitude makes him weep generous tears, although his notion of how to love one's wife comes from sadomasochistic porn. In a terrific scene, Marty comes home and the doubles confront each other. "Why have you stolen my life?" asks the killer.

This time the Stillwaters manage to escape—barely. The rest of the novel is, in the main, given over to the killer's pursuit of them, their attempts to escape or ambush him, near misses, violent collisions, bystanders killed off right and left, the killer as relentless, as hard to destroy and as quick to recuperate as the Terminator. The final conflict, against a background of ice and snow (as in *Frankenstein*), is all it should be. It occurs in the deserted compound of a cult once led by a man named Caine, who turned out to be a child molester. The dark and ruined chapel is now polluted by the obscene graffiti written all over everything in luminous paint, images that flicker evocatively before the mind's eye.

There are other nice touches. One is the muted suggestion that it is Stillwater's interests as a writer, which are those of Mr. Koontz, that call up the monsters. Another is the genuinely funny and charming bedtime poem Stillwater reads to his daughters, a poem in which "Santa's evil twin" breaks into the Stillwater house to do mischief. For all that, *Mr. Murder* is no post-modernist comment on itself, no exercise in camp. Mr. Koontz plays it straight: there are no sly winks to the reader, no signals that although someone wrote the novel and someone is reading it, they are both above this sort of thing.

On the other hand, there are touches that get in the way of Mr. Koontz's best effects. I, for one, could do without the pregnant similes ("The metrical susurration of the night surf was like the slow and steady beating of a great heart"), or the melodramatic one-line paragraphs ("Nightmares were real. Monsters existed"), or the potted homilies ("While sociopaths stalked the modern world, the judicial system operated on the premise that evil was spawned primarily by societal injustice").

But these distractions count for little against the resounding variations Mr. Koontz plays on this good story, here craftily retold. They allow him to counterpoint the new horrors about us with the old horrors always inside us.

IV

THRILLERS

"Thrillers," *Columbia Forum* Vol XIII, No. 4, Spring 1970.

Although avant-garde writers have been claiming the opposite for one hundred years or so, popular, rather than esoteric, fictions are more likely to be abstract, to be forms without content, to be beautiful shapes with empty heads. Popular fictions are more likely to be conventional in character, technique, and plot, to be without those deviations from an expected norm that propel us into meaning. And in the history of any art form I can think of, the greater the reliance on convention, the greater the abstraction. A purely conventional fiction would not be an imitation of any single actuality, real or imaginable; it would be a system of counters for a whole class of attitudes toward and ideas about a condition that has endured for some time in the society that produced the conventions. A purely conventional fiction would be a kind of paradigm.

So it is, more or less, with the popular fictional forms—westerns, tales of outer space, thrillers, and the rest. As distinct from the highbrow writing of this century (at least in its heyday), popular fiction is like folk literature, is in a certain sense classical, in its reliance on a repertoire of characters, techniques, settings, plot formulae that pre-exist the appearance of any individual work. That is one reason why we tend to feel that the "meaning," the social function, of the popular literary forms is generic rather than individual. The differences among the thousands of Gothic romances seem less important than the similarities, except when the form is used by someone like Henry James or Iris Murdoch, in which case the differences are more important—even if it is the similarities that make the differences most visible.

Popular literature is literature read in a certain way; that is, one can read Henry James as one reads Charlotte Armstrong, or read Joseph Conrad as one reads C. S. Forester, and to do so is to turn them into popular writers. But it is not so easy. James and Conrad have built in certain kinds of meanings and provided for only certain kinds of satisfactions, so that the essential quality of their work resists attempts to turn them into popular writers (in the generic sense). The most satisfying popular literature has none of these built-in meanings. Tendentious popular literature is simply bad literature. The merely verbal joke, Freud says, is funnier than the pointed one; so in adventure fiction, the naked event is more like what we want than the edifying one: in neither case do we want to be distracted by a need to evaluate an attitude or to appraise a doctrine. Ideally speaking, popular literature is like a certain incident in Samuel Beckett's *Watt*, "of great formal brilliance and indeterminable purport."

The indeterminable purport explains why so many critics on the make have turned to the popular arts as pretexts for advertising some doctrine or other. The less meaning an author has wrapped around his story, the more room for the reader or critic to decorate the story with whatever gladdens his eye. Perfect criticism of great literature, on the other hand, is nothing else than perfect fidelity. When every rhythm, every action, every inflection, every relation among elements, every displacement of an expectation, is significant, nothing is as meaningful as the work itself. Merely to describe is to violate, to distort, to fall short. All that is left for a critic with an impulse toward commentary is to translate the language of the fiction into some discursive equivalent, to make the implicit explicit, to turn image into idea. (I am speaking of the ideal, not the practice, of course. But for critics to have written so much about *Hamlet*, for example, they had either to reduce it to popular literature first or they had to break faith with the relations among its elements.) Faithful criticism is low on short-run ego gratifications: it requires that the critic suppress whatever it is that makes him in his own eyes most himself—his attitudes, his values, his biases, his opinions, his philosophy, his very personality. To write pop criticism one does something else.

To write pop criticism of pop you make a display of hot items manufactured according to a pattern lifted from your favorite *couturier* of ideas—Sorel, say, or Derrida, Foucault, Susan Sontag, Kahlil Gibran. You talk fast and sell short, lest the market move on, lest the items cool, lest someone actually gets a chance to inspect your wares. And since your items, your notions, will not, in the form you have them, stand on their own, you string them on a fiction, which you jiggle to give them the illusion of independent life. The trick, then, is to find Durkheim in Dagwood, the church fathers in Chaplin, Bakunin in Bomba the Jungle Boy—or to find Heidegger in thrillers, as Ralph Harper does, for example, in a recent study, *The World of the Thriller*:

> All thrillers are basically concerned about two things: death and responsibility. Tillich may be right in thinking that the anxiety of meaninglessness is the characteristic anxiety of our time. The popularity of the "death of God" debate seems to confirm this. Few of us talk about personal death or guilt, or seem much concerned about either. But we read about them in thriller literature. What we do not acknowledge openly and directly, we at least read about. The thriller

world is Heideggerian rather than Tillichian. Its categories do not include meaninglessness, but rather Care, Dread, Death, Guilt, Time, and a Being-unto-Death, all the categories of contingency and resolution that we find in even the run-of-the-mill detective or spy story. If the categories of danger, tension, death, heroism are Heidegger's, the mood and momentum are Dostoevsky's.

Suppose one were to begin with the formal brilliance rather than the indeterminable purport? Suppose one were to isolate the conventions that make up thrillers and to outline the typical plot in which they are embedded. Suppose, that is, one were to build a model of the thriller, a model based on what seems most satisfying in existing thrillers. One might then be able to see what they are good for, what they can do for us. For strictly speaking the forms of popular fiction have functions, not meanings, except in the sense that a thing means what it does. In the following sketch I assume that the work of writers like Eric Ambler and Andrew Garve constitutes something like a norm; that Helen MacInnes stretches the norm in one direction (toward the romance) and Ian Fleming in another (toward science fiction); that Dashiell Hammett, Raymond Chandler, and Ross MacDonald write fusions of the thriller and the private-eye form; that Graham Greene and John Le Carré do with thrillers what Henry James in *The Turn of the Screw* and Charlotte Brontë in *Jane Eyre* do with the Gothic romance—fill them with content.

The prose, first of all, would be of a certain kind. It would be as transparent as possible; it would be as without tone (the author's attitude toward the reader), as without mood (the author's attitude toward his material), as without irony, mannerism, cliché, nudgings of symbolic import, as language will allow. Ideally, it would be without the refractions of class bias in diction and syntax that, in detective novels, we get on one end of the scale from the high-toned British ladies (Tey, Christie, Marsh, Sayers) and on the other from the low-brow American men, led by Mickey Spillane. It would have to be without any complication of arrangement or trope that might impede an urgent forward propulsion. It must do nothing to call attention to itself. It must in the main be made up of statements as to what someone saw, did, or said: nothing is so inscrutable as a perception flatly asserted. When a writer's prose is working for him, he can make a statement such as "Groddeck spat neatly into his handkerchief" or "the pigeons took flight amidst a clatter of wings" as luminously ambiguous as a dream. A certain amount of humor, preferably grim, in keeping with the action, is not only allowable, but desirable: it works as a dividend of pleasure to keep the reader going through passages of otherwise dull but essential exposition. It keeps the reader both alert and uncritical. Above all, the prose should be terse, if not in style, in effect: the author must allow for menace to flood the spaces left by what he does not say.

For a sense of unassignable menace, of anxiety produced by external rather than internal circumstances, is the generic effect of thrillers. This effect distinguishes thrillers from fictions in which the threat to the hero is experienced as either horror or terror. *Horror* is fear mixed with loathing. It occurs when a tenaciously repressed wish takes on perceptible form; it usually involves the threat of a sexual violation consciously loathed and unconsciously desired. *Terror* is fear at a distance—fear of annihilation, perhaps, but fear of a tangible and distinctly external agent. A charging grizzly produces terror, not horror, and not anxiety, exactly, either. When in a thriller, the sense of a menace whose center is everywhere and whose circumference is nowhere turns to simple terror, we can be sure that the anagnorisis—that sudden mind-boggling and stomach-sinking recognition of who's who and what's what—has occurred, or is about to. But when unassignable menace is mixed with an inadmissible wish, when the settings and characters out of which the menace flows offer what a decent person wants only a little less than he does not want to want it, the threat is thought of as *sinister*, a quality that defines the thriller's most delicious *frisson*.

The hero most in keeping with a world entirely sinister is not that distillate of brain and eccentricity in the tale of ratiocination, not the walking truncheon of the American private-eye novel, not the blighted absurdist of the European big caper type, not the obsessed quester of adventure yarns, not the intrepid loner of westerns, not the mad doctors of one kind of science fiction or the masters of technological white magic in another, not even a secret agent, unless he is on vacation or retired or recuperating, but an ordinary citizen, which in Western society means a businessman. He should not even believe that the world he will be sucked into exists. He is usually no longer young; overtly conventional in thoughts, attitudes, values, allegiances, sexual interests; of average intelligence and moderate education—accidentally sometimes because the author is that way, functionally so that he will be without the resources of youth or of special knowledge and abilities, and so that the reader can more easily share his experiences. Canny authors often introduce a hero who has just undergone a crisis, physical or spiritual, brought on by divorce, the death of a wife or son, a respectable illness. He begins isolated, empty, weak, ready to be filled in and filled out by what he undergoes.

The other characters are conventional in a different way: one learns how to put them together not from introspection or from observation, but from other literature and from fantasies, which are only less derivative than paintings by monkeys, paranoid delusions, and other products of minds devoid of intelligence. The most effective female characters, for example, appear under the aspects of pipe dream and daymare, the shape of a wish and the embodiment of a fear—from the male's point of view. Half the fun is that until the end you do not know which is which, and most of the unease comes from the fact that one could so easily have been the other. Nor is it easy to tell which is more satisfying to behold: the hero's embracing of his pipe dream or the exquisitely elaborate punishing of her anti-type, which punishment is usually brought on by either her own devices or by those of other villains—lest the hero's gratification be contaminated by responsibility for her undoing.

The other characters, villains and suspected villains mostly, are conventional in the way of caricatures and grotesques. In them human nature is pressed into an exemplary posture by an overriding humor, frozen into the shape of a deviation, softened by vice, deformed by obsession. They are either obese or gaunt, if not phthisic, if not bodies in which muscle has crowded out mind. If they are not grossly uncouth, they are finical: debauchees or dandies, or both. The major antagonist is often a connoisseur, a gourmet, an aesthete. He has a taste for esoteric learning, dangerous liquors, suspicious tobaccos. If he is not perversely sexless, he is simply perverse. He is Sidney Greenstreet or Peter Lorre. Around him hangs the savor of ruined 12-year-olds, of either sex. He and his colleagues are negative definitions of middle-class morality; that is why they are sinister.

In that respect they are like their environment, out of which they scarcely emerge. A flotsam world of official corruption, metropolitan squalor, sleazy finance, implacable lust, sordid opportunity, ancient grievance, casual violence, universal dispossession, and galactic ambition gathers in these characters to questionable shapes that are never seen but in a bad light, out of which they slide back into their element. They are spawned in some estaminet of Ankara, blistered in Baghdad, patched and peeled in Latakia. They can be bought for a drachma, sold for a dinar, rescued by a piaster. They operate in Shanghai, Hong Kong, Macao, Casablanca, Singapore, Tangier, Istanbul—wherever reason, rectitude, and restraint, the three R's that Westerners live by and hate, seem to count for nothing; wherever the political and moral anarchy that Westerners have longed for, feared, and rushed toward for at least two hundred years is alleged to be a fact.

Our hero does not think of himself as rushing toward this world. He is not an adventurer. He is an ordinary man travelling for business or for health. His passport is in order. His outlook and values have been certified by the perfection of their fit with the stable and daylight realm he had, for the moment, to leave. He orders his exotic dinner in confidence. But a slight misunderstanding, a comic and trivial case of mistaken identity, an absurd coincidence, a snatch of conversation overheard, the most trifling of accidents, and he is tripped into the ambiguous, the questionable, the menacing, the sinister, into a realm wherein no one and nothing can be relied upon, least of all to be one thing or the other for once and for all. The smallest step out of phase and the solid ground of saving illusions on which he lived and moved and had his being dissolves into its substratum. A dream of unease becomes the actuality that dreamed it.

He thrashes around at first, as he sinks through layer after layer of illusion, queer fish floating by all the while, until he begins to move downward on his own volition, driven by fear, drawn by a secret wish. When the pressure becomes unbearable he pops through the other side to stand upright on the solid ground that had first parted beneath him. The badly-shaven man in the rumpled Panama suit turns out to have been on his, and our, side. The pipe dream only lied to him because in his ignorance lay his salvation. The forces of order had been working for him all along and would have rescued him far sooner, had he not perversely insisted on getting to the heart of the matter on his own. Things are, after all, pretty much as they had always appeared to be, that is, how we hope they are—with reservations.

Thrillers, in brief, and the other genres of popular fiction, are in their public functions like rituals, and in their private functions like daydreams. When a society wants something very badly, something such as rain or prowess or public order, it produces a rite or a story in which the wish is accomplished mimetically. The rite or story may at the same time help its inventors to absorb, domesticate, reduce, live with, a fear—by containing it in a form, by affixing it to a mortal agent, by rubbing it into the public nose until the body politic gets used to the smell. But in thrillers, as in many rites, that which is feared, that which is brought forward only to be cast out, is also attractive. Its attractiveness is imprinted upon it by that to which it is sacrificed. Vice and disorder are cast out so that virtue and order can prevail, but vice and disorder are attractive to the extent that virtue and order do prevail, and vice and disorder are menacing and sinister to the extent that they are attractive. And because they are so very attractive the thriller gives them world enough and time to romp through the Casbahs of our longings.

To each reader as a private person, to that portion of each reader's character that is uniquely his own, thrillers will function as he needs them to function. Thrillers are abstract enough, paradigmatic enough, sufficiently empty of content for him to use them as pretexts for having whatever daydream will do him good. He can flesh them out with whatever wishes and fears, with whatever intellectual debris, is weighing him down. If the reader, then, like Ralph Harper, finds that more than in any other part of his intellectual life, in his reading of thrillers he is brought face to face with what he really is, that is unfortunate, but not surprising: we look for in literature what we need to find. If, however, what I take to be the public function of thrillers is really something private to me, I am in even worse trouble.

RATNER'S STAR

Review of *Ratner's Star* by Don DeLillo. The *New York Times Book Review*, June 20, 1976.

Don DeLillo's first three books had the feel of novels straining to be something else, of energies out of their element, tadpoles in a cocoon. If what novelists did was to round characters, set scenes and plot consequences, DeLillo was willing, but he did not seem happy doing it. He seemed happiest when careening off into a detour.

In *Americana* (1971), for instance, an executive at a TV network drops out of the rat race to drive cross-country in pursuit of reality, America, himself. He finds them, but the news is not good. In *End Zone* (1972), a flakey halfback at Logos College in Texas jukes his way through a rough season. There are many references to war-games and to Vietnam. And in *Great Jones Street* (1973), a rock star, tout of rout and impresario of zonk, silences himself, retreats to a dingy tenement. His reputation catches up to him, with sinister effect. These plots, with all their insistent but familiar purport, don't count for much, even with the author. What counts is the aside, the digression, the excursus—the set-pieces of bravura craziness and inspired quackery, the rapid-fire dialogue of pointed indirection and baited indiscretion, the displays of learning twisted just enough to reveal the obsession behind it.

DeLillo's new book is the something else his others were

straining to become. In *Ratner's Star* his energies are turned to Menippean satire—an ancient form invented by a Greek Cynic philosopher and ex-slave, developed by Lucian and Petronius and Apuleius, revived by Erasmus and Rabelais, preserved by Swift and Lewis Carroll, Americanized in *Moby Dick* and *Invisible Man* and *The Dream Life of Balso Snell*. This last was written by Nathanael West, to whom DeLillo is very close in mood. He is close in subject matter to Thomas Pynchon, who seems to have learned how to use the form through a study of William Gaddis, a presiding hidden genius, as it turns out, of post-war American fiction. The Menippean satire, in short, is the exemplary form of the moment.

It is the right form, that is, for fiction writers who have little interest in fitting together rounded characters, social relations and sequential plots—or who see little evidence of them in experience. It is the right form when experience seems to consist of discontinuous selves, collapsing institutions and arrested developments, which is how it seems to seem right now to our best fiction writers. In Menippean satires characters are reduced to the attitudes or theories for which they stand. Vice and folly are situated not in human nature or in social relations, but in distempers of intellect. Occupational bias and fantastic learning take the place of manners and morals. Plots are dislocated by juggernaut structures of ideas. Reality, social or other, is swallowed up by mind. And that is the way of things in Don DeLillo's new book.

The main mind in *Ratner's Star* is Billy Twillig, mathematician, specialist in zorgs, inventor of the stellated twilligon and the twillig nilpotent element, alumnus of the Center for the Refinement of Ideational Structures, Nobel laureate, a legend in his own time, but small for his age, which is fourteen.

He is called to a huge research complex to decipher what seems to be a signal from outer space. The year is 1979. Among his 2,000 colleagues are the beautiful Thorkild, expert in decollation control, who unfortunately has no lap; J. Graham Hummer, who provoked the famous "language riots" at M.I.T. with the claim that "what there is in common between a particular fact and the sentence that asserts it can itself be put into a sentence"; U.F.O. Schwartz, head of the Space Brain Complex; Siba Isten-Esru, a number shaman; Armand Verbene, S.J., who finds evidence of God's plans in the secretions of red ants; Sweet Jean Venable, author of "Eminent Stammerers," but suffering from a writer's block; Maurice Wu, archeologist, who discovers in a bat-loud cave that the earliest hominids devolved from creatures much like ourselves; and Orang Mohole, two-time winner of the Cheops Feeley Award for his contributions to alternate physics, a pill-popper and dispenser of rubber goods. These characters, and numerous others, are unstable; they tend to decompose and recombine—like portions of the universe they are trying to limn.

In particular, they are trying to limn a glim from the area of Ratner's Star. It is a signal made up of 14 pulses, a gap, 28 pulses, a gap, 57 impulses—or 101 bits of information. One-zero-one is the same number forward and backward, rightside up and upside down, before a mirror and in it. It is symmetrical and uncanny, like much else in the book. But 142857 is a repeating decimal (or "surd")—it follows the decimal point if, say, you convert twenty-two sevenths (makeshift pi) or if you divide the number of days in the year by the number of days in the week. It is one of numerous equally disturbing refusals of symmetry in the book. (It is very upsetting to DeLillo's characters, for example, that the left testicle customarily hangs lower than the right.) Like the universe it reflects, 142857 is both absurd and discouraging: it diminishes in value each time it reiterates itself, as on and on it goes toward an infinity it cannot reach. The number might also refer to the fourteenth hour (2 o'clock), plus 28 minutes and 57 seconds, when something awful will happen.

The signal is one problem; its source is another. Ratner's Star seems to be in a mohole. A mohole is a void core, an unoccupied negative energy state, a value-dark, multidimensional non-dimension, the origin, substratum and fate of the universe, the final inconceivable blank, black truth of things. Our own solar system seems to be in another mohole, if not the same one.

Ratner's Star is not only interesting, but funny (in a nervous kind of way). From it comes an unambiguous signal that DeLillo has arrived, bearing many gifts. He is smart, observant, fluent, a brilliant mimic and an ingenious architect. Too often, however, the razzle-dazzle seems that of a child prodigy, the conspicuous originality somewhat derivative, the dollar unearned, the desperation routine. And the flashbacks to Billy Twillig's family life seem vestigial remains, non-functioning traces of the novel this Menippean satire overgrew. All of DeLillo's books are in an anxious sweat for direct confrontations of the Zeitgeist—which, however, is like a nebula most clearly seen when you look past it or to its side. In *Americana*, the narrator tells us that "one of my main faults was a tendency to get blinded by the neon of an idea, never reaching truly inside it." and there is some of that in *Ratner's Star*. But the flashy neon seems pale amid the deep incandescence of this red giant of a book.

MYSTERIES OF A HARDCASE

Review of *Dashiell Hammett, A Life*, by Diane Johnson. The *New York Times Book Review*, October 16, 1983.

I f you were to go merely by the quantity (rather than the quality) of his imitators, you could argue that Dashiell Hammett was a more important writer than James Joyce. There were one or two writers of at least parboiled crime fiction before Hammett, but Hammett gave his imitators more than an attitude. He gave them a cast of characters, a resilient plot, a setting, a repertory of images, a style, a keyhole view of society, an ethos and, above all, a hero. Sam Spade is an old American type brought up to date, Hawkeye become private eye with fedora and street smarts instead of leatherstockings and wood lore, his turf the last frontier of San Francisco. The invention of a new popular genre is to the lesser world of literature what the invention of a new form of government is to the larger world of institutions—and just as rare. There are good reasons, then, for reading or writing a biography of Hammett, and Diane Johnson's cool, steady-eyed and engrossing *Dashiell Hammet* is the third in as many years.

There are reasons other than the interest of his work. From a distance, anyhow, Hammett looks as "wild and unpredictable," as much fun to read about, as Sam Spade. Here is what Ms. Johnson has to tell us. He was born In Maryland in 1894 and considered himself a Southerner, like his drinking companion, William Faulkner. His father, whom Hammett hated, tried many things and failed at all of them. His mother, with whom Hammett sided in an undemonstrative sort of way, considered herself superior. He quit school at fourteen, worked at odd jobs (to the extent that they did not interfere with his drinking) and in 1915 caught on with the Pinkerton detective agency in Baltimore. He liked the work, but that's pretty much all we know about it. The Pinkerton files seem to have been lost in a fire, and Hammett's wry accounts of his adventures attest mainly to the fertility of his imagination.

In 1918, he enlisted in the Army, served in the ambulance corps stateside, came down with TB, spent nearly three years in and out of veterans' hospitals, commenced his lifelong course in reading (the one activity his drinking never interrupted), got a nurse pregnant, married her by and by, rejoined the Pinkertons, quit them for good in 1922, began to write advertising copy freelance and to send poems and prose sketches to H. L. Mencken's *Smart Set*.

In 1923, the magazine *Black Mask* published the first of Hammett's stories to feature his detective, the Continental Op. During the next ten years he wrote five novels, more than eighty stories, novellas and articles, and more than forty reviews. After 1933 he wrote practically no fiction, except for a comic strip, and not much else, except for open letters on political matters—though, God knows, he tried. Hammett's writer's block lasted nearly thirty years, until his death in 1961.

One theory is that he burned himself out by riotous living. Certainly he did his best. After the publication of *The Maltese Falcon* in 1930, the money poured in, from royalties, from magazines, from radio serials and movies based on his fiction, from work on movie scripts (he was at one time among the dozen or so highest paid writers in Hollywood). He made over a million dollars, but he spent and gave away more than he made. He surrounded himself with loungers and spongers, with a chauffeur, a cook, a factotum, with secretaries (some of whom had to sue him for back wages), with actresses (he had walked out on his wife and two daughters, who never got to see much of his money), with call girls (he liked black and Asian prostitutes best), with women writers (first Nell Martin, then Lillian Hellman, whom he met in 1931). He had his own table at swanky restaurants and charge accounts at fashionable stores. He ran up huge hotel bills and then snuck out without paying. He lost large sums playing poker and betting on the ponies.

Above all, he drank. When drunk, the otherwise untalkative Hammett became noisy and argumentative. He made scenes, broke windows, tyrannized waiters, slugged women, made plays for his friends' wives and passed out flat on his face, in barrooms, in living rooms, in publishers' offices, on streets. He died broke, owing the Government $163,286.46, plus interest, in back taxes.

Probably in 1937, and out of the blue, this carouser, this hardcase, this individualist, this apolitical repudiator of all allegiances, this creator of heroes whose professional code comes before or goes beyond good and evil, this believer in nothing but good prose—"literature, as I see it, is good to the extent that it is art, and bad to the extent that it isn't"—joined the Communist Party and damn well toed the line. He wanted to go to Spain to fight against Franco, but the party said he would be of more use at home, so he stayed. Soon he was going around "as kind of an enforcer, making sure people coughed up their weekly dues of $15 to the Party."

He signed petitions, wrote propaganda, chaired meetings, swelled rallies. He defended the Moscow trials. During the period of the Hitler-Stalin nonaggression pact, he took the line that America ought to skip World War II rather than aid imperialist Britain or pursue its own "course of imperialist expansion." After Hitler's invasion of Russia In 1941, he argued that America had to join the peoples of China, Great Britain and Russia in their heroic struggle against Fascism. He tried a number of times to enlist in the Army, and finally, in 1942, at forty-eight, talked himself past a medical officer. "This is the happiest day of my life," he said. He served mostly in the Aleutians, where he edited a daily paper. When asked by a general why he wrote so much about Russian advances and so little about American victories, Hammett replied, "Well, sir, this paper has a policy not to publish ads."

After the war, Hammett went on a three-year binge—until he collapsed, d.t.'s and all. A doctor told him he'd be dead in a month or two if he didn't stop drinking. So he stopped, just like that, and for good. Instead, he resumed his errands for the Party, but in a half-hearted way, so it seems to me—as though work for the Party were a substitute for activities he preferred but could no longer perform, like writing, detecting, soldiering, drinking and entertaining prostitutes, for on top of everything else, Hammett was now impotent.

In 1951, he was subpoenaed to testify about the Civil Rights Congress bail fund, of which he was a trustee. He took the Fifth Amendment, was cited for contempt and served five months. He came out of prison broke and broken in health. For the next 10 years he lived, comfortably enough, on handouts from friends and a Government pension of $131.10 a month. Through it all, he never grew morose or bitter or self-pitying, never complained, never explained. His equanimity under pressure had always been remarkable. Whatever else he was, Hammett was a good soldier.

So much, and much more, of course, we learn from Miss Johnson's narrative, but she does not tell us all she knows. She is herself a considerable novelist and a critic one has learned to trust, but the novelist is far more evident in this biography than the critic. At some point and for some undeclared reason, she decided not to interpret or evaluate Hammett's books. I, for one, would like to know what she thinks of them, although her few scattered interpretive remarks suggest that the novels have begun to fade a bit in her mind.

She goes out of her way to note that "the central crime" of *Red Harvest*, the murder of a son by his father, is "a theme unusual in literature"—a remark that would be more to the point if that murder were the central crime or if the father had, in fact, committed it. And she misreads Sam Spade's story (in *The Maltese Falcon*) of Flitcraft—the most important single passage in all of Hammett's fiction. It has nothing to do with "the brevity of life," in Miss Johnson's phrase, but with, in Spade's phrases, the "random" and "haphazard" nature of existence. Flitcraft, a man who thinks life is "a clean orderly sane responsible affair," is nearly killed by a falling beam. "He felt like somebody had taken the lid off life and let him look at the works." He tries to live according to his new understanding of how things are ruled by "blind chance," but can't do it. He drifts unconsciously back into his old rut.

There are other reticences. The book begins with an acknowledgment of Lillian Hellman's "gracious cooperation" (something no previous biographer has received) and goes on to note that Miss Hellman has herself written about her relationship with Hammett. "I have seldom ventured into this preserve," says

Miss Johnson, but I wish she had, if only to snare what looks from the outside like "a pride of mythical beasts." Of Hammett's political career, Miss Johnson gives a full enough account, at least with respect to what he did and what was done to him, but she gives practically no account of his motives or the quality of his commitment. Was the man a saint, a fool, a true believer, or just contrary? Was he led to Communism by moral indignation or by Lillian Hellman, as another biographer has suggested? It may be that these things are unknowable; it is certain that Miss Johnson's method leaves Hammett more elusive than ever, but possibly more lifelike. Because of her efforts, we now know more about Hammett, although we understand him less.

Her method is a novelist's method, one Hammett perfected in *The Maltese Falcon* and *The Glass Key*, the method of the camera eye. We see what the characters do, hear what they say, note their gestures and postures, watch them assume positions toward each other, record their suspect attempts to account for themselves and each other. Hammett developed this method because he had come to see human motives as unknowable, human behavior as inexplicable, and all existence as random. For the author to explain was to add one more untestable hypothesis. The result is that his readers must play detective, must suspect the detective's motives as well as those of his suspects. The result of Miss Johnson's employment of this method is that her readers must decide for themselves what made Hammett tick.

My untestable hypothesis is that Hammett was more radical in his skepticism than in his politics. Thoroughgoing skepticism is a strenuous philosophy; it offers no grounds for making choices; the freedom it offers is dreadful; living by it requires more stamina than Hammett, unlike Sam Spade, could muster. Thus Hammett was happiest, most sober and least self-destructive when someone else made his decisions for him—in the Pinkertons, in veterans' hospitals, in the Army, in the party, in prison. "Going to prison was like going home," he said. "I like ruts." The philosophic skeptic also has no grounds for affirming his own existence, the reality of his own perdurable self. He suffers from a kind of ontological insecurity. Thus the impression Hammett gives of having no interior life; thus his signing his first stories "Peter Collinson," underworld slang for "nobody"; thus his inability to write about his own past, which had no reality for him; thus his self-deprecation, his disparaging remarks about his fiction, his invidious comparisons between his wealth or fame and his worth; thus his attempt, probably in 1931, at suicide, by means he never revealed. Thus, perhaps, Miss Johnson's refusal to sum him up, except through one desperate reach for a containing epithet. "Authentic" is her final word for him, an exclamation rather than a conclusion.

This biography is better written and more shapely than its predecessors—Miss Johnson is especially artful in arranging documents, letters and choruses of testimony by Hammett's friends so that they all comment, usually ironically, on each other and on her own narrative. She adds many new facts and gets very few of the old ones wrong. But we still do not know out of what in himself Hammett forged a new genre or what made him tick.

COP TRISTESSE AND ONE-LINERS

Review of *The Delta Star* by Joseph Wambaugh. The *New York Times Book Review*, March 20, 1983.

Near the beginning of the first Sherlock Holmes yarn, A *Study in Scarlet*, Watson comes across a magazine article entitled "The Book of Life." Its anonymous author claims that "from a drop of water, a logician could infer the possibility of an Atlantic or a Niagara without having seen or heard of one or the other." What is more, "All life is a chain, the nature of which is known whenever we are shown a single link of it." Watson snorts and slaps down the magazine:" What ineffable twaddle!"

But Holmes demurs; "As for the article, I wrote it myself"; and then he makes a momentous announcement: he is a detective, the world's only consulting detective, the detective others come to when they are stumped. He is the last court of appeal. In what follows he makes good on the claims in his article. Wildly disparate and scattered objects and events become links in the chain of logic with which he manacles an ingenious murderer. Given the earnest agonies of Victorian doubt, the Holmes stories must have been reassuring: the world is after all intelligible, logical, in order. If God's not in his heaven, at least Holmes is on earth. Without someone like him, the wicked would go free and innocent victims of the secular stupidity of the police would go to jail.

The classical British detective story, from Dorothy Sayers to P.D. James, offers similar reassurances. *The ABC Murders*, written by Agatha Christie, the world's all-time best-sellingest writer of whodunits, is a fair example. Just before the unravelling, Mr. Cust, thought to be a multiple murderer, goes to the movies. The theater is the *Regal*; the heroine is Katherine *Roya*l; the scene is at the Van *Schreine*r mansion; the title of the movie is *Not a Sparrow*. This movie makes Mr. Cust think of a fond quotation: "God's in His heaven. All's right with the world." Right now Mr. Cust has his doubts; the evidence around him, rather, is that all's wrong. Hercule Poirot, however, rights Mr. Cust's wrongs and restores his faith—and relieves our anxieties. The murders were not random eruptions of madness, as everyone else in the novel thought, but perfectly logical. If a sparrow falls, you can be sure that M. Poirot knows all about it.

From the outset, American hard-boiled detective novels have eschewed such reassurances. In the first of them, *The Maltese Falcon*, Sam Spade's story of Flitcraft argues the "random" and accidental universe that the rest of the novel depicts. Human motives are unknowable; Spade himself doesn't know whether or not he loves Bridget; whether or not the jewel-encrusted falcon ever existed is unknowable. Joseph Wambaugh in his new detective novel goes a step further. The connections among objects and events in *The Delta Star* may or may not be accidental; there is no doubt that they are absurd.

Early on, the Bad Czech, a cop, gets a chopstick caught in his shoe. This accident is the first in a series of "tiny vagaries of fortune" with immense consequences. Mario Villalobos, Wambaugh's detective, who works out of the Rampart Division, LAPD, mulls these vagaries over. They bring him to "the inescapable and troubling conclusion that most Big Events are decided by the falling of *less* than a sparrow," by something so small that even God wouldn't notice it, if, that is, there were a God. That's one way of looking at it. But the momentous consequences of another tiny vagary (a drunk relieving himself against a tree) seems "to indicate that all men are linked in a great and mysterious chain." So it seems. "Either that, or as cops tend to believe, it's all a freaking accident."

Mysterious chain or freaking accident, existence is absurd, in that the course of events has no relation to human intentions and values. Certainly the links (if that is what they are) in the chain (if that is what it is) are in the main ghastly or grotesque, as though forged by a sardonic and malevolent demiurge. A prostitute who takes a header off a roof, a Russian nuclear submarine, a lost Timex, a lecherous private eye, a magnet, a man in pinstripes and false mustache, a worthless credit card, a hysterical homosexual sure that spies are after him, the kinky sex life of a Nobel Committee member, a failed pacemaker, a woman named Lupe Luna with a fetching overbite, a delta to delta-star excited state, a Peruvian chemist who is determined to prove that there is no "grand design . . . no prime mover. . . no *mysterium tremendum*," but inadvertently offers evidence that there is—these are the links that Detective Mario Villalobos first uncovers and then tries to join. But he happens to live "in the emotionally perilous world of the policeman, where *nothing* is as it seems."

From this view of things stem the two distinguishing characteristics of Joseph Wambaugh's police novels: gallows humor, on the one hand, and on the other, what John Gregory Dunne, in an allusion to Mr. Wambaugh, calls "cop *tristesse*." Mr. Wambaugh's cops are genuinely funny—to us, but not necessarily to themselves. They speak in one-liners worthy of a Redd Foxx at a stag party and they have names like Rumpled Ronald, Pipeline Jones (a snitch), Too-Tired Loomis. The Gooned-Out Cop, Dolly and Diford (partners who hate each other), Chip Muirfield and Melody Waters (partners who lust for each other), Hans and Ludwig (a K-9 cop and his handler who smell alike and have the same sexual disturbance), and Jane Wayne, the New-Wave Bionic Bitch.

Their sayings and doings are very funny, but they think of themselves as "cripples and misfits and losers." They are cranky and grouchy and gloomy; they are "angst-ridden" and hungover when they are not drunk; they call their watering hole "The House of Misery"; they are paranoid and apocalyptic and apoplectic, particularly over Jerry Brown and his Chief Justice of the California Supreme Court ("Rose Bird and the Supremes"). They are broke and divorced and suicidal; what they see on their daily rounds leaves them with counter-sunk eyes and sinking stomachs. What we see through their eyes are winos and muggers and dopers, suicide and homicide and severed heads, mangled children and savaged fathers and wailing mothers, a chaos of uprooted nationalities and ruptured lives preying on each other out of need and psychopathy and despair. All this is convincingly and economically represented by Mr. Wambaugh, who has become a wonderfully skillful novelist.

For all its representations of moral and cosmic disorder, this novel is by no means a downer. It is, in fact, great fun to read. For one thing, the humor by far outweighs the *tristesse*; there is even a happy ending—of sorts. For another, there is an interesting mystery here, and the sleuthing of Mario Villalobos (a housebroken wolf) provides all the satisfactions proper to the whodunit genre. Above all, the formal elegance of this novel is a separate pleasure in itself. The order of its rendering is more than equal to the disorder it represents. Evidence of design, of providential links between part and part and between part and whole, may be hard to come by in life—but not in Mr. Wambaugh's new novel.

INTRODUCTION TO A CLOSER LOOK AT ARIEL: A MEMORY OF SYLVIA PLATH

Introduction to *A Closer Look at Ariel: A Memory of Sylvia Plath*, by Nancy Hunter Steiner (New York: Harper's Magazine Press, 1972).

Sylvia Plath would have been a good poet even if she had not committed suicide, but not exactly the poet she has since become. Our knowledge of her suicide comments on the poetry as we read it. The image of the poet that rises out of the poetry as we read it wears the aspect of her fate. Our knowledge of her suicide not only clarifies what she said and what she meant—it also certifies that she meant what she said. Or so it seemed. Additional knowledge of the poet as it comes to us has had the effect of suggesting that she meant something else, or at least something in addition. Even the suicide that seemed to clarify the poetry is no longer the one we first read about, that of a dissenting voice refuting a bad world by silencing itself, according to some, or that of a desperate woman signaling for help with a gesture that put her beyond the reach of any helping hand, according to others.

Moreover, the image of the poet that rises out of the poetry and the memory of Sylvia Plath as recorded by her friends never quite came together, even when they did seem to cast a kind of light on each other. But Nancy Hunter Steiner's *A Closer Look at Ariel* increases the area of overlap considerably; and it helps us to understand why the poet in the poetry and the poet in the memoirs of her friends often seem like two different people. It suggests a way of fitting the biography in the memoirs and the autobiography in the poems into the figure of a single life, although one that experienced itself as double. For Sylvia Plath was not only aware of an opposition between the life of her poetry and the life she led—she harnessed this opposition to charge her themes and to shape the forms of her verse.

Ted Hughes, in some remarks on the chronological order of Sylvia Plath's, his wife's, poetry notes that "the opposition of a prickly, fastidious defence and an imminent volcano is, one way or another, an element in all her early poems." The earlier the poems, as we can now see, the more powerful the defensive forces of containment. In the poems up to about 1961 or so, the defense is both formal and thematic. Those elaborate stanzas, the measured harmonics, the connoisseur's diction helped to keep the volcano from becoming more than imminent. "Throughout *The Colossus*," says A. Alvarez, "she is using her art to keep the disturbance, out of which she made her verse, at a distance." But in "Ouija," a poem written after most of those in *The Colossus*, a poem that displays the fops and gauds of Wallace Stevens' "Le Monocle de Mon Oncle" only to bring them down, we can see the distance close. We can see the defensive aureate poetry absorbed by the forces it contains, not only in what she says, but also in how she says it:

> The old god, too, writes aureate poetry
> In tarnished modes, maundering among the wastes,

> Fair chronicler of every foul declension.
> Age, and ages of prose, have uncoiled
> His talking whirlwind, abated his excessive temper
> When words, like locusts, drummed the darkening air
> And left the cobs to rattle, bitten clean.
> Skies once wearing a blue, divine hauteur
> Ravel above us, mistily descend,
> Thickening with motes, to a marriage with the mire.

Two poems written by Plath in March 1961, a year or so after "Ouija," and while she was in a hospital recovering from an appendectomy, were, says Ted Hughes, "the first sign of what was on its way." She wrote these at top speed, without her usual studies over the thesaurus, "as one might write an urgent letter. From then on, all her poems were written in this way." One of these two poems, "In Plaster," alludes to the condition of a woman in a bed near Plath's own, but takes the form of a monologue by the imminent volcano on the subject of its relations to the prickly defense—relations that have become close, explicit, and murderous:

> I shall never get out of this! There are two of me now:
> This new absolutely white person and the old yellow
> one.

The white person, notes the lady within her cast, "is certainly the superior one." "She is one of the real saints." At first the old yellow one didn't like the plaster saint. She thought her cold; "she had no personality"; she took punishment without complaint— "you could tell almost at once she had a slave mentality." But the yellow one comes to realize that what her visible (and showy) saintly self wanted was to be loved by her. She begins to take advantage of the situation. She allows the plaster saint to wait on her, to put "her tidiness and calmness and her patience" at the yellow one's disposal, and the saint just adores being so used. But in time their relationship becomes "more intense":

> She stopped fitting me so closely and seemed offish.
> I felt her criticizing me in spite of herself,
> As if my habits offended her in some way.

The trouble, as the yellow one begins to understand, was that her beautiful façade "thought she was immortal":

> She wanted to leave me, she thought she was superior,
> And I'd been keeping her in the dark, and she was
>   resentful—
> Wasting her days, waiting on a half-corpse!
> And secretly she began to hope I'd die.

But the buried self is not in any position to dispose of her character armor—"She'd supported me for so long I was quite limp"—so she lies low, takes care not to do anything that might upset her domineering and fastidious slave, and plots her revenge. For the meantime,

> Living with her was like living with my own coffin:
> Yet I still depended upon her, though I did it
>   regretfully.

Old yellow is forced to give up the idea that the two of them might make a go of it, even if they were so close, even if what they had between them was a kind of marriage—"Now I see it must be one or the other of us":

> She may be a saint, and I may be ugly and hairy,
> But she'll soon find out that that doesn't matter a bit.
> I'm collecting my strength; one day I shall manage
>   without her,
> And she'll perish with emptiness then, and begin to
>   miss me.

For a poem written quickly, as one might write an urgent letter, "In Plaster" is remarkable for its control, its intelligence, its grim humor and wry self-consciousness, all of which make it that much more chilling. The spiteful childishness of the anticlimactic last few words ("and begin to miss me"), an expression of the sentiment that lies behind many suicides, shows that the author, if not the speaker, realized how unlikely it was that the yellow one could dispose of the plaster saint without disposing of itself. And in *Ariel*, in which the ugly and hairy repressed self exacts its revenge against the restraints that had held it both down and together, the special horror and fascination derive from the fact that Sylvia Plath knew what was happening to her, knew where it would end, but could or would not do anything about it.

Could or would not do anything, that is, but find words for what was happening and anticipate the end. In poem after poem, from about 1959 on, one self will emerge into words and note that

>   I inhabit
> The wax image of myself, a doll's body.
> Sickness begins here:

Old yellow may pause on a bridge and look down out of its stiff cast toward the water, only to

>   encounter one
> Blue and improbable person
>
> Framed in a basketwork of cattails.
> O she is gracious and austere,
> Seated beneath the toneless water!
> It is not I, it is not I.

Instead of disavowal, there may be a reluctant recognition:

> This woman who meets me in windows—she is neat.
>
> So neat she is transparent, like a spirit.
> How shyly she superimposes her neat self
> On the inferno of African oranges, the heel-hung pigs.
> She is deferring to reality.
> It is I, it is I—

Most commonly, however, a tense and lucid intelligence will gather to a point from between and around the opposed selves to observe how

> Daylong a duet of shade and light
> Plays between these.

or to ask "What am I to make of these contradictions—" or eagerly to watch "My selves dissolving, old whore petticoats," or to note, with distaste, how

>   the same self unfolds like a suit
> Bald and shiny, with pockets of wishes,
>
> Notions and tickets, short circuits and folding mirrors.
>
> Or to explain to a lover
>
>   how you insert yourself
> Between myself and myself.

In "Two Sisters of Persephone," a poem written after those in *The Colossus* and before those in *Ariel*, the consciousness hovering in the charged area between herself and herself looks both ways, drawn by the positive but held back by what Sylvia Plath took to be the negative pole of her being. One sister of Persephone, "Bronzed as earth," out in the bright air, couched in grasses, lulled by poppies, becomes the sun's bride, bears him a king. The other sister, a poet of sorts, sits in a dark room, works problems on "a mathematical machine," her squint eyes rat-shrewd, her meager frame root-pale, until finally, bitter, "sallow as any lemon,"

>   wry virgin to the last,
> Goes graveward with flesh laid waste,
> Worm-husbanded, yet no woman.

The persona speaking out of any given poem by Sylvia Plath, then, may be either sulphurous old yellow, or the plaster saint, or a consciousness that sometimes contains these two and sometimes lies stretched between them. In the course of a given poem, especially if it is a later one, any of these personae may dissolve, re-form, take on novel shapes, fuse with whatever it is not, or reverse its charge, so that the plaster saint becomes a golden girl and squint-eyed old yellow becomes a queen bee, a comet, God's lioness. The outer shell of consciousness may be completely or dimly aware of the chthonic presence within: it may feel itself a puppet jerked by strings receding into an interior distance where a familiar demon sits in possession, or it may try to locate the menace outside of itself, among shadows, thin people, reflections in water, ghostly presences glimpsed from the corner of the mind, but always with a sense of *déjà vu*.

As they appear in the poems and prose, these opposed selves are fabulous, mythological in their dimensions and resonance; it is easy enough to sink them in traditions and arrange them among analogues. Sylvia Plath was a well-read woman. At one time she had a liking for D. H. Lawrence, in whose work a black, father-haunted, sexy troglodyte strives to break through the encrustations of a white, supercivilized consciousness, which he associated with his mother. Before her breakdown and suicide attempt in 1953 Sylvia Plath was doing research for an honor's thesis on twins in the works of James Joyce; she eventually wrote her thesis on the double in Dostoevski. And she was interested in witchcraft, the occult, astrology, and the like, traditions which at many times and in many places have taught that the body is the coffin of a spirit fed by chthonic energies. But her opposed characters have also a personal reference and source. They carry with them into the prose and poetry contours of the persons, incidents, and landscapes amidst which they were formed, no matter what the distorting pressure of the new contexts. The opposed characters are each associated with a separate cluster of attendant persons, incidents, and landscapes; they are associated with successive periods of Sylvia Plath's life. A closer look at the separate worlds of old yellow and the plaster saint may tell us something about what the opposed forces in Sylvia Plath meant to her and what they may mean to us; it may also tell us something about why we read the poetry and why we brood over her life.

At the age of fifteen, Otto Plath emigrated to the United States from Grabow in the Polish corridor. "My German-speaking father," says Esther Greenwood, heroine of Sylvia Plath's autobiographical novel, *The Bell Jar*, "came from some manic-depressive hamlet in the black heart of Prussia." He became a professor of biology at Boston University, an expert in insects, especially bees, a fact commemorated in a series of poems by his daughter, who commemorated the fact further by keeping bees herself after moving to Devon in 1961. He also taught German. In a poem, Sylvia Plath remembers his voice as "Gothic and barbarous, pure German"; and the one subject in college Esther Greenwood cannot master, although, like her author, she is a great getter of straight A's, is German: "the very sight of those dense, barbed-wire letters made my mind shut like a clam." While studying for an M.A. in German, Aurelia Schrober, born of Austrian parents, met her husband-to-be.

Their daughter was born on October 27, 1932, and spent the first eight or nine years of her life in the seashore town of Winthrop, Massachusetts; but she was frequently a guest at the home of her maternal grandparents at Point Shirley, where the sea is on one side and the bay on the other. Point Shirley, and "the beautiful formlessness of the sea" around it, appears more often than any other landscape in Sylvia Plath's poetry and prose. In an autobiographical essay, "OCEAN 1212-W," which gets its title from her grandparents' phone number, she begins by explaining that "My childhood landscape was not land but the end of the land—the cold, salt running hills of the Atlantic. I sometimes think my vision of the sea is the clearest thing I own." In her recollection, at least, her fascination with the sea began quite early: "When I was learning to creep, my mother set me down on the beach to see what I thought of it. I crawled straight for the coming wave and was just through the wall of green when she caught my heels." What would have happened, she wonders, "if I had managed to pierce that looking-glass?"

She goes on to describe how when she was two and one-half years old, on the day her brother was born, she walked along the beach and saw for the first time "the *separateness* of everything. I felt the wall of my skin: I am I. That stone is a stone. My beautiful fusion with the things of this world was over." On this day, the "awful birthday of otherness," she became "my rival, somebody else." When her mother read to her from Matthew Arnold's "The Forsaken Merman," she felt shaken, as by a chill; the gooseflesh rose; she wanted to cry: "I had fallen into a new way of being happy." And on the day she suffered the awful birthday of otherness, she looked to the sea for "a sign of election and specialness." The sea threw up to her a forsaken merman of sorts, a "totem," a carved, wooden sacred baboon: "So the sea, perceiving my need, had conferred a blessing." This account strikes me as more parable than history, its truth more imaginative than literal. It is a myth whose incidents and images express how the sea had come to saturate her sense of identity as well as her sense of being her rival, somebody else, and how the sea had come to represent for her the depths of poetry, in which literal losses underwent a change into symbolic recoveries. "OCEAN 1212-W" ends with these words: "And this is how it stiffens, my visions of that seaside childhood. My father died, we moved inland. Whereon those nine first years of my life sealed themselves off like a ship in a bottle—beautiful, inaccessible, obsolete, a fine, white flying myth."

A week after her eighth birthday, her father died, she moved inland, her childhood sealed itself off, in something like a bell jar, inaccessible except as myth. "After that," says Esther Greenwood, whose experiences are a pointed version of her author's, "I had never been happy again"—not since "I was about nine and running along the hot white beaches with my father the summer before he died." He died, in fact, after a long illness, but in the myth a mature Sylvia Plath created of her childhood he becomes a victim of suicide or murder (in each case usually by drowning), or both at once:

> I am the ghost of an infamous suicide,
> My own blue razor rusting in my throat.
> Oh pardon the one who knocks for pardon at
> Your gate, father—your hound-bitch, daughter, friend.
> It was my love that did us both to death.

These lines are quoted from "Electra on the Azalea Path"; in other poems old yellow speaks out to her "Father, bridegroom" as Clytemnestra raging how she loves and hates him, how she killed him and how he is killing her.

Her own explanation of her love and her hate is one that any amateur Freudian might give. To Nancy Hunter Steiner she said, "He was an autocrat. I adored and despised him, and I probably wished many times that he were dead. When he obliged me and died, I imagined that I had killed him." And so "I Dream that I am Oedipus":

> What I want back is what I was
> Before the bed, before the knife,

> Before the brooch-pin and salve
> Fixed me in this parenthesis.

She is fixed in a parenthesis because she is sealed off from her childhood—"O I am too big to go backward"— and because in the only future she can imagine her father rises from the waters of her past:

> The future is a grey seagull
> Tattling in its cat-voice of departure, departure.
> Age and terror, like nurses, attend her,
> And a drowned man, complaining of the great cold,
> Crawls up out of the sea.

Even when she longs for death, for "the black amnesias of heaven," when she thinks of getting "through to a heaven/Starless and fatherless, a dark water," the heaven is black, her father's color, and it is a dark water, her father's element. Fixed in this parenthesis, all she can do is

> walk dry on your kingdom's border
> Exiled to no good.
>
> Your shelled bed I remember.
> Father, this thick air is murderous.
> I would breathe water.

Whether Laius, Agamemnon, Proteus, a colossus, a vampire, or murdered god, always, "This is the tongue of the dead man: remember, remember" and always,

> It is a chilly god, a god of shades,
> Rises to the glass from his black fathoms.

In his essay on the uncanny, Freud argued that the apparitions of a subconscious wish, as in a dream, say, or in hallucination or a work of art, are distorted by the disapproving superego into malevolent and sinister shapes that threaten with what they promise, that insinuate the desire beneath the fear. The superego turns into a source of revulsion what the subconscious finds attractive. But the case of Sylvia Plath is all the more unsettling in that neither the attraction nor the revulsion is subconscious. She knows perfectly well that what her submerged self wants the plaster saint disapproves of, and she knows why, too. No matter how deep her self-analysis, no matter how great her self-knowledge, and it was very great, the black, watery, malevolent, timeless world of raging, lustful, childish old yellow remained the *thesis* of her poetry and of the dialectic that shaped her life, as she understood it. To the antithesis we now turn.

Within a few months of her father's death, Sylvia Plath published her first poem (in the Boston *Sunday Herald*) and her first drawing, for which she won a prize. Those perfect report cards began coming in, with always an "A," a "100," an "excellent" after every subject, including deportment. There followed an unbroken string of awards, prizes, scholarships, elections to honor societies—the goads and lures for what are now called aggressive achievers. No doubt this inexorable academic success was encouraged by a mother who had become a schoolteacher, who had wanted to be a professor, and who was making many sacrifices to ensure that her daughter's life would be less restricted than her own, less dependent upon men. Says Esther Greenwood,

"My mother had taught shorthand and typing to support us ever since my father died and secretly she hated it and hated him for dying and leaving no money because he didn't trust life-insurance salesmen." Listening to her mother's stories about her marriage, Esther Greenwood comes to feel that being a wife was "like being brainwashed, and afterward you went about numb as a slave in some private, totalitarian state." She decides that she "hates the idea of serving men in any way," and as for the consequences of serving men—"children made me sick."

Such passages led one critic to praise *The Bell Jar* as a chronicle of "genuinely feminist aspirations." They have led some feminists to find in Sylvia Plath a heroine and others to find in the course of her life a cautionary tale with a moral. Germaine Greer, for example, has claimed that if the new feminists had been around in 1963, Sylvia Plath would not have had to commit suicide. The claim seems excessive. Certainly Sylvia Plath did not herself see the demons that attended her as vengeful spirits conjured up by the social status of women. And she attributes Esther Greenwood's attitudes toward men, marriage, and children to the bad air inside the bell jar of neurosis.

Poems such as "Lesbos" suggest that she would not have liked Women's Liberation and that she did not like the feminist streak, such as it was, in herself. She wrote to friends that she married Ted Hughes in part because "He was very simply the only man I've ever met whom I could never boss." She turned out to be an exceptional cook, an efficient housekeeper, and a loving mother. The attitudes toward men most persistently expressed in her writing, rather than comprising a spinsterish resentment or a feminist demand for justice, add up to something more like the female equivalent of misogyny, which is not male chauvinism, but the outcome of a need and a longing so urgent and so fantastic that no living woman can satisfy it. The size of a misogynist's hatred of women is equal to the distance between the compliant creatures of his fantasies, who exist only to gratify him, and actual women, who exist in their own right. And yet living women remind him of his fantasies more than anything else. So it seems to me with Sylvia Plath's misandry. For one thing, no living man could measure up to the colossus that bestrode the fantasy world of her childhood, dripping salt water. And yet it was only living men who partook of his quality, no matter how far they fell short. Because she understood all this, and because she had no gift for evasion, she could not lull herself into that daydream first worked out by Charlotte Brontë, whose situation was similar, and since reworked by a host of imitators: in Sylvia Plath's writing there is no Rochester— no hawk-nosed, piercing-eyed, awesome father/lover is turned into a doting and diminished husband/child. The longing and the hate remain, unresolved, and assume in the poetry the lustful and avenging shapes of vampires, witches, and Medusa.

Sylvia Plath's mother, then, in the poems and in *The Bell Jar*, is associated with the antithetical go-getter's plaster saint of a self, that stiff, driven, and spinsterish achiever of goals set for her by other people. It is probably no confusion of art and life to say that she was unfair to her mother, as she was unfair to her father, who after all did not die just to make his daughter miserable. During the late forties and early fifties the prevailing winds of opinion were especially such as to confirm and accelerate the tendency of any teenager who began with private reasons for becoming a dissatisfied satisfier of other people's expectations.

She became, said Sylvia Plath, "a rabid teenage pragmatist." The rabidity, which turned the pragmatism into something else, was unusual, but the pragmatism was not. The social pseudosciences, for example, were pragmatical as can be. They advertised the notion that all people at all times and in all places inevitably conform in one way or another to the mores that define the societies in which they live. Whether inner-, outer-, or other-directed, you are directed to defer private inclinations to the public welfare, upon which your own depends. Utopia had never been, nor would be, so the argument ran; there were certain minor injustices in the United States, and a certain amount of inefficiency, as was bound to be the case in a democracy. But if your antennae were sensitive, if you learned the rules, if you did in public what "society" required of you for its own well being, "society" would reciprocate with material compensations and with an unprecedented freedom to do whatever you wanted in private. The concrete application of these lessons, among the representative men who graduated from college in 1955, the year of Sylvia Plath's graduation (and my own), was to look for a job with a large corporation, so that if you were careful not to wear brown socks with a blue suit during the weekdays, you were allowed and could afford to spend the weekends behind your curtained picture windows, watching dirty movies. Representative women looked for such men to marry. As Sylvia Plath wrote of that period, "The Times Are Tidy":

> There's no career in the venture
> Of riding against the lizard,
> Himself withered these latter-days
> To leaf-size from lack of action:
> History's beaten the hazard.

We get a sense of how well she learned the lessons of her tidy times, and how thoroughly her rabid pragmatism applied them, from a summary by Lois Ames (from whose excellent biographical essays[1] I have taken many facts and quotations) of Plath's high school years:

> She played tennis, was on the girls' basketball team, was co-editor of the school newspaper, *The Bradford*, joined a high school sorority, Sub-Debs, painted decorations for class dances, went on college weekend dates, was Lady Agatha in the class play, *The Admirable Crichton*,

and got terrific grades. At Smith, Nancy Hunter Steiner reports, the majority opinion was that, except for the intelligence and the poetry, Plath "could have been an airline stewardess or the ingenuous heroine of a B movie." Robert Lowell, who met her a few years later, noted "the checks and courtesies" of a laborious shyness, "an air of maddening docility." And A. Alvarez, who met her a few years later still, noted "That curious, advertisement-trained, transatlantic air of anxious pleasantness." Pragmatically perhaps, but rabidly for certain, she was "Adhering to rules, to rules, to rules." She was, she came to feel, as though dead, but

> unbothered by it,
> Staying put according to habit.

The social cast of her personality, anaesthetic, frozen in a cover-girl smile, mother-directed rather than father-haunted, historical

---

[1] "Notes Toward a Biography" in The Art of Sylvia Plath, *Charles Newman*, ed. (Bloomington: Indiana University Press, Midland Paperback, 1971), pp. 155-173; and "Sylvia Plath: A Biographical Note" in The Bell Jar, *Sylvia Plath* (New York: Harper & Row, Inc., 1971).

and local rather than mythographic, pragmatic in its protective coloring but rabid in its need for such coloring, fiercely self-denying and self-controlled, anxious, up-tight, and doomed, seems to have remained in charge during her first three years at Smith College, where she continued to do what you were supposed to do, only better than anyone else, and where she wrote stories and poems that were published in *Seventeen*, *The Christian Science Monitor*, *Mademoiselle*, and *Harper's Magazine*. In the summer of 1953 she was chosen to serve as a guest editor for *Mademoiselle*. Her scrapbook description of that month in New York would be funny if it had come from a character in a novel by, for example, Mary McCarthy, but coming from Sylvia Plath it is both sad and infuriating. The accents are those of the American Girl as we want her; it is infuriating that we want her that way, as it is infuriating and sad that Sylvia Plath was so anxious to comply with what we want:

> I won a guest editorship representing Smith & took a train to NYC for a salaried month working—hatted & heeled—in Mlle's airconditioned Madison Ave. offices.... Fantastic, fabulous, and all other inadequate adjectives go to describe the four gala and chaotic weeks I worked as guest managing Ed... living in luxury at the Barbizon, I edited, met celebrities, was fêted and feasted by a galaxy of UN delegates, simultaneous interpreters & artists... this Smith Cinderella met idols: Vance Bourjaily, Paul Engle, Elizabeth Bowen—wrote articles via correspondence with 5 handsome young male poet teachers.

The Bell Jar gives us some idea of what old yellow was doing while the Smith Cinderella was fêted and feasted by a galaxy of idols. It was emerging through the cracks that opened all over the plaster saint from the shock of its collision with New York City. In New York, Plath ran smack into the reality principle, as though it had been lurking in ambush to exact revenge for having been so long and so relentlessly denied. She had knocked into her how little she would be prepared upon graduation to make her way in New York as an editor and writer. "I felt terribly inadequate," says Esther Greenwood. "The trouble was I had been inadequate all along, I simply hadn't thought about it. The one thing I was good at was winning scholarships and prizes and that era was coming to an end." She feels her carefully built up public personality dissolve as, she says, "all the little successes I'd trotted up so happily at college fizzled to nothing outside the slick marble and plate-glass fronts along Madison Avenue." Above all, her Betty Coed prudishness found itself squeezed between the lusts and kinks of New York swingers from without and her own awakening sexuality from within.

"When I was nineteen, pureness was the great issue," says Esther Greenwood. From a poem ("Fever 103°"), old yellow answers: "Pure? What does it mean?" Wedged, for the time, between countervailing forces of equal potency, Esther Greenwood can move neither way:

> ...I wondered why I couldn't go the whole way doing what I should any more. This made me sad and tired. Then I wondered why I couldn't go the whole way doing what 1 shouldn't, ...and this made me even sadder and more tired.

But old yellow begins to break through "yellower than ever," takes charge, decides to seduce a simultaneous interpreter from the U.N., fails, and, according to the logic of such things, suffers in return a beating and attempted rape, in a patch of black mud, by a South American playboy woman-hater, who acts as though he knew what secretly she was after. "Slut!" he says: "Your dress is black and the dirt is black as well." She leaves New York to return to her home and her mother, but that whole life now seems "vacuous." She goes, for the first time, to her father's grave: "I laid my face to the smooth face of the marble and howled my loss into the cold salt rain." The next morning she squeezes into the crawl space beneath her house, where "a dim, undersea light filtered through the slits of the cellar windows." She wraps her black raincoat around her "like my own sweet shadow," and swallows, one by one, a bottle of sleeping pills: "The silence drew off, baring the pebbles and shells and all the tatty wreckage of my life. Then, at the rim of vision, it gathered itself, and in one sweeping tide, rushed me to sleep."

That sea imagery and an enveloping blackness accompany old yellow's return to her element is what we might expect. Sylvia Plath herself understood the suicide attempt as an effort to rejoin her father, to appear before him free from the tight, but life-preserving, social self she had wrapped herself in, pure once more:

> And I, stepping from this skin
> Of old bandages, boredoms, old faces
>
> Step to you from the black car of Lethe,
> Pure as a baby.

The suicide attempt of 1953, however, did not succeed. She was found, hospitalized, and subjected to a course of therapy that included treatments of electric shock. By midwinter she was back at Smith, "Facing & reconstructing the old wrecked life—new

& strong." And at the end of the term, the false, flat, bright, insistent voice of the go-getter is back in the scrapbook to claim that "exams & papers proved I hadn't lost either my repetitive or my creative intellect as I had feared .. : a semester of reconstruction ends with an infinitely more solid if less flashingly spectacular flourish than last year's." But Nancy Hunter Steiner's *A Closer Look at Ariel*, the closest and most clear-eyed look at Sylvia Plath we have, tells us that the reconstructed "typical American girl, the product of a hundred years of middle-class propriety," was suffering from something like ontological insecurity. She hangs on, as though for life, to the material possessions that constitute the visible reaches of her reconstructed identity. She is roused to a shrill passion when another girl merely observes that their hairdos are the same. She would have felt "raped intellectually," as she puts it, had anyone disturbed the finicky arrangement of her dresser drawers. She sets up little melodramas to test the loyalty of her friends. And at the same time, old yellow, "the blond bitch," as she is called by the wife of a Harvard professor, becomes yellower and yellower, reveals a special interest in older men, especially professors, and gets herself raped by the sinister and repulsive Irwin, professor of biology.

A Closer Look at Ariel, besides giving us the most vivid and most understanding account we have of how the opposed twin poles that charge Sylvia Plath's writing alternated in the currents of her life, also gives some insight into how she reshaped the life to heighten the significance and tighten the forms of the writings. In the novel, as distinct from the life, the Irwin affair and its consequences neatly conclude the old life that the fictional heroine, as distinct from the real woman, sloughed off and left behind. Esther Greenwood's best friend at the time is Joan Gilling, who insists on accompanying a cool Esther to the doctor when Irwin's rape causes her to hemorrhage, but Sylvia Plath hysterically would not allow Nancy Hunter to leave her for a minute. She tells us that Sylvia Plath "referred to me in letters to her mother as her alter ego and often remarked that we presented a mirror image or represented opposite sides of the same coin." Esther Greenwood tells us that "sometimes I wondered if I had made Joan up." Of herself and Joan she says, "we were close enough so that her thoughts and feelings seemed a wry, black image of my own." But Joan is entirely different from Mrs. Steiner in physical appearance, character, and personal background. Joan is a childhood friend, a constant reminder to Esther "of what I had been, and what I had been through"; she had wanted to marry the suitor whom Esther rejects; she especially loves the suitor's family, which Esther Greenwood scorns, unlike Sylvia Plath, who described in her scrapbook the family of the young man on whom the suitor is modeled as her ideal. Joan turns out to be a lesbian. When Joan commits suicide, right after and partially in reaction to Esther's hemorrhaging, Esther feels the bell jar lift; she decides for life; she feels that a surrogate self had died so that she might live, whereas Nancy Hunter is forced to put some distance between herself and Sylvia Plath so that she might continue to live her own life, rather than serve as a portion of her friend's. It is clear that Joan's character is a kind of disposal unit for traits that Sylvia Plath came to reject in herself. Mrs. Steiner was nothing of the sort, although it is also clear she would have been just that had Sylvia Plath gotten her way. To the extent that she did get her way Nancy Hunter was cast in the role of the plaster saint, so that Sylvia Plath might be free to play old yellow with a single mind.

A Closer Look at Ariel, then, tells us much about Sylvia Plath of which we would otherwise have no inkling and about much that other sources only imply, such as the hypochondriacal fear and fascination with which she regarded the functions and malfunctions of her own body. One is especially grateful for the episodes of mundane happiness, as on the giggly afternoon when Miss Plath and Miss Hunter sat white-gloved in the cavernous parlor of Olive Higgins Prouty, devouring platters of cucumber sandwiches under the disdainful eye of a cartoon butler. For its intelligence, its sense of the historical moment, its clear-eyed sympathy, tact, and narrative pace, the memoir would be worth reading, even if it were about some anonymous college girl of the fifties, even if it were a piece of fiction, rather than the best-informed account we are likely to have of crucial events in the life and art of an important poet and notorious suicide.

There were occasions enough for more than mundane happiness in the eight years or so Sylvia Plath lived after she and Nancy Hunter went their separate ways. The prizes and fellowships continued to come. The poems also continued to come, and as time went on they came easier; good as they had been, they got better. They were accepted for publication in many journals. *The Colossus* and *The Bell Jar* were favorably reviewed, for the most part. She married a man she could respect as well as love. She traveled—"so much! the whole world coming alive, banging through my eyes and fibers!" She returned to Smith as an instructor, triumphantly successful in the role of "triple-threat woman: wife, writer & teacher (to be swapped later for motherhood, I hope)," as she described her aspiration. After she swapped teaching for motherhood she seems to have felt, sometimes at least, that her children rounded her completeness, that they demonstrated to herself and to the world how the squint-eyed poet was also a golden girl. Ted Hughes describes the births of the two children as crucial stages in his wife's movement toward self-acceptance.

She even seems for a time to have found formulas for exorcizing the ugly and hairy underside of her personality, for converting the blasting furies into bountiful eurnenides. Freud explains in *Beyond the Pleasure Principle* and in a number of essays how in play, in dreams, or in art, we may mime the ghosts of traumas that hold us in thrall. We may confront or manipulate in play, or dreams, or art the representation of what in life was or is traumatically unbearable so that it becomes familiar, domestic, bearable, a source, even, of aesthetic pleasure. Plath's note on "Daddy," written for a BBC audience, is Freudian in this sense, among others:

> The poem is spoken by a girl with an Electra Complex. Her case is complicated by the fact that her father was also a Nazi and her mother very possibly part Jewish. In the daughter the two strains marry and paralyze each other—she has to act out the awful little allegory once over before she is free of it.

In the same exorcizing mood she wrote *The Bell Jar*, which she described as "an autobiographical apprentice work which I had to write in order to free myself from the past."

And while she was trying to free herself from the traumas of her past by discharging them into the forms of her art, she and her husband "devised exercises of meditation and invocation," as he tells us, to help her "break down the tyranny, the fixed focus and the public persona which descriptive or discursive poems take as a norm" and to help her "accept the invitation of her inner world." That she accepted that invitation the poems written in the last two years of her life and *The Bell Jar* testify well enough. A number of passages celebrate the exhilarating sense of release that sometimes accompanied the breakdown of the fixed focus and the public persona. In the novel, for example, Esther Greenwood's one moment of unqualified happiness occurs when on skis she doesn't know how to use she schusses down a slope:

> I felt my lungs inflate with the inrush of scenery— air, mountains, trees, people. I thought, "This is what it is to be happy."
>
> I plummeted down past the zigzaggers, the students, the experts, through year after year of doubleness and smiles and compromise, into my own past.

Similarly in "Years" she writes that

> What I love is
> The piston in motion—
> My soul dies before it.
> And the hooves of the horses,
> Their merciless churn.

In "Stings" she has "a self to recover, a queen," a queen bee, whose wings, like the hooves of her horse Ariel, rush her past the boundaries of selfhood into new dimensions:

> Now she is flying
> More terrible than she ever was, red
> Scar in the sky, red comet
> Over the engine that killed her—
> The mausoleum, the wax house.

But in other poems, the crumbling of the public persona and the solicitations of the inner world are experienced not with exhilaration, as a soaring release after long confinement, but with anxiety and dread, with a sense of being in the grips of an implacable force riding her irresistibly to no good end:

> the wind
> Pours by like destiny, bending
> Everything in one direction.

Then the pistons shriek and the hoofbeats appall:

> The train is dragging itself, it is screaming—
> An animal
> Insane for the destination,
> The bloodspot,
> The face at the end of the flare.

The ego is reduced to numb helplessness by the solicitations of the ghosts it called up but cannot control—"the dead injure me with attentions, and nothing can happen." It stands helpless before its own dissolution:

> See, the darkness is leaking from the cracks.
> I cannot contain it. I cannot contain my life.

In the winter of 1962-1963, the coldest in a century, the dread and depression found allies against the exhilaration. She was cold, ill, lonely, separated from her husband, unable to sleep. More than ever, as Ted Hughes said, "She had none of the usual guards and remote controls to protect herself from her own reality." Once again, death began to impend like "A Birthday Present," a promise of a condition in which "split lives congeal and stiffen to history." When A. Alvarez visited her near Christmas, her hair, the exclusive styling of which had formed part of her reconstructed identity and which she later wore in a finicky bun, hung loose down to her waist and gave off "a strong smell, sharp as an animal's." Six weeks later she killed herself.

> From the bottom of a pool, fixed stars
> Govern a life.

SEX IS EVERYTHING

Review of E.E.Cummings's *Complete Poems, 1913-1962*. The *New York Times Book Review*, July 22, 1973.

The odd look on the page of E. E. Cummings's poems is best understood as an attempt to apply the theory of the Symbolists to particles smaller than the traditional elements of poetry. Like his Symbolist predecessors and modernist contemporaries, Cummings will jam words into novel contexts so that peripheral or buried possibilities are forced into prominence. He will juxtapose heterogeneous elements without providing the trope that yokes them together. He will violate the habits of English syntax so that semantic units can float free of any grammatical setting that might anchor them to single meanings. He will use adverbs as nouns, prepositions as adjectives and articles as verbs. He knows all the devices that for a long time now have led the ordinary reader by his expectations to where the pie will hit him squarely in the face. Cummings said that he could express his theory of technique in fifteen words, "by quoting The Eternal Question And Immortal Answer of burlesk, viz. '*Would* you hit a woman with a child—No, I'd hit, her with a brick'"

But Cummings also has his own special devices, mostly typographical. In his typographical extravaganzas everything the mind can isolate for inspection is significant, down to the size of the letters and the shape of the spaces around them. He has densified, so to speak, the formal properties of poetic meaning, as a mathematician might densify infinity for us by pointing out that between any two of the infinite series of whole numbers there is an infinite number of fractions. Cummings rescued typography from the confinements of conventional usage and thereby multiplied the means through which poets can construct forms, communicate ideas, and violate conventions. It is his major achievement and one of which he was justly proud: "It is a supreme pleasure to have done something FIRST," he wrote his father in 1920 about the placement of a comma.

A poet, said Cummings, is "somebody who is obsessed by making." He is obsessed in part because the traces of his technique on the finished product demonstrate his individuality: "By technique we do mean one thing: the alert hatred of normality which, through the lips of tactile cohesive adventure, asserts that nobody in general and somebody in particular is incorrigibly and actively alive." But the traces in Cummings's poems of his own individuality, which was often petty and smug, are not the main source of their appeal. The appeal, for me at least, lies rather in traces of something else, of that mysterious delight humans take in making and watching bravura displays of dexterity, of an exacting skill that triumphs neatly over reluctant words and recalcitrant matter. As Cummings put it, "acrobats have always been, & will always remain, the only truly and honestly miraculous things."

Cummings's exercise of his skill was as gratuitous and absorbing as that of men who make cathedrals out of toothpicks and as finely focused as that of men who etch the Lord's Prayer on the heads of pins. He would take three hours to write three sentences for an essay and then rewrite the essay nine times. He would put his poems through fifty to a hundred drafts, some of them on graph paper. He would tinker for hours over the placement of a semicolon. Before signing with publishers he would insist on a guarantee that they send him proof until he was satisfied, although for one reason or another satisfied he never was.

Except with himself. His self-confidence, his complacency even, was such as to inspire awe. Unlike his modernist contemporaries, who also took pains, Cummings seems never to have doubted the reality of words or the worth of poetry or the truth of his perceptions or the adequacy of his powers. He wrote no poems that cancel themselves out, that demonstrate the impossibility of poetry. Among modernist poets, Cummings is unique for the extent of his appeal to readers who have no professional interest in poetry. One reason may be the absence, in his poetry, of an informing anxiety about itself.

He suffered from none of the anxieties that curse and blast poets who think they have something urgent to say, but no medium ready at hand through which to say it. Cummings did not seek new techniques so that he might express new perceptions or new ideas, but to highlight the curves of his personal bent—"so far as I am concerned, poetry and every other art was and is and forever will be strictly and distinctly a question of individuality." His poetry, in any case, is not notable for the freshness of his perceptions or the novelty of his ideas. On a quick count, I would say that the whole body of his verse contains maybe seven Ideas; at least four of which are in Wordsworth and two in Donne. One of his favorite ideas was that Ideas are bad for you. "Think twice before you think," he said. "THE MORE WE KNOW THE LESS WE FEEL!!!!!!!!" he wrote his sister. Intellectually speaking, Cummings was a case of arrested development. He was a brilliant 20-year-old, but he remained merely precocious to the end of his life. That may be one more source of his appeal.

Instead of ideas, or anxiety, his poetry is informed by what we might as well call the spirit of play. Cummings was a transcendent doodler, in his life as well as in his poetry. He never once assumed a responsibility, not even of earning a living—in spite of three wives, he was always, as he said, "a bachelor incapable of occupation"—and the irresponsibility of his verse is the kick in its hop and skip. There is something exhilarating about a man who never scrupled to vent a prejudice. But best of all, like much play, like much doodling, much of Cummings' poetry is graced by an expansive or graphic eroticism.

"SEX IS EVERYTHING" is another of the maxims Cummings sent to his dubious sister, and he seems to have meant it. Numerous drafts of his poems are decorated with sketches of naked women and of lovers going at it. (His favorite position: man supine on a bed, pillows propping his upper torso; woman riding the man and leaning forward so that a breast may reach his mouth.) His carnal, as opposed to his platonic, love poems strike me as on the whole Cummings's best. In these poems he allows himself to feel what he feels rather than what he thinks he should feel. For once, he does not strike attitudes. He has his eye on the subject rather than on himself. His carnal love poems, I am happy to say, violate most local community standards.

I certainly hope it is Cummings's gratuitous and exacting virtuosity, his irresponsibility, his playfulness, his carnality, that allows Harcourt Brace Jovanovich to sell 10,000 or so copies a year of each of three collections of his verse and allows Grove to sell 25,000 copies a year of the collection they publish. Cummings's amoralities are valuable and hard to come by. What I fear is that much of his popularity lies rather in the Rod McKuen dimension of his poems, especially those about sunsets, snowflakes, landscapes, about his parents, and other disembodied loves.

Let's hope especially that his popularity does not lie in his jokes about "niggers" and "kikes"; or in his sneers at democracy and the common man, or in his grouses about "Kumrad" Roosevelt who made the dollar worth only thirty cents; or in the imbecile shrewdness of his position on McCarthyism, which is that where there is smoke there is fire; or in the congratulations he offers himself for being the only man personally alive among non-humans in an unworld of "dollars and no sense"—"my speciality is living said/a man /who could not earn his bread/ because he would not sell his head)"; or in his hatred of ideas, his ignorance, his perpetual adolescence; or in the pop mysticism that advertises those mythical and mindless moments when "forever is now" and "everywhere is here" and one (lover) plus one still equals one and to die is to be born into a new self. Such matter is all too easily come by elsewhere.

But such matter weighs heavily in the 866 pages of his complete poems, recently published and excellently produced. It depresses the ardor of a reader ready to celebrate with Cummings the ruts and splendors of a consort's body; and it inhibits the applause of a reader roused by the acrobat who sails with debonair ease over the vertigoes of a verbal space nearly empty of content.

MANISM IN RETREAT

Originally published as "Men, Boys, Wimps." The *New York Times Book Review*, August 12, 1984.

Two chapters into James Dickey's novel, *Deliverance* (1970), the classic moment of classic American fiction recurs, perhaps for the last time. Our hero and narrator Ed Gentry has a case of the middle-age megrims, a stifling hopelessness, a stomach-sinking sense that nothing matters, least of all anything he routinely does himself. He therefore accepts an invitation to go white-water canoeing with three friends. On the morning of his departure, his wife asks him whether he really wants to go. Not much, he says, and then he tells her how low he feels. "Is it my fault?" she says. "Lord, no," he says to her, but to the reader he confides that "it partly was, just as it's any woman's fault who represents normalcy." So he takes off.

Similarly, during the second quarter of the nineteenth century, James Fenimore Cooper's hero Hawkeye (or Leather-Stocking or Pathfinder or Deerslayer or whatever his name was) took off again and again with his Indian friend Chingachgook (pronounced "Chicago," according to Mark Twain) whenever good women, churches, or game laws began to close in on him. Similarly, in mid-century, Herman Melville's Ishmael, "a damp, drizzly November in my soul," as he puts it, signs up with Queequeg to pursue the great sperm. "I love to sail forbidden seas, and land on barbarous shores"—where there are no respectable women. At about the same time, Walt Whitman, in the opening lines of *Leaves of Grass*, invited his readers to go along with him "to the bank by the wood and become undisguised and naked." For "Houses and rooms are full of perfumes"; you've got to get them behind you: "Washes and razors for foofoos...for me freckles and a bristling beard."

By this time (1855) Edgar Allen Poe had been dead for a half dozen years; but in his one completed novel, *The Narrative of A. Gordon Pym*, the "gloomy" young hero wants to go to sea. "My mother went into hysterics at the bare mention of the design." But he stows himself away and has his most extraordinary adventures alone with the racially mixed hardcase Dirk Peters, whose name means, roughly, "stone knife." Half a century later, Huckleberry Finn had his most extraordinary adventures in the company of Jim, a runaway slave. In the first paragraphs of his narrative, Huck tells us how Aunt Polly, Miss Watson, and especially the Widow Douglas, want to "sivilize" him. "But it was rough living in the house all the time, considering how dismal regular and decent the widow was in all her ways; and so when I couldn't stand it any longer, I lit out." And in the last paragraph of his narrative, in the grips of another respectable woman, he declares his intention "to light out for the Territory ahead of the rest." His reason: "Aunt Sally she's going to adopt me and sivilize me and I can't stand it. I been there before."

By that time (1885) the changes on our tune had been rung so often that when (ten years later) Stephen Crane's young hero mounts a "firm rebellion" against his pious, anti-alcohol, nose-to-the-grindstone mother to enlist and prove himself on the battlefield; when Faulkner's tall convict returns to do an extra ten years in prison rather than set up housekeeping with the woman—"this millstone which the force and power of blind and risible Motion had fastened upon him"—he has rescued from a flood ("Women ----t!" are his last words); when Hemingway's Nick Adams runs away from his henpecked father, a doctor, and his hectoring mother, a Christian Scientist, and from his girl friend, Marjorie, who wants to marry him—when he takes off to have adventures among criminals, hoboes, athletes, and soldiers, we can hear the old chords behind the thematic variations. And we are meant to hear the same chords, for all the dissonances, when Saul Bellow, Norman Mailer, and Jack Kerouac send Augie March and Henderson the Rain King, Stephen Rojack and D.J., Sal Paradise and Dean Moriarty away from smothering and mothering women to the African or asphalt jungle, the Alaskan wilds, or simply on the road—to anywhere, so long as it is away.

Recurrent as this moment or movement is in our classic novels, it occurs still more often in our popular fiction, wherein the heroes do more than leave their women behind them. In *The Maltese Falcon.* for instance, Sam Spade sets out to find his partner's murderer, who as it turns out, is the woman he's fallen for, the beautiful Brigid O'Shaughnessy, betrayer of many men. At the unravelling, he tells her that he is going to turn her in. "You didn' t—don' t 1-love me?" she says. "I think I do," he says. "What of it?" She wants him to run away with her. He gives her seven reasons why he won't. "If you loved me you'd need nothing more," she says. Spade's last words on the subject are these: "I won't play the sap for you"—the implication being that sapdom is the invariable condition of men too weak to leave 'em just because they love 'em.

In Mickey Spillane's *I, the Jury*, the plot of which is borrowed, shall we say, from *The Maltese* Falcon, Mike Hammer sets out to find his partner's murderer. She turns out to be the woman he is madly in love with, wants to marry, the gorgeous

Charlotte Manning, enslaver of many men through drugs, hypnosis, and psychotherapy. At the unravelling, he strips her morally, by enumerating her crimes, while she does a striptease, to distract him ("*And she was a real blonde*"). Hammer's indictment builds to this damning conclusion: "You no longer had the social instinct of a woman— that of being dependent upon a man." So he shoots her in the belly. "How c-could you?" she says, a moment from death. "It was easy," he says.

Whodunnits with similar plots have been written by Raymond Chandler, Ross MacDonald, and a plague of imitators; equivalent moments occur in westerns, tales of adventure, spy thrillers, and especially gangster epics. The climax of *The Godfather*, for example, comes not when Michael Corleone wipes out half of Little Italy in a glorious and gory orgy of revenge, but when he declares his moral independence from his genteel New England WASP of a wife—by lying to her, by denying that he bumped off his treacherous *brother-in-law. When I saw the movie, the audience—mostly Hispanic—loudly cheered Michael's barefaced lie. Kay Adams Corleone, the kill-joy, deserved what she got, we all felt, for trying to interfere with Michael's "business," which, when you come down to it, means living adventurously. All that Kay and her predecessors stand for is the nemesis of adventure; to have the one you must reject the other.

This antithesis in American literature between women and adventure, this rejection of an allegedly feminized civilization for an urban underworld or natural wilderness has been long noted (primarily by Leslie Fiedler) and frequently lamented. American men, say both foreign observers and our own pop sociologists (is there any other kind?), never grow up, are perpetual adolescents. And our classic literature, highbrow and low, rehearses again and again that moment when the adolescent cuts apron strings to embark on the great adventure of growing up. In *Deliverance* which is both an instance and an investigation of the American adventure novel, the hero early on catches a reflection of himself in a car window. He has a bow in his hand and a knife at his hip. He likes what he sees, then feels self-conscious, then apologetically reminds himself "that all men were once boys, and that boys are always looking for ways to become men."

If all men remain boys trying to become men, all literature should reflect their arrested condition--and so it does, sporadically. The very earliest secular literature we have, the Sumerian yarns about Gilgamesh, tell how Gilgamesh and Enkidu light out from the city to pursue immortality. They have to—because Enkidu, a kind of noble savage, has fallen into mortality and alienation from nature by coupling with a townswoman. And in Wolfram's *Parzival*, the greatest of the medieval romances, Parzival must wrench himself free from a doting mother before he can ride out to win a seat at King Arthur's table. D. H. Lawrence's Paul Morel goes further: he has to poison his mother (and break with Miriam) before he can become free to "drift," even if the drift is toward death. Just the same, in British and Continental fiction, it is the provincial young man's pursuit of the lady, rather than his flight from her, that constitutes the adventure. In American literature the "moment" I have been describing is not sporadic, but pervasive, and not only because American men are more adolescent than others, although they may be.

Only in America, so far as I know, were the formative years of a modern national literature tied up in apron strings. During the two middle quarters of the nineteenth century, the American literary marketplace was bullish on women. Middle-class women from the Northeast produced and consumed the best-selling novels. They edited, wrote, and above all bought the magazines with the largest circulations. They and their allies, liberal Protestant ministers, established the characters, situations, themes, conventions, and attitudes that governed our literary culture. The term commonly used to sum up this mass of largely-forgotten fiction is "sentimental." But I prefer a term introduced to literary discourse by Alice Walker. The subtitle of her recent collection of essays, *In Search of Our Mother's Garden* is "womanist prose." By "womanist," says Alice Walker, she means "a woman who loves other women, sexually and/or non-sexually. Appreciates and prefers woman's culture, woman's emotional flexibility (and values tears as natural counterbalance of laughter), and women's strength...*Loves* the spirit... Loves herself. *Regardless.*" The bulk of nineteenth-century American fiction was womanist in this sense: it was sentimental, narcissistic, domestic, suffused with a diffuse religiosity, and female chauvinist.

In womanist fiction, the occasional Byronic brooder may at first seem deliciously dangerous, but in the long run the only acceptable men are ministers and other easily housebroken types. So it is that in Alice Walker's celebrated womanist novel, *The Color Purple* (1982), the only men allowed to hang around after Celie and her female lover establish their Utopian commune are Samuel, a big, tame, tabby cat of a minister, Harpo, who likes to do housework, the de-fanged Mr._____ who likes to sew—and all of whom defer to the women. Given the prevalence of womanist fiction, male writers had a number of choices. Some wrote womanist fiction themselves; they are justly forgotten. Others, like Hawthorne and Henry James, grumbled about the "damned female scribblers," but co-opted and adopted womanist conventions and attitudes. Still others, like Poe, Melville, and Twain, rebelled: they wrote what, by analogy, we may call manist literature. The classic "moment" of American fiction may be a male adolescent fantasy; it is also a stroke of literary criticism, a manifesto, a gesture of repudiation, of self-definition by negation.

American manist fiction may not be as grown-up as the great European novels, but there are times when the adolescent vices are preferable to the middle-aged virtues. In any case, I doubt that manist fiction has done much harm, that the classic novels of our male writers have moved many men to leave their wives—as I doubt that the novels of Barbara Cartland, say, move women readers to get themselves ravished. One of the many good things about literature is that it stimulates you to do in your imagination what for good reasons you will not allow yourself to do in the flesh. The main just charge against manist fiction is that it offers women so little in the way of imaginative indulgence. That deficiency, during the last twenty years, has been made up—by a flood of neo-womanist novels that are also acts of criticism, manifestos, gestures of repudiation and self-definition. There are now many novels in which women light out from those tyrannical fathers, those inadequate husbands and presumptuous lovers who get in the way of a heroine's growth into full personhood, as it's called.

That is as it should be. One may note, however, that the new womanist heroine flees into the embrace of a regular occupation or another woman, precisely what the old manist hero fled from. One may also note that our male writers have not reacted to the second wave of womanist writing as they did to the first. Their male protagonists no longer venture forth; they retreat, admit defeat, take the heat, and with a crow-eating grin. They break down, instead of breaking away. They are flighty and futile, their large-gestured adventurousness and heroic defiance shrunk to restlessness and petty spite.

The last three novels of Philip Roth, for instance, and the most recent novels of Joseph Heller and Saul Bellow, read like apologies for the way these formerly manist writers treated women in the novels that made them famous. The female leads are likeable, often admirable; the male protagonists are lamentable. In John Updike's *The Witches of Eastwick* (1984), three women become witches by divorcing their husbands. "Men aren't the answer," says one of them, and the men know it. Against the magical powers of these witches, no man, and all the men in this novel are figures of fun, stands a chance—except for Darryl Van Home, a kind of warlock. He is also a homosexual, thus his immunity. "They don't bring to it"—meaning heterosexual sex—"the illusions that normal men do," says one of the witches.

In Moon Deluxe (1983), Frederick Barthelme's collection of stories, most of which were first published in the *New Yorker*, the women are wrestlers and weightlifters; they are mail carriers and wheeler-dealers; they are self-confident and always hungry; they pat men on the bottom and make the advances; the men decline; they hide behind the curtains, take baths, or watch late night T.V.; they are awkward and wistful. In C. D. B. Bryan's *Beautiful Women; Ugly Scenes* (1983), the narrator-protagonist places the blame where it belongs from the outset: "my unsatisfactory relationships with women were my own fault." His wife is more specific: "The reason why you don't turn me on is because you're too sweet and you talk too much"—but for all that he keeps working on his "sensitivity." When a randy and good-looking girl grabs him by the behind, he jumps—in the other direction. "We're going to be friends who don't happen to go to bed with each other," he says, a line traditionally assigned to female characters. His earnest conversation with a male friend reads like an excerpt from *Ms*. This novel is not meant to be funny.

In Leonard Michael's *The Men's Club* (1981), seven men, and a sorry lot they are, gather together in imitation of women's consciousness-raising klatches. "I envied them," says the narrator, thinking about women. "It seemed attractive to be deprived in our society. Deprivation gives you something to fight for, it makes you morally superior, it makes you serious. What is left for men these days?" What is left is remorse—"I'm ashamed. Also guilty"—and abject spite. In a positive orgy of it they gobble down a feast the host's wife has prepared for a meeting of her women's club the next day. They wreck her triumphantly feminine living room. When she comes home, she conks her husband, hard, on the head, with a black iron pot. "I feel you're feeling anger," says the husband, blood streaming down his face. "You clean up," she says; so he gets right down to it, head bloody and bowed.

There is no relief from this sort of thing anywhere—not even in hard-boiled detective fiction, once the preserve of manly men strong enough to go their ways without women. Robert B. Parker is probably the hottest writer of tough guy detective novels around, "the legitimate heir to the Hammett-Chandler-MacDonald tradition," says one critic. Parker's private eye, Spenser, is a broken-nosed ex-boxer who still lifts weights. Professional enforcers cringe when he frowns, but only because they can't see what mush Spenser has turned to inside. In his last few outings, he has concentrated more on becoming "sensitive," lest the beauteous (and liberated) Susan Silverstein leave him, than on getting down to cases. He uses a Cuisinart she's given him, drinks Soave Bolla, and reads Simone De Beauvoir. Reading one of these novels is like discovering that someone has poured out your Jack Daniels and then refilled the bottle with diet Pepsi.

It is now the turn of men to complain that American fiction

offers them little in the way of imaginative indulgence. The classic moment of American fiction has finally passed. Writers who try to bring it back, like Jim Harrison, often seem quaint, purveyors of nostalgia. Novels by writers like James Morrell, Robert Stone, and William Kennedy get over-praised, just because there is so little other decent fiction around to tickle a jejune man's fantasies. But before we congratulate our male writers for having at last grown up, we might notice that their male characters, at least, have not. They seem, rather, to have regressed further, to the preadolescent condition of momma's boys, alternatively bratty and eager to please, one testicle undescended. Certainly recent fiction by male writers has an air of sidling up to women, one cheek or the other presented for a kiss or a spank. It's easy enough to understand, if not forgive: now, as in the nineteenth century, women consume more fiction than men. Writers, like the rest of us, need to eat, want to be stroked.

And certainly there has been a gain in realism: the protagonists of our recent male writers are no doubt truer to life than Cooper's Hawkeye or Bellow's Henderson, than all those other guys who answered the call of the wild. But realism is not everything. Fantasies are also real. With the gain in realism has come a loss of resonance. And if literature (and its derivatives, like movies and T.V.) do not offer to our imaginations what we deny ourselves in the flesh, what will? Male writers of America! You are not doing right by us. We need something from you, who knows what, and we are not getting it.

THE 'NICE GUY' WHO TOUCHED OFF McCARTHYISM

Review of *The Redhunter*, by William F. Buckley Jr. The *New York Times Book Review*, June 7, 1999.

It takes chutzpah to attempt a rehabilitation of Senator Joseph R. McCarthy. Most Americans, after all, take it for granted that he was guilty of, well, McCarthyism, or witch hunting, a species of virus that erupts on the lips of the body politic in times of stress. But rehabilitation is precisely the goal of William F. Buckley Jr.'s new novel, *The Redhunter*.

We should not be surprised: Mr. Buckley has long had the courage of people who never doubt their own convictions. And the particulars of *The Redhunter* are organized by the conviction that "atheistic Communism" is unqualified evil; to those dedicated to the "noble cause" of eradicating this evil, it follows, nothing can be forbidden, certainly not McCarthyism. The mitigations of historians and the waffling of liberals are irrelevant to anyone whose peripheral vision does not extend to the gray areas that surround all secular issues of importance.

As the novel opens, in June 1991, Harry Bontecou, pretty much Mr. Buckley's stand-in, is sitting in a London pub, reading a newspaper. He is reading about the capture of Pol Pot, who is alleged to have executed one to two million Cambodians, from twenty to forty percent of the population. Such numbers lead Bontecou to reflect on the 25 million thought to have been shot or starved to death by Stalin. This sampling of Communist atrocities helps to prepare us for all that follows: starting with the arrival of Bontecou's host, one Alex, Lord Herrendon, a former Communist spy.

By way of atonement Lord Herrendon is writing a book on which he wants Bontecou to collaborate, its subject "the Communist scene in the West." He wants to sort out "the history of Soviet suffering and to analyze compliant responsibility for it by the West." Above all he wants to answer "the great question raised by the 20th century," the attraction to totalitarian movements, especially Communism, of not only "multitudes of people, but of intellectuals." These interests lead Lord Herrendon to the question of "the delinquency of the loyalty security practices of the Federal Government" and therefore to McCarthy, and therefore to Harry Bontecou, the Senator's closest aide and speechwriter.

After this introduction to the issues, Mr. Buckley skillfully alternates chapters devoted to the biographies of Bontecou and McCarthy, until the former writes the latter for a job. "The highest calling of our time is to contribute to the anti-Soviet cause," Bontecou writes. McCarthy wastes no time in hiring him.

Along the way there are constant references to the advances of Communism along the road to world domination ("the loss of China," for example), the growing influence of Communism within the United States (the Presidential campaign of Henry Wallace), the subversions of its agents (Alger Hiss, the Rosenbergs and a lengthening list of "Communist front" organizations), the ineptitude or worse of our leaders (who let us down at Potsdam and Yalta, who lost us "Poland and Bulgaria and Czechoslovakia and Romania and East Germany"), and so much more, all of it aided by pinkos and fellow travelers and abetted by dupes like Protestant clergymen ("the largest single group supporting the Communist apparatus in the United States today"), by "professors, scientists, artists, critics," by "liberal Commie-smoochers" in general.

In Mr. Buckley's view, the threat was dire enough not only to explain but to justify the emergence of Joe McCarthy. His fame (or infamy) began with a speech in 1950 in Wheeling, West Virginia, to 275 members of the Ohio County Women's Republican Club. "I have here in my hand," he is reported to have said, a list of 205 known members of the Communist Party who are still shaping policy in the State Department. (He later said he had spoken of 57 "loyalty risks," not 205 Communists.)

Mr. Buckley is at his best in serving up the resultant brouhaha, hearings and behind-the-scenes maneuverings, the meat of the novel, the rest mere condiment and garnish by comparison. Certainly he has done his homework—mostly way back in 1953 when he was working on the hard-hitting *McCarthy and His Enemies*, written with L. Brent Bozell and published in 1954. Passages from that book are carried over verbatim to *The Redhunter*.

Mr. Buckley deserves praise for giving equal time to McCarthy's enemies, if only to dismiss them. Through various spokesmen he derides the notion that "there never was any reason for a Red scare," scoffs at the claim that "McCarthyism is a greater threat to America than Communism," and ridicules Joseph Welch's memorable rebuke—"Have you no sense of decency, sir, at long last? Have you no sense of decency?"—which finished off McCarthy and in fact made him a liability to other Red hunters.

The portrait of McCarthy that emerges is of an essentially

"nice guy," generous and loyal, even honorable, utterly without malice or rancor when offstage, ambitious, hyperactive, indifferent to money, admittedly capable of the occasional stretcher, of jumping to conclusions, of fudging evidence, goaded into intemperate rejoinders, hounded into alcoholism and an early death.

At the end he is undone by Commie-smoochers, by vengeful Democrats, by blowhard journalists, by the machinations of Eisenhower, by his own "foibles," by his 5 o'clock shadow, above all by his quixotic loyalty to the sinister and sleazy Roy Cohn. Thus a righteous crusade gets stuck in the muck. If Mr. Buckley's McCarthy were entirely a fictional character, one would feel sorry for him.

But Mr. Buckley's McCarthy does not quite square with the McCarthy who appeared on the tube back there in the early '50s. Worse, Mr. Buckley's McCarthy, although he has a style and a mission, has no psychology or inner life. We never learn what drives him. To the end he remains only an assortment of traits. And as much may be said about the other characters, including Bontecou, for Mr. Buckley has no interest in subjectivity, no free-floating curiosity of any kind. Everyone and everything is subsumed under a moral-political-theological idea.

Maybe that is why Mr. Buckley, like Lord Herrendon, has no idea as to why an American intellectual might have become a Communist in the '50s or ten or twenty years earlier. Similarly he has no clue as to why an American who abhors Communism might want to accord sympathizers the usual rights under the law.

At one point the novel's single sympathetic intellectual tells a story about an "old colored gentleman" who asks whether it is true that "there's people who want to overthrow the

Government by force and violence?" When assured that there are, he says, well, "Why don't we just run them out of town?" The intellectual then tells his fellow members of the Columbia political science department that the old gentleman "has a more sophisticated understanding of democratic theory than any of you gentlemen."

Mr. Buckley likes this story well enough to have repeated it from an earlier novel, *Tucker's Last Stand* (1990), where, however, the interlocutor is "an elderly Negro lady." But Mr. Buckley has no inkling that the tenor of this story is—to use a word of the time—profoundly un-American, in law and spirit, if not, alas, always in practice.

VI

INTRODUCTION TO SIX MODERN BRITISH WRITERS

Introduction to *Six Modern British Novelists* (Columbia University Press, 1974).

The great English literature of the modernist era, from about the 1890s until World War II, was written by Irishmen, Americans, a Welshman, and a Pole. It is hard to think of an important English contemporary of Stevens and Williams, of Eliot and Pound, of Faulkner, Fitzgerald, and Hemingway, for example, who was as representative, as exemplary even, of the prevailing English type as these Americans were of the era's prevailing American type. It is hard, that is, to think of an important English writer of the modernist era who openly qualified for membership in the caste that set the styles, determined the values, and wielded the power that showed the world just what it meant to be English: it is hard to think of a modernist who was at once English, Protestant, male, middle-class, and heterosexual.

If the writers were not American or Polish or from one of John Bull's other islands, they were Catholics (usually by choice rather than by birth), like Ford, Waugh, and Greene, or from the working class, like D. H. Lawrence, or women, like Virginia Woolf, or homosexual, like Forster and Auden (and, perhaps, Lawrence and Woolf). Successful writers who were indeed examples of the prevailing type, like Galsworthy and Bennett, showed the others what they had at all costs to avoid, and what they had above all to subvert. Self-consciously, deliberately, with programmatic zeal and polemical emphasis, the others, those who were not of the prevailing type, made clear in their writing just how little they were Galsworthy or Bennett or their equivalents among poets. And those writers of the younger generation who by birth and sexual preference qualified for membership in the dominant caste declined the honor; they exiled themselves in one way or another: by identifying themselves with the working class, like George Orwell, by leaving the country, like Robert Graves (who in any case thought of himself as spiritually an Irishman), or by pursuing strange gods, like Aldous Huxley—to single out one in a crowd.

The prevailing type, although in fact he still prevailed, seemed somehow to have outlived his historical moment. The complex of ideas, values, and relations to his culture, the set of practices and attitudes that constituted his typicality and guaranteed his prevalence, no longer seemed the ones from within which anything of moment could be written. When the prevailing type appeared in modernist fiction it was as a figure of fun or as an occasion for justifiable parricide. To write anything of moment seemed to require at least the adversary edge of Irishmen or Americans trying to cut themselves free from the cultural imperialism of a mother country whose language was the one they had perforce to use. Or it required the implacable antagonisms of class conflict, and with it that freedom from official pieties that sometimes comes to people who have been deprived of the advantages that make the pieties plausible. Or it required the cool refusals of feminist resentment, the withering glance of someone who has discovered that what the emperor's clothes no longer hide had never been worth looking at. Or it required the satirical disenchantments of homosexuality, the oblique and disabused perspective of an abused outsider on that massive system of erotic, domestic, social, and artistic conventions built upon an alleged attraction between the sexes. Or it required a hatred of the present and a nostalgia for the past desperate enough to drive one into the arms of the Church.

Analogous things might be said about French and German writers, about writers from portions of what used to be the Hapsburg Empire, and about Americans to the extent that they worked at becoming English or European, in the style of Henry James and T. S. Eliot. Writers became modernist wherever advanced Western civilization had taken firm enough hold for advanced people to wish it were in decline. South American writers, for example, seem now to be in a modernist phase. Their felt relations to Spanish and Portuguese must be something like the Irishman's or American's felt relation to English during the days of Joyce and Pound. But the resentful love and reciprocated hate that modernist writers feel toward their own countries seem to have been especially pervasive among English moderns, perhaps because in the period just prior to the onset of modernism England was by most standards the greatest nation in the world. Its decline, or appearance of decline if you will, was that much more dramatic.

The decline of nations is like the decline of fathers, at least to boys and girls growing up. The children of discredited fathers and fatherlands seem both more free and more driven to do unheard-of things and to imagine compensatory worlds more attractive— more free and more driven, that is—than solid citizens assured of their succession. An astonishing number of writers—among them Shakespeare, Dickens, and Joyce, to name three of the greatest to write in English—had fathers whose fortunes declined as the sons were growing up. And Western modernists, especially those born near the end of the nineteenth century, clearly felt that their fatherlands were coming down in the world, that their cultural patrimonies had become debased coin, that the very principle of authority had compromised itself, that their release from filial piety had only delivered them into the anxious compulsions of a world whose center no longer held, that the aesthetic order of their work would have to compensate for the actual chaos of the world their fictions represented. During the modernist period, fathers, fatherlands, principles of authority, conventions and traditions were still there, sometimes insistently there, but discredited. The insistent presence of these, and with it the itch to subvert them and the longing for substitutes, is one thing that distinguishes modernist literature from what followed it.

The most general common characteristic of the modernist writers, then, was an adversarial or alienated relationship to their own cultures. The most general common characteristic of their work was the inverse relation between the rendered aesthetic order and the represented chaos. The more disordered the world represented, the more ordered the rendering of the work. In this respect *The Wasteland* and *Ulysses* are exemplary, but so are the novels of Ford, Conrad, Woolf, Forster, and Waugh. The very techniques used to represent a world of dissolving appearances and discontinuous selves, of crumbling institutions and discredited authorities, of the ruin of all space and time, shattered glass and toppling masonry, are also the techniques that bind part to part and part to whole with an unprecedented adhesive force. For esemplasticity the modernist classics are unequaled.

This very esemplasticity, unlike Coleridge's organic variety, has something un-English about it, as do the techniques used to produce it. The techniques of the English modernists are not simply those of their nineteenth-century predecessors brought up to date. The English modernists did not look toward their immediate past for hints as to how to make it new. They wanted nothing to do with "the eunuch century, the century of the mealy-mouthed lie, the century that has tried to destroy humanity, the nineteenth century," in the words of D. H. Lawrence. They looked around them at new occasions calling for new practices. Or they looked toward the fiction of France, America, and, Russia. They looked at Post-Impressionist painting, Russian ballet, Chinese ideograms, African masks, Japanese drama, and American movies. They looked toward psychology, anthropology, and physics. They looked everywhere but at Meredith, Thackeray, George Eliot, Tennyson, and Browning. "We are sharply cut off from our predecessors," said Virginia Woolf. "Every day we find ourselves doing, or thinking things that would have been impossible to our fathers." As a result, she continues, "no age can have been more rich in writers determined to give expression to the differences which separate them from the past and not to the resemblances which connect them with it." That determination required not only techniques different from those of the past, but techniques that called attention to themselves for their ostentatious and subverting differences.

The prevailing type of Englishman, who did not look at his past as across a chasm but as the ground under his feet, has still not forgiven the modernists for their ostentation and foreignness. If he reads twentieth-century literature at all, he prefers Georgian poets and realistic novelists, John Betjeman and the small portion of D. H. Lawrence that looks like Thomas Hardy, or, among more recent writers, those antimodernists who used to be called Angry Young Men. It is no accident that John Wain, whose practice as a novelist may be described as antimodernist and who used to be called an Angry Young Man, chose Arnold Bennett to write about. Mr. Wain can look at Bennett, "this most prosaic of novelists," as the ground under his feet, as a predecessor in the great tradition of English realism stretching without break all the way back to Defoe, if not to Chaucer. Great as that tradition has been, impressive as its achievements continue to be, the modernists rejected it, and at the same time rejected the assumptions about nature, human nature, and human society upon which that tradition is based. "Can it be," asks Virginia Woolf, "that owing to one of those little deviations which the human spirit seems to make from time to time Mr. Bennett has come down with his magnificent apparatus for catching life just an inch or two on the wrong side? Life escapes; and perhaps without life nothing else is worth while." D. H. Lawrence's disparagement of Bennett, who had been characteristically generous in trying to help Lawrence out, is on the same ground of technical obsolescence as Virginia Woolf's: "Tell Arnold Bennett that all rules of construction hold good only for novels which are copies of other novels. A book which is not a copy of other books has its own construction, and what he calls faults, he being an old imitator, I call characteristics." The prevailing type of Englishman has never forgiven the modernists for their rejection of the assumption about nature, human nature, and human society upon which realism has rested. Modernism, like psychoanalysis, was and is more congenial to Americans.

The reasons for that congeniality can be explained without recourse to invidious myths of national character. In his discussion of "the negative side of the spectacle on which Hawthorne looked out," Henry James remarks that "one might enumerate the items of high civilization, as it exists in other countries, which are absent from the texture of American life, until it should become a wonder to know what was left." James's enumeration of thirty-five or so absent institutions moves from "No state" to "no Epsom nor Ascot!" The natural remark in the face of such an indictment, says James, "would be that if these things are left out, everything is left out." Such was the natural remark of the prevailing type of Englishman, which James strove to become, in the face of all that the modernists left out. But what the modernists left out was all that had been removed from the texture of national life by recent history. And recent history had Americanized the Western nations, so to speak, by cutting them off from their own institutions, those which America had never had. Americans are the oldest people in the world, said Gertrude Stein; they have been in the twentieth century for over one hundred years. Looking through America to the future, Tocqueville fearfully predicted "that the productions of democratic poets may be surcharged with immense and incoherent imagery, with exaggerated descriptions and strange creations; and that the fantastic beings of their brains may sometimes make us regret the world of reality." As D. H. Lawrence put it, "the European moderns are all *trying* to be extreme. The great Americans I mention just were it." European and English modernism soon enough achieved American extremism, and in the same way: by adapting a parricidal relation to whatever had spawned them, by developing techniques for expressing an adversarial relation to those items of high civilization in the texture of their national lives that recent history had discredited.

In spite of its international or alien or American quality, or perhaps just because of it, there is in English modernist fiction a slow return of the native. He wakes up like old Rip to discover that he is no longer at home in his home, and his unease is precisely what makes him a subject of interest. The prevailing type became a subject of interest at precisely that moment when his prevalence could no longer be taken for granted. The great nineteenth-century English novelists revealed national character—they represented it through their characters and expressed it by being themselves—without having to look for it. They did so by the way, usually while setting out to do other things. But writers like Ford, Conrad, Woolf, Forster, and Waugh, like indeed Gide in France and Mann in Germany, and like American writers from the beginning, found national character not only a problem but problematic as well, something to be discovered and defined. The English modernists again and again posed their national types against a background of others, Americans, Irishmen, Europeans, Indians, Africans, South Americans, and these home-grown New Men of relentless aspiration. The idea was to throw the native into sharp relief, to see what in fact was the design in his lineaments. Ford's Tietjens, Conrad's Jim, his Gould, his Lingard, Woolf's six characters in search of a Percival who died in India, Forster's Wilcoxes and Ango-Indian boors, Waugh's landed gentry and traveling rascals, however, are thrown by what surrounds them into an ambiguous light that makes vices of their virtues, and vice versa. The native type became most illuminating just as his light began to fade, when like Lord Jim he found himself "under a cloud."

Even Arnold Bennett was enough of a modern to measure the vices and virtues of his provincial English town of Bursley against the more flamboyant ones of Paris. But his conclusion showed that even Paris had no lasting effect on the Bursley principle in wise Sophia, who at the end of it all remained inwardly identical to the stay-at-home and constant Constance. Bennett did not have an adversary relation to his own culture; his liberalism is the thing itself. The aesthetic order of his novels is not extraordinary;

the disorder they represent is ordinary. Conversely, the other writers discussed in this volume (*Six Modern British Writers*) tended to be as conservative in their politics as they were radical in their aesthetics. Whether from the right or from the left or from somewhere beyond the pale, what the modernist writers hated most in politics was liberalism, although the Bloomsberries sometimes pretended otherwise; what they hated most in fiction was realism, which according to them left reality out.

FANTASTIC LESSING

Review of *Shikasta* by Doris Lessing. The *New York Times Book Review*, November 4, 1979.

Doris Lessing's new novel has this in common with its predecessors: it forces us to think about first and last things, about what we are, how we got that way and where we are going. It forces us to look into the depths of the apocalyptic tide washing round us.

It forced me, at least, to remind myself that all predictions of a worldwide cataclysm have so far turned out to be false. Until just the other day, however, such predictions were engendered not by material evidence but by heated imaginations. From the Book of Daniel to the Book of Revelation, from the revelations of quakers and shakers to ghost-dancing Indians and cargo-cultic New Guineans, from the Son of Man to Charles Manson, apocalypse has been a pathos, a hunger, a wish, an expression of unendurable grievance or grief, rather than a reasoned conclusion. It has been a desire parading as fear, yearnings disguised as warnings. The giveaway, of course, is the accompanying fantasy of a saving remnant of the virtuous, among whom the predictor is prominent. The Days of Wrath, so apocalyptics tell us, will eliminate the bad guys and elevate the good guys, sole possessors of a pastoral paradise regained.

But it is no longer just the crack-brained who imagine a global disaster slouched waiting for us to turn the next corner.

Nothing short of a disaster, after all, is likely much to reduce the disastrous world surplus of births over deaths. You don't hear much talk anymore of a world government emerging to make peace and keep it, or to distribute resources so that everyone has enough and stays satisfied with it. Remember when even smart people used to think we would outgrow the murderous fanaticisms of nationalism and religion? When was it (40 years ago?) that we suddenly realized that from now on our efforts to improve things through science, technology and industry would only make them worse? Ah, for the good old days, five decades back, when we children of violence could deny we were chips off the old block! And then there is the bomb.

My complaint, then, is not that Doris Lessing's new novel (the first of a tetralogy) is a forecast of doom. She has been forecasting doom for a long time now, ever more insistently these last dozen years or so. And she has had her reasons, those enumerated above. My complaint, rather, is that our Grand Mistress of lumpen realism has gone religious on us. Her reasons are no longer historical but astrological. The great diagnostician of what ails us has become a symptom of it.

At the turning point of her first novel (*The Grass Is Singing*, 1950) the protagonist is finally able to look at herself "without a shadow of false hope, as honest and as stark as truth itself." But this new novel is saturated with false hopes, and the ultimate truth is a system of theosophical emanations, cosmic influences, occult powers, spiritual visitations and stellar vibrations. In that same first novel the author asks (rhetorically), "What is madness but a refuge, a retreating from the world?" But in this new novel, madness is an attunement to the real extrasensory reality, a possession of "the Capacities of contact," a receptivity to messages from outer space.

In 1957 Doris Lessing could say (and point to her fiction as proof she meant it) that "the realist novel, the realist story, is the highest form of prose writing." Now she tells us in a preface that her models are "the sacred literatures of the world" and science fiction, through which "the human mind is being forced to expand: this time star-wards, galaxy-wise, and who knows where next." The former Marxist now tells us that "politics is a mistake," ersatz religion "a crippling partiality," and reserves her harshest satire for the left. The sometime humanist, champion of responsibility, dramatist of modern humankind making and unmaking itself, the radical individualist who used to say that "what is dangerous is the inner loyalty to something felt as something greater than oneself," has become a religious totalitarian.

Now, through her mouthpiece, the archangelic Johor, she tells us that "to identify with ourselves as individuals — this is the very essence of the Degenerative Disease." Yes, "disobedience to the Master Plan was always, everywhere, the first sign of the Degenerative Disease." In this novel Doris Lessing stands back so that she can look down at us, *sub specie aeternitatus*, from "a realm where the petty fates of planets, let alone individuals, are only aspects of cosmic evolution expressed in the rivalries and interactions of great galactic empires." In this new novel the old aching concern for human self-destructiveness is mixed with a distant and glittery-eyed glee.

The great galactic empires in question are the benevolent Canopus, its ally Sirius and its rival Puttiora, from which criminals escape to colonize Shammat, planet of evil. The novel is in the form of a primer for "first-year students of Canopean Colonial Rule," a collection of documents, reports, diaries, letters, case studies, synoptic histories and explanatory notes, all relating to the planet Shikasta, which its inhabitants call Earth.

The story these documents tell is this: When, as a result of prolonged radiation from an exploding star in Andar, the protohuman inhabitants of Shikasta first show the potential of developing into "a Grade A species," Canopus moves to absorb it into its empire. It subjects Shikastans to "an all-out booster, Top-Level Priority, Forced Growth Plan." It sends giants, wise and good, from Colony 10 to tutor the Natives. It incorporates Shikasta into the Lock, a network of emanations, a cosmic dance a radiation of SOWF, the "substance-of-we-feeling" that holds the Canopean empire together, doing good.

Not only were there giants on earth in those days, there were also the Little People, from Sirius, who taught crafts to the slow-witted Natives, and a good time it was. Harmonious vibrations from the shining and symmetrical cities, built to receive astral currents, drew animals to the suburbs, where lions lay down with lambs, for they, too, were vegetarian. The eight-foot tall Natives could each look forward to 500 years of unrelieved health, virtue, and happiness.

But then a disaster occurs, unexpected even by the omnific Canopeans—a sudden mal-alignment among the stars. The flow of SOWF is radically diminished. From then on, until after the cataclysm perhaps 10,000 years later, everything goes downhill. Without that substance-of-we-feeling, Shikastans gradually become as we now are: greedy, gluttonous, lustful, treacherous, fractious, violent, vain, stupid, meat-eating, scientific and political—and all "due to circumstances beyond their control and for which they bore no responsibility at all." In this novel, Doris Lessing both indicts and exculpates us. We are vicious, but not to blame. Her mood is like that of St. Augustine when he told the women who had been raped by barbarians not to worry: they were only in a state of sin if they enjoyed it.

Most of the documents in *Shikasta* deal with the Penultimate Time and the Wrath, the second half of the twentieth century, that is. It is a time of general break-down and chaos, of revolution, terrorism, random slaughter and atomic warfare; of famine, epidemic and natural catastrophe; of poisoned air, contaminated water, death rays and deadly sound impulses; of paramilitary youth gangs, of a Chinese takeover of Europe, of such destruction that finally nothing remains "alive across continents but an occasional diseased animal, a demented child."

When the survivors, about one percent of the world's former population, creep out from their ruined cities, the stars have shifted. The malalignment becomes benign. There is once again enough SOWF to go around. The survivors instinctively rebuild their cities on the pattern of the First Time. They are once again healthy, virtuous,and happy. A jaguar shuns meat, settles for porridge.

From the First Time to the Last, Shikasta is busy with thousands of emissaries from outer space, which in this novel is a metaphor for religious or inner space. Envoys from Canopus bustle around on errands of mercy; those from Sirius engage in "breeding experiments"; those from Shammat sow discord and fatten on evil.

The busiest of the Canopean envoys is Johor, from whose reports we get much of the action. He is on the scene to decide who deserves to survive the Deluge (a "useful means for separating the superior from the inferior") and to survive the Time of The destruction (by space ship) of Cities, among them Sodom and Gomorrah. During the Wrath, Johor, incarnate as George Sherban, works for "the preservation of adequate representative genetic material." He warns the worthy (the sign of their worthiness is their willingness to respond), prominent among whom are telepaths and schizophrenics, including Lynda Coldridge, a survivor from *The Four-Gated City*, a novel Doris Lessing published in 1969.

Doris Lessing endorses Johor entirely (for the wages of sin is death), but not his old friend Taufiq, who falls, through "pride," to Shikastan enticements, becomes a lawyer, a figure in world politics, Satan's realm. He redeems himself during the Wrath when he teams up with Johor to save the white race from extermination by justly enraged third-worlders. Such, then, is Doris Lessing's angelology.

I disapprove of this novel, but that doesn't mean I didn't enjoy reading it. This is not the first book of Doris Lessing's to succeed, sometimes brilliantly, in spite of the author's manifest intentions. Once again, the natural storyteller triumphs over the prophet. Besides, there are ways of leaping into transcendence that enable you to see what is transient more clearly, as in the theosophical excursions of D.H. Lawrence and W.B. Yeats.

Doris Lessing's satire has never been sharper, particularly of neo-Marxist jargon and the pretensions of the powerful. Chen Liu, the humane and cultured Governor-General of Europe, who in his letters home to Peking tries hopelessly to justify mercy on the grounds of expediency but still wastes no time in ordering the execution of troublemakers, is one of Doris Lessing's best creations. And her old secular realism would not have allowed for the scenes in Zone 6 (where souls await reincarnation), which have the eerie beauty of ancient Gnostic texts. It would not have allowed her glance to swivel so effortlessly back and forth in time and space.

But the new unearthly perspective reduces the size of her earthlings. Their fates too often seem beneath our concern. And that is sufficient reason in itself to regret that reality has grown soft for Doris Lessing, whose other main characters seldom failed to move us, one way or the other. In describing the outlook of decent humans during the Penultimate Time, she finds words, I believe, for her own: "Nothing they handle or see has substance, and so they repose in their imaginations on chaos, making strength from the possibilities of a creative destruction."

ROMANCE FOR HIGHBROWS

Review of *Nuns and Soldiers*, by Iris Murdoch. The *New York Times Book Review*, January 4, 1981.

Iris Murdoch's new novel is an epitome and sum of its nineteen predecessors. It provides us, therefore, with an opportunity to formulate some constants among this round score of fictions and to see what they add up to. The first of her novels, *Under the Net* (1954) won her immediate acclaim as one of the Angry Young Men—a confusion of sexes that anticipates a number of her characters. Since then, as usual, critics have disagreed about what is good and what bad in her work. But they have agreed above all else to take Iris Murdoch *seriously*, to take her as among "the most accomplished British novelists to come to maturity since the close of World War II," to quote one of her critics.

Professors of English, understandably, have been grateful for novels that provide them with obscurities to elucidate, learned allusions to identify, and post-modernist techniques to get solemn about. Baffled and busy reviewers have been pardonably respectful of a novelist about whom monographs and dissertations are written, who is supposed to be a professional philosopher, whose Muppet characters and loop-the-loop plots have all the air of eschewing plausibility to espouse profundity The good-natured general reader has been told so often not to sneer at what he can't take time to understand that, regrettably, he now keeps his mouth shut entirely. And then there are the closet Christians, to whom Iris Murdoch (like Graham Greene and Muriel Spark) sings Come out, come out, you are just as modern, messed up and godforsaken as anyone else. Aside from all that, Iris Murdoch has had a number of genuine, if modest, popular successes. I think I know why.

On the one hand, she writes Harlequin romances for highbrows (as defined by Brander Matthews: "a highbrow is a person educated beyond his intelligence"). Secular love is the efficient cause of what goes on in her novels, as when Paul loves Paula, who loves Paulo, who loves Pauline, who has a little something going with Saul, who falls into a sudden passion for his pretty nephew Apollo when, one portentous day ("a strange mystical light pervaded London"), he finds Pauline in the arms of Paulette. Apollo, meanwhile....

On the other hand, Iris Murdoch is a neo-Christian apologist. Her fictions, I mean, argue a Christianity that has become so much more *interesting*, don't you know, since God took a powder, a Christianity that substitutes a diffuse religiosity for a formulated religion, that approves your belief according to the rigor of your disbelief. The final cause of what happens in her novels is not the earthly Aphrodite, as at first you might think, but the heavenly Eros, obscurely apprehended. "I feel that some god is playing a game with us," says one lover to another, who in turn says, "God sent you to me" to still another lover, who in her turn notes, "How strangely interlaced all these histories were."

The strange interlacings of these characters, then, their sudden twists and kinks, occur not to reveal the workings of unconscious forces—Iris Murdoch's novels are pre-psychological—but to illustrate a dogma, which boils down to this: "There was no God, but Christ lived." The heavenly Eros is Jesus, who plots our love, in, through, and for which He lives.

Iris Murdoch's novels, in sum, are primarily for people who can't take either their romance or their religion straight, who need the one to justify to themselves their indulgence in the other. The religion is shy, sly, elusive, oblique, as neo-Christians, I believe, find it in real life, and as well as they might. The intimations of Immanence allow you to take the romance allegorically. ("There was something almost allegorically sad about her," we read of a lovelorn lapsed nun who is elsewhere compared to Martha and whose beloved is very Christlike.) There are some people, are there not, who won't permit themselves to enjoy a thing unless they can first convince themselves that it is also improving them. ("How mysterious religious people were.") Therefore we have the whole elaborate defense system of covert apologetics—the coy allusions, the pregnant names, the cute in-jokes, the cluttering symbolism, the cloying play on the language of devotion, secular and/or sacred, the name-dropping.

"Wittgenstein" is the first word of Iris Murdoch's new novel, for it's time we got down to cases. That name is taken, not in vain (for did he not argue, in effect, that you can neither prove nor disprove the existence of God?), by Guy Openshaw, who is dying of cancer and tends to wander. Guy, who has been like a father to most of the other characters, dies on Christmas Eve, and in many other respects turns out to be like the Christian deity. He's half-Jewish, for instance.

While the old Guy is dying, we meet his circle of friends, who are all related, as we gradually learn, by descent or marriage or adoption, the point being that we are all God's chillun. As we piece together their biographies we gradually learn that they are nearly all orphans, the point being that Guess Who has absconded. "The father was absent," we are told, more than once, much more. And then the sexual ringalevio begins.

Guy and his wife Gertrude had loved loving each other. ("They confessed to each other and redeemed each other.") But with her husband dead only a few months, Gertrude takes a bath in a magical pool and falls suddenly in love with Tim. Tim, having had his "baptism" in a canal, falls just as suddenly in love with Gertrude. ("She was as if shriven." "He was transfigured.")

The main impediment to the marriage of these two wimps is the famous circle of friends, *les cousins et les tantes*, as they are called, none of whom considers Tim worthy of Gertrude, who is rich. And Gertrude, of course, still loves Guy, in a way. Tim, in his way, still loves Daisy, who still loves Tim, although she is too proud to stand in anyone's way. Worse, Peter, a melancholy Pole, has long loved Gertrude with a soldierly and honorable reticence that makes you want to kick him. Anne, a convent dropout, who loves Gertrude and is loved by Gertrude, also loves Peter with nunnish devotion and the same kind of reticence. Ned Openshaw and Manfred, both of whom love Anne, don't declare themselves either. The silent and scrupulous suffering of these characters is much admired by their creator and, by implication, their Creator. Mrs. Veronica Mount, however, has no qualms about declaring her love for Manfred, but then she is neither a soldier nor a nun.

She is, in fact, a character lifted from T. S. Eliot's play, *The Cocktail Party*, where she goes by the name of Julia Shuttlethwaite. Both Julia and Mrs. Mount are widowed busybodies, comic versions of St. Mary the Intercessor. On the whole, I would say that Iris Murdoch's character has the cuter name. But I might be wrong.

Because of the mostly well-meant meddling of their friends,

Tim and Gertrude are kept apart, until Iris Murdoch decided that the novel had gone on long enough. Peter in his soldierly way settles for the role of intimate family retainer. He is also cheered by the announcement that the new Pope is a Pole. Anne goes off to help a group of religious do-gooders in America. Daisy goes off to join a female commune, also in America, which in this novel is a symbol. These two women, you see, are nuns *and* soldiers. We are supposed to hope that some day, somehow, somewhere, they will meet again.

There are lots of symbols in this novel. There are symbolic rocks, rugs, birds, an orchestra of china monkeys, a patch of cliff that looks like "a head wearing a crown," its brow creepy with vines and its cheeks weepy from a hidden spring, things like that. When standing there before that face, even Tim feels "full of grace."

My favorite symbol is that of the dog. There's a dead one in the fast-rushing canal the first time Tim nearly drowns in it and a live one the second time, much later in the novel, when Tim and dog are swept through a symbolic tunnel and deposited miraculously on a stony beach. These anointings immediately precede dramatic changes in Tim's spiritual state. The dead dog and the live one signify the disappearance and return of divinity because of what "dog" spells backward. In case by this time you have begun to skip, there is another dog, named Barkiss, that disappears at the beginning of the novel and returns at the end, signifying the same thing. The absence and return (from America) of a mysterious and all-knowing character named Balintoy signify the same thing too, just to make sure. These dogs are lifted from the Proteus episode of James Joyce's *Ulysses*.

Speaking of Joyce, I should mention the prose of *Nuns and Soldiers*. Mostly it is nondescript. But when it dwells on the characters' transports of silent suffering or loquacious rapture ("He wanted to cry aloud and fall down and embrace her knees and kiss her feet"), when it dwells on the costumes of the women, then the prose is like that in the Nausikaa episode of *Ulysses*, but without the irony. Joyce himself, in a letter, described it as a "a namb-pamby jammy marmalady drawersy . . . style with effects of incense, mariolatry, masturbation, stewed cockles...." Iris Murdoch's style is more genteel, however: stewed prunes instead of cockles.

I do not mean to imply that Iris Murdoch is a cynical exploiter of high-toned old Christian women, of all four sexes. Writing this bad cannot be faked; more likely it gushes straight from the unrelieved sincerity of an author who needs mostly to deceive herself. A (rhetorical) question of Anne's, I take it, puts into words the conscious informing sentiment of these novels: "Can anyone who has had it really give up the concept of God? The craving for God, once fully established, is perhaps incurable." No doubt, but my own feeling is that sex this far sublimated is not more than the thing itself, but less. I much prefer to take my erotic fantasies raw. They are more nutritious that way.

VII

FAT-CHEEKS HEFTED A SNAKE; ON THE ORIGINS AND INSTITUZIONALIZATION OF LITERATURE

"Fat-Cheeks Hefted a Snake: On the Origins and Institutionalization of Literature," in *English Literature: Opening up the Canon*, eds. Leslie A. Fiedler and Huston A. Baker Jr. Baltimore (Johns Hopkins University Press, 1981). Originally a paper read before the English Institute.

I'd be in for an easier time of it today were it not for this dismal notion I have that institutions don't exist— materially speaking, of course. Marriage, for example, surely doesn't exist, although people exist, and some of them get married. Marrying, I mean, is to people as bouncing is to balls: balls exist, and some of them bounce, but for all the ways of handling a ball, there's no way to lay a hand on its bounce. Again: red lights exist, and cars stop at them, but though you can shoot out the light or abandon the car, there is nothing material you can do to the stopping itself, although it's what constitutes the institution. From the point of view, I regret to say, the English Institute doesn't exist either. Certainly there are people who read aloud words about other words—the words they read headed by titles with colons in them. And certainly there are listeners, or it would be foolish indeed for the readers to be reading aloud. But the English Institute is not its readers or listeners or colons, for these might be exchanged for other people, or for semicolons, without our wanting to say that the English Institute no longer is what it was, or rather wasn't. Nor is an institution a law or system of laws, for much of what goes on regularly at the English Institute is not governed by law; for although brides and grooms kiss after saying "I do," on this matter the law is silent.

To an alien intelligence, then, to an intelligence that knew neither our language nor our motives, what we call our institutions would look like a tangle of group habits. It would look as though humans had dispositions to do certain things in certain places at certain times. Our institutions would mostly look like behavior patterns activated by endogenous or environmental stimuli according to seasonal or diurnal rhythms—although habits, dispositions, patterns, and rhythms don't exist either, materially speaking. In this respect, we would look to the alien as animals look to us; for the institutions of animals don't exist in the same way ours don't, and for similar reasons.

Those reasons are evolutionary: the institutions or behavior patterns of animals fit them out for survival; so presumably did ours, once upon a time. Some behavior patterns equip an animal to survive the pressures exerted upon it by the other members of its species, its conspecifics, as biologists say. Such patterns, that is, evolved in response to intraspecific selective pressures. Pressures such as these we can fairly call social. Other patterns equip an animal to interact adaptively with everything outside of its population. Such patterns, that is, evolved in response to extraspecific selective pressures. Pressures such as these, for the sake of simplicity, we can call economic or natural, although among animals, at least, social patterns are anything but unnatural. Once any animal institutions had evolved, whether they were social or natural, they exerted selective pressures in their own right. New behavior patterns as well as new physical traits would evolve in response to them, for although institutions are immaterial, they have material consequences.

Some of these consequences are spectacular, the tails of peacocks, for example, and the equally gorgeous behinds of baboons. Neither attraction is of much use to peacocks and baboons in their struggle with nature; their function, rather, is to stimulate meaningful interpersonal relationships. So it is with the red breasts of robins, which exist strictly for the sake of other robins. So it is with the animal or human institutions made notorious by ethologists, those dominance joustings and territorial displays, those appeasement gestures and courting rites—all of which indeed have functions that are mainly social, but not necessarily the function of maintaining the society we happen now to have. So it is, less dramatically, with the red dot on the end of the herring gull's bill. When the parent gull returns from a search for food to its nest, it leans forward so that the chicks will see its bill. The chicks thereupon peck at the red dot. The parent thereupon regurgitates whatever it had been eating. It then picks up a bit of food, so that when the chicks once again peck at the red dot, they are rewarded with something to eat. The red dot is what ethologists call a social releaser: it releases the social activity of pecking, which then releases the food, so to speak. Red dot, pecking, regurgitation; social releaser and behavior pattern; physical trait and institution—these evolved in response to each other, reciprocally. They help animals get on with each other, but as a general rule what helps animals get on with each other also helps them get on in the extraspecific world around them. So it must have been with protohumans, whose institutions, like ours, are indistinguishable from behavior patterns, to the alien observer.

Protohumans, that is, presumably had protohuman institutions; they were a part of what made them protohuman. Once some of them had evolved, protohuman institutions became a part of the protohuman's environment. Like the rest of his environment, they exerted selective pressures. Behavioral and physical traits that meshed adaptively with the social or institutional environment survived and multiplied. Among such traits are an ability to visualize what is not perceptible and funny vocal cords. Maladaptive behavioral and physical traits became extinct or vestigial or suppressed, for we carry much of our pasts within us. Among such traits, we gather, were a disposition to express rage physically rather than symbolically and those stiff but powerful facial muscles that limited the protohuman's range of expressions. Protohuman institutions, on the one hand, and protohuman physical and behavioral traits, on the other, evolved in response to the pressures they exerted upon each other; they evolved reciprocally, or dialectically, like everything else, so it seems.

The notion I have been arguing against, then, is that the first human institutions were post- or transevolutionary. I have been denying that we got pretty much to where we are now physically, and only after that flew or fell into culture. To see institutions such as language and literature (neither of which, materially speaking, exist) as postevolutionary, after all, is to see them as related to the physical human as the classless society is related to history, and as the City of God is related to the other one. It is to see them as related by a leap into the absurd. The more likely alternative is that our institutions are part of what got us to where we are, physically and otherwise. It is more likely that our institutions, to begin with, functioned adaptively, whatever they do now.

Among the protohuman institutions that didn't exist, materially speaking, was the behavior pattern of storytelling. Modern anthropology, in any case, knows of no society (no matter how "primitive" it might otherwise seem to anthropologists) that is without storytellers and willing listeners—or, I might add, without critics, those second-storymen; for tribal people, like other kinds, like to comment on stories almost as much as they like to listen to them (and it is the social function of such commentary, of course, to turn stories into institutions). Storytelling, then, is a species-specific behavioral trait; at least we don't know of any other animal that tells stories, except for animals *in* stories. Storytelling is as definitively human as fully opposable thumbs and rounded buttocks, which, though not as gorgeous as the baboon's, have enabled us to rise above him. If storytelling had no adaptive function, it would be proof of the existence of God; it would be a miracle, a suspension of the laws of nature, the only gratuitous species-specific behavior pattern in the world. In sum, although, materially speaking, stories and storytelling do not exist, they function: they are functions. They are functions of our need to get on intraspecifically so that we can get on cooperatively in the extraspecific world around us.

That literature has social functions is no longer news, although storytellers often deny it. They deny it because their private interests in their stories are at odds with the institutional ones—for humans differ from animals in that the interests of the individual human, if only to the individual human, are often at odds with the interests of the group. Among such interests is the interest in stories. The private functions of literature, I am going to argue, are at odds with the institutional functions, or there would be no need for critics, whose institutional function is to co-opt private subversiveness for the public interest. At the same time, it is in the public interest for private individuals to enjoy subversive fictions—just as it is in the interest of private individuals for public institutions to function, so long as they also remain adaptive. These paradoxes require evidence and instance, for which I now turn to the first story ever told.

The protohumans who invented literature lived before the great leap forward during the Paleolithic plenitude of big game protein. They were wee, timorous, and cowering, no longer able to scamper up into the safety of trees, nor yet big or cooperative or smart enough to stand off predators. They called themselves "the People," so as to distinguish themselves from other protohumans, whom they considered fair game. But most of their words were exclamatory or imperative or hortatory, signals mostly, equivalents to such things as the crow's warning caw or the baboon's amorous display of his engorged and gorgeous rump. One word, for example, might mean "Duck, there's a python at ten o'clock!" while another might mean, "Come on, baby, and knock me a kiss." Just the same, the People had syntax enough to organize exclamations and the names of things into conceptual units, into sentences. And the words they liked to organize best, the words that carried the greatest payload of emotion, were the quasi-exclamatory names of the things upon which the People depended for survival.

Their word *stake*, for example, was not the name for just any old stick. It was the name of their only implement and a man's most valuable possession, materially speaking. It was the name used for a found object of a certain length, thickness, rigidity, and toughness, good for digging up grubs and roots, for poking around in anthills and in bee hives, for bludgeoning frogs and overturning porcupines. Intraspecifically, it could be used for a cane or billy club or swagger stick. Or take the People's verb *heft*, which did not mean to dandle something in the hand as though to estimate its weight. It was, rather, a technical term used solely for the act of picking up and testing a *stake*. It meant to pick up a *stake* and mime its uses, to poke, swing, shake, lean on, and swagger it. The People's Alpha male, name of Fat-Cheeks, had the best of *stakes* and no one was his equal when it came to *hefting* one. On the whole, Fat-Cheeks was satisfied with his *stake*, his people, and himself, but he was not happy.

The impediment to his happiness was Short-Shanks, the Omega male, whose *stake* was a disgrace. It was altogether too thin, limber, crooked, and worm-eaten. It offended Fat-Cheeks's aesthetic sensibilities; it detracted from his sense of pride in the People, upon which his own self-esteem was dependent. One day, when he could stand it no longer, Fat-Cheeks broke the miserable Short-Shanks's miserable *stake* over his knee. He pulled Short-Shanks by the ear as a signal that he should come along. His intention was to find and *heft* for Short-Shanks a *stake* commensurate with the dignity of the People. Half-hidden under a thicket of brush, he saw something like what he had in mind. As much as he could see of it was thick, straight, strong-looking, a dark olive in color, nearly black. He reached down, put a hand around it, and started to *heft* it. The damned thing reared back with forked tongue, bared fangs, and a bloodcurdling hiss, for this was no *stake*, but a black mamba, deadliest of serpents. Fat-Cheeks whirled the mamba once over his head, so that centrifugal force would keep the fangs away from him, and then let go. He scuttled back a few steps, tripped, and sat down hard on his fat and rounded buttocks. Short-Shanks said not a word, for Fat-Cheeks, like most Alpha males, was thin-skinned and short-tempered.

But that evening, when Short-Shanks hunkered down for a soothing session of lice hunting with his consort, name of Turtle-Neck, because that's the kind she had, he finally spoke. His momentous words were these: "Fat-Cheeks *hefted* a snake." Turtle-Neck froze, dropped the louse she was about to eat, gaped at Short-Shanks, tipped over on her back, kicked her feet in the air, and whooped with laughter, for she was jealous of the charms and privileges of Fat-Cheeks's latest consort. Only then did Short-Shanks begin to laugh, for storytellers derive their pleasures not so much from their own stories as from the imagined or material reactions of their audience. And a storyteller is what Short-Shanks had just become, the very first. "Fat-Cheeks *hefted* a snake" was the world's first work of literature.

On what grounds, you may ask, do I call this literature. How, you may want to know, does it differ from humbler sentences. After all, it doesn't look any different. Certainly I will agree that, materially speaking, there is very little to distinguish it from a sentence such as this one: "Fat-Cheeks *hefted* a *stake*" (with a t), which is not literature. And certainly I would agree that it is not fiction, in one sense of the word, because it is not false; when uttered, it was about as true as sentences get. I might claim, however (if I were an historical critic), that Short-Shanks's epical sentence, like all other literature, so bears the imprint of its *sitz im Leben*, like a nudist who has been sunbathing on gravel, that you can't understand it unless you know whence it arose. To understand the sentence's original meaning, at least, you would have to know something about the People, their economics and institutions, their superstitious horror of black mambas, the vortex of feelings and ideas that whirled around the words *heft* and *stake*, the social status of Fat-Cheeks and Short-Shanks and Turtle-Neck, the relations among them, the whole history of the universe until the moment of the sentence's maculate conception. But who cares about the original meaning of anything any more? Besides, you would have to know the same things to understand the original meaning of a sentence such as "Fat-Cheeks *hefted* a *stake*" (with a t), which, we agreed, is not literature.

Or I might claim (if I were a formalist) that Short-Shanks's epochal sentence, like any poem, is a self-contained verbal universe characterized by tension, irony, and paradox. 1 might point out how the swift final anapest, "ed a snake," rears back on the lumbering trochees behind it, as the black mamba reared back on Fat-Cheeks. I might point to the gustatory pleasures of the mouth in moving from the low back vowel in "Fat" to a high front vowel, to a middle front, to another low back, to the final low, low front vowel of "snake," never mind the laxative roughage of the consonants. I might point to the buried pun in the buried rhyme between "snake" and the absent word *stake*. But these features of the sentence do not make it literature, although they encourage us to make literature out of it. A work of literature is not a form, but a function, although its form may signal its function.

Or I might claim (if I were a Laconian structuralist) that the sentence derives its uncanny power from the fact that the snake is all the more present for being absent; that, like all literature, the sentence recapitulates that awful moment when the little boy first saw his sister naked, only to be confronted by an absence where there should have been a presence, thus undermining his own sense of reality. Or (if I were a Derridean structuralist) I might claim that the difference between "snake" (with an *n*) and stake (with a *t*) reenacts the portentous difference between *difference* (with an *e*) and *differance* (with an *a*) and thus, like all literature, is a reflexive commentary on the language that comprises and compromises it. If I were an Aristotelian I would have to settle for the claim that the sentence, like all comedies, has a beginning, a middle, and an end, a doer, a doing, and a done to—unless I wanted to dwell on the cathartic qualities of the consonants. If I were an archetypal critic there would be no end to the things I might claim. All these are much-mended nets to bag literature for institutional consumption. Finally, if I were a pragmatic critic, which I am, I could claim that the sentence is a paradigm of all stories in that it is a something told by someone to someone about an absent someone else— but (if I were an aesthete) I might add, for no utilitarian purpose. If I were to add that, however, I would not be telling the truth. For the sentence does have a practical function, if not a material one, and it is that function that makes it literature. For a story, like any work of art, becomes a story or work of art by virtue of how it is used. This dark saying calls out for a short excursus.

If some dodo, for example, finds a bent and rusted Mack truck muffler in a suburban dump, and solders bottle caps on it, and displays it in a gallery; and if another dodo buys it, puts it on a pedestal in his living room, evidences pride in it, shows it to friends, who stand back to inspect it with solemn looks on their faces; and if he then wills it to a museum, so as to beat the inheritance tax—then we know that the muffler has become a work of art. Or if we see overdressed people sitting quietly in Carnegie Hall while some guy on stage tortures a whoopee cushion, or if we see the same people listening attentively to forty-eight minutes of silence while the musicians on stage, also overdressed, sit with their hands in their laps—then we know that the noise of the whoopee cushion and the forty-eight minutes of silence have become works of musical art, to the dodos that listen to them. For things that are visual, auditory, or verbal become works of art when they are used the way works of art are used by the society that considers them works of art.

Similarly, the sentence "Fat-Cheeks hefted a snake" is literature because it functioned the way what we call literature functions, because it was used the way literature is used. But it did not function in the same way for Short-Shanks and for the rest of the People. Its private and institutional functions, that is, were different; its private function, in fact, was anti-institutional, but that is how, as it turns out, it served its institutional function.

Luckily, we can recover the use to Short-Shanks of his momentous sentence, and without any recourse to depth psychology. It was used by Short-Shanks as a substitute for murdering Fat-Cheeks. Like all literature, it was a substitute in words for what the author couldn't or wouldn't do in the flesh, just as E. H. Gombrich's hobby horse was a substitute for the kind its owner couldn't afford or wouldn't want to clean up after. And like all literature, Short-Shanks's substitute was overdetermined. He acted in words rather than in the flesh because he was already so protohuman that his disposition was to express intraspecific rage symbolically rather than physically; because he partook of the institutional awe that hedges an Alpha male; because he was not sure he could bring it off; because he was not sure that if he could bring it off, he would get away with it; because he was lazy. Short-Shanks's feat was to express his anti-institutional resentment without the risk of guilt, failure, retaliation, or fatigue. And there were side benefits: the pleasure in mouthing a well-turned phrase; the admiration in Turtle-Neck's eyes; the chance that, for once, she would not repulse his amorous advances.

That's how literature functions for the individual, then, as a substitute in words for an action he can't or won't perform in the flesh. And that is in part how it serves his institutions. After suffering Short-Shanks's amorous attentions, Turtle-Neck ran off to tell her story to other women, who told it to their men. In the days that followed, many of the People used Short-Shanks's story as he had used it: to express their private resentment toward their institutional chief—but the effect was to consolidate that worthy's position. Fat-Cheeks could have censored the story, but unlike many of his successors, he was shrewd as well as strong. He was quick to notice that those of the People who repeated the story afterwards became easier in his presence, found ways of making up to him—perhaps because they were after all human enough to feel guilt over symbolic aggression, and not just the material kind. This (so far) natural process of socialization was too full of ambiguities for one of Fat-Cheeks's flunkies. He improved the original sentence with a commentary in the form of an addition. His edition of the sentence went like this:

> The least of men can heft a stake
> But only Fat-Cheeks hefted a snake.

This became the official version; when it became the only version, the institutionalization of Short-Shanks's opus was complete.

Fat-Cheeks's flunky, by the way, founded the school of criticism that looks at all works of literature as commentaries on other works of literature, and that looks at commentary as literature in itself. He later wasted away, I understand, under the anxiety of influence. But his lasting achievement was the first systematic perversion of literature for an institutional purpose, which achievement, ever since, has been the institutional function of critics. The inevitable, and adaptive, response of individuals is to deinstitutionalize. Take, for example, that dreamy-eyed protohuman girl, overweight and clumsy, a future storyteller herself, who when she heard the Authorized Version, immediately revised it into an erotic fantasy. She revised it into a fantasy of Fat-Cheeks hefting his snake for her sake alone, thereby instituting a tradition of revision faithfully honored by undergraduates ever since, much to their credit. By virtue of its availability for such usage, good literature survives institutions and their flunkies, for this is not yet the end of our story.

Once the ice had been broken, new works of literature gushed from many a sacred fount. Fat-Cheeks, for example, after driving Short-Shanks into exile (for Alpha males were protohumans as well as institutions), noticed how subdued and retiring Turtle-Neck had become. He waited for a moment of silence, cleared his throat, looked around to make sure he had everyone's attention, and in an unnaturally loud voice said this: "Turtle-Neck has withdrawn into her shell." He thus inaugurated the tradition of institutional art, which is dull because it has no personal or anti-institutional edge.

Those of the People who followed Short-Shanks into exile preserved the original form of the story, but they lost its original meaning. Over millennia they became bigger from big game protein, more cooperative through hunting it, and smarter in response to the intraspecific pressures of their evolving language and literature. They threw away their *stakes* for a tool kit of bone and stone. Their word "stake" now meant what it means to us, a kind of pretentious stick. Their word "heft" devolved to something like our "lift." Their catchphrase, "Fat-Cheeks hefted a snake," took on the functions, pretty much, of our catchphrase, "He walked into an exploding stove." If Blow-Top, for example, kicked a porcupine, or Lump-Jaw slapped at the mosquito on his ear but forgot to let go of his stone axe first, you could count on some wiseacre to say, "Fat-Cheeks hefted a snake."

Millennia still later, the People left their ancestral home to escape the descendants of Fat-Cheeks's followers, who considered them fair game. They migrated north, turned the lower right corner of the Mediterranean, and spilled into the Near East, although it was not yet near to anything. They learned how to tame and ragout the dogs that scavenged their campsite detritus. They learned how to scratch out furrows, how to plant the alien corn that had become their staple, for big game was getting scarce thereabout. The hefty stick used for scratching out furrows they called a *stake*, around which a new vortex of feeling and idea began to whirl. But the first story ever told was forgotten, except by a guild of sorcerers, who gave it an esoteric meaning now beyond recovery. An early scholiast, sure enough, explains that the sorcerers read *Fat-Cheeks* as a synecdoche for robust health and beauty; *hefted* as archaic for "plowed"; and *snake* as figurative for "stake," for over millennia the repressed slowly returns, even in language. The scholiast's full translation of the sorcerer's alleged meaning goes like this: "Pleasing Plumpness plied his plow," or 'Through work wax wonderfully." For a long time this reading held, but a noisy group of revisionists have recently denounced it as a euphemism at best and at worst, propaganda, an attempt to reconcile workers to their chains. Thus literature evolves dialectically with the institutions that co-opt it and with the critics who denounce them.

The descendants of Fat-Cheeks's followers preserved the Authorized Version of our story. Over millennia they evolved a snake-handling ceremony to drive the message home. Each year, at the spring equinox, the Alpha male, whose royal or institutional name was Fat-Cheeks, handled a black mamba that a flunky had secretly defanged. Following the ceremony, everyone got a piece of black mamba to eat, like it or not. Millennia still later, they evolved a substitute for the snake, a hobby snake, a *stake* in fact, for over millennia the repressed slowly returns—or did I say that? By now the People of Fat-Cheeks had killed off the big game around their ancestral home, so they too moved to the Near East, which was getting nearer. There they quickly conquered the descendants of the People who had gone into exile with Short-Shanks. The victors continued to call themselves "The People," but they called their victims "The Others," so as to signify that they were fair game. For the sake of convenience we will follow this nomenclature, if it is understood that my doing so implies no valorization of either party. The People, then, pressed the Others into service as slaves and serfs, for being warriors and hunters, they considered farming beneath them. But being also shrewd, like their culture hero, they recruited promising young Others for the lower clerisy.

One unemployed young Other, who had been trained as a scribe, refused the role of flunky. Besides, no one would hire him. He was untidy, gaunt, eloquent, and sexually ambiguous. Millennia before, he would have been a berdache or shaman, except that no matter how hard he tried, he just couldn't bring on a vision. He tried hacking off a finger, starvation in the desert, and forbidden mushrooms, but the vision never came. Finally, in desperation, he sought out the last of the sorcerers, a blind ancient who lived in scrofulous poverty and in a batty cave. The young man stood before the sorcerer and spoke these words: "What is to be done?" The sorcerer, who was senile, mumbled his answer: "Fat-Cheeks hefted a snake," by which he seems to have meant, "Go find a job." But the young man fell in a fit and thrashed around for a while in the bat guano. When he woke up, he began to preach, for he had at last had his vision.

He travelled among the flotsam of the city and the jetsam of the countryside, calling himself Son of Others, spreading the good news. For his vision had revealed to him how in the beginning the Great Goddess danced in the void. She called herself Fat-Cheeks because, like many dancers, she was both steato- and calli-pygous. Her pirouettes created a whirlwind, which she rolled out between her hands until it was very like a snake. When it reared up with forked tongue, bared fangs, and a blood-curdling hiss, she mounted it. From this union came all things, including the Others, whom the Goddess chose for her own. Under Her mild sway, the Others at first lived in a pastoral paradise of polymorphous perversity—until they were conquered by the People, who bowed down to male demons, ate meat, and were otherwise disgusting. Their Alpha male had usurped the Goddess's name and prerogatives, had expropriated the sacred black mamba, symbol of Her power and instrument of Her bounty. But now Son of Others had been elected to prepare the way for Her return. The Days of Wrath were upon us. Soon she would ride in on a whirlwind. She would blow the People away and restore the Others to their pastoral paradise. This gospel spread like wildfire. Disciples swelled the ranks and purged deviationists. And so it was that "Fat-Cheeks hefted a snake" became the world's first revolutionary slogan—equal to "Thou shalt have no strange gods before me" or "Death to the infidel" or "Workers of the world unite." For in their way with literature, anti-institutional institutions are like the other kind.

There is no need for me to go on with how Son of Others and *the* Others took charge; how they began to call themselves "the People" and to call other people "the Others"; how in the fertile valleys of the Meander they established the world's first oriental despotism, thus bringing the Near East still nearer; how cadres of untidy heretics met secretly to expound the true gospel, which told how Fat-Cheeks, Father of all things, puffed out his face like a black mamba to blow life into the first clay men, ancestors of the Others, whom He chose for his own. I have already said enough to illustrate my point, which has nine parts: 1. Literature doesn't exist. 2. It is an institution. 3. It is anti-institutional in origin. 4. It is a substitute. 5. That is its institutional function. 6. The institutional function of critics is to convert it to other institutional functions. 7. The disposition of individuals is to deinstitutionalize it. 8. The disposition of anti-institutional institutions is to reinstitutionalize it. 9. Thus literature survives by adapting itself to intraspecific pressures.

I don't suppose I can get out of declaring myself on the question as to whether or not the institutionalization of literature is a good thing. I could evade the issue for a moment by observing that it is as inevitable as aging: if you live, you get old; if literature lives, it gets institutionalized. But you don't have to like something just because it's inevitable. All right, here goes: my answer to the question of whether or not the institutionalization of literature is a good thing... depends. It depends on which I value more, literature or institutions; and that depends on which literature and which institutions are in question; it depends on whether or not the institutions in question are adaptive. Suppose I leave it for you to decide whether or not our literary institutions are adaptive. I have already hefted more than one snake too many.

K. LORENZ, AND THE DOG BENEATH THE SKIN

"K. Lorenz, and the Dog Beneath the Skin," The *Hudson Review*, Vol. XXVI, No. 1, Spring, 1973.

Ethology is the biology of behavior, the science of "comparative behavioral physiology." Its particular objects of study are the forms and movements of animals in their natural settings. Its point of departure and of rest is in the theory of evolution. The first and last thing an ethologist wants to know about the morphological or behavioral characters of a species is how these help the species to survive. For an evolutionist, to ask what a thing is for is to ask how it got that way; to investigate the adaptive function of a trait is to investigate the process that brought it into being. But between his first "what is it for" and his final "how did it get that way" the ethologist wants to know many other things.

He wants to know whether a sequence of behavior is set off by stimuli from within or from without the animal. He must concern himself, that is, with neurophysiology and endrocrinology on one hand, and with ecology and the psychology of perception on the other. He wants to know whether a trait is peculiar to an individual or characteristic of its species, its genus, its order. He must concern himself, in other words, with ontogeny (the developmental history of an individual) and phylogeny (the evolutionary history of a species), with genetics and taxonomy. He wants to know how fur, feather, or fin, how a disposition, capacity, or habit, is related to the whole of the animal, to the animal's conspecifics, and to the animal's extra-specific environment ("specific" is an adjective derived from "species"). Somewhere along the way he inevitably asks how what he has learned about other animals will apply to humans.

The founder of ethology and its greatest practitioner is Konrad Lorenz. The recent publication, in a scrupulously accurate English translation, of his collected papers, dating from 1931 to 1963, is an important event.[1] They reveal the variety and complexity of the data, as well as the theoretical finesse, upon which ethology is founded, but they also reveal the fissures and soft spots underlying Lorenz' books for the general reader, *Man Meets Dog* (1953), *King Solomon's Ring* (1952), and *On Aggression* (1963). They reveal how the methods and concepts that now make up the ethologist's equipment gradually emerged from patient observation; and in the process of showing that ethology has a past, they make clear how promising is its future. They require no more special knowledge from the reader than did, say, *The Interpretation of Dreams*, but they demand an equal willingness to engage difficult and unfamiliar ideas; they are equally concerned with the intricacies, rigidities, and fragilities of the mechanisms of behavior.

Among the rigidities of behavior the most rigid is the *fixed*

---

[1] *Studies in Animal and Human Behaviour, by Konrad Lorenz. Translated by Robert Martin. Vols. I and II. Harvard University Press, 1973.*

motor pattern,[2] "the Archimedean point on which all ethological research is based," as Lorenz puts it. Fixed motor patterns—these "innate action and response norms," these "ready-formed species-specific functional lay-outs," these "rigidly-structured, phylogenetically inherited behavior patterns," as Lorenz variously refers to them—are inherited in the sense of being common to all healthy members of a species (like an infant's nursing movements), rather than special to individuals (like an ability to swallow swords). Each animal brings into the world a repertoire of fixed motor patterns that defines his membership in a species as precisely as do his morphological features. Such patterns evolve among the members of any species by the same processes of mutation and selection that shape bones, teeth, and silhouette. They are as invariable, in their temporal unfolding, as are the markings of a duck in their spatial distribution, and they are as immutable in the face of experience.

Once set off, in fact, a fixed motor pattern is very little subject to deflection by an internal or an external stimulus, unless the stimulus is as irresistible as, say, a ruptured aorta or a round of buckshot. Certain insects will continue their mating ceremonies right to the end, no matter what—long after, for example, their prospective mates have been conspicuously removed. A fixed pattern is an indigestible chunk; it is virtually autonomous; it behaves "like an inorganic inclusion in the ambo-ceptor causal

---

[2] *The German word is* Erbkoordination, *or "inherited coordination." Ethologists writing in English usually write "fixed action pattern." In his earlier papers Lorenz used the terms* Triebhandlung *("drive-operated activity") and* Instinkthandlung *("instinct activity") and* angeborne Verhaltenwese *("innate behavior pattern").*

reticulum of the organic system." So long as the environmental conditions in response to which fixed patterns evolved remain unchanged, the rigidity of the patterns is of great survival value to the animal. They enable him to do things that he could never learn to do through insight, imitation, or trial and error:

> A young swift reared in a narrow cave in which it cannot extend its wings (far less beat them up and down), in which it cannot attain a sharp retinal image, as the farthest point of the cave is much nearer than its shortest focusing distance, and in which it cannot gain any experience on parallactic shifting of retinal images, nevertheless proves to be perfectly able on the very moment it leaves the nest cavity to assess distances by the parallactic shift of the object's images. It can also cope, in its rapid flight with all the intricacies of air resistance, upcurrents, turbulence, and air pockets and can "recognize" and catch prey, and finally effect a precise landing in a suitable place. The information implicitly contained in the adaptive molding of all these forms of behavior to the environmental givens to which they indubitably do fit would fill many volumes. The description of the innate distance computers alone would contain whole textbooks of stereometry and that of the responses and activities of flying, an equal number of data on aerodynamics.

Thus knowledge stored in the genome, or set of chromosomes, and acquired through phylogeny is more subtle and more extensive than anything an animal can pick up in its lifetime; but it is like the knowledge that might allow a dancer to get up and pirouette in her sleep, rather than like the kind that allows a choreographer to organize pirouettes into a significant form. Animals run through their fixed patterns like sleepwalkers; they give no sign of an awareness that they go through these innate motions for a purpose—a purpose either of their own or of their species. Birds, for example, build nests not to provide for their young, but from a compulsion to build nests. They build them even if they have never seen eggs, even if they have been reared away from all other birds and every kind of nest. A female canary pushes loose strands of material into the cup of her nest with a special weaving movement. If reared in isolation it will still perform this weaving movement on the floor of its cage—but without strands and without nest. The bird knows neither what it is doing, nor why; neither what set the action off, nor what it is good for.

For all the zombie-like aspect of an animal enacting its fixed patterns, these are not reflexes, or unconditioned reflexes, or even chains of reflexes, though this is what for a long time Lorenz assumed, even asserted, they were. Reflexes can only be set off by external stimuli, but fixed patterns sometimes "explode" *in vacuo*, as Lorenz puts it, without any observable stimulus whatsoever:

> A hand-reared starling that I owned many years ago had never in its life caught flies nor seen any other bird do so. All his life he had taken his food from a dish, filled daily. One day I saw him sitting on the head of a bronze statue in my parents' Viennese flat, and behaving most remarkably. With his head on one side, he seemed to be examining the white ceiling, then his head and eye movements gave unmistakable signs that he was following moving objects. Finally he flew off the statue and up to the ceiling, snapped at something invisible to me, returned to his post, and performed the prey-killing movements peculiar to all insect-eating birds. Then he swallowed, shook himself, as many birds do at the moment of inner relaxation, and settled down quietly. Dozens of times I climbed on a chair, and even carried a step-ladder into the room— Viennese houses of that period have very high ceil-

ings—to look for the prey that my starling had snatched: but not even the tiniest insect was there.

Such *Leerlaufreaktion*, or "vacuum activity," poses a problem. Lorenz, at first tentatively, but with increasing confidence as the evidence from neurophysiologists (especially Paul Weiss and Erich von Hoist) began to accumulate, and as the opposition of behaviorists stiffened, postulated the "spontaneous, automatic-rhythmic" production by the central nervous system of "energy parcels" allotted to particular fixed motor patterns. These are produced automatically once the animal has reached a certain stage of maturation, no matter what its experience, or lack of it. They appear spontaneously and rhythmically even if the piece of spinal chord producing them has been severed from the animal's brain and from the nerves reaching to the animal's sensory receptors—its sole means of contact with the outside world. The *reaction-specific energy*, as it's sometimes called, accumulates between performances of the fixed pattern to which it is allotted. The pattern, once elicited, uses the accumulated energy up. But if after a critical period of time the pattern is not elicited, if, that is, the animal is isolated from the kind of natural situation in response to which the pattern evolved, the action specific energy may "overflow"; the pattern may explode in a stimulus vacuum. The canary then weaves invisible strands and the starling catches invisible flies.

The reaction specific energy is "dammed up," in other words, and the fixed pattern it tenders is "inhibited," by a "higher," or more centrally-organized, structural or functional system.

Each system is at once a part of another system and a whole made up of sub-systems. The function of any one sub-system is alternately released or inhibited by the more inclusive system of which it is a part, but once released it acts with relative autonomy, according to the instructions fed into it by its evolutionary history. The automatism of an instinctive behavior pattern, says Lorenz, "is virtually a closed system. It is subject to the systemic control of the central nervous system only with respect to the timing and degree of disinhibition." Although each functional or structural component is relatively autonomous, or closed, the components together form "a complex hierarchical system of reciprocal inclusion and exclusion of sequences of more restricted behavioral motivation." Imagine a tree growing upside down, the thickest part of the trunk on top and the branches spreading downward. At each junction of branch with trunk or branch with branch, there is a "center" that inhibits or releases the activity of the center below it and coordinates the activities among its various branches. Without this system of inclusions and inhibitions, the gazelle, say, might stop dead in its headlong flight from a lion to munch tender shoots from the top of a bush or to put on a courtship display before an enticing female.

Lorenz' centers, hierarchies, and levels of integration at first had roughly the status of Freud's topographical metaphors for the structure of the human psyche. Like Freud, Lorenz had hoped from the beginning that the physiological basis for his functional topography would ultimately be discovered. Like Freud, he had assumed from the beginning that "all 'pure' psychological processes are simultaneously neuro-physiological processes." Freud died still hoping, but neurophysiologists seem to have given Lorenz what he was looking for. I quote from Paul Weiss's *ex tempore* summing up of conclusions reached during the celebrated Hixon Conference of 1948, among whose participants were such distinguished scientists as H. Klover, Wolfgang Kohler, K. S. Lashley, W. S. McCullock, and Linus Pauling:

> ...A few things have come out... for instance, *the relative autonomy of structured patterns of activity, and the hierarchical principle of their organization*.... The nervous system is not one big monotonic pool whose elements can be freely recombined in any number of groupings, thereby giving an infinite variety of nervous responses. This used to be the old idea of the associationists, and it is utterly incompatible with what we have learned about the development of the nervous system and its function in animals.
>
> The working of the nervous system is a hierarchical affair in which *functions at the higher levels do not deal directly with the ultimate structural units*, such as neurons or motor units, but operate by activating lower patterns that have their own relatively autonomous structural unity. The same is true for the sensory input which... operates by affecting, distorting, and somehow modifying the pre-existing, performed patterns of central co-ordination.... The final output is then the outcome of this hierarchical passing down of distortions and modifications of intrinsically preformed patterns of excitations which are in no way replicas of the input. *The structure of the input does not produce the structure* of *output, but merely modifies intrinsic nervous activities that have* a *structural organization of their own*....
>
> ...Any group of bulbar or spinal nerves taken from vertebrates, if deprived of their structural bonds of restraining influences and allowed to undergo a certain degree of degradation, will display permanent automatic, rhythmic, synchronized activity of remarkable regularity. Rhythmic activity, therefore, *seems* a *basic property of pools of nervous elements*.... The rhythm is not something generated through an input rhythm, but is itself a primary rhythm which may be released and even speeded up or retarded by the input, but is not derived from the input. So we have experimen-

tal evidence that *rhythmic automatism, autonomy of patterns, and hierarchical organizations are* primary attributes of even the simplest nervous systems, and I think that this unifies our view of the nervous system.

According to Weiss, and Lorenz, this unified view of the nervous system gives the *coup de grâce* to the behaviorist and reflexologist notion that animals, including human animals, do whatever they do just as they do it only because of stimulus input. They do as they do because of patterns of central co-ordination preformed by phylogeny and subject only to modification and timing by sensory input. The animal is not passive in the face of experience; it is not infinitely malleable; it is not silly putty or a bank of buttons and levers and slots. Against the contingencies of its individual experience it asserts the practical lessons built into its species by evolution.

II

We need to look at a few more items in the animal's behavioral repertoire before we can say which, if any, of them are also in the human's bag of tricks. The center governing a fixed pattern, then, is primed by endogenous-automatic nervous impulses. Its load may also be affected by hormones, by the integrating center above it, and by local stimuli from its chemical environment within the animal. The various centers are primed in sequence according to the workings of an internal clock, which has been synchronized by evolution to the normal seasonal and diurnal changes in the animal's ecological niche. Birds look for nesting materials *when* the weather is right; male mammals look for females *when* females are in estrus; frogs look for insects *when* insects have hatched; but not *because* the weather is right or females are in heat or flies are buzzing. Birds, males, and frogs look for nesting materials, females, and flies because of a kind of "arousal pressure"; the priming of particular centers with reaction-specific energy has given them something like an "appetite" for a performance of the fixed patterns that those centers control.

The arousal pressure nudges the animal off in search of the very particular set of external circumstances that will release the pattern under pressure. This search for a releaser, this *appetitive behavior*, as it is called, has the look of being purposive, because it exhibits "adaptive variability whilst the goal remains the same." The animal seems to know what it is looking for. Evolution, or conditioning, or individual experience, or the habits of the tribe, has taught the animal where to look for what it needs—such as a nest site or appropriate prey—but the animal can circumvent obstacles on its way and choose among alternative routes; it can explore and try things out. It seems almost human.

The whole sequence of actions, from the point of arousal to the discharge of the fixed motor patterns—from the migration north to the completion of the nest, from the meowing at the kitchen door to the slaughter of the field mouse—is usually made up of various behavioral elements intercalated with one another, some innate, some relatively *ad hoc*. In the appetitive behavior of higher animals, for example, there may be intercalation, in variable sequences and combinations, of reflexes, of conditioned responses, of subordinate fixed patterns, of *taxes* (or orienting responses, some of which are like what used to be called "tropisms"), and of intelligent or "insight-controlled" behavior, actions that solve problems without the governance of fixed patterns, or an antecedent term of learning. Appetitive behavior, says Lorenz, "extends from the simplest motor restlessness to the complex, purposive behavior patterns of human beings, involving an enormous variety of functions." From the abrupt turning of a frog toward a fly so that it may discharge the fixed pattern of shooting out its tongue, to Konrad Lorenz struggling to solve the mind-body problem, we have only differences of degree. "From the standpoint of objective ethology, no distinction can be made between the simplest orienting response and the higher form of 'insight' behavior."

All forms of appetitive behavior are alike, then, in that their goal is the discharge of reaction-specific energy. Prior to discharge, the accumulating energy is felt as a kind of tension or unease; discharge of the energy through the final motor pattern, or *consummatory act*, feels good. Because the consummatory act feels good, it serves as a reinforcement of the behavior that led up to it. The animal is therefore "driven and attracted" to perform the fixed patterns necessary for the survival of its species. And every fixed pattern, as Lorenz says, "is in itself an autonomous purpose as well as an autonomous reinforcement of precedent behavior." If you are an animal, at least, it feels good to do what is good for you, and what is good for you is also good for your species.

Under normal conditions, the consummatory motor pattern is performed not *in vacuo*, but amidst the particular kind of environmental situations in response to which it evolved. In most cases the animal does not recognize the situation as being of a certain kind, one in which, for example, its particular food is available or in which it is in danger from a predator; such recognition would depend on an ability to abstract and generalize that few animals have. Instead, most animals have an innate capacity to recognize certain representative elements, or *key stimuli*, as English-writing ethologists call them, that are regular concomitants of the situation. An ethologist with a literary bent might call them "synecdotal stimuli." They are called key stimuli because they fit an innate receptor correlate as a key fits a lock. When stimulus key fits receptor lock an *innate releasing mechanism* is activated. The innate releasing mechanism removes the block that had been inhibiting the fixed motor pattern in question. Upon disinhibition the animal pecks, gapes, preens, bristles, broods, flees, fights, copulates, displays its colors, tends its young, or changes color, depending on which fixed pattern in which animal has been released.

One category of triggering stimuli has especially interested would-be ethologists of human behavior, mostly cranks. Such stimuli are the morphological or behavioral features that coordinate the fixed patterns among members of a given species. A scent, a sound, an electrical charge; the display of a marking, a silhouette, a configuration, or a fixed pattern, will under appropriate circumstances and at appropriate stages in the animal's maturation, release a reciprocal fixed pattern in a conspecific. A herring gull chick pecks at the red dot on its parent's bill; the parent regurgitates food; the chick eats. Both the red dot and the chick's pecking are what Lorenz calls *Auslöser*, usually translated as "social releasers." The red dot releases the pecking; the pecking releases the regurgitation (which, so to speak, releases the food). But most of the gorgeous colors and improbable shapes of animals; their various ritualized motor displays of presenting, appeasement, enticement, and challenge; the perfume of their ruts and the accents of their cries—all these are likely to be social releasers. They are most likely to be social releasers if they seem unadaptive, if they seem to reduce the animal's ability to function and survive, if, for example, they make him conspicuous to predators or clumsy in form or movement.

Social releasers and their receptor correlates differentiate through a kind of dialectic and along parallel lines; they evolve in response to a selection pressure working out of relations among members of a specific population, rather than in response to pressures working out of the relations between a population and its environment. The pressures making for differentiation, that is, are intraspecific rather than extraspecific. The gratuitous quality of many social releasers, their quality of *gestural exaggeration*, results from the relative strength of intraspecific, as compared to extraspecific, selecting factors, and makes them that much more useful as signals. They differentiate in the direction of maximal simplicity of structure with maximal improbability of form. Lorenz cites the yawn as an example of a social releaser among humans. A number of his popularizers cite the breasts of human females, which are the only kind that remain extended all year round and which would be easier for babies to nurse on if they were smaller; and popularizers cite the buttocks of human females, which in their gratuitous bloom have no equivalent in the animal world—the popularizers cite breasts and buttocks as social releasers of, at the least, appetitive behavior in human males. The consummatory act is released by something else.

III

The paradigm of a typical behavioral sequence, then, is as follows: (1) at a certain stage in the animal's maturation, a stage synchronized by evolution with a certain point in the day or year, (2) an accumulation of reaction-specific energy leads to a state of arousal or motivation, which (3) generates appetitive behavior consisting of various intercalated motor components, some innate, some learned, until (4) the animal comes upon the key stimulus (which may be a social releaser) that 5) activates the particular innate releasing mechanism whose function it is to disinhibit 6) the consummatory act, a fixed pattern concluding the sequence and using up the reaction-specific energy.

Many contingencies may complicate the paradigm or interfere with the sequence of its unfolding. If the reaction-specific energy for a certain fixed motor pattern is low, either because not much has yet accumulated or because repeated performance of the pattern has exhausted it; or if the key stimuli releasing the fixed pattern are either partial or of weak intensity, the pattern may only begin to go off. The animal only gets as far as an *intention movement*. If the intention movement occurs frequently enough, it may take on signal functions. The jackdaw's crouch preparatory to flight may warn its fellows that a predator is in the distance. Through selective pressures the intention movement may jell, differentiate further, undergo gestural exaggeration, and become the kind of social releaser called a *symbolic motor pattern*, now entirely distinct from its initial function. If conversely, the reaction-specific energy for a certain fixed pattern becomes unusually high, the pattern may go off *in vacuo* or in the presence of inappropriate stimuli; the energy may "overflow' (In the hydraulic metaphor) or "spark over" (in the electric metaphor) and release a different fixed pattern. Such *displacement activities*, such sparking over, may also occur when a single situation activates the innate releasing mechanism for two fixed patterns. A bird equally motivated to fight and to run may instead peck at the ground, or even fall asleep. Displacement activities may also jell, differentiate, encourage the selection of receptor correlates, and become ritualized into symbolic motor patterns. In situations of extreme conflict or deprivation or novelty, a fixed pattern may be activated that is not normally in the species' repertoire but that was in the repertoire of the genus from which the species differentiated. Extreme conflict, or deprivation or novelty, that is, may produce *regression*, a return to the phylogenetic past. A habit accidentally acquired may inhibit the fixed pattern adaptive to the situation; one fixed pattern accidentally triggered may inhibit or deform the adaptive one; the slightest inherited or acquired physical defect may twist fixed patterns into amazing behavioral oddities. Innate "gaps" left in motor patterns, normally filled by experience, may be filled with the wrong objects. An animal may *imprint* its caretaker; it may become permanently fixated on him, so to speak, as the proper object of an innate pattern, rather than on another member of its own species; it may then act toward the caretaker as if he were its mother or its mate. "Greater snow geese (*Anser hyperboreus atlanticus*), and probably many others possess perfectly good phylogenetic information about how a fellow member of the species behaves when inviting copulation, but they have to learn what a fellow member of the species looks like." Case histories of fetishism, of animals fixated by imprinting on substitute objects, abound in the literature of ethology.

The literature of ethology, in fact, demonstrates vividly enough just how easy it is to make animals do things that among humans would be called neurotic or crazy. The fixed patterns of animals are so dependent for their regular functioning upon a normal upbringing and upon a characteristic set of experiences; they are so intricately meshed with the different action patterns of mates, rivals, parents and offspring; with prey and predator, host and parasite; with the lay of the land and the course of the season; that only minor modifications of these by natural accident or experimental design may shock the animal into an exemplary lunacy. Animals so shocked become compulsive, as though gripped by an obsession. They burst into inexplicable rages or fall into fatal melancholias. They seem to hallucinate the key stimuli they are deprived of; they court phantoms, joust with shadows, feed on air, and display before mirages. They cower, shaking before their natural prey. They brood stuffed replicas of their natural enemies and murder their offspring. They develop ovarian cysts, prostate trouble, and various kinds of cancer. They scratch, peck, claw, and bite themselves or each other bloody. They treat everything presented to them as though it were a threat; they become as though suspicious and fearful of everything. They develop an anxiety that seems to float free of any external cause or past experience. Above all they act like characters in Bergson's treatise on comedy. In their solemn self-absorption, their mulish lack of self-awareness, their fits and starts, they blunder along as mute and dead-pan as Buster Keaton, like wind-up toys with rusty springs, like puppets jerked by strings in the hands of mischievous children, like victims of demonic possession, like comic humors in ritual bondage to fixed ideas.

They only seem to act that way in the eyes of a human observer, no doubt. My language, no doubt, has been unscientifically anthropomorphic. What we call neurotic, an ethologist would call unadaptive. But by "adaptive" he means no more than "just good enough for the survival of the species." And even under the best of conditions, there are endless opportunities for behavior that at the very least has a low survival value, given the way evolution puts things together:

> Organisms are *never* built on the principle which must be postulated on the basis of preformationist concepts, that is to say, like buildings whose function a far-seeing architect

foresaw, whose smallest details were agreed upon before the first stone was laid, and whose actual erection then took place all in one sitting. Organisms are always constructed on the principle on which a house is built by a settler, who first erects a simple provisional shack in which to live, and who later on, as his affluence and his family increase, adds one piece after the other to the building. In such a house, many parts will, in the course of time, change their functions completely. What first was the living room, may become the stable or even the lumber room; compromises and temporary shifts will become necessary. The efficiency of the building as a whole will necessarily remain inferior to that which could be achieved by the construction of a planning architect, but the latter is unobtainable just *because the house has* to be lived in all the time and can never be torn down altogether and wholly reconstructed.

We have to revise, therefore, our first provisional topography of the systems that govern and execute an animal's behavior. Instead of one neat functional hierarchy, each sub-system of which is integrated by a center subordinate to centers above it and in control of the centers beneath it, we must think of many hierarchies, at all angles to each other and some of them not so hierarchical. The hierarchies are all of different sizes, shapes, powers, and ages—in both the history of the species and the history of the individual. Any two of them may intersect here, overlap there, interlock there, and share a part somewhere else. The waxing of one may famish another and fatten still a third. Any new one may make an old one vestigial, make another hyperactive, and fight still another to a standstill. Any hierarchy may release, inhibit, encroach upon, and cooperate with, others, or parts of others, to different degrees, at different times, under different conditions, and not always to the animal's benefit. We have to imagine, then, not a single tree growing upside down, with the thickest part of the trunk on top and the branches spreading downward, but a whole forest of trees and shrubs of different kinds, ages, rates of growth, fruit, foliage, pliancy, and rigidity, all crowded together in all the possible permutations of symbiosis, parasitism, and competition, stealing light and nourishment from each other or sharing it, the branches inextricably tangled or connected by creepers hung with tropical moss.

This monstrous contrivance, assembled in a fit of distraction by a stinting and impatient Frankenstein (as passages in Lorenz make us see it), works well enough to preserve if not the animal, at least the population of which it is a member, so long as the conditions that brought the machinery into existence prevail. But any contingency not prepared for by phylogeny, any deprivation of nourishment or experience, any shock or set of conflicting key stimuli may drive the whole contraption careening off course, spilling gears and flywheels, or pull it apart. As W. H. Thorpe, an English ethologist, notes, "In some species of starfish the lack of coordination between the arms occasionally results in the animal actually being pulled in two merely by the antagonistic activity of its own tube feet." Analogous things happen to all animals. When such things happen, they are unadaptive, sure enough, but they occur because of what successive adaptations have put together. The provisions for something like madness are species-specific to all species of animals, including the human animal.

IV

At the moment, says Lorenz, the scientific investigation of human behavioral specifics has only stumbled a step or two beyond Darwin. So far, the drafting of a detailed and complete human *ethogram*, or behavioral map in evolutionary perspective, is no more than a program, although there is no more urgent a need. It takes years of patient observation before an ethologist is ready to rough in the behavioral contours of one simpleminded bird or fish; a scientifically respectable ethogram of *homo sapiens* will require the life work of many cartographers of behavior—among whom Lorenz expressly does not include the social scientists, who in his eyes are mostly not scientists at all. Even when the work of psychologists, sociologists, and anthropologists meets the standards that apply in the natural sciences it does not furnish the ethologist with what he needs. And because ethology operates on a "more general" level of explanation, it would similarly be "an illegitimate extension" for ethologists to explain ethologically "any complex special principles governing human intellectual or social life"; at the same time it would be an avoidance of responsibility were ethologists, or students of "comparative behavioral physiology," as Lorenz often describes his field, not to explain what they can about the more general processes underlying those specifics of human intellectual and social life:

> If we, as natural scientists, wish to provide a natural explanation for the special, immeasurably complex principles governing human behavior and the human mind (i.e. by tracing them back to the adjacent, more general level of natural principles), then we are faced with the question: "What are these more basic principles?" There can be no other answer: "The principles concerned are *those which govern the behavior of living organisms in general.*"

When the social sciences begin to elucidate human social and intellectual life on the basis of principles that in theory at least can be traced back to those governing the behavior of living organisms in general, which latter principles can themselves be traced back to those governing the movements of inorganic matter, there will be at last a unification of the sciences, and the social sciences at last will become natural.

Lorenz' argument to this point is professionally self-serving but plausible, especially if one is not a mystic. Certainly the absence of an inclusive theory, against which both the unlikely and the significant might leap into focus, explains as well as anything why the data amassed by the social sciences are in the main either soft or trivial. Lorenz feels that much of Marx and Freud will survive the unification, or naturalization, so to speak, of the social sciences. He speaks with enthusiasm of "the progressive unification of ethology and psychoanalysis," and of Marx he says: "Everything he said in *Capital* is right, but he always made the error of forgetting the instincts." In my opinion a unified theory of human behavior built up on what is consistent in psychoanalysis, Marxism, and ethology would be something worth having, but I doubt that it would look like anything either psychoanalysts, Marxists, or Lorenz have in mind.

In any case, Lorenz is very anxious to counter the charge that measuring the degree of human singularity against the principles that govern the behavior of living organisms in general is a way of shortchanging that singularity. Far from trying to make the human element fade into the background, ethologists, says Lorenz, provide the point of view from which human singularity is thrown most dramatically into relief. We can only see what constitutes the naked and native dignity of man, and where it comes from, against the background of those evolutionary processes in which all animals live and move and have their being. All human traits, whether they are universal, such as the facial expressions that accompany anger or terror and such as incest taboos, or whether they are culturally diversified, such as ideas of history or definitions of incest, are either the direct products of evolution or are based on dispositions and capacities that are themselves the direct products of evolution. "Behavior is adapted to environmental givens and it can only be thus adapted by two well-defined processes, phylogenetic adaptation and adaptive modification"—by habits picked up during the evolutionary history of the species and by social and individual modification of these habits.

As it turns out, the human elements in human behavior that comparative behavioral physiology throws into relief are both disappointing and reassuring in their familiarity. They are as follows: (I) The degree to which humans are capable of reason, the most complex kind of appetitive behavior, and are capable of "insight," the sudden apprehension of relations and analogies, (2) "The unique, phylogenetically unprecedented phenomena of rational responsibility," through which men may repress a natural inclination in behalf of an ethical idea or social imperative. (3) Culture, which is based on an "accumulation of tradition [that] is practically equivalent to the inheritance of acquired characteristics," and which is as essential to the mind as food is to the body. Because "man's whole system of innate activities and reactions is phylogenetically so constructed, so 'calculated' by evolution, as to *need* to be complemented by cultural tradition," anyone so unlucky as to be reared without it would be a "poor cripple," functionally indistinguishable from an idiot whose cerebral cortex had been destroyed in some intra-uterine disaster. (4) Speech, which seems to have evolved for the express purpose of handling and passing on culture: "It was indubitably the selection pressure of accumulating tradition which caused the rapid growth of the human telencephalon," which contains the speech center. (5) Self-awareness, the human's capacity for objectifying himself, "The best definition of man is that he is the one creature capable of reflection, of seeing himself in the frame of reference of the surrounding universe." To the extent that a man is self-aware he moves out of the realm of irony, in which he is possessed and driven by demonic obsessions, to the realm of comedy, in which his pretentions are mocked, although his impulses are confirmed, by natural energies. (6) Most inclusive among the human elemental capacities and dispositions, one that amounts to "the constitutive character of man," is an innate, unique, and lifelong curiosity, a drive to investigate and explore, which impels any healthy human into a "continuous, inquisitive communication with extra-subjective reality," into an "active, dialectic construction and dismemberment of the environment," so that information may be picked up and stored as engrains in the central nervous system for future use, and so that bit by bit a significant, thoroughly objectivized world solidifies to enclose the very animal who alone can see it in the round.

All this amounts to the conclusion that human action when exemplary in its humanity, rather than human-all-too-human in its subservience to the dog beneath the skin, is a full, delicate, finely attuned, continuously adjusting responsiveness to all the particulars of whatever the situation, as successively it unfolds. But this singular responsiveness is no miracle, the product of a cosmic purpose or occult will; it is in theory perfectly explicable by a convergence of certain of the processes that shape the differentia of all species. Neoteny, for example, the preservation throughout maturity of traits that in ancestral species were only characteristic of infants and foetuses, has been observed in numerous species, but only in conjunction with the other adaptive strategies that shaped humanity did it make possible the lifelong playfulness and curiosity of men and women. Similarly, our descent from a tree-living primate that climbed by means of grasping extremities, rather than by hooking claws, explains, given everything else, our capacity for stereoscopic depth-perception, for a central representation of spatial relations that developed finally into a sort of "imaginative space," in which hypothetical situations might be visualized. "And this is the beginning of all thinking processes," as well as the prerequisite for the making of tools. Again, the evolution of our versatile, non-specialized physical traits included the development of an equal behavioral versatility. The fact that we adapted to no one environment means that we can adapt to many. We are, says Lorenz, "Specialists in nonspecialization." No other animal can climb twenty feet up a rope *and* swim fifty feet under water at a depth of two fathoms *and* walk twenty miles in a day; our modes of perception and conception are correlative in their range and plasticity. Finally, domestication is primarily a condition in which selection by extra-specific pressures no longer takes place; "human self-domestication produced effects homologous to those that domestication produced in barnyard fowl and dogs." Domestication is accompanied by increased physical and behavioral variation among individuals within a species; by the atrophy of more recent drives, such as those having to do with brood care and social life; by the hypertrophy of more primitive drives, such as those having to do with feeding and mating; by a reduction in the selectivity of innate releasing mechanisms by a general dismantling of fixed patterns and inhibitions, so that substitute stimuli may serve as releasers; by a general dismantling of fixed patterns and inhibitions so that the patterns and bits of patterns may be employed for novel situations and in novel combinations, and so that intelligence and improvisation may fill the gaps. "The constitutive *freedom* of human behavior is the direct result of domestication-induced reduction of rigid instinctive behavior," but it is a freedom as phylogenetically adapted as the opposability of our thumbs.

Less familiar, less reassuring, and more difficult to take, is Lorenz' insistence that much of human behavior, especially human social behavior, is directed by a complex of releasers, innate releasing mechanisms, motor display patterns, endogenous-automatic accumulations of reaction-specific energy, and dispositions to learn only certain kinds of things under only special circumstances at only specific stages in the course of individual development. Imprinting-like phenomena, or fixations, sometimes seem to occur at various more or less well-defined points from infancy through adolescence, and movements like those of swallowing and ejaculation may be genuine fixed patterns; but for the most part the accumulation of reaction-specific energy in a human does not lead to the performance of a fixed motor pattern. More characteristically it leads to an intention movement that has evolved into a motor display pattern—one of those postures, gestures, or facial expressions that can tell us at a glance whether a fellow human from anywhere in the world is angry or happy, hostile, or flirtatious. According to Iranaus Eibel-Eibesfelt, one of Lorenz' students, "smiling, laughing, and crying, also the expressions of anger, pouting, fear, and sadness, looked the same in blind-born children, although they could not have imitated anyone." When display patterns are genuine social releasers they fit receptor correlates that evolved along with them and that enable us to understand the "meaning," in one sense of the word, of the display. We do not have to learn, for example, that a snarl is a snarl. Reception of the display (the snarl), activates the appropriate innate releasing mechanism, which in a human, however, releases not a fixed pattern (another snarl), but an *emotion* (fear or anger). The emotion had been the "subjective experiential correlate" of a fixed pattern that has since dropped out, thus leaving the emotion as the sole automatic component of any response. Lorenz argues that the qualitatively separable human emotions are each based on "an action-specific arousal modality and behavioral motivation. With very many of these specific behavioral motivations, assumption of an endogenous-automatic basis is supported by the fact that the stimulus threshold shrinks during periods without response and rises following abreaction of the drive concerned." After a good venting of fear or anger, for example, we feel relieved, all passion spent.

In some cases, then, endogenous-automatic stimulation generates a motive and primes an emotion. Not all physiological processes prime motives, but all emotions are signs of an instinctive process. Our gut reactions, whether aesthetic or moral, to fellow humans comprise an especially instructive category. "The close interaction and the far-reaching analogies between instinctive and culturally determined norms of behavior notwithstanding, I am quite convinced that, at the root of every emotional value judgment, an innate releasing mechanism lies concealed." Lorenz goes on to argue that the aesthetic and ethical emotions are logically distinguishable but functionally inseparable. Aesthetically speaking,

> our emotional value judgment categorizes as repulsive characters which have arisen through typical domestication effects, whilst characters which are threatened by the same

effects of domestication are classed as desirable. There is scarcely one typical domestication effect in the morphological realm, which does not evoke our pronounced aesthetic revulsion. Almost more important than this statement is the fact that the converse also applies; virtually all characters which we perceive as specifically ugly are genuine domestication effects.

Muscular flabbiness, a hanging stomach, weak connective tissue and their side-effects such as flabby skin, bow-leggedness and so on, relatively small looking eyes, expressionless facial features lacking in "striking" qualities, pug head and many other "ugly characters" are typical results of domestication. If a large series of wild forms and their domestic derivatives is assembled, one is again and again amazed by the "beauty" and "nobility" of the wild animals in comparison to the domestic forms.

...The same correlation exists between our ethical evaluation feelings and domestication-induced alterations of behavior as between aesthetic feelings and morphological domestication characters. In this case, too, the ethically highly valued behavior patterns are just exactly those which are adversely affected by domestication-induced deficiency, whilst those judged to be "bad" and inferior are those which tend toward hypertrophy through domestication.

Among the endogenous-automatic behavior patterns of human beings, each was originally equally valuable and necessary for the preservation of the species—food-uptake and mating just as much as parental care responses or more highly differentiated social impulses. The fact that we perceive one to be ethically valueless, indeed sinful, and the other as a highly estimable moral attribute, is no doubt closely related to the fact that the former are over-developed in civilized human beings just as in domestic animals, whilst the latter tend to disappear.

I quote this passage at length because it is probably wrong in detail and just possibly sinister in implication. The domesticated thoroughbred horse, for example, is more "noble" in appearance than the wild hammer-head cayuse. The German Shepherd dog is at least as noble as the jackal, from which, says Lorenz, it was bred. And it is unlikely that domestication can worsen the looks, or the morals, of the hippopotamus. Further, the flabby muscles, hanging stomachs, and so forth, of humans are not effects of domestication in the same sense that they are in, say, the Muscovy duck: in humans they are not inherited, they are not universal, and they can be eliminated during the lifetime of an individual by exercise and diet. At the same time, I find it plausible that, cosmetic fashions aside, the people of all cultures respond with innate approval to the athletic type of body that is best adapted to grapple with a rigorously selective environment. And I find it plausible that if, as Chomsky says, the child is born "with a perfect knowledge of universal grammar, that is, with a fixed schematism that he uses...in acquiring language," he is also born with a fixed inclination to approve some kinds of human actions and bodily shapes and to disapprove others.

If Lorenz is right, our innate approvals and disapprovals will often conflict with precepts we arrive at through reason and with injunctions that support the institutions of our society. We may find ourselves liking people whose morals we consciously disapprove of and disliking people whose morals are irreproachable. We find it hard not to sympathize with violent men, if they are also men of "honor," by which I mean the constellation of values that tends to prevail among primitive hunters, rather than among agriculturists. Those groups and individuals who are driven above all by a desire to amass or preserve honor, usually by counting coups or exacting revenge, tend to get our imaginative sympathy and our moral disapproval. To most people the ferocity of ancient Greeks, questing knights, Renaissance princes, Plains Indians, Italian *mafiosi*, Japanese samurai, teenage gangs, western heroes, and private eyes is both attractive and lamentable. We are likely to think that there is something wrong with a young man who would rather have been St. Francis than Achilles, but it is not so easy to say why. The examples are mine, and I am not sure that Lorenz would endorse them, but the point is his: our innate judgments in practice often over-ride our rational commitments and social allegiances.

None of that is news. More unexpected is Lorenz' argument that as much trouble is caused by the loss of certain innate action-and-response norms as by the preservation of those that have become dysfunctional under the conditions of advanced industrial society. A whole set of "the more finely differentiated social instincts and inhibitions" has been dismantled by domestication, or has been gradually selected out by the increasing human reliance for behavioral directives on abstract principles, social imperatives, cultural ideals, and novel ecologies. At one time, presumably social instincts and inhibitions made relations between men and men, men and women, parents and children, brothers and sisters, the individual and his group a kind of dance in which everyone knew the steps and the musicians always played in tune. Life was no doubt short and harsh; not, however, because of the way individuals within a group treated each other. But for a long time now, except among a few forest peoples, freedom from social instincts and inhibitions has had a positive selective value. The behavioral traits that on ancient grounds we still judge to be ugly or wrong have become the very ones that enable those who have them to sit pretty. Avarice, treachery, cowardice, ingratitude, assertiveness, disloyalty, random promiscuity, ruthless ambition, "emotional deficiency and value blindness," neglect of young children and aged parents, were once as unadaptive as they were repulsive—repulsive because they were unadaptive. Now they are just repulsive. At one time, again presumably, they were held in check or were selectively and adaptively directed by superordinate instinctive mechanisms. But in some cases "headlong, culturally determined changes in human sociology and ecology" have at once routed the inhibitions and inflamed what they were inhibiting.

Lorenz' remarks about the "pervading degeneration" of our social instincts under the effects of domestication probably sound cranky, the sort of thing one might expect from a man who has spent fifty years studying animals and noting how much more healthy and attractive they are in the wild. But it has been easy for many people to arrive at similar conclusions on different grounds. It is not only students of animal behavior who have observed "how abjectly stupid and undesirable the mass behavior of humanity actually is." Lorenz is not the first to have commented on "the pathological disintegration of our social structure" or the "catastrophic social confusion of mankind." All kinds of people agree that, "at the moment, humanity represents a functional entity which has gone fundamentally awry." Lorenz is not the only student of behavior who has been led to conclude that "discomfort within our culture" is inevitable, that neurosis, given the social circumstances within which our natural inclinations must now express themselves, is also inevitable, that, in sum, "we are all—without exception—psychopaths." Neither is he the only observer to have pointed out that the conditions of advanced industrial society bring out the worst in people. And I find it hard to see how one can disagree with his claim that "the danger to modern man arises not so much from his power of mastering natural phenomena as from his powerlessness to control sensibly what is happening in his own society."

For all that, Lorenz and his conclusions have been attacked with some heat, mostly on political grounds. The ethologists' claim that individual behavior and social institutions are still shaped by instinctual residues, and especially Lorenz' claim that aggression is caused by the endogenous-automatic accumulation of reaction specific energy, have led to charges that his attacks on modern social conditions are merely the grumbling of a conservative, if not the bile of a reactionary or the ravings of a fascist. The charges would hold better if Lorenz were a conservative or if the implications of ethology were not in fact revolutionary. So far as I can tell the charges are supported mostly by rumor, by a confusion of Lorenz with Robert Ardrey and Desmond Morris, both of whom he disowns in the introduction to Volume I of *Studies in Animal and Human Behavior*, by a misreading of the first eleven chapters of *On Aggression*, and, more reasonably, by reference to the traditional connection between conservatism and some sacred or secular notion of original sin.[3]

The conservative tends to assume that we are naturally vicious and that only good institutions can keep us in line; the Left usually assumes that we are naturally good or naturally nothing and that only bad institutions make us vicious. Lorenz for his part insists again and again that "the imagination of man's heart is not really evil from his youth up, as we read in Genesis." In various works and in different words he keeps saying, "we fundamentally disagree with the biblical thesis defended by

---

[3] See Ashley Montagu, ed., Man and Aggression *(Oxford University Press, 1968).*

some child psychologists and psychoanalysts, that man is utterly 'wicked from childhood on.'" Lorenz' opinion, rather, is that "man can behave very decently indeed in tight spots, provided they are of a kind that occurred often enough in the paleolithic period to produce phylogenetically adapted social norms to deal with the situation," or provided that stress, overwork, hunger, anxiety, hopelessness, and overcrowding have not subverted his reason or his instinctive aestheticoethical value judgments.

I have not been able to find anywhere a full statement by Lorenz of his politics, but it is easy enough to judge where he stands from his scattered remarks on the issues of the day—he stands in that, shifting and uncircumscribed zone in which left-liberalism, social democracy, and democratic socialism jostle one another. He is, in short, a Western European: He supports, for example, much of women's liberation: he speaks of young wives as "a whole class of people who are treated as slaves and who are exploited shamelessly." He attacks as he tries to account for "demagogically directed mass cruelty, such as witchcraft trials or anti-semitic persecution." He has no use for nationalism, imperialism, or racism: "National ideas were still serviceable for our grandparents. During the time of Rudyard Kipling, the norms of social behavior he wrote about were valid for his epoch and his country. Transposed into our time, Kipling results in Hitler—just as imperialist and just as racist." In the early 1960s he observed that "the way in which huge numbers of young Americans have recently identified themselves with the rights of the American Negro is a glorious exception" to the political apathy of the young; and now in the 1970s he supports the "student protestors"; he believes that "youth sees very clearly the great faults committed by the 'Establishment'"; he believes that the accusations of the young are "frequent, necessary, and absolutely just"; he joins with them in trying to expose "the real obsolescence of many social norms and rites still valued by some of the older generation." He has written at considerable length and with some vehemence against the evils that accompany military fanfare, militant enthusiasm, and charismatic leaders. He is pacifistic and perhaps a pacifist (he managed to stay out of World War II for the first few years and then served as a field surgeon). His arguments with behaviorists are more than academic: their ideas, he says, are helping to bring about "the best of all possible worlds for the Russian apparatchiks or the American monopolists"; for "as far as mass manipulators are concerned, the Pavlovian dog is the ideal citizen." And his remarks on the consequences of domestication do not constitute social Darwinism, but the opposite.

All this does not amount to a politics, of course, but it disqualifies Lorenz for fascism. Although his feelings on the practical issues of the day are those characteristic of left-liberals, his deepest impulses, I suspect, are anarchic. To an interviewer from *L'Express* he said, "I'm against everything, against all the ideologies, all the regimes in the world. Except perhaps the Dubček regime, which no longer exists. It's the only regime that would have been able to get my vote." An anarchist maybe, or simply a political *naïf*, but a humane, humanistic, kindly, and even tender-hearted one, as every page of his writings on humans and animals shows. There is a grave and rich music to Lorenz' pessimism; it is orchestrated by an old-fashioned love of humanity and counterpointed by the "Avowal of Optimism" that concludes *On Aggression*, an avowal based on the virtues built into us by our evolutionary past. And it was precisely because he believes in those virtues, and because he is so "naïve" as to be appalled by the universal slaughter and disorder that he wrote *On Aggression* (although his evidence, as he knew, was far from conclusive) rather than because he believed that since our nature is fixed and fallen, social revolution is useless. In fact, his avowal of optimism rests on the belief that our evolutionary past will demand a revolutionary future.

More important than Lorenz' personal feelings about things are the political implications of ethology. These are, simply, that we have ineradicable needs and inclinations. Societies vary in the extent to which they permit the irreducibly human in us to find satisfaction. Societies that satisfy the irreducibly human in us very little turn us into psychopaths. Such ideas strike me as comprising a basis for slogans as good as any we have around.

I also think we are ready for the ethologist's shift of emphasis from the socio-historical dimension in people to the individual and human dimensions. I, for one, am tired of being encouraged to think of myself as entirely the product of historical accidents and social contingencies. The ethologist redirects our attention to "the influence exerted by the structure of the individual within an organic system upon the structure of the super-individual society." He insists that "there are very many qualities of an individual which can indeed only be 'understood' through the structure of the total entity, but which the individual possesses as innate, inherited features and not as traditionally transmitted acquisitions." The ethologist also insists that what the individual asserts against the crush of his society is precisely what he shares with the individuals in all societies. He insists further that what humans share unites them with nature: "We consider the moral law within us not as something given, *a priori*, but as something which has arisen by natural evolution, just like the laws of the heavens." Ethology provides the philosophic basis for an ethic that shares Spinoza's main assumption and some of his sublimity:

We all agree that the greatest and most precious freedom of man is identical with the moral laws within him. Increasing knowledge of the natural causes of his own behavior can certainly increase a man's faculties and enable him to put his free will into action, but it can never diminish his will. If, in the impossible case of a Utopian, complete, and ultimate success of causal analysis, man ever should achieve complete insight into the causality of earthly phenomena, including the workings of his own organism, he would not cease to have a will but it would be in perfect harmony with the incontrovertible lawfulness of the universe, the *Weltvernunft* of the Logos.

Bibliographic Note

Besides the volumes under review I have quoted or paraphrased from the following works of Lorenz: *Evolution and Modification of Behavior* (Chicago University Press, 1965); *King Solomon's Ring*, trans. Marjorie Kerr Wilson (New York: Apollo Editions, 1961, first English edition: 1952); *Man Meets Dog*, trans. Marjorie Kerr Wilson (Baltimore: Penguin Books, 1964, first English edition: 1954); *On Aggression*, trans. Marjorie Kerr Wilson (New York: Harcourt, Brace & World, 1966); "Rats, Apes, Naked Apes, Kipling, Instincts, Guilt, the Generations and Instant Copulation—A Talk with Konrad Lorenz," *New York Times Sunday Magazine Section*, July 5, 1970, pp. 4-5, 27, 29-30 (translation of an interview with *L'Express*).

The following compendious texts give some notion of the volume and variety of work being done more or less along lines laid down by Lorenz and along some divergent and intersecting lines: Eibl-Eibesfelt, Iranaus, *Ethology: The Biology of Behavior*

(New York: Holt Rinehart and Winston, 1970); Hinde, Robert A., *Animal Behavior: A Synthesis of Ethology and Comparative Psychology*, 2nd ed. (New York: McGraw-Hill, 1970); McGill, Thomas E., ed. *Readings in Animal Behavior* (New York: Holt, Rinehart and Winston, 1965); Marler, Peter and William J. Hamilton III, *Mechanisms of Animal Behavior* (New York: John Wiley & Sons, 1967); Thorpe, W. H., *Learning and Instinct in Animals*, 2nd ed. (London: Methuen, 1963). The following attempts a synthesis of ethology and psychoanalysis: Fletcher, Ronald, *Instinct in Man* (*In the Light of Recent Work in Comparative Psychology*). New York: Schocken paperback, 1966. First published in 1957.

The following strike me as the two best recent books on human evolution and on evolutionary theory, respectively: Campbell, Bernard G., *Human Evolution: An Introduction to Man's Adaptations* (Chicago: Aldine, 1966); Mayr, Ernst, *Animal Species and Evolution* (Cambridge: Harvard University Press, 1963). The following strike me as the best argued and best informed essays contra Lorenz in English: Alland, Alexander Jr., *The Human Imperative* (New York: Columbia University Press, 1972); Lehrman, D. S., "A Critique of Konrad Lorenz' theory of Instinctive Behavior," *Quarterly Review of Biology*, XXVIII (1953), 338-363.

DESPORTMENT

"Desportment" in the *Hudson Review*, XXII, No. 4, Winter, 1969-70.

"Athletes are excellence in the guise of men," says Paul Weiss. They define themselves by a dedication to the project of achieving perfection "in and through their bodies." They enter contests in order to discover what they are by what they do, and thereby to reveal "what man as such can be and do"—so far as man is a body moving in accordance with the "vectoral thrust" of his mind. And because, as he plays, the athlete assumes a representative role, he "makes all of us vicariously completed men." The excellence he embodies is the form of our humanity perfected in action.

With such assertions *Sport: A Philosophic Inquiry*[1] opens. And they are promising enough in their fusion of classical and existential assumptions for the reader to want to see what Weiss will do with them. We are presently told that the rest of the book, another two hundred pages or so, will make the promise good. But it does no such thing.

It moves instead through a series of distinctions among related forms, as might an argument by an ordinary language philosopher, except that Weiss's distinctions do not correspond

---

[1]Sport: A Philosophic Inquiry, *by Paul Weiss. Southern Illinois University Press.*

very well with those of common usage and do not make anything very distinct, least of all sport. When we have finished reading J. L. Austin's essay on excuses, say, we feel both invigorated and relaxed; our minds are sharp, clear, ready to perform with dispatch and precision. A conceptual blur has been brought into focus, dissected, and its components labeled for future reference. The words *excuse, justification, extenuation* become rich and grave with the generations of human experience that went into their making; they hop with energy amidst the forces that hold them together and keep them apart. But Weiss's distinctions numb the brain, chill the heart, and irritate the sensorium; reading them is like listening to a man play your favorite piece on the clarinet, a quarter-tone off on each important note, or like watching a painter with much schooling and no talent do a portrait of your mistress.

Athletes are attentive, says Weiss. *Attention* "involves a focusing on a future prospect and an elicitation of acts, usually bodily acts." Without the elicited acts, there is only *alertness*, but not attention. If there is attention and *desire* the "elicited" acts are "relevant to the realization of the prospect focused on." *Wish* differs from desire in that it does not involve acts "relevant to the realization…." etc. *Intention* assures that the acts "are relevant not only to the desired prospect but to oneself"; in intending, "one reads into a prospect something of himself." *Commitment* guarantees that one will not give up a long-range project even while he is busy with immediate intentions. Above all, "it is the *dedication* of the athlete that marks him off most conspicuously from those who have the same commitments, intentions, desires, objects of attention, and inclinations." The dedicated athlete "adds a self-determination by which he supports that which he aims at with inclinations in that direction."

And so we go, through strategy and tactics; to practical judgment, common sense, wisdom, skill, habit; to decisiveness, will, control, mastery; flexibility, suppleness, relaxation; skill, gracefulness, accuracy, correctness; chance, luck, good fortune ("Good fortune is a steady run of luck"); and many others. The pages on equipment are as brain-softening as the others, but at least have a certain charm:

> A boxing glove in the store is not yet equipment; if it is torn, without stuffing, it is no longer to be used in a match; if made for a man, it is not equipment for a normal child; if designed for the training camp, it is not usually suitable for the ring. Equipment not used is equipment capable of being used only if it is available, in working order, and suitable to the individual and the situation.

None of this is false, exactly; nor is it exactly true, either; it is simply not to the point. *Sport: A Philosophic Inquiry* is both internally consistent and systematically wrong, as are an endless number of books by philosophers on art, sociologists on movies, behaviorists on emotion, theologians on love, and Marxists on the poor, and for the same reasons: there is a relentless conceptual machine, a repertoire of all-purpose abstractions, intellect a-plenty; but also an atrophied intelligence, a flight from the observable, a casting-out of common-sense, an absence of first-hand experience. "I am not an athlete," are the first words of this book, and the sequel goes on to prove them.

A philosophical inquiry into sports has yet to be written, then, and we are entitled to feel annoyance with Weiss to the extent that we had hoped his book would be it. The real thing, I should think, would have to begin by pointing out that what we call sports form among themselves a disjunctive category, one in which there is not a set of shared features, no common denominator, among the items in the category, but only "similarities, relationships, and a whole series of them at that," to quote Wittgenstein on games; "we see a whole network of similarities overlapping and criss-crossing: sometimes overall similarities, sometimes similarities of detail"—family resemblances, in short, but no one feature common to them all. Sports A and B may have a dozen things in common, and sport C may have a half-dozen things in common each with A and with B, but not have any of the things in common with A that it has in common with B. And it is doubtful that fishing, say, has as much in common with football as it has with many activities not usually considered sports, as it is doubtful that fishing "means" the same to all the men who regularly hunt fish. It might turn out to be more profitable to characterize as sports not certain activities, but any activity performed in a certain "spirit," in a certain frame of mind.

A proper inquiry would also have to take into account that any particular sport is over-determined, is as it is because it came into being in this or that historical circumstance; because it is maintained by this or that national life-style; because it satisfies this or that psychological need; because it is an expression of this or that disposition programmed into our genetic structures; because the pelvis and muscle fiber of women are different from those of men; because of all these at once. A man who took such matters into account might be able to explain why football is becoming more popular than baseball, why baseball was once so popular, why baseball is transportable, although football is not, what the rest of the world sees in soccer. He might then proceed to the proper business of philosophy, which is to conceptualize experience, to turn what is lived into what can be thought. And if he had either experience as an athlete, a gift for observation, or a sympathetic imagination, he might be able to give us a phenomenology of sport—which would be something worth having.

My guess is that such an inquiry would come to rest in a conceptual area adjoining the one blocked out by Weiss's opening and concluding remarks on the relations between athletics and excellence. For the Greeks, excellence, *areté*, denoted a perfect fit between a thing's achievement and its *telos* or generic end, a realization of its *raison* d' *être* without overlap or insufficiency. It could describe the cutting of a knife, the swoop of an eagle, the mettle of a horse. But among humans, to have *areté* was in a very special sense to excel; it was achieved only through increasing strife for supremacy, through fierce and relentless *agon*, conflict, through unremitting competition. For to be entirely a human was to engage in a struggle to be more than one. Above are "the immortals," the gods, personifications of energies that survive beyond the seasons and the individual men who from time to time embody them. Below lies nature, also immortal in that it is reborn yearly, in that the unit is the enduring species, rather than the perishing individual. Between are "the mortals," individual men who die. Their condition is unstable; unless they achieve god-like immortality they sink back into the anonymity of nature.

In the flesh, of course, men fail; they die; their condition is tragic; unlike gods, no man is omnipotent or omniscient. But to test the limits of human knowledge and power, to excel, to become through conflict the best among men, is the only way to leave an imperishable trace, to achieve immortality, to detach one's *areté* from the dying animal, to be properly a man. It was in honor of the immortal *areté* of dead heroes and warriors that the Greeks built their shrines and poured their libations, as it was to honor the *areté* of athletes that Pindar wrote his odes.

Only to the extent that he was honored could a man know that he had achieved excellence; his honor was the reflection of his *areté* in the eyes of his peers. "Men seem to pursue honor in order to assure themselves of their worth—their *areté*. . . . For honor is the prize of *areté*," said Aristotle. I confess to believing that this view of the task of being human, if stated in an up-to-date idiom and laced with an ironic awareness of its convenience to aristocratic self-congratulation, its naïve reliance on the ability of humans to recognize excellence or to honor it once they have recognized it, is still a pretty good one. It at least has the look of explaining much about soldiers and athletes—not to mention Mafiosi Sicilians, coup-counting primitive hunters, teenage gangs, all of whom seem ready to risk everything for honor.

"The skill and strength of a warrior or an athlete," then, adds Werner Jaeger, is what the Greeks meant most of all by *areté*. The honor a Greek won through excellence was the shape of his visibility as an individual while he lived and the measure of what would survive in him when he died. But the honor awarded athletes was not, and is not, the same as that awarded to men who achieve excellence in warfare, or, for that matter, in statesmanship or science or play-writing. Athletes play games; and although games, as schoolmasters used to say, are a preparation for war, they are not the thing itself.

The victories won in games are neither ambiguous nor Pyhrric; history cannot turn them into defeats. Defeat itself is redeemable. The players know in advance the rewards of victory and the penalties of defeat; these are not inevitably transformed by the course of the struggle. There are rules; they are known;

there are referees to enforce them; there are penalties for those who do not play fair. A game has neither a past in what caused it, nor a future in its effects on games to come. One's opponents are entirely visible and of one's own kind. The field of endeavor is circumscribed by visible and immobile boundaries. The players need not fear falling into a hidden dimension. They can be confident that training will be of use, will not hamper them with propensities in the wrong direction, that skill, strength, courage, and dedication will give one an advantage, that the best man will win. Above all, they can count on being seen, at least by their opponents; they can rely on their efforts being recognized and their achievements acclaimed. They can feel the bracing presence of an audience that has come for the express purpose of watching them do what makes them all they are; even in defeat they need never feel the special despair that haunts those who struggle for self-determination out of sight and out of mind. These traits of games separate the playing-field from the other arenas in which men pursue honor. No matter how much life is a game, games only mime life.

Athletes, in short, win their excellence in a controlled environment, one that is artificial in the way of laboratories, plays, rituals. The risks they run are of a different kind from those run by men who try to domesticate nature by thought or action, or who assume the responsibilities of leading and misleading other men, or who in sounds or words or paint struggle to fix in a memorable form the shapes of human experience. We honor our athletes with shares in soft drink empires and fried chicken chains, with appearances on television commercials and gab-fests, with harems of airline stewardesses; the Greeks did much the same. But no tragic poet celebrates their excellence. No Herodotus writes in their honor. The folk mind of no culture immortalizes them in legend. Once a great athlete's own contemporaries have died, his achievements survive only as bare entries in a record book

GAME THEORY

"Game Theory," in *The Lively Rhetoric*, eds. Alexander Scharbach and Ralph H. Singleton (New York: Holt, Rinehart and Winston, 1968).

There are many ways in which football is unique among sports, and as many others in which it is the fullest expression of what is at the heart of all sports. There is no other major sport so dependent upon raw force, nor any so dependent on a complex and delicate strategy; none so wide in the range of specialized functions demanded from its players; none so dependent upon the undifferentiated athletic *sine qua non*, a quick-witted body; none so primitive; none so futuristic; none so American.

Football is first of all a form of play, something one engages in instinctively and only for the sake of performing the activity in question. Among forms of play, football is a game, which means that it is built on communal needs, rather than on private evasions, like mountain climbing. Among games it is a sport; it requires athletic ability, unlike checkers. And among sports, it is one whose mode is violence and whose violence is its special glory.

In some sports—basketball, baseball, soccer—violence is occasional (and usually illegal); in others, like hockey, it is incidental; in others still, car racing, for example, it is accidental. Definitive violence football shares alone with boxing and bullfighting, among major sports. But in bullfighting a man is pitted not against another man, but against an animal, and boxing is a competition between individuals, not teams, and that makes a great difference.

If shame is the proper and usual penalty for failures in sporting competitions between individuals, guilt is the consequence of failing not only oneself and one's fans, but also one's teammates. Failure in football, moreover, seems more related to a failure of courage, seems more unmanning than in any other sport outside of bullfighting. In other sports one loses a knack, is outsmarted, or is merely inferior in ability, but in football, on top of these, a player fails because he "lacks desire," or "can't take it anymore," or "hears footsteps," as his teammates will put it.

These physical and mental risks, the fact that pain and injury are not only commonplace but inevitable, dignify the game, give the playing of it gravity and the watching of it zest. For in sports, as in gambling, and as in most of the activities that we think of as peculiarly masculine, the greater the risk, the more serious the play, the keener the fun. But what the football player risks and the activity in which he risks it are not in the first place symbolic, like the risks and activities of gamblers, captains of industry, and intellectual explorers. These stand to lose or gain money, or power, or communicable truth, and take their risks through verbal and human intermediaries. The football player, on the other hand, risks the violation of his being, and risks it in public. Every forty-five seconds or so he must endure the intimacy of a violent collision with another man; he must pit his skill, courage, and strength, the qualities that define him, against another's, and then consult his flesh and emotions to see whether he has been diminished or increased in the process.

Many sports, especially those in which there is a goal to be defended, seem enactments of the games animals play under the stimulus of what ethologists, students of animal behavior, call *territoriality*—"the drive to gain, maintain, and defend the exclusive right to a piece of property," as Robert Ardrey puts it. The most striking symptom of this drive is aggressiveness, but among social animals, such as primates, it leads to "amity for the social partner, hostility for the territorial neighbor." The territorial instinct is closely related to whatever makes animals establish pecking orders: the tangible sign of one's status within the orders is the size and value of the territory one is able to command. Individuals fight over status, groups over *lebensraum* and a bit more. These instincts, some ethologists have claimed, are behind patriotism and private property; and also, I would add, codes of honor, as among ancient Greeks, modern Sicilians, primitive hunters, teen-age gangs, soldiers, aristocrats, and athletes, especially football players.

The territorial basis of certain kinds of sports is closest to the surface in football, whose plays are all attempts to gain and defend property through aggression. Does this not make football *par excellence* the game of instinctual satisfactions, especially for Americans, who are notorious as violent patriots and instinctive defenders of private property? (At the same time, in football this drive is more elaborated than in other sports by whatever turns instinct into art; football is more richly patterned, more formal, more complex, in the functions of its parts, which makes football *par excellence* the game of aesthetic satisfactions.) Even the unusual amity, if that is the word, that exists among football players has been remarked upon, notably by Norman Mailer.

And what is it that corresponds in football to the various feathers, furs, fins, gorgeous colors by means of which animals puff themselves into exaggerated gestures of masculine potency? The football player's equipment, of course. His cleats raise him an inch off the ground. Knee and thigh pads thrust the force lines of his legs forward. His pants are tight against his rump and the back of his thighs, portions of his body which the requirements of the game stuff with muscle. Even the tubby guard looks slim of waist by comparison with his shoulders, extended half a foot on each side by padding. Finally the helmet, which from the aesthetic point of view most clearly expresses the genius of the sport. Not only does the helmet make the player inches taller and give his head a size proportionate to the rest of him; it makes him anonymous, inscrutable, more serviceable as a symbol. The football player in uniform strikes the eye in a succession of gestalt shifts: first a hooded phantom out of the paleolithic past of the species; then a premonition of a future of spacemen.

In sum, and I am almost serious about this, football players are to America what tragic actors were to ancient Athens and gladiators to Rome: models of perennially heroic, aggressive, violent humanity, but adapted to the social realities of the times and places that formed them. For only American money, only the American educational system, only the American life-style could have produced football or created an audience capable of responding to its unique beauty. Who else but a people now grown sedentary on profits from the violence that continues to be their national habit are likely to feel the psycho-social relevance of football with any sort of poignancy? Who else but a people whose deepest social dream is of a condition in which prodigies of individualism are still teamwork, in which the fiercest acquisitiveness of any individual advances all the members of his group, could see in football the testing of their national aspirations? Who but such a people could be absorbed enough in the visible strategies of the game to take in, enjoy, thrive on the instinctual, the sub-social gratifications that inform the social ones? Only Americans could. And that is why, every year from July through January, American men neglect their wives and daydream at their jobs.

And so they should; nothing so easily pursued is as good for a man as football. I take it as axiomatic that play is good, whether one participates in it directly or as a spectator. And I take it as self-evident that anything which allows a man to take an unabashed delight in masculine display is for the good, as is anything that allows a woman to take delight in feminine display. But football is good for us in other ways. Freud noticed that humans have what seems like a species-characteristic way of dealing with realities too painful—too immense, too chaotic, too revealing—for them to be confronted directly. They return again and again to analogies of the painful situations through forms created by the individual and social imaginations. They confront and master in dreams, rituals, works of art, and games the transpersonal and unconscious forces that are otherwise as much resistant to the hopes of reason as intractable to the instruments of science. Football, in the course of giving pleasure, allows us Americans to domesticate and for the moment to bear those keenly felt but elusive forces that have largely made us what we are without quite being either what we are or what we want to be. Football is at once the expression of what has made us Americans and our human response to what has made us Americans. It is the product of a perfect fusion of our human nature with our national character.

So there is no use asking whether football is immoral or brutal or costly. No use asking whether it is a sign of health or disease in our civilization. It is a part of things as here and now they necessarily are. And it is one of the few things of that sort that can make you feel good.

ON EXPERT WITNESSING

Remarks given to an organization
of lawyers specializing in
Intellectual Property Law, 1995.

From a quick glance backward, I'd say I learned more about expert witnessing from the dozen times I've served as a juror than from the half-dozen times I've been served up as an expert. What I've learned, mainly, is that the skepticism of jurors is exceeded only by the cynicism of judges. Jurors and judges doubt us from the moment we swear to tell the whole truth and nothing but—as well they might. For it is just about impossible to tell the whole truth, assuming it were knowable, from the witness stand, the truth being invariably complex, ambiguous, and relative, cluttered with technical distinctions and dispersed amid the detail. Trying to tell it in response to a lawyer's questions would turn off the jury and turn on the peremptory impatience that judges seem to put on with their robes.

This skepticism, I would say, derives less from a philosophic belief in the imperfection of all human attempts to formulate the truth than from the situation, which includes the layman's sense that all lawyers are rascals and includes the other side's expert witness, whose equally impressive credentials lead him to conclusions that make you out to be a special pleader or fraud. Worse yet, in my experience a jury pays less attention to what the expert witness prides himself in knowing than to how he says it, to his manner, his posture, gestures, expression, to his dress and diction and demeanor, all of which it is impossible to get right.

A professor who dresses as professors usually dress will seem not to respect the dignity of the court, that legal fiction, or will look too bohemian to trust. But dress as well as the lawyers, and the jury will wonder how you got your money. Accept in silence the opposing lawyer's imputations of incompetence or sleaze, and you thereby imply they are deserved. But sass him back, and you seem defensive or defective in scientific impartiality—not to mention the openings you provide for further insult. Dramatize your material and you seem like a ham half-baked by the spotlight. But present it without emphasis and you seem like a robot, a wind-up toy, an alien who doesn't know the human meaning of what he knows. The witness chair, in sum, often feels as though surrounded by an aura that magnifies character flaws, turns what would otherwise be virtues into vices, all your carefully constructed poses and defenses transformed into the emperor's new clothes.

Clearly, what's needed is an impersonal method, a screen the expert witness can hide himself behind, a security blanket he can rest his cheek upon—and by "cheek" I mean chutzpah, for that's what it takes. The problem is that in the whole of literary scholarship there is no agreed-upon method for proving the degree of relatedness between two works of the imagination, barring the rare case of an extended passage of close verbal similarity. If a student comes to me and says he wants to write a paper arguing the influence of X on Y, say the influence of a poem by Keats on a poem by Yeats, there is no industry-wide test for deciding whether he has a case, as there is in forensic science for deciding whether or not two bullets were fired from the same gun. Yet professors of English make that kind of decision all the time.

The question is how they do it. In practice I would read the two works, the poem by Keats, the poem by Yeats, unconsciously absorbing a hundred particulars, unconsciously organizing them according to habits formed by experience, and unconsciously arrive at a decision. If some wiseacre student were to ask me how I arrived at this decision, I would not be able to tell him, but I think I could demonstrate to him that the decision is the right one. As Aristotle said, the truth is not arrived at through logical method, but that is how it is demonstrated. The most primitive (and common) way of demonstrating the relationship between two works of the imagination, whether to a student or from a witness stand, is to divide them into components, say twenty a piece, and see how they match up.

In both Hammett's *The Maltese Falcon* and Spillane's *I, the Jury* for example, we have a hard-boiled private eye, a secretary with a crush on him, a partner whose murder gets the action started, a widening web of crimes and criminals, some of whom are homosexual, a *femme fatale* who gets the detective to fall for her, but whom in the final scene he exposes as a multiple murderess, for starters. You could make a fairly convincing case… until the opposing lawyer started to work you over. He would surely get you to admit that between *The Maltese Falcon* and *I, the Jury* there had appeared so many films and novels graced by some or all of these components that they had become a floating repertoire of motives for makers of crime fiction, as the Hopi potter has a repertoire of designs to grace his pots. He would surely get you to admit that two new lists could be drawn up, such that no component in the first list matched any component in the second. There is no black bird, for example, in *I, the Jury*, nor is the criminal ringleader a sinister fat man. And the *femme fatale* is not a Park Avenue shrink in *The Maltese Falcon*, nor is she dispatched by a .45 slug in the navel.

The expert witness might therefore want to sophisticate the matching-columns test, which is essentially one of quantity, by adding the test of salience. Are the components that match up those that stand out, arrest the attention and stick in the mind; are they the most original? If in two works, and in only those works, a pubescent girl possessed by a demon swivels her head 360 degrees, you have good evidence that the later work copied at least something from the earlier. But it is no use pointing out that both works use the word "the" a lot.

The expert witness can sophisticate his method still further by applying the test of homology to that of quantity and salience: do the similar components occupy the same position within the structures of the two works, as the wings of a bat, the forelegs of a lion, the arms of a human occupy the same position on the bodily structures of these very different animals. Rochester in *Jane Eyre* and Max de Winter in *Rebecca* are in that sense homologous, as the triangular bit of blue tile in the eye of a saint in this mosaic and the triangular bit of blue in the robe of a saint in that mosaic are not. There are other ways of sophisticating this method, but I want briefly to mention a different method entirely, one more sophisticated to begin with, one that allows the expert witness to pretend that literary investigation is after all a discipline, not just a pastime, with an ancient tradition and a technical vocabulary. The method is pilfered from Aristotle, a good man to pilfer from, and not just because his works are out of copyright.

Aristotle divides tragedies into six constituent parts or elements, which we can modify so that they apply to any narrative fiction, whether in words, on a screen, or over the air. His first, *mythos*, is usually translated as plot or story, the structure of events as they unfold in time. His second element, *dianoia*, can be translated as theme, meaning, message, the point, a discursive correlation of the plot. The third element, *ethos*, means "character," the personalities of the players, but can be extended to include such matters as the ethnic, occupational, and socio-economic status of the characters, whether they are rednecks or bluebloods. Aristotle attaches less importance to his next three elements, but they can be of crucial importance in modern narratives. By *opsis*, for example, Aristotle means "spectacle," but we can extend it to include everything that may be taken in by the outer or inner eye, imagery, scene, setting, the characters' style of dress, an urban backdrop, the hazy atmosphere of cyberpunk movies, the dark corners of *film noir*. Similarly, by *melos* Aristotle meant "music," but we can take it to signify whatever is apprehended in time, the score, but also pace, rhythm, recurrence, a ticking clock, an amplified heartbeat. The last element, *lexis* we can translate as "language" or rhetoric, diction, style; the *lexis* of *Cyrano de Bergerac*, for example, is easily distinguishable from that of a Three Stooges film.

We can top off Aristotle's six elements with two of our own. *Mood* is the attitude of the writer toward his material, whether he satirizes his characters or celebrates them, whether he looks down on their world or looks up to it with longing. *Tone* is the writer's attitude toward his audience, which he may schmooz, like Dickens, or try to convert, like Harriet Beecher Stowe, or shock, like William Burroughs.

If an expert witness for the plaintiff can show that in the two works at issue these six-plus-two elements are much alike, that they are so systematically interrelated as to form a structure, rather than a heap, he will have earned his fee. He will have applied his expertise in a way that would not have occurred to the non-expert, but in a way that any judge or juror can repeat for himself, can test by common sense, once it has been done. He may not prove the plaintiff's case, but he will make life more difficult for the defense. A lawyer who expects more from his expert witness is as optimistic as people who believe the blurbs on the covers of paperback thrillers.

ACKNOWLEDGEMENTS

The author and publisher gratefully acknowledge the following for permission to reproduce previously published material:

The *New York Times Book Review* for:

"Fiction in the Modernist Mood," "A Luminous Parable," "William Gaddis's Frigicom," "A Fiction Made of History which in Turn was Made of Fictions," "His Alter Ego is a Killer," "Monsters Have Needs, Too," "Ratner's Star," "Mysteries of a Hardcase," "Cop Tristesse and One-Liners," "Sex is Everything," "Manism in Retreat," "The Nice Guy who Touched Off McCarthyism," "Fantastic Lessing," "Romance for Highbrows."

Turtle Point Press for:

"Parable of the People," from *Sex and Violence, A Love Story*, by George Stade, (New York: Turtle Point Press, 2005).

Partisan Review for:

"Snot, Navel Fluff, Toe-Jam, and the Uncensored Body of *Ulysses*," *Partisan Review*, Vol. LIX, No. 2.

Godine for:

"Afterword to Two Novels by Friedrich Dürrenmatt," Afterword to *The Judge and His Hangman* and *The Quarry* by Friedrich Dürrenmatt, (Boston: Godine, 1983).

New York University Press for:

"Horror and Dissociation," in *Split Minds/Split Brains*, ed. Jacques M. Quen (New York and London: New York University Press, 1986).

Yale University Press for:

"Dracula's Women, and Why Men Love to Hate Them," in *The Psychology of Men, Psychoanalytical Perspectives*, eds. Gerald I. Fogel, Frederick M. Lane, and Robert S. Liebert, (Yale University Press, 1986).

***Columbia Forum* for:**

"Thillers" *Columbia Forum*, Vol. XIII, No. 4, Spring 1970.

Harper's Magazine Press for:

"A Closer Look at Ariel: A Memory of Sylvia Plath." Introduction to *A Closer Look at Ariel: A Memory* of *Sylvia Plath* by Nancy Hunter Steiner. (New York: Harper's Magazine Press, 1972).

Columbia University Press for:

"Introduction to *Six Modern British Novelists*," Columbia University Press, 1974.

Johns Hopkins University Press for:

"Fat Cheeks Hefted a Snake: On the Origins and Institutionalization of Literature," in *English Literature: Opening*

Up the Canon, eds. Leslie A. Fiedler and Huston A. Baker, Jr. (Baltimore: Johns Hopkins University Press, 1981).

Hudson Review for:

"K. Lorenz and the Dog Beneath the Skin," *Hudson Review*, Vol. XXVI, No.1, Spring, 1973.
"Desportment," *Hudson Review*, Vol. XXII, No. 4, Winter, 1969-70.

Holt, Rinehart, and Winston for:

"Game Theory," in *The Lively Rhetoric*, eds. Alexander Scharbach and Ralph H. Singleton. (New York: Holt Rinehart and Winston, 1968).

Pari Publishing is an independent publishing company, based in a medieval Italian village. Our books appeal to a broad readership and focus on innovative ideas and approaches from new and established authors who are experts in their fields. We publish books in the areas of science, society, psychology, and the arts.

Our books are available at all good bookstores or online at
www.paripublishing.com

If you would like to add your name to our email list to receive information about our forthcoming titles and our online newsletter please contact us at **newsletter@paripublishing.com**

Visit us at **www.paripublishing.com**

Pari Publishing Sas
Via Tozzi, 7
58040 Pari (GR)
Italy

Email: info@paripublishing.com

TAMARIND ACHE

TAMARIND ACHE

SRUSHTI DHOKE

Foreword by
Ruskin Bond

Published by
Rupa Publications India Pvt. Ltd 2018
7/16, Ansari Road, Daryaganj
New Delhi 110002

Sales centres:
Allahabad Bengaluru Chennai
Hyderabad Jaipur Kathmandu
Kolkata Mumbai

Copyright © Srushti Dhoke 2018

This is a work of fiction. Names, characters, places and incidents are either the product of the author's imagination or are used fictitiously and any resemblance to any actual person, living or dead, events or locales is entirely coincidental.

All rights reserved.
No part of this publication may be reproduced, transmitted, or stored in a retrieval system, in any form or by any means, electronic, mechanical, photocopying, recording or otherwise, without the prior permission of the publisher.

ISBN: 978-93-5333-285-3

First impression 2018

10 9 8 7 6 5 4 3 2 1

The moral right of the author has been asserted.

Printed in Parksons Graphics Pvt. Ltd., Mumbai

This book is sold subject to the condition that it shall not, by way of trade or otherwise, be lent, resold, hired out, or otherwise circulated, without the publisher's prior consent, in any form of binding or cover other than that in which it is published.

*For all the legends based on
whose lives this story has been built.*

Contents

Foreword by Ruskin Bond / ix

1. Sundown / 1
2. Wishes / 12
3. Velvet Malice / 23
4. Torrent / 41
5. Venom / 53
6. Granny's Wedding / 63
7. Tang / 84
8. Mail / 94
9. Tamasha / 109
10. Reminisces / 127
11. Stiff / 143
12. Marooned / 155
13. A Lucky Stroke / 167
14. Unfinished / 177

Acknowledgements / 189

Foreword

I have had an old love or two. But I shall not take the luxury of calling myself lucky in love. Because if I were that lucky, I wouldn't be a bachelor today…would I? But I do have with me some great memories of those days of my youth right here in Mussoorie.

There was Miss Bun, the baker's daughter. Of course, that was not her real name. Her real name was very long and beautiful, but I won't give it here for obvious reasons. She would sit at the foot of my bed, always looking radiant. She wore her raven-black hair loose on her shoulders, and her eyes always looked large and innocent when she applied kajal. I still remember her pretty glass bangles and her silk kameez. She would bring me a bag of samosas every evening. I hate samosas, but I would keep ordering them because it gave Miss Bun a pretext for visiting me. It was all in the way of helping the bakery get by. When she would leave, I would give away the lot to any of the children in town.

Long, long ago, there was also an unknown girl who once kissed me in the dark. The lights had gone out, there was some amount of chaos all around and someone kissed me and disappeared. It's a nice mystery to have in one's life, I feel. I can wonder who it was—and there lies a tale in the not knowing. Once upon a time, the year of the kissing was also quite famous. But that was well before my time. The accounts of those who met happily or tragically at this time, and of those who stayed on, and those who came by many years later looking for them, are vivid and dramatic.

Falling in love is one of the most inspiring experiences for a young writer; it brings along with it a certain kind of spontaneity and intensity. My own life has been one long love story—I have loved people, I have loved books, I have loved flowers, the sun, moon and stars, trees and towns, children and grannies, birds, fairies... For home is where love is.

As you turn the page over, you'll find yourself in another such story of love—the story of Shiva and Suchita; love that transcends generations. I do not wish to divulge any more details to you before you even begin, or delay you from beginning. A tale of desolate fancies and unfulfilled promises, Srushti Dhoke's *Tamarind Ache* will bring to you the charm of old-fashioned love and longing. And I predict that it will make a great movie!

> Somewhere in life
> There must be someone
> To take your hand
> And share the torrid day.
> Without the touch of love
> There is no life, and we must fade away.

Ruskin Bond
17 October 2018

1

Sundown

THE SKY GRUMBLES for an eternity before pouring down on the frantic earthlings, as if to mock their minuscule existence. The first, most-celebrated shower satiates the parched earth, erasing all evidence of soot from the air, bathing the trees and the houses, and making every soul rejoice.

As shades of grey hijack the sky, parents make futile attempts to hold their children back from getting drenched. Animals, too, seem filled with a renewed joy, happily bleating, clucking and mooing. The calves leap around in elation, escaping their frantic masters and racing all around the village lanes. While bees and dragonflies rule the air, smiles reign over the land.

The first shower also means an end to the mile-long walks village women have to embark on in summer to fetch potfuls of water for everyday use from the nearest water source. Farmers groom their equipment, getting ready for another season of hard labour—and, hopefully, its fruit. The cattle's year-long wait for green, crunchy grass finally comes to an end. Bugs and beetles, at long last, bid farewell to months of aestivation, now ready to brave the world.

It is time, too, for children to bid adieu to the fun-filled days when they were the masters of their time. With the vacation now over, school has pushed open its formidable doors once again, pulling them back into a hellish world of harsh rules and incomprehensible books. The reluctant teachers, too, have managed to overcome their lassitude and drag their feet to the village school, which is now filled with a chattering, if unwilling, crowd.

The wedding season has just drawn to a close and a few houses have added members to their families. The new daughters-in-law are hard at work, slogging day in and day out to win over their still-stranger husbands and critical mothers-in-law. The matriarchs, settled all day on moth-eaten cots, watch them with hawk eyes to find any chink in their shy and obedient armours. The husbands seem self-conscious in the presence of their new wives and have temporarily stopped drinking and gambling to impress their unfamiliar spouses. Another activity they've stopped—again temporarily—is working; the leftover rations from the wedding celebration are more than enough for the family, at least for a while.

◈

Looking at the landlord's mansion, the first word that escapes any onlooker's mouth is 'abundant'. Stepping inside, into a compound almost as large as the village school's, one is taken aback for a moment. Most of it is open field. One boundary wall is lined with cattle sheds, with a full, mooing herd. The cemented house is two-storeyed, with a brown and green garishly patterned 'Welcome' mat at the doorstep—an invite to either walk out richer or lose whatever one takes inside with them, maybe more. Dusty rubber slippers lie in a dishevelled heap on either side of the heavy wooden door, through which hesitant villagers move in a sluggish line—some holding close to their chests the precious metals their daughters-in-law brought with them, some clutching the dog-eared documents of their family's land to give up as mortgage, and some others with their sons in tow to offer as free labour to the god of money, before they are demanded to sacrifice a more prized possession.

'I swear, Shiva, if I have to come here one more time, which I already know I will, I'm going to lose my mind. How am I going to pay him back? I knew those blue bulls would be the end of me.'

'It will all be fine, brother. Don't worry.'

'Yes, I hope so. But tell me, what brings *you* here?'

'Oh, the usual. I plan to sow cotton this time, and you know how much they charge per packet...'

'High enough to kill you! Never in my life have I known prices this astronomical.'

'And to top it all, the interest Rao Saheb charges is touching the sky. *Kasam se*, Sitaram, I don't know how we farmers are supposed to carry on. The government pretends to help, but...'

'So right you are. That's all it does—pretend.'

◈

It's almost noon but the sun still hasn't risen to its full glory. The night before had seen a sudden downpour and clouds still shade the sky. A moist breeze blows through the trees. Perched on the branches, birds create quite an uproar, as if holding a parliament to comment on the spectacle taking place below.

'Catch me if you can! Catch me if you can!' a girl's shrill, taunting cry rends the air.

'Forget it, Palak. I won't be able to, not in a thousand years,' a boy replies, with his hands on his knees, panting heavily.

'Come on! You can do it, Chintu, I know you can,' Rehan encourages.

'Ugh. Here goes nothing.'

Palak easily evades him. Her adroit dodging confuses Chintu and he slips, falling headlong into the mud.

Palak sits on a boulder nearby and waits for her brother to draw the courage to lift his mud-caked self off the ground. Chintu looks up at her, a lean girl, with her brown hair tied up in the usual tight ponytail.

She has an air about herself, he thinks, *the way she walks, talks, carries herself. It's like she's an adult already.*

Chintu, hardly a year and a half younger, has, on the other hand, managed to paint a different picture of himself in the eyes of his peers. Nobody has ever heard anything uplifting from him—neither about himself, nor about anybody else. However, despite being an object of constant ridicule among his mates, he loves to hang out with them.

Chintu groans, managing to haul himself out of the mud and wiping the slime off his clothes. 'See? I told you, it's a sheer waste of time!' He leans against a tree, defeated.

'Yes, yes, okay.' Palak dismisses him.

Chintu lets out a sigh of relief, which soon turns into a gasp of dread. He sees two boys approaching from a distance. He doesn't mind one of them—he's quite fond of him, actually; it is the other that scares him out of his wits.

'Oh, thank god.' The promise of a fun afternoon ahead is evident on Rehan's face. 'There they are, Raghu and Ansh.'

The two boys are best buddies, despite their divergent personalities. Ansh looks timid and introverted, the kind everyone considers harmless, silent—and non-existent—company. His friends, however, know better. Once he gets into one of his moods, there's no escaping his true maddening self. But that rarely happens, so it's nothing they have to worry about—not too much, anyway.

Raghu, with his rebellious and—to some—daunting nature, is a sharp contrast to Ansh's timid self. He is not intimidating, given the mediocrity of his looks, but his domineering attitude easily makes up for that lacuna. He can resolve fights in the blink of an eye, except when they get interesting. Then he just lets the show go on.

Despite this mismatch, Ansh and Raghu get along well. Their friendship is an unusual one, but then, some people are meant to be.

Raghu has an enormous tattered shirt on, probably a hand-me-down, which dangles just above his knees. The breeze makes his long hair dance. Ansh, as is his wont, wears a clean shirt buttoned all the way up to the neck, tucked neatly into his shorts. His hair is oiled and meticulously parted on one side.

'Hello humans...and Chintu.'

Chintu cowers behind the boulder.

'How are we all today, hmm?' Overdramatizing conversations is Raghu's forte.

He raises his left eyebrow and thrusts a hand into one of his pockets, pulling out a handful of gleaming sea-green marbles and jingling them like coins. 'Who's up for a game?'

'Come on, Chintu, we're just playing, it's okay,' Ansh tries to pull the much heavier boy and fails miserably.

'Get in here, you big marble,' says Raghu, as he slaps his thighs and doubles up laughing. 'God, I'm funny.'

All through the evening, Chintu is attacked with ruthless comments and names but the poor boy doesn't dare protest because of his fear of Raghu. He keeps everyone entertained at his own expense, until it's time to go home.

After an unwilling departure, Palak flings her arm over her brother's shoulder and starts singing, in no particular order, the verses of a song whose name she can never remember. She soon runs out of the lyrics and starts humming instead.

'So...how's school going?' she asks after a long silence.

'Oh, don't ask! The teacher took a Math test today, and everyone seemed to know about it, except me.'

Why am I not surprised. Palak rolls her eyes.

'All my classmates were saying that the teacher had announced it day before yesterday, but then how come I didn't know? All of them had certainly ganged up against me, I'm sure of it.'

'Well, have you considered the possibility that you weren't paying attention when the teacher told the class?'

'What?!' Chintu shoves Palak in the shoulder. 'Are you on my side or theirs? I thought you, of all people, would support me. All those boys make fun of me and you're the only one I thought I could trust. But I guess I was wrong,' Chintu sulks.

'Okay, little brother, I am sorry,' says Palak, exasperated.

'Anyway,' Chintu continues with renewed passion, 'when I failed with flying colours, the teacher gave me such a scolding! He hit both my palms so hard with that wooden stick he carries around, I felt like my hands would fall right off. And the worst part is he made me hold my ears and stand on the desk for two whole classes! He said...he said that I am a good-for-nothing fool and that-that-that my brain and body are the same—round and useless. Everybody was laughing... Oh, Palak, it was so humiliating!'

Palak sees her brother's lower lip wobble as he recalls the incident. But then his expression slowly changes; he looks angry now.

'I tell you, Palak, if I had my way, I would beat those kids to a pulp! I would just...' He punches the air, as if his conspirators are standing right in front of him.

'Hmm...good luck with that,' Palak giggles.

'What do you mean? Why are you giggling? Here I am, confiding in you, and all you do is giggle?' Chintu looks wounded.

'Oh, no, you get me wrong. Look, we're finally home, and I'm famished.' Palak ducks her head to enter their two-room house.

◆

'How many times have I told you to not play with that twisted boy, huh, Palak? What's his name?'

'Raghu,' Palak replies, morosely. Baba scares her when he's in a bad mood.

'Children today, they think they're smarter than all of us. Fine, then! Do as you please.'

The gap in the conversation is filled only by Baba's heavy breathing and Palak's defiance.

'But remember this,' Baba continues after a short pause, 'we've seen more of life than you have, Palak. Chintu, this is for you too. Listen, and listen well. I do not approve of that disrespectful, dishonest, discourteous boy. He has "bad influence" written all over him and I don't want you two to turn out to be vagabonds like him one day.'

He pauses, and then, with a sigh, he says, 'I tell you all this for your own good, don't you see? Palak, at least you should try to understand. You're the elder one.'

Palak bites her lower lip, looking at the ground.

'I should not see you both playing with him any more, is that understood?' His voice turns harsh.

'Yes, Baba,' the two say in unison, but it seems to Palak that Chintu says it a bit too happily. She makes it a point to chide him later. And, as for the matter at hand, Palak thinks it unfair of her father to judge Raghu without really knowing him. She knows all too well that whatever he has just said is based on stories he has heard in the village. Raghu is a close friend of hers and there's no way she'll let him go.

Her mind is made up, but she knows better than to say it out loud. This isn't the first time Baba has told her this, anyway. It hasn't worked before and it won't work now.

'Hurry up with the tea, Kamla,' he says.

❖

'Oh, Raghu! You're back!'

'Yes, Ma.' Raghu gives Yashoda a big hug, while reaching out to yank his sister's hair.

'Ow!' Kavita pulls away and tries to dig her nails into Raghu's arm but he is too quick for her. He jumps behind his mother to dodge her claws.

'Why do you always come back so late, Raghu? If you return even half an hour earlier, you can read a page or two before going to sleep.'

'Hmm, I'll try from next time,' Raghu nods gravely, putting on his most earnest look.

'This, Ma, this is what I always tell you! Why don't you ever scold him? See, this is what I mean when I say I'm the only one you have a problem with.'

Raghu sticks his tongue out from behind his mother.

'Raghu!' His mother's fake anger makes him snap back to attention. 'Go and change,' she adds, without lifting her eyes from the utensils she's washing.

Kavita storms out of the house, while Raghu sniggers his way to the makeshift wooden bathroom his father has built out of dried branches of the arjun tree.

A little while later, a visibly tired Shiva steps in through the door, a sulking Kavita in tow. She glares at Raghu, who is now sitting quietly in a corner, trying not to look his father in the eye. Shiva drops his farming tools on one side of the room and sits down heavily on the floor, his eyes closed.

Yashoda cooks on the chulha as the family huddles around on the mud floor. The smoke the burning wet wood gives off irritates their eyes and makes Yashoda cough even more. She has recently been diagnosed with tuberculosis but they are far from mustering up the money to get it treated.

The one-room hut is separated into the kitchen and the living area by just an old bed sheet—there is no wall, no door. It is covered by a steep, slanting, dexterously woven straw roof. The gap between the wall and the ceiling provides perfect ventilation but also an easy entryway for mosquitoes and bugs. The roof threatens to leak in the monsoons, so Shiva covers it with blue plastic sheets on risky days.

The kitchen is an unorganised, shabby mess. Tin drums of varying sizes holding grains and pulses, and heaps of firewood, line a wall blackened with soot. A voluminous brass pot is mounted on a stand to store drinking water and is distinguished from the others by its golden sheen.

Another wall is pierced with hooks and nails to hang clothes on. Axes, spades and sickles are stacked in a corner. The mattresses, blankets and bed sheets are folded neatly and piled on one side of the room. They are spread out at night and shared by the whole family to sleep upon.

'Hear this,' Shiva says, after a while. He looks flushed, as he often does when he comes back home at the end of the day—even though home should be a welcoming haven after a day's hard work.

'Really? Haridas is going to town?' Kavita cuts in, forgetting all the injustices against her.

'Yes, yes. And to cel—'

'And he found a job? What kind of job?'

'Patience, my dear girl. It's not exactly a job. He's opened a small eatery of his own there. A dhaba. So, anyway, as I was saying, to—'

'This is great! Haridas owns a dhaba now! I wish we could go and visit him. It's been so long since we last went to town!'

'Well, there's no need for that. If only you would let me finish!' Shiva thunders, losing the little patience had left.

'Sorry.'

'So, I was saying, to celebrate this news, we must go to Kisna sometime soon to offer our wishes. Haridas is visiting the village this very week.'

'Really? Oh, Baba, you made my day! When will we go?'

'Tomorrow night, maybe.'

'I can hardly wait,' Raghu beams.

2
Wishes

KAVITA AND RAGHU drag their feet along the dusty pathway. The bright morning sun illuminates the apology of a structure—a brick-and-clay building with half a dozen rooms, a broken compound wall and a dry, parched playground in front with kho-kho poles at its two ends. A small lavatory near it is divided into compartments for girls and boys. The floor is covered with cracked, chipped tiles, which, not very long ago, were a proud cream in colour but are now a sorry, faded brown. The emaciated cows, goats and occasional pigs that had made the school compound their home over the holidays have been shooed out of their summer kingdom.

The school lies on the edge of the village. A few hastily built cowsheds have come up next to the school building, with cattle on one side and cartloads of fodder on the other.

Heaps of dung lie strewn along the sheds, attracting flies and other insects.

The siblings idle around the school ground for a while. Soon, clusters of children start showing up. Very few bring their books and slates in school bags; some bring them in worn plastic bags, while others simply carry them in their hands.

When Kavita catches sight of Nirmala, she merrily ditches Raghu and skips away with her friend to their usual corner on the extreme right of the hallway—their very own private spot—where they prattle away about all possible things under the sun till the assembly bell rings. Their laughs and giggles have an almost ritualized flavour—the two friends know every little thing about each other and yet their secrets and whispers continue endlessly.

In a bit, Ansh and Rehan show up at the school gate. They seem to be talking about something; Raghu suspects it's Haridas, and rightly so.

'Do you know what the best part is?' squeaks Rehan. 'My brother, he's thinking of joining Haridas's dhaba!'

'Just when I thought this couldn't get better!' exclaims Raghu.

Tun-tun! The school bell rings out, the cue for the children to line up height-wise for the morning prayers, a row for each grade. Rehan and Ansh are still busy making plans, when they feel the headmaster's piercing glare on them. They immediately stop chatting and look down at their feet, sweaty hands clasped tightly behind their backs.

Not many students are concerned with studying; in fact, quite a few attend school just for the heck of it. They make merry and kill time all day, bunk way too often and hate to sit still in any of their classes. Raghu has always considered these students with tremendous regard, with a desire to follow in their lead someday. However, he is scared to upset his parents, especially his father. He's sure Kavita understands, even if she says his aspirations are worthless. He himself has seen her gaping at them, admiring their guts to do what they do.

Gangadhar, the headmaster, is one of the very few in school who care about the betterment of the students, their surroundings and the future of education in their area.

And in this snakes-and-ladders situation, Hiraman is the longest, most venomous snake. Being sarpanch, or head of the village, doesn't deter him from paving the way for his own profits—it rather facilitates him. Though his position is that of a teacher, like any other, he bosses over his colleagues—and in times even over Gangadhar. Teaching is very low on his list of priorities in school; conveniently, he provides the students with answers scribbled in chits and whispered into their ears to help them pass their exams. This, quite understandably, makes him the students' all-time favourite. He would have been fired ages ago, but nobody has the courage to take on the sarpanch.

It pains Gangadhar to see Hiraman and the other uncultured villagers imprint their petty values on their children. He feels crushed when he sees them throw away their opportunities, their lives, straight out of the window, opting to waste it all in mere folly. It almost feels to Gangadhar that even though there is just enough opening for progress, the villagers don't *want* to avail it. They want to continue living in the supposedly incurable filth that they have created for themselves and not even attempt to rise above it. Not one person in the past decade has taken up a worthwhile, respectable job.

The teachers stand in a herd behind Gangadhar, as he faces the students. Everybody folds their hands. A teacher begins the prayer and the children follow. The army of harsh-sounding notes wage a war on their ears, attacking in all their deadly unpleasantness. When the prayer is done, everyone looks up at the headmaster for dismissal. Generally, all it takes is a slight nod, but today, Gangadhar steps up and clears his throat. There is a long, awkward pause.

'Namaste.'

'*Namaste, sir*,' the children sing in a chorus.

Gangadhar clears his throat again, coughing a little.

'As you might know, the dropout rate of students at this school is escalating by the day. It's sad to see the value of education drop in the eyes of this village,' he says.

'I'm sure you are all giving your best, but you must have the will to do better. Everything that you do in this school will take you one step closer to a finer life... I know that to think that any of you will understand—truly comprehend—what I am saying is unlikely, but I'm still giving it a shot.'

Kavita could almost see the thoughts inside the headmaster's head whirring in a nervous mess.

'You must have all seen lotuses. They grow in muddy swamps and yet, when they bloom, are completely untouched by the dirt. They are spotless, beautiful. Despite the muck, they flower, and draw all eyes to them when they do. Everything around you here—the poverty, the illiteracy, the fruitless gossip—all of it is mud. Now it's up to you to decide whether you want to spend your entire life suffocating in the mud or blossom your way out of it.'

He scans the crowd for any trace of comprehension or enthusiasm, but finds nothing but unfulfilment. He lets out a deep breath he doesn't know he has been holding.

'Okay, then. Proceed to your classes.' He waves his hand in dismissal.

❖

Gangadhar has been posted in the village for the past six years and now lives with his wife, Anjani—they have no kids—in a rented house close to the school. Kavita visits Anjani every now and then, and their relationship, bordering almost on friendship, grows deeper with every meeting. Anjani narrates tales from her past to Kavita, who listens with rapt attention.

'It was the month of May. We used to live in Mahugiri when I was pregnant,' she had told her once. 'Piya's father didn't want the delivery to happen at home, with just the midwife present, so we travelled to Bhimpur. The bus was jam-packed—there were twice as many people standing as those sitting. Add to that the intolerable smell of dust and soot in the air and the heat of the afternoon sun. We didn't have other options available at the time. The potholed roads were such a pain. I remember it was such a bumpy, almost violent, ride that Piya's father had to grab my shoulders to stop me from bouncing too hard, and I had to hold on to my tummy for dear life. Your headmaster had a habit of worrying too much—he still does. He straightaway took me to the nursing home, where I was examined and admitted.'

Anjani had slipped into a trance-like mood. She gazed up at the vast, open skies and Kavita could see the tufts of slow-sailing clouds reflected in her deep brown eyes.

'Then one day, our grey world was blessed with an angel. Nothing felt the same again. There I was, holding my baby girl, my sweet girl. Her father,' she had giggled, 'bought boxes of sweets and offered one to everyone who happened to cross his way—doctors, nurses, patients. He said Piya's feet were just like his and her nose just like mine. No matter who came to us, friend or stranger, they were greeted with exorbitant hospitality and warmth, with extra-large smiles. Those were the happy days, Kavita. I often see Piya's face in yours, you know. You look a lot like her.' Anjani had cupped Kavita's chin lightly in her hand as she had said the words. But the mood had shifted; darkness had overshadowed her smiling words.

Kavita knew the story already—and so did everyone else in the village. What she didn't know, however, was how to handle it. A surge of poignancy had engulfed her and she'd decided to remain silent and listen on.

'One morning, I woke up around 3. Piya's cheeks were a little warmer than usual. I thought it was just the heat, so I fanned her with my pallu while she slept. But soon, sleep overtook me. I woke up a little late that day, around 8, I think, and Piya was burning up by then. It couldn't possibly have been because of the weather. I rang the bell and called for the nurses and the doctors. I shouted and screamed. They checked her and noted her pulse while I stood in a corner, numb at how careless I had been.'

She had paused, perhaps reliving the pain of the moment. 'My baby, she didn't even last a week in there. All those doctors, bending over her little body...'

She'd let a tear escape. 'If only I had been more careful, she would've been with us today, Kavita. She could've been in my arms at this very moment. She could've been here. If only I had been a better mother...' That thought had been all that was needed to trigger her heart-wrenching wails.

'You can't blame yourself, didi. What had to happen happened.'

'Oh Piya, I'm so sorry...'

Kavita had never asked her to stop crying. She had never told her that it was okay, that everything would be fine. Because she knew it was not, and that it would never be. Though young and never having lost a loved one, she knew there could never be an easy way out of such sorrow.

And so, instead, she'd just kept her hand on Anjani's shoulder and let the pressure that had been building inside the broken woman find an escape. She'd just held her hand and let the tears flow.

◆

The small village, Nimkhedi, is nestled in the foothills of the Satpura range.

The kuccha huts, interspersed with very few pukka houses, are connected by a web of unpaved stone lanes. The village has had a history of malicious droughts, but that was a quarter of a century ago. Although to say that Nimkhedi is now thriving would be somewhat of an overstatement, it is not doing too poorly either.

The village is at its best and most serene during the cool, misty dawns, when cattle quietly line the streets like well-parked cars and the villagers' everyday troubles are cloaked by the morning silence.

The family wakes up before daylight. It is drizzling outside and the village is covered in a misty blanket. Shiva's cotton crop is currently tender and needs to be protected from invasive wild grass. To promptly carry out the task at hand, he has decided to involve the children as well. They all set off together on their mission, with just the leftovers from the previous night to fuel them.

Three back-breaking hours later, Kavita and Raghu sprint back home. They are late for school. Both of them take a quick bath and head out in a rush, knowing they are late by around half an hour and have already missed their first class.

'I don't feel like attending the second one either. Will you bunk with me?' Raghu asks Kavita expectantly.

'You'll never learn, will you? I'll tell Gangadhar sir,' Kavita retorts.

'Aw, come on! It'll be fun! We even have an excuse that nobody will have reason to disbelieve—a perfect alibi.'

'If you want trouble, go ahead, but leave me out of it.'

'Hmph, fine! You win,' Raghu grumbles. 'But next time I'll be sure to get my way.'

Kavita rushes, almost tripping, towards her classroom, only to find her class teacher, Mr Kumble, in his usual surly mood. He is sitting on a chair and looks at her from above his spectacles perched precariously at the tip of his nose, in danger of falling right off. In front of him is a table smaller than what would generally be considered normal in a classroom, with a thin attendance register on top. The drawer is open and Kavita can see the mess of pens and papers inside.

Kumble is a cantankerous, middle-aged man, with more hair on his moustache than on his head. He wears almost the same, drab clothes every day—a light blue half-sleeved shirt, grey trousers and soiled brown leather slippers. Chewing betel leaves with superfluous amounts of tobacco is his one true hallmark. What he is especially good at doing is teaching while showing off the amount of spit he can hold in his mouth at any given point. He isn't very strict, though he does have his fair share of tantrums. Kavita, of course, is his favourite student. She gets the privilege of writing the date and the day on the top left corner of the blackboard every day, the milky white chalk turning her fingers ghostly pale. It is she who is sent to fetch whatever he needs from the staffroom, sometimes even asked to get him a tumbler of water from the pot in the hallway. This gives her a chance to step out of the class and catch a breath of fresh air, while the rest of the children sit in the jumble of letters and numbers. Her fellow students turn all shades of green at this privilege that is denied to them.

Their classroom is quite small, considering it has to accommodate twenty children on thin mats across the floor. A placard saying 'Education is power'—a sad attempt at inspiring the insipid children—hangs above the blackboard, like it does in every other class. Carved into a nicely finished wooden board in a childlike, yet tidy script, this somewhat dusty placard is, probably the neatest thing in the room.

Kavita stands in the doorway, conscious of all eyes on her. *Oh, this is bad.*

But being the teacher's pet has its perks. She is gently rebuked and sent to sit down. Stalked by disappointed looks, she walks through the maze of bags and fellow students to an empty space on one of the mats at the back.

Kumble opens his textbook and orders them all to do the same.

'Did I finish Chapter 2, Nirmala? I think I did.'

'No, sir. We still have a page left.'

'Okay. Everyone, listen up!' he says, clapping his hands. 'I believe we finished reading about the Ganga-Brahmaputra basin. Let us start with the Indus River. Who would like to read?'

Since no hands are raised, he picks a student at random, and the class begins.

However, Kavita's mind is somewhere else altogether. The delicious smell of the school khichdi wafts in and fills her eager nostrils. The midday meal is what really motivates many students to come to school every day.

She fantasizes about the soft, delicate rice melting in her mouth, the mellow taste of the dish, the satisfaction of a full tummy. She thinks of the agonizing 120 minutes she still has to endure before she finally gets to taste the delicacy.

No, Kavita. If you don't pay attention in class, you know better than anyone what you'll be up against in the test. Concentrate!

'...a very gentle slope. With a total length of 2,900 km,

Indus is one of the longest rivers in the world. A little over one-third of the Indus basin is located in India in the states of Jammu and Kashmir, Himachal Pradesh and the...'

Kavita couldn't care less about the Indus basin. It is impossible to focus in class, knowing that hot, freshly made khichdi is being stirred at that very moment in a big brass pot just a few metres from her. To make matters worse, thin wisps of smoke from the pantry fire stealthily creep into the class. The aroma of the khichdi gets her stomach rumbling. It almost seems to control Kavita; she even feels slightly ashamed of it. The morning weeding had proved a little too much exertion, with just the meagre serving from the previous night in their bellies.

Kavita's stomach is going haywire now, making all sorts of gurgling, wailing noises; sounds she is scared are loud enough for the others to hear.

Time stretches to infinity and beyond, but the bell for recess just doesn't seem to be in the mood to ring. *If only I could somehow go back in time,* she thinks, *I would go back and forth from break to now as many times as I would want, so I could have infinite plates of khichdi.*

Kavita now can't stop herself from fiddling around. She rocks back and forth, flips through the pages of her textbook, fidgets with her pen and doodles in her notebook. At long last, when the bell finally rings, Kavita quickly sits up on her knees, ready with the steel bowl in her hand, waiting for what seems like another eternity for Kumble to finally shut his book and wind things up, before she dashes off to her favourite place in all of the world—the school kitchen.

3
Velvet Malice

'RUN, CHINTU!' PALAK jumps and claps her hands. 'Run!' she yells in an effort to make herself heard over the other shouting, hooting bystanders. Chintu zigzags through the line of opponents and sprints like a mad dog. Every inch of his being—his hair, his face, his clothes—is drenched in sweat.

'Rehan! Catch him!' A pint-sized boy standing behind Palak cheers, and she gives him a dirty look.

Kho-kho is by far the most serious sport in the village, and although there isn't any other local competition, the one school that the village has to its name takes part devotedly in the annual interschool kho-kho tournament, visiting nearby small towns every year without fail to battle their players.

New members for the boys' team are yet to be selected, though the practice sessions have already begun in full swing.

The eager contestants spend hours together on the field, even when the teacher-in-charge, Amit, isn't around—which is most of the time. Amit is, in fact, a History teacher; hiring an actual sports teacher, especially to train the children, is beyond the school's budget. Even those who are no good at any kind of sports activity, including the teachers, do their best to blow their own trumpets by assisting Amit, while at the same time trying not to annoy him—which makes for quite a bit of entertainment for the potential team between practices. While the aspiring team members perspire day in and day out, others who are interested in the game but aren't good enough to be shortlisted line the field to watch. And though Gangadhar protests meekly, the staff downright refuses to listen.

At present, Rehan is the one chasing Chintu. In no time, he tags a boy called Ali, who, after pursuing Chintu for a while, tags their most trusted player, Raghu.

'Phew! I wonder what's biting him,' exclaims Ali, as he squats in the space left vacant by Raghu. Beads of sweat cling to his forehead.

Chintu is galloping across the field with surprising abandon, and the spectators are beginning to wonder if the spirit of an athlete has taken over Chintu's body.

'He can't run from Raghu for long,' replies the boy beside Ali.

Raghu is charging Chintu like a ravenous predator desperate for its prey. Chintu skips over to the other side, expecting Raghu to tag someone else. Raghu, however, seems to have taken it upon himself to finish the game. No matter how much Chintu tries, Raghu is still slicker than him, faster than him. The distance between them keeps reducing by the second, and the audience goes crazy with the tension.

Chintu seems to be on the verge of collapsing, and Palak knows for a fact that he will, if this doesn't stop soon. His face is red with exhaustion and it's quite evident that he can't take it any more. He slows down a bit, giving Raghu an unwilling chance to catch him and get it over with. Raghu, who does not see this coming, can't manage to slow his pace accordingly and slams his palm into Chintu's spine. Chintu tumbles and falls face down on a stone wedged into the ground right beside the kho-kho pole.

Everybody gawks at Raghu.

Chintu's face is a bloody mess. A gross sludge of saliva and blood drips from his mouth; tears and snot follow soon after. Palak runs to him and gets him up on his feet.

'*Hay bhagwaan*, this can't be happening!'

Chintu is wailing like a banshee and it is evident that it'll be a while before he stops. One of his incisors is broken. 'He...' Chintu points at Raghu, 'He did ith! Ith his faulth!' Speaking while crying has always been a challenge for him, and the broken tooth isn't helping.

Palak glowers at Raghu, who is standing right where he'd stopped, shocked. 'I... No... I-I didn't...' is all he says to defend himself.

Kavita bends down to pick up the broken piece of tooth. She tries to hide it from Chintu but is too slow—he freaks out when he sees how big a chunk it is, and his wails intensify. It takes a lot of consoling, and double the attention and sympathy, to get him to not act like the sky is falling.

Palak's gaze turns tender as she looks at her bleeding

brother. 'Come, let's go home.' Palak places her hand on Chintu's shoulder, trying her best to soothe him.

Meanwhile, a teacher with an unpleasant expression, wades through the sea of children, heading straight to the kho-kho team.

Raghu gulps. It's Amit.

'What's going on?' He sees Raghu standing beside the puddle of red, and groans. 'What have you done now?'

'I haven't... I mean, I have, but...'

'He pushed Chintu! That's what happened!' someone shouts from the crowd. Everyone starts muttering.

'Is this true?'

Raghu sees Ansh and Rehan standing nearby, looking at each other, concern writ large on their faces. 'Actually, sir...' Ansh starts to speak but Amit's hard stare shuts him up.

'Is this true?' he repeats.

'No, sir... Although, yes, he might've fallen because of me, but—'

'You admit that it was your fault?'

'What? No! No, that's not what I meant. It was an accident, I promise, I...'

'So you're saying that everyone here is lying, huh?' Amit shouts. 'Is that what you're saying?'

'No, just listen to me, please... I didn't mean to...'

Smack!

His cheek tingles and his ears ring in the aftermath of the slap. He feels a little dizzy—that was a hard one. He can sense all eyes—some mortified, some curious—on the fingermarks on his face that he's sure will dominate his entire profile for the next couple of days. Stunned, he keeps standing where he is, not sure what to do next. He has never been shamed like this before in all of his 15 years.

'Shut up! You don't get to say another word. How dare you justify yourself? I thought you were just naughty, you know? But you've hurt someone today—badly. That boy is bleeding. Do you hear me, he's bleeding! Even from you, I didn't expect this. You play well, no doubt, but this has gone way out of hand. If you ask me, you don't deserve to play any more.'

Raghu seethes, and the anger finds its way out of his mouth. 'Fine! I did it, okay? I pushed him! Yes, I'm evil, and I'm crazy, and nobody can do anything about it!' He walks past the startled teacher, and the crowd parts, silently, to let him pass.

He storms into an empty classroom and sits in a corner, against the wall. He shuts his eyes and tries to think of anything but the last five minutes. All he wants to do is go back home, curl up on his mattress and lie there forever. He didn't mean to harm Chintu; why would he? He hadn't done it on purpose, everybody had seen that. Why does Amit suddenly care so much for Chintu? He has himself been heartlessly indifferent in matters much more serious than this.

Raghu is sure that he's deliberately being targeted. He knows Amit won't last a minute in front of him if he were to truly get down to it. But it seems now that that's what he'll have to do. The wound on Raghu's self-esteem can only be healed by the salve of vengeance.

◈

Palak looks at the branches of the gulmohar tree as the sparrows fly across the lilac sky. She sees the young ones reaching out of their nest to pick at the swaying yellow flowers and the fresh green leaves. A tinge of orange has lit up the horizon—it's the sun, bidding Nimkhedi a good night.

She stands across from Chintu, on the other side of the road, fiddling with a handful of pebbles. Chintu had wanted to complain to Baba as soon as he got home, deciding he would wait right at the gulmohar tree so he could cry out his story as soon as Baba came home. He is absorbed in inspecting the broken fragment of his tooth from all angles; his lower lip looks like it's been bitten by a wasp.

'You're wrong about this one, Chintu,' she says.

'Don't you tell me what's wrong and what's not! Raghu has been after my life for as long as I can remember! But you've always been siding with him. *Him*, instead of me, your own brother! You're the one who's wrong, Palak.'

'Okay, yes, I agree Raghu makes you feel a little uncomfortable sometimes, but it's all fun and games, Chintu. Today was definitely an accident, though. I was right there; he never meant to hurt you, I can swear on that.'

'Well, it's too late now, isn't it? The deed is done. It's been six hours since it happened and my lip still feels like it's on fire. I'm going to have a crooked tooth for the rest of my life, and it's entirely his fault!'

'Fine, complain all you want. But we surely don't need to stand here waiting for Baba. You can complain once he's home.'

'No, Palak, you don't understand. I've waited long enough.'

They stand silently for a while. Palak says softly, 'You know this will get Raghu into a lot of trouble, don't you?'

Chintu defiantly stares at the ground, refusing to look Palak in the eye. 'That's his problem,' he mutters under his breath.

Palak steps away. 'Okay, that's it. You can keep waiting here, I'm going home.'

She marches off, and Chintu is left standing alone under the tree, with the nestlings for company.

Soon, he sees two figures walking towards him, silhouetted against the setting sun. Baba looks quite weary and Ma looks even worse; but this is an emergency, something he should've done a long time ago. He thinks back to the night Baba had scolded both Palak and him for keeping Raghu's company. He opens his hand to examine the half of his tooth for the hundredth time that day.

You have gone too far this time, Raghu, Chintu shakes his head. *Watch me now.* He knows his father won't go easy on Raghu's, who in turn would definitely not let that bully off without a nice, long shouting, maybe even a thrashing.

'Chintu?' Ma seems puzzled.

They're coming closer now. One step, then another. This is it. Finally, his moment of salvation is here.

'What happened to your face?' Baba enquires, frowning.

'I have a lot to tell you,' Chintu says proudly.

He narrates the entire story to them and Sitaram's face contorts with every word Chintu utters. Kamla, however, is just concerned about her son, not bothered one bit about how all the drama might end.

'How many times have we told you, huh?' she chides him. 'We have told you a hundred times not to play with him. Have we or have we not?' She blows on her pallu and holds the warm cloth against Chintu's swollen lip. 'Oh my dear, poor boy.'

Sitaram, on the other hand, is fuming. 'That scoundrel! He has the audacity!' he bellows. 'Come on, come with me, Chintu. We're going to Shiva. Now!'

Chintu gladly follows, with Kamla trailing behind them.

When they arrive, Sitaram knocks a little too vigorously on the open door. An annoyed Yashoda replies from somewhere out of sight, 'For the last time, no, I'm not giving you rascals your ball back. Enough is...'

She appears at the door with a cup of tea in her hands. It is only now that she realizes who the visitors are.

'Namaste. How come you are here?'

'Where is Shiva?' Sitaram demands.

'Hold on, he must be around here somewhere...' She arches her neck to look outside. 'Mmm... There. He's coming right here.'

Shiva's exhaustion is obvious, and it's clear from his face that he is in no mood to entertain frivolous talk.

'Yeah?' he says without preamble, looking at Sitaram droopily.

'Your son is causing a lot of trouble,' Sitaram starts.

'I know,' comes the reply.

Sitaram, not expecting such a matter-of-fact response, is taken aback momentarily but recovers in the next minute and pulls Chintu out of his mother's arms. He makes him stand between the two men, holds his chin tightly and angles his lip so Shiva can see the damage his son has done.

Yashoda is standing beside her husband, sipping her tea nervously.

'Look at the boy's lip.'

'So, a bee bit him. Why are you here, again?'

'It wasn't a bee. It was your son.'

'Uh... Raghu bit him?'

'You think I am here to joke? Don't fool around with me. Raghu pushed Chintu, and he fell and broke his tooth. Look at what your son has done to my boy. Is this what you've taught him?'

'Yes, you're right. This is what I've taught him,' Shiva says, putting away his tools by the wall.

Chintu's parents gawk at Shiva, offended, while Yashoda tries to hide her nervous giggles by sipping her tea noisily.

Shiva exhales and crosses his arms. 'Fine. I apologize on his behalf, okay? I'm really sorry. But I am sure you also know that this isn't my teaching. He just...I don't know, taught himself. And if you think of a way to straighten out his completely twisted sense of fun, please do let me know.'

He pats Chintu's head and walks into the house. As he thinks for the umpteenth time about how to handle Raghu, he looks right through Yashoda and her meek offerings of tea as she follows her husband inside.

◈

The following day, Raghu makes it to school early. The sweeper is the only one in sight, which is a good sign. Just to be sure, he peeps into the staffroom. He finds it all clear, so he jogs through the corridor and unbolts the door to his classroom, careful not to touch the fine bristles of the velvet pods he is carrying. He can't be found scratching his own hands; he might as well wear a placard saying he did it. He walks up to the teacher's chair and takes a deep, long breath. The first period is Amit's.

Here we go.

He cautiously holds the petioles and brushes them against the flat wooden seat of the chair.

What Amit did yesterday was not right. This is what he deserves, Raghu convinces himself once more. This is his idea of revenge, of settling scores.

Raghu recalls Amit's smug look from the day before and brushes the pods with renewed anger against the chair, so every inch of the seat now has a generous sprinkling of the pods' fine hair.

In case Amit does not sit on the chair—he usually takes classes standing—the next teacher, the village sarpanch Hiraman, will. That surely will not end well, but the satisfaction is worth the risk, Raghu thinks.

After his work is done, Raghu sits down on the floor, stares at his handiwork and waits for the other students to start trickling into class. But the assembly bell soon echoes through the school corridors and all the students rush out to line up for the morning assembly. Raghu sees some latecomers darting to reach before the daily prayer starts.

He saunters out to the school ground and joins a random line at the back. They are soon dispersed and now it's time for classes to begin.

He takes his usual position at the back of the room and watches the yapping children file in; they have no clue whatsoever about the event of a lifetime he has lined up.

The children are followed by the stout Amit, with a stay-away-from-me vibe. 'Listen, everybody,' Amit addresses the class. He doesn't have to make much of an effort to make himself heard, unlike the other teachers. Everyone stops fidgeting at once. 'Open your books. You're all familiar with the usual rule—shut up or get out.'

The class turns silent.

Raghu looks at Amit's muddy feet.

He must've gone to the field this morning, Raghu thinks, expectant now. *Please be tired, Amit, please be tired. You are an old man, after all.*

'Rehan!' Amit barks, swiftly scanning the class. 'Where's Rehan?'

Rehan meekly raises his hand. 'Y-yes, sir?'

'Hmm. Read.'

Rehan obeys.

Raghu turns to his book, seeking shelter from the teacher's hawk-like eyes. The last thing he wants is to be picked on in public again, which he knows Amit will willingly do if given the slightest chance. Both of them keep stealing glances at each other, though.

Raghu catches Amit wincing once, hunching over to keep his hand on his left knee, and his heart does a little anticipatory dance. 'Yes,' he whispers to himself, 'sit down...sit down...'

However, it turns out to be just an itch on Amit's calf, and Raghu's spirit falls.

This cycle of anticipation and disappointment continues through the class. Amit, as is his habit, rests his elbows on the backrest of the chair as he explains the concepts from the textbook or walks around the classroom as Rehan reads. Every time the teacher comes within a foot of the chair, the hair on Raghu's arms stands on end, but his hopes are dashed every time Amit's lazy strides resume across the classroom floor. One time, Raghu sees Amit's face contort heavily as if from joint pain, and for a fleeting moment it seems to him that he will finally sit on the chair, but he soon discovers that the facial animation was just for a wimpy sneeze.

In what seems like no time at all, the gong of the school bell announcing the end of the period reaches Raghu's ears.

NO!

All the people are looking at him now, even Amit.

'Is there a problem, Raghu?' he asks, with a comically raised eyebrow.

It is only then that Raghu realizes that he had, very stupidly, shouted out loud in class.

'Uh... No, sir.' He drops his gaze.

When he looks back up, Amit is gone.

'What!' Raghu elbows his neighbour. 'Ali! W-where did Amit go?'

'Well, the class got over. He can't stay here forever.'

'Oh, this is not how it was supposed to happen...' he mutters, getting up. 'God, no.'

'I didn't know you liked Amit's class this much,' Ali says, confused.

'Yes. Better you think that way,' he says, hopping and jumping between the rows of children, desperate to get his hands on the chair. When he finally reaches it, he lifts it with utmost care and rushes out of class with it.

He pushes past everyone in his way and goes straight to a corner of the school, holding on to the chair tightly.

They do keep a broom here... he thinks, looking around. *Aha!*

Feeling on top of the world, he stands there for a glorious moment, holding the broom in one hand and the chair in the other, relieved that for once in his life he has managed to handle a problem by himself.

'Raghu?'

Dread swallows him whole. A timid 'yes, sir' escapes his mouth. He quickly turns around, almost smacking the broom into the teacher's face.

'What do you think you are doing?' Hiraman is puzzled at seeing the boy so flustered. 'Do you mind taking the chair back to class?'

Raghu doesn't reply; he just stares back.

'Did you hear what I said? Take the chair back.' This time, the command is firm.

Raghu silently obliges. He drops the broom and turns back towards class, cursing under his breath. Hiraman follows him with furrowed brows.

Placing the chair back at its unfortunate place, Raghu sits as quiet as a mouse, watching the horror of the seated teacher's changing expressions. *Oh god, already? This was supposed to take time!*

It seems like in his excitement, Raghu had overdone the coating. There's a strange frown on Hiraman's face and he shifts into a wider posture.

'Uh...Ali! I expect you know where we left off last time. Stand up and read to the class. I, uh, forgot something in the staffroom. I'll be right back,' he says, with uncomfortable pauses.

Hiraman makes quite a spectacle of himself as he gets up and walks out with an awkward gait. Raghu dashes to the door and peeps outside, careful to stay hidden. A few others join him and they can hardly stifle their amazed laughter, as Hiraman takes a turn into the washroom instead of the staffroom, his hands hovering in a protective way around his behind. He doesn't come back.

A little while later, Raghu is sitting in a corner of the class, when the message that he has been summoned to the headmaster's office is delivered to him. Certain that his life is now about to end, he prays to god and asks for absolution for all his sins.

He stands for a moment outside Gangadhar's room, takes a deep breath and knocks on the door—which is more of a pat, really. But he doesn't need to ask for permission to enter; he knows his teachers are waiting for him inside. So he closes his eyes and walks straight into the room of doom, home to dusty cabinets, a disproportionately large table, a picture of Goddess Saraswati, a rickety fan and mountains of orderless papers. While the headmaster looks exasperated, Hiraman appears ready to lunge at Raghu's throat. But that's not all. There's a third person in the room too, who is almost crimson with rage—Amit himself.

So they've figured it out, Raghu thinks bitterly.

'YOU! HOW DARE YOU DO SOM...'

'Hiramanji! Please calm down!' Gangadhar jumps in and, for a fleeting moment, Raghu feels relieved. 'I'll talk to the boy.'

Desolation once again.

'I expect that not a word you say now is going to be a lie, young man. Do you understand?'

Raghu nods, keeping his gaze down.

'Were you the one who did it, as we all know and believe?'

Silence.

'Did you do it, Raghu?' Amit demands.

Raghu exhales. 'Yes. I did.' He looks straight at the headmaster. Kavita had told him once that the headmaster's wife, Anjani, is the friendliest adult alive. Raghu hopes Kavita has unknowingly managed to put in some good words for him to Anjani, and that Anjani has mentioned it to Gangadhar.

'Why did you do it?' Gangadhar asks.

'I thought you already knew,' he says, looking at Amit.

Hiraman is getting impatient now. 'Just say it, boy,' he urges, giving his behind a little scratch.

'Okay then. I did it because Amit sir wasn't particularly nice to me on the field yesterday.' Amit rolls his eyes. 'This was my retaliation. I sincerely apologize to Hiraman sir, though. I didn't mean for him to sit on the chair. I'm really sorry.'

'Sorry my bloody foot! You don't get to say sorry after embarrassing a teacher—hell, the sarpanch of your goddamn village—in this manner!'

'In my opinion,' Amit tries to sound wise, 'as punishment, Raghu should be kicked out of the kho-kho team without any second thoughts. First, that poor boy Chintu, and now this. This is setting a very bad example. We better hope other students don't follow his lead.'

'I agree! Throw him out! Who cares?' mutters Hiraman.

'I do,' Gangadhar intervenes again. A long, long debate follows these two words in Raghu's defence, most of which eludes Raghu's understanding, thanks to the oh-so-articulate nature of the teachers' speech. Amit and Hiraman thunder through their arguments and the headmaster, after quietly listening to them, explains his own stand and leaves all three of them mum.

'I'm afraid you're being a little too harsh,' he begins calmly. 'We can't kick him out of the team. He's the best we've got, after all. We have to think of the school too.' He cuts off Amit by bluntly telling him that he, in this case, is wrong—he shouldn't have slapped Raghu without knowing the whole story. He expresses his deepest regret over what Hiraman had to endure and manages to convince him that the incident was not related to him whatsoever—it was just horrible luck, if it may be called so. As for Raghu, he is too overwhelmed to say much, except a mumbled 'thank you'.

'Life isn't that easy, young man. Your parents and I are still going to have a nice cup of tea over this.' Gangadhar nods at the door, dismissing him.

◈

Ansh hangs on to every syllable attentively. Raghu mimics the way Hiraman had marched out of class, describing to his friend the thrill he had felt feeding off the teacher's embarrassment. And although Ansh feels a little guilty, he can't help but giggle at the older man's ignominy.

As they walk through the village, everybody seems to be

staring at the notorious lad. It had slipped Raghu's mind that stories such as this spread like wildfire.

The schoolday had passed in a rush of laughs and praises from his fellow students for his act of pure brilliance. Home, however, is not as sweet.

The ghastly silence is broken only by the sound of the utensils Ma is washing. Baba is sitting in one corner, mute, staring at Raghu with a gaze so cold, Raghu shivers.

'Sit here,' Baba motions to him to join him on the floor.

'I just remembered,' Ansh, who had tagged along, stammers, 'I-I need to go, uh, get something.' He flees out of the house, leaving Raghu alone to face another apparent session of therapy.

'Why did you do it?' Shiva asks.

'I'm sorry I did it,' Raghu mumbles, rooted to the spot.

'I asked why.'

'Well...Chintu accidentally fell because of me and broke his tooth. It happened unintentionally, I promise.'

'Yes, so I've heard, directly from his parents. I'm surprised you remembered to mention it at all.'

'I was just going to tell you.'

'*Bakwaas*! What rubbish! Are you sure it was purely an accident? Do you swear by it?'

'I am. I do.'

'But I'm still not able to see why you would even think of putting velvet pod hair on the sarpanch's chair!'

'You will if you just listen to me,' Raghu whispers.

Shiva looks offended but Raghu continues anyway.

'So, Amit gave me a—'

'Amit *sir*.'

'Yes, yes, Amit *sir* slapped me in front of the entire school. He wasn't even ready to listen to my side of the story. I got angry, obviously, so I brushed the itchy pods on the chair. They were meant for Amit...um, Amit sir, not Hiraman sir. But then Amit sir didn't sit, and Hiraman sir did, so...here I am.'

'Do you think what you did was right?'

'I'm not sure.'

Silence.

'Get out.'

'Okay.' Raghu gratefully obliges.

4

Torrent

RAGHU OPENS HIS eyes in the morning to discover that he's the only one still on the mattress, which makes him smile. He had almost forgotten what day it is. He scrambles out of bed and peeks out the door to see where the elders of the house are. Ma is by the well, chatting with a group of women. Dadi is with her. Raghu has learnt the hard way, over the years, that with great celebration comes great work. Kavita is sitting in their courtyard of sorts, grinding dal for puran poli, the sweet queen of chapatis; but she is neither old enough, nor important enough to assign him tasks, so he lets her be. Baba is nowhere to be seen.

Good. The road's all clear.

He tries to tiptoe out without being too conspicuous, when Kavita spills water on all his hopes—Raghu suspects it to be deliberate—by squealing out, 'Oh, you're awake! Finally!' As if seeing him really makes her that happy.

Ma spins around almost like it was him she had been waiting for, and Raghu curses his sister under his breath.

'There you are! Take the bullocks to the river and wash them well.'

'Right now?'

'Yes, right now. Also buy paint on your way back, okay? Your father is very busy today.'

I think you mean drunk.

Annoyed, he runs up to his sister in full speed, smacks her on the back of her head and escapes from her furious claws even faster.

'Hey!' Kavita screams, massaging her head.

He unties the beasts and heads for the river, taking a small bucket and a stick with him.

'Be careful!' Yashoda yells after him.

Preparations are on in full swing for Pola, the most widely celebrated festival in the village, in which the bullocks are worshipped. After being bathed and adorned with embellishments, the bullocks are allowed to rest for a day as a token of gratitude for all the hard work they do throughout the year.

On his way to the river, Raghu makes a stop at a crowded little shop.

'I want two garlands, and…uh… What oil paints do you have?'

'Blue, green and red.' The shopkeeper yawns.

'I'll take blue and red. Charge my father for it.'

As he walks with the plastic bag, bucket and stick in one

hand, and the bullocks' ropes in the other, he notices for the first time that the ground is all mushy.

It must've rained last night.

When the river comes into view, a refreshing breeze blows over him and the leaves rustle invitingly. He can hear the waves splashing over the smooth, black pebbles on the bank.

Sunlight reflects off the water and dazzles him, forcing him to squint. Raghu ties the bullocks to a nearby tree and drops the plastic bag beside them, happy that at least for a day, Baba won't have any chance to point a finger at him.

He wades into the river till the water is knee-deep, trying hard to stay put. He reaches out as far as he can to dip his stick in to check the depth, and realizes it's a tad deeper than he had expected—he has to plunge half his arm in to make the tip touch the riverbed.

The current, however, is surprisingly harsh as that depth and Raghu loses his stick to the frenzied waters. It resurfaces a moment later at some distance, floating away swiftly. Raghu loses hope of ever finding his dear stick again.

'Okay, bullock,' he says, as he steps back on to the bank. 'Let's take you in.'

He drags the reluctant animal into the water, with his little bucket in one hand. Now that he has learnt his lesson from the stick, he tightly holds on to the bucket and dips it into the water. Thankfully, he manages to hold on to it, and pours the stingingly cold water on the bullock's back. It does a little shaky dance, which Raghu assumes to be a shiver.

He repeats this cycle a few times, painstakingly washing and rubbing the animal's back, moving on to the neck. The next bucketful catches the bullock by surprise and it gives its head a nice, strong shake, startling Raghu. The horns swipe inches from his body.

Not having learnt from what just happened, he pours another pail right into the bullock's face, which now gets extremely agitated and shoves its broad muzzle straight into Raghu's chest. Raghu crashes into the perilous waters, splashing around for something to grab on to.

'Help!' he yells out. 'Some...'

But the torrent takes him under. The chilly water floods his senses. He can't breathe; he can barely see. Terror grips him and he struggles against the angry river, fighting against its flow. His chest burns with the pressure, just about ready to burst.

He can't take the torment any more. He goes under. The surface of the river now seems distant, moving farther away as the seconds tick by. He loses focus, and there's a ringing in his ears. He can feel losing himself in the water, slowly drifting away. His limbs go limp, and then...

Darkness.

◆

'You... How dare you?' he says, drunk silly. 'How dare you say that? You don't know a thing about...about Rao Saheb, okay?' His speech is slurred. 'You don't get to say a word against him, you...'

A day off for the bullocks means a day off for the farmers as well. Having nothing else on their hands, they turn to their ever-ready friend, Vasudev, who keeps a whole lot of his speciality freshly brewed for the day.

'Oh, shut your mouth!' says the other, slapping his thigh, his condition no better than his companion's.

'No, you shut...you shut your mouth. Sure, his interest rate is...stupid, but you know what? I. Don't. Care. Nobody's perfect.'

'Rao is a talking...swine, that's all. Hiraman is a million...' A hiccup interrupts him. 'Trillion times better... You understand?'

'Hmm, yeah,' the others nod.

'No!' He realizes he's on his own now. 'No. No. No.' He looks at his opponent, and anger wells up inside him. He throws his bottle aside and it shatters to pieces. He dives at his opponent's face and they both tumble to the ground, fumbling around for each other's collars and throwing excited but mostly futile punches.

'Fight! Fight! Come on!' The onlookers, one of whom is Shiva, hoot and cheer, happy to have found their own private little show. Even though both the drunk men land a few good punches, it's mostly just talk about how they would love to crush each other's heads.

One of the few things Shiva is truly grateful for in life is liquor. The escape it provides from his dreary reality is worth the frivolous things it makes him do and the exceptionally dim company he keeps during the time. His mind wanders to the first time he had picked up the bottle, how hard he had pressed it against his palm in anger and loneliness...

'Yes! That's what I'm talking about!' someone shouts, jolting Shiva out of his reverie. He's so engrossed in the tussle that he doesn't notice two men, soaking wet, come straggling into the village, carrying his boy in their arms. One of them runs up to Shiva and shakes his shoulder so bad it almost takes him off his feet.

Shiva spins around and tries to focus on the man with an intense expression—which he fails at miserably, so he starts giggling instead.

'Shiva, no. Listen. Your son... We found him in the river.'

'Raghu? Oh yes, he is a naughty one,' he says, waving his hand dismissively.

His eyes shift to the other man, standing a few feet behind the first. A boy, who seems to be either sleeping or drunk, is leaning against him.

'Why is Raghu standing like that? What has he done *now*?'

'It's nothing like that, lis—'

'Oh wait! I don't care. Sorry, I'm not taking in any complaints today. Come tomorrow!' he says, waving them goodbye.

'No! Listen to me!' the other man yells, grabbing hold of Shiva's face tightly. 'Look here, Shiva.'

He does so, slightly annoyed now. 'What is it? Go mind your own business.'

'Your son almost drowned, okay? Raghu. Was. Drowning.'

This seems to catch his attention.

This is another good thing that Shiva has noticed about the nature of liquor. Its effect overpowers you, makes you do frivolous things and keep dim company; but when you desperately need it gone...*poof!* It disappears. Just like that.

The other man lays Raghu on the ground—15-year-old boys aren't easy to carry.

It's only then that Shiva realizes what the situation really is. He looks down at the boy lying at the men's feet—his eyes closed, body pale and unmoving. His state is such that he looks almost…dead.

'Raghu!' he cries, squatting beside his son.

'His breathing is very faint.'

Shiva doesn't know whether to be relieved or worried.

'We need to do something, quick,' says one of the men.

'I…I'll take you home, Raghu, I'll…' He tries to lift his son up but it proves to be too much for his wobbly legs.

'Allow me, brother.' The men who'd brought him in pick him up again and, without further ado, carry him home. Among gasps and screams from the household's women, Raghu is laid down on the floor.

'Well, don't just keep looking! He's breathing, don't worry. Yashoda, get him dry clothes. Kavita, go get a blanket,' Shiva commands. 'Our poor boy almost drowned today. Ma, help me massage him.'

Whimpering, and scared out of their wits, everyone quietly obeys. In the next couple of minutes, Raghu is lying on the mattress in a fresh set of clothes, wrapped in the thickest blanket Kavita could find, with the family collectively rubbing his arms, chest and soles of his feet. Kavita vaguely remembers learning in school about the techniques to save someone from drowning and starts pressing Raghu's stomach.

Soon enough, little coughs start issuing from his mouth, turning into louder ones, and eventually Raghu vomits out a lungful of river water. Raghu's eyes pop open. And while he can still barely breathe, everyone is relieved that the boy is, at least, alive.

Yashoda runs to the kitchen to make her son a hot cup of tea and the others sit around to listen to what had happened. While Raghu is sure the story will make him the talk of the village for at least the next week or so, his father does not look quite so happy.

As he squats on the doorstep, Shiva sees people rushing up to the gothaan, the open area where the cows assemble before they are taken out to graze, with a few eleventh-hour preparations for the festival. His obligation to stay at home due to his half-dead idiot of a son has crushed his hopes of attending the favourite part of the festivities.

He sees Sitaram jogging up to him and envy burns inside him.

'Do you want me to take your bullocks for you? The function is about to begin,' he says in a haste.

'I don't seem to have a choice, thanks,' Shiva replies.

'No problem. Tell Raghu to look after himself!' With that, Sitaram, now with two extra bullocks, hurries away.

What luck. Even the bullocks get to go, but not me.

Shiva digs out dirt from under his fingernails, as if his life's mission is to get them spotlessly clean, trying to rid his mind of the recent miserable turn of events. A tantalizing roar of elation rings out not far from him and he has to press his head between his knees to block out the sound of merriment.

'There must've been a fight...'

He shuts his eyes tightly. More shouting. He can feel the frustration building up inside him, steadily, like the waves of a river.

'Aaaahh! Raghu!' he explodes into an impulsive burst of

anger. He swings back to face his son with the most unloving glare he can manage. But this isn't like the other times—it isn't just to show him the extent of his fury. Shiva is surprised that he genuinely doesn't feel any affection for the sallow, wide-eyed boy wrapped in sheets, sitting on a mattress and sipping tea. Shiva hopes, at the back of his mind, that this is all just the effect of liquor. 'Is it too much for you to just stay alive? Are we asking for too much here? Why did you take the bullocks to the river?'

Raghu looks at his mother. 'I-I was just trying to help.'

'Well, you did a good job, didn't you? I never would've thought handling cattle could be life-threatening.'

Raghu's breaths pick up speed. A tear streaks his face.

'Don't try these tricks with me, Raghu. I've seen it all before. Of all the days you could've chosen to drown, you chose today! Now, thanks to you, I'll have to stay tied to the house... *Today!* I have been looking forward to these celebrations for weeks, and now, all thanks to you...'

'Well, go, then. I never asked you to stay,' Raghu mutters, hurt.

Shiva looks taken aback. 'What? What did you just say to me? Did you just answer back?'

'Yes. Yes, I did. Go if you want to. I haven't stopped you.'

'Oh, I would have, believe me. But it so happens that I care about what people say behind my back. This is where I'm supposed to be right now, so this is where I will stay—only because of you and your warped sense of timing.'

'I didn't know it was possible for you to care.'

'About others? About myself? Yes. Yes, I do. But *you*?' He

says it with such contempt that Raghu almost recoils. 'For you I feel nothing!'

With that, Shiva stomps out. He walks up to the well next to the house, sticks his face in and screams into the bottomless darkness. Breathing heavily, he slumps to the ground. Sitting with his back against the hard wall of the well, he bites his lip and tastes blood on his sharp tongue. He wishes he could be anywhere but here, with anyone but this cluster of people he has had to call family.

Meanwhile, inside, Raghu's guilt has left him wailing for sympathy.

'Oh, Ma, what have I done? I hate myself.'

'Why do you say that, Raghu? It was an accident, right? There's nothing you could've done about it. Your father knows that too.' She coughs. 'It's okay, don't worry.'

'How can I not worry? I've ruined everybody's day.'

'Just try to forget about it. Think of the puran poli you'll have for dinner. It always makes everything better,' his mother smiles.

'But you are all missing the celebrations only because of me,' he sobs.

'I'm telling you it's fine. Won't you listen to me? You know I hate tears. I'll go talk to your father. You rest. Kavita, take care of him,' Yashoda walks out.

'Tell Baba I'm sorry!' he shouts after her.

'I will,' he hears her say.

◆

'He apologized, you know.'

'Hmm.' He avoids eye contact.

'Why do you have to be like this? He's only a child. You must be more understanding,' she says, squatting beside him.

'Why did he even go this morning? Doesn't he know I do the washing?'

'He went because I sent him.'

'What?' Shiva looks at his wife. 'Where has all your sense gone, Yashoda? You think sending a child to that raging river to wash two grown bullocks is the perfect "motherly" thing to do?'

'You were drunk,' she says, softly.

'Don't blame this on me.'

'I could say the same, you know.'

'On what grounds? Did you not see the way he was talking to me? That awful, insolent boy. Whose values are those, huh? Not mine, I can tell you that. You've been sheltering him from every slight inconvenience, Yashoda, but you won't get to do so henceforth. You've turned our son into a nasty little brat and I feel like it's up to me now to set things straight.'

'Wow, that doesn't hurt at all. You tell me now, what about all the times I've seen him cry to sleep because you're such a great father? While you're lost in your drunken world, it's always been me who's done all the raising! I am sure even you can't argue with that. All *you've* ever done is pile up expectations on the poor boy's head and think that magic is how things work. Has it ever occurred to you that you actually have to work towards what you want in life, put in some effort? It certainly doesn't seem like it.'

In that moment, there's nothing more that Shiva wants

than to run away. From everything. In that moment, he realizes that no matter what he does or can do, no matter what anyone can do, nothing *can* be done. His family has been on its way to eternal damage for years, right in front of his eyes, and he has just been standing by and watching the mayhem unfurl.

Maybe he deserves this. Maybe if he hadn't made that decision years ago, his life would have been different.

The silence that follows is evidence of the fierce cracks and fissures that have appeared in their weary marriage.

Yashoda gets up, wipes a tear with her pallu and walks away.

I never wanted you to be my wife. I never wanted this life.

5

Venom

CUCKDOO-KOO! THE rooster screeches.

Shiva lies on the mattress, stretching his stiff body. He tries to overcome the laziness that seeks to control his drowsy mind with a long, loud yawn. The well is crowded with chattering ladies and the atmosphere is rife with their high-pitched banter. The clatter of utensils mixed with the animated conversation between his wife and daughter drifts in through the door. Kavita is helping Yashoda with the chores.

What a good girl, he thinks. *Always ready to lend a hand, never says no... Unlike her brother.*

He stands up and stretches, throwing out his arms and filling his lungs with the clean morning air. He turns his head and looks down at Raghu, who is sprawled on the thin, worn-out mattress beside him, snoring lightly. Shiva smirks, shaking his head. He can't even recall the last time he had days as carefree as his son's.

'Uncle!'

He turns around to find his puffy-eyed neighbour's son, Ansh, half running towards him.

'Raghu is still asleep,' Shiva says dismissively.

'I'm not here for him. Ma sent me for some smoked tobacco, to clean her teeth. She told me to hurry because she has to go to work. I need it fast, or she will taunt me about it for a week.' His words are accompanied by a dramatic eye roll.

'I don't have any left. The stock got over yesterday. I could smoke some fresh but it will take time.'

'Ohhh...' the boy says, mulling over the offer.

Not waiting for a reply, Shiva takes out his chillum and starts cleaning it with a piece of cloth, which itself is not particularly clean either. He inserts a small stone and then fills up the pipe with the mustard-coloured tobacco. He lights a piece of cotton with a chakmak, his very own flint and steel lighter, and brings it close to the head of the chillum. The orange flame engulfs the tip, and Shiva takes a long, satisfying drag. After he's had a couple of puffs, he takes out the smoked powder and hands it to the boy, who races towards his house without another word.

Shiva squats on his doorstep, cleaning his teeth with a neem twig, and glances around. His neighbour, Ansh's father, is clucking at his cattle to goad them out of the shed. The women at the well are busy discussing their husbands and mothers-in-law, critically describing every little trait and exaggerating some to gain sympathy from their fellow sufferers.

Some boys, complying with their mothers' commands, are carrying little paper bags of grocery back home, stealthily munching on small chunks of jaggery as they go.

This bustling cacophony is what Shiva calls home. His infancy, boyhood and adult life have all been spent here; he loves this place. But he knows now is not the time to get nostalgic. He has work to do. He sets out to go from house to house—his mission is to look for someone willing to labour in his field for a nominal pay. Half a dozen doors later, Sitaram, along with his wife Kamla, agrees to help reap the crop. Shiva's offer makes Sitaram uncomfortable, but he has seen worse.

Shiva makes his way back home and after a quick bath, sits beside Kavita to have his breakfast. He steals a quick glance at the now-awake Raghu. Shiva smiles at Kavita and puts his arm around her shoulders, squeezing affectionately.

He helps himself to a mouthful of warm poha from the plate. He notices that Yashoda has added extra peanuts, some lemon juice and chillies—just the way he likes it. He watches his children eyeing the dish, their mouths watering, so he feeds them spoonfuls too. But, as always, it proves to be too spicy for Raghu, who rushes to the kitchen with red eyes and a runny nose, seeking solace in mugs of water. Shiva shakes his head and continues eating, with a tiny hint of a smile on his lips.

Suddenly, realizing that he may get late for the fields, Shiva hurriedly shoves the rest of the poha down his throat, while Yashoda ties their afternoon meal—sorghum bread, potatoes tossed with brinjals, onions and green chillies—in an old piece of cloth.

It takes them half an hour to reach their farmland. Sitaram

and Kamla are already there, awaiting Shiva's instructions.

An immense sky stretches endlessly above their heads, over the trees and beyond the hills. Rivulets of sweat run down Shiva's forehead and find their way down his kurta, which is soon drenched. The heat scorches his skin and he feels like he'll melt any time now.

By early evening, he decides to take a break. His throat feels dry as sand, so he goes to the stream to have a sip and then sits under a tree along the river bank, gazing at the undulating mountain range silhouetted in the horizon.

The trees sway in the breeze; the lull of the soft flow of water makes his lids leaden and, soon, sleep engulfs him. He doesn't feel the reptile slithering up his foot. A sudden, sharp pain jolts him awake. Locating the painful area, he spots two little pinpricks of red just above his left ankle. The snake glides away unnoticed.

It takes a few seconds for him to realize what has happened.

'Sitaram! Yashoda! Help! Kamla bhabhi!' He wants to run but his feet refuse to budge—partly because of the stabbing ache, partly because he is so mortified.

They come to him running.

'Hay bhagwaan...' Sitaram mutters, as he notices the serpentine trail on the wet soil. 'Kamla, quickly run to Sonu—he's in the next field—and ask him to rush here with his bullock cart. Tell him it's an emergency. Go! Hurry!' he commands.

Kamla dashes off, hitching up her sari so she doesn't trip. In the meantime, Sitaram tears off a piece of his dhoti and wraps it tightly just above the bleeding wound.

Yashoda is frozen with shock. Her expression is one that

Sitaram will remember all his life—pooling tears threaten to spill out on to her sun-tanned skin, which suddenly looks a shade paler; her eyes are wide in shock and horror; her eyebrows are arched high on her forehead and her mouth hangs open.

Fellow farmers from adjoining fields rush to Shiva's rescue, fear writ large on their faces.

'The cart is here!' shouts Sonu, from the road.

'Come on! Lift him up!' yells Sitaram.

The men hoist up an immobile Shiva, put his arms around their necks and carry him as fast as their weary legs can to the squeaky cart. Yashoda trails behind, sobbing.

'Everything will be okay,' Yashoda manages to mumble to Shiva in soft whispers, as he lies on the wooden planks of the cart. They're both drenched in cold sweat.

The cart rattles away, rocking in rhythm with the tinkling bells around the bullocks' necks. Nausea engulfs Shiva and he starts retching, but in vain.

When they finally reach home, the traditional healers, the vaids, are waiting at their doorstep. The news of Shiva's snakebite has already reached them and there is quite a hullaballoo in the village.

A swelling crowd surrounds Shiva's house, as dusk descends on the village.

Kavita and Raghu are standing in a far corner, in their grandmother's arms, too dazed to speak, not wanting to watch the goings-on. Yashoda runs to them and holds them in her arms. 'Everything will be fine.'

Shiva can vaguely see his family, scared and helpless, in

the distance. He wonders if they will ever sit together as a family again.

The treatment starts and Shiva is given bitingly acrid neem leaves and pungent green chillies to chew on. The villagers expect to see a cocktail of bizarre expressions flashing on Shiva's face, but none of that happens—Shiva's tongue fails to detect either the leaves or the chillies. Everyone knows that he will not be out of harm's way until the procedure bears the desired results.

And so it begins.

While Shiva sits as still as stone, the local snakebite experts take their positions and start whispering the crucial snakebite-survival incantation—one in each ear, and one right in front of his mouth. They chant with their eyes closed, in complete synchronization; if any of them falters, the chant will not work.

'What am I going to do? God help us!' Yashoda's wails punctuate the procedure.

It is now Shiva's turn to perform. Sitaram proceeds to pull up a bucket of water from the well; a woman is asked to sacrifice a few strands of her hair, which are then put in the water, and Shiva is asked to look at it.

'Snake! It's a snake!' he shouts, his eyes wild with terror. 'Save me, somebody! Hay bhagwaan, have some mercy.'

Kavita realizes that the effect of the snakebite has still not worn away. She sees somebody hand her father two glasses full of cooking oil. She can read on his face that while he is unwilling to go through this part of the treatment, he wants nothing more than to be done with this whole nightmare. As she watches silently, Shiva grabs the brass glasses and gulps the contents down in one go.

Come on, come on, come on.

Everybody seems to be thinking the same thing.

Come on, come on.

Nothing.

Everyone looks on in dismay.

But then it starts. Shiva's eyes bulge, his hands clutch his stomach and he finally disgorges a waterfall of vomit.

The poison's out! The temple proceedings are all that is left now. Yashoda is overjoyed.

Shiva looks weak, pale and pretty much done with life. Everybody is delighted that he's vomited, and the experts are wearing proud smiles.

But it's not over yet. The poison may be out but the snake still possesses Shiva's soul. Leading the way, he is made to hike all the way to the temple at the edge of the village. Lord Hanuman is invoked to cast mercy on the poor man, to free him of the snake's charm, to keep him hale and hearty for the rest of his days. With the prayers now ascending to a crescendo, the bucket of water is shown to Shiva again.

This time, however, much to the relief of everyone present, Shiva identifies the strands of hair in the water. The villagers let out a collective sigh of relief.

Yashoda and Kavita run to Shiva, and his mother follows. Kavita pulls him into a tight hug. Shiva realizes that when everything goes downhill, the light at the end of the tunnel is nothing but the people you love. Yashoda has always been a constant pillar of support in his life, irrespective of whether he has reciprocated. His mother's sacrifice and care is beyond description. His daughter is the sweetest little angel the world has ever seen. And Raghu...

He sees Raghu standing beside them awkwardly, not knowing how to act, not sure whether he can do what his sister is doing. Remorse stabs at Shiva like a million knives—he has led his own son to distance himself from him. He extends an arm to Raghu, who smiles and takes it, and is pulled into the warm family huddle.

Following the obligatory overflow of emotions and a tearful thank you to the vaids, Sitaram and Sonu, the crowd disperses for the night.

◆

She sits under the mulberry tree with a pen in her hand and a diary on her lap. It had been a parting gift from Anjani, a remembrance of sorts. Anjani had known that Kavita could be made to leave home any moment. The past year had been her last in school. Her parents work as labourers for most of the year, doing odd jobs here and there. So money, like the devil it is, tends to put them in a fix. Her dropping out of school means that they now have one more member who can earn and one less child to pay school fees for. This has alleviated the stress on their pockets. Moreover, Kavita would've had to go to Mahugiri for her Class XI, which would've required even more money—and this was just not feasible.

She sees weary children returning home from school as she sits in the shade, pondering over what to pen next—maybe a beautiful theme for a mesmerizing piece of art.

Lost in the rabbit hole of her mind, she is jolted back to reality by her mother's shouts. Yashoda is running down the street.

'Kavita!' The children around her stare and snicker, but she pays no attention to them.

'What, Ma?' Kavita calls, slightly annoyed.

'There you are. Get up now, hurry. Run back home and change into the green sari I have kept out for you. Wash your face and tie your hair into a braid. The family is reaching in an hour. I'll go get some milk.'

'Oh, okay.' She walks back home, diary in hand, the pen wedged between the pages, the dream of creating something beautiful lost in her head.

The next sixty minutes pass in a blur. She reaches home, sweeps the floor, sets everything straight, gets ready, prepares the customary poha, makes rangoli at the doorstep and basically tries to pretend that their life is lived in an organized manner, instead of being a series of spontaneous ideas and actions.

When everyone is ready, the family sits in a corner like neat showpieces, trying not to mess anything up at the last moment. Ansh's grandmother had told them about a boy. She had said didn't know much about his family, other than the fact that they live in Khapa and are considered relatively well-off—they have half a dozen buffaloes and six acres of rain-fed farm, and plan on building a new house. Ansh's grandfather had been a good friend to their family, but after he'd passed away, communication between them had ceased.

After a few more moments of bated breath and smoothening of crinkled clothes, there's a knock on the door.

'Come, come, please come. We have been waiting.'

Ansh's grandmother has been summoned too, to keep the small talk going.

Kavita walks in, holding a steel plate on which sit six glasses of water. Even with her eyes down and her head covered with her pallu, she can feel every move of hers being observed. The pressure is colossal; her palms begin to sweat and while handing a glass out to her potential mother-in-law, she almost drops it, which would have surely led to the death of the proposal.

The two families wear their best smiles and demeanours, and adhere to every courtesy demanded by social norm, all the while dissecting every significant detail of the others' lives. And, of course, both parties scan the other with critical eyes and conspicuous scrutiny—every single gesture has to be perfect, there is no scope for unimpressive moves.

The meeting is adjourned with promises to get back to each other with the next step, if any. Kavita knows that her own opinion does not matter and that if her parents miraculously agree with each other, there is nothing she can do to prevent the marriage. And this is exactly what happens as soon as the boy's family leaves—Shiva can't stop smiling, which is rare, and Yashoda's excited banter seems without end.

6

Granny's Wedding

IT STARTS WITH a breeze.

The children engage in their usual frivolity around the tall wooden Jari pole. It's a little time-worn now and has lost the smoothness it once possessed, but it still is a crucial part of the villagers' life.

The breeze picks up, bringing with it dust and sand, which prickle the children's faces and irritates their eyes. They morosely decide to end their games for the day and tread back home with dejected faces.

Later that evening, all hell breaks loose. Dark, heavy clouds swirl over the tiny village and break out in such angry downpour that it becomes difficult for the people to hear one another over the thunder and lightning. Unlike the clouds and the rain, the lightning and the thunder, the wind, miserable in its loneliness, howls all night, uprooting trees, banging on windows and tearing leaves off branches.

Dawn brings with it the full realization of the terrible scene outside. It seems as if the whole village has been ransacked by a giant bratty child. Raghu carefully ventures out of the house, trying not to step on anything sharp. There seems to be a lot of commotion, and he somehow feels the storm isn't the only reason. People are crowded around in a clearing, with creased foreheads and squinting eyes, trying to peep over each other's shoulders. Raghu pushes his way through the crowd to see what the racket is about.

What he finds leaves him gawking. The fifty-foot-tall Jari pole, which had been standing proud for as long as the villagers could remember—the one constant reason for them to celebrate every year, the one whose strength had been taken for granted by all of them—has been broken in half by the ruthless storm. The upper part lies on the ground, while the lower jagged end, now slightly tilted, sticks out of the soil, forlorn and defeated. It seems to Raghu that it is looking to the heavens and cursing the sky.

The Jari pole had always been the centre of all village activity. From playing children to chattering oldies, from dispute settlements to weekend markets, everything had happened around the pole. There was a time, years ago, when its main purpose was to set up marriages. But now with the pole gone, the very soul of the village seems to have lost its mirth.

People start whispering about how this is a bad omen, that it is the harbinger of nasty days to come, something that will leave a dreadful scar on their tranquil home.

Hiraman arrives in the next fifteen minutes, accompanied by other members of the panchayat. They gaze at the broken pole for a while and then huddle in a small group, whispering.

'Quiet, everybody!' the sarpanch shouts when they're done. He whistles to grab everyone's attention. 'What has happened is indeed very sad. The pole has been part of our tradition and culture for ages, and it is thus our moral duty to not let this tradition die. I, along with my fellow panchayat members, have taken the obligatory decision to find another pole to replace this one. For this, we will first need to survey the forest thoroughly for a tree that is worthy of being a replacement for our beloved Jari pole. All kind men and women who wish to volunteer for the worthy cause may report to the gram panchayat office to register. Registration for fetching the tree will take place separately, at a later time. Thank you.'

The people disperse, some going straight up to the office without a second thought and some heading back home to ponder whether the idea of preservation of culture is worth the effort.

Shiva reaches home, only to find his mother sitting on the mattress and sobbing. When she sees him, her sobs turn into loud wails.

'What's wrong, Ma?' Shiva rushes up to her.

'Oh my dear Shiva,' she wipes away a tear. 'I'm surprised it hasn't occurred to you yet.'

'Shh! Calm down. People will hear.'

'To hell with them! You listen to me. Your father and I, we got married, thanks to that very pole.'

This, to him, feels like the greatest epiphany of all time. 'Of course!'

In the earlier days, young women would be given three-metre-long sticks to poke and jab at the boys trying to climb the grease-coated pole. If any boy succeeded, he would have the right to choose a bride then and there, from among the girls jabbing their sticks at him. If he failed, well, better luck next time.

'I remember how valiant he had been, fighting against all us girls to climb that tall pole. He did slip, though, sometimes dangerously low, but I never once saw a hint of defeat on his face. To tell you the truth, I didn't really do my part trying to bring him down; he had to make it to the top, for me.'

People are peeking in through the window now, and some even through the door. Children are stealthily snaking into the room to enjoy the show.

'Did I ever tell you what he did when he got the money kept at the top?' She pauses for effect. 'He bought me my wedding sari. He was a noble man, Shiva. And now that the pole is broken in two, so is my heart.' She sniffles and continues, 'But I wish for you to be part of the search for the new Jari, Shiva, in your father's memory. You will help out, won't you?'

'Later, not now,' he sighs.

'Please? You can do this much for me, can't you?'

He stares at his mother, exasperated. 'Fine, I'll do it. But I won't waste my time looking, because I know you'll ask me to go and help with setting up the pole too, once it's found. So I'll go when the actual job starts, okay?'

'Okay. You don't know how much this means to me.'

She makes her way out of the house, wiping her face with her pallu.

◆

Almost half the village has shown its willingness to search for the perfect tree out of which the replacement pole will be carved—which is quite an overwhelming number. They split up into teams of two and look in all possible direction, combing every inch of the surrounding forest, but to no success. After quite a few days of fruitless perspiration, most of the pairs bail out.

One fine evening, though, two of the volunteers emerge at the village boundary, dusty and tired, but with jubilant expressions. People crowd around them, praying for some good news.

'We found one, yes. You people don't know all the things we went through for the sake of this village,' says one, gloating.

'It's a teak tree in a valley on the other side of the state border,' says the other. 'It's a beautiful site but the locals told us not to be fooled by what meets the eye. They say the place practically swallows people up; it's a dangerous place. Apart from a few exceptions—us included—the jungle doesn't show much mercy. Many people who have ventured in in the past have not returned.'

'That doesn't sound like a big deal at all!' Shiva exclaims, sarcastically.

'But I'm not sure if any of this is true,' says the gloater. 'Maybe the locals don't want us taking anything from their "precious" forest, so they made the whole thing up. He makes a face at his partner.

'But there is still a chance he could be right,' says the sarpanch. 'Let us not dismiss the information we have. We have no reason to be disheartened. We will definitely be cautious, yes, but this is something that really needs to be done. Tell me now,' Hiraman turns to the heroes of the day, 'how tall is the tree?'

'Around sixty feet, I think.'

'So after cutting off the excess, we should be left with a little over forty feet. That's good enough,' says Hiraman, nodding.

'Good enough?' says the pompous one. 'It's perfect.'

'Yes, yes, perfect. Now we must take action soon. The day of the Jari is fast approaching. We have just half a month to prepare the pole. Again, all men who would like to go should inform the gram panchayat office. You two will be going, of course,' he says to the exhausted pair. 'Also, there's one more thing...' Hiraman hesitates. 'It would be preferable if all of this is carried out on a voluntary basis. Free liquor will be provided to all those willing to go, to keep them pumped. However, village funds are running low, so if you had been hoping for money in return, I am sorry to disappoint you. I just wanted to make that clear.'

A collective groan goes around the crowd.

'That's a shame.'

'I was hoping that...'

'How do they expect us to...'

The men burst out in protest, but the parsimonious sarpanch silently slips away.

◆

The sky is bright and clear, in sharp contrast to Shiva's current mood. He is standing at the gram panchayat office gate, along with twenty other men. He had known this day would come but he hadn't expected it to arrive so soon. He makes a disgusted face at the sun and then turns his back towards it, which soon feels baked.

Hiraman smiles. 'I am extremely happy to see you all. Respect for one's culture is rare these days. We've all gone through what needs to be done, so I hope there's no confusion. Remember, wait till it's dark. We don't want any trouble with the Forest Department. I wish you victory. Be successful and, of course, be careful. Don't go missing.' He ends his 'motivating' speech with a laugh.

On this happy note, the men start off on their journey into the deep forest. They are all carrying with them one bedsheet each, which they know will come in handy later. The more spirited ones among them are also carrying axes—they'll be the ones bringing the tree down. Accompanying them are five bullock carts, trundling along the kuchcha path, the bullocks munching away on every grassy patch they can find.

While the others are enjoying their day out, singing and joking around, to Shiva, their seemingly endless walk seems like a punishment for a crime he hasn't committed. When they finally reach the edge of the forest, they set up a cosy little camp, spreading their bedsheets on the ground and waiting for dusk to descend. Shiva's continuous yawns are punctuated with annoyed groans as he swats away mosquitoes and flies. Vasudev passes bottles of liquor around. Shiva sees the others smoking their chillums and regrets not bringing his own, reluctantly asking to share theirs.

When night settles and the crickets begin to chirp, the men tie their bullocks to their carts and march into the woods fearlessly. Lighting their way are flame torches, their unpredictable flickerings threatening to start a forest fire if the villagers aren't careful. Once they find the tree, a few of them attack its tough bark with their newly polished blades. Within half an hour, the trunk gives way and the tree falls to the ground. Small animals and birds screech and scuttle away in fear.

Here comes the work. Shiva grudgingly gets up from his seat and wedges his torch firmly between the branches of a nearby tree. Taking a swig of the glorious grape water, he hauls an axe over his shoulder and walks up to the giant of a tree, contemplating what the right angle would be to start chopping. Once decided, he takes a deep breath and lands his first blow, chopping away at the branches, careful not to hit the main trunk. Neither the humidity, nor the teeming insects deter the men from their mission. Sweat and a few occasional cuts are, of course, part of the package. It takes the twenty grown men two full hours to get the job done. Even Shiva admits, despite all the hard work and whining, that the tree really is a fine piece of nature's work.

But little do the men know that this is just the beginning—the hardest part of the expedition is yet to come.

The men start to collect the newly hacked-off branches, cutting off the tender shoots and leaves to smoothen out the wood as much as possible without affecting the toughness of the branches.

At long last, when they've collected just enough, the real work begins.

With the bedsheets folded on their shoulders to cushion the weight, the two men who had found the tree walk up to either side of the trunk and place a branch across their shoulders, ready for the challenge. The others lift one end of the trunk up, position it above the branch the two men are carrying and let the weight fall on their shoulders. Then all the men steadily take up their positions behind the first two. It is soon Shiva's turn.

'This looks like so much fun,' he groans.

Using all of his remaining strength, he pitches in. The breath is knocked out of Shiva's lungs as the full weight of the tree falls on him; he feels suffocated. He knows that within the next few minutes his face will go embarrassingly red, and thanks his stars for the cover of darkness. Maybe they would've done better to bring more men. If they give up now, all their effort will come to naught. But the load is just too much to handle.

'Jai Jari Mata!'

The voice comes from behind Shiva. He doesn't know who has said it but he knows why. Shiva, too, feels like screaming would be a great idea.

'Jari Mata ki...!'

Without thinking twice, the others follow with a loud 'Jai!'.

'Jari Mata ki...!'

'Jai!'

Their rhythmic chants echo through the woods. The men manage to haul the huge tree's weight with just their bare backs and hands, trudging across the uncertain forest floor.

Dawn sneaks in through the canopy of trees, lighting up, even if slightly, the grateful men's way, who have had to leave their torches behind. But the sunlight also means they're short of time. The forest guards will soon be on their rounds, and they don't want to land into a soup.

'Time for a break. I can't take it any more,' says Shiva's partner in between desperate gasps, after nearly an hour of the herculean task. No one complains.

They try to carefully put the trunk down but it proves too much for their weary shoulders and the tree hits the ground with a thud.

'Ow! My shoulder... I think I'm bleeding.'

Shiva's own shoulder and head feel like they're on fire. They all try to look at their wounds, giving in to the human tendency of comparing their agonies.

'I never thought it would be this bad,' says one, hissing as he touches his injury.

'This couldn't get any better,' says another, wincing. No sooner are the words spoken than a few nimble drops of water fall right on his nose.

'Oh god, you must be kidding!' Another one cries out, looking at the raindrops on his bruised arm.

Before long, rain drenches the men, dousing out any remaining zeal.

'I never should've come,' mutters Shiva.

'Watch your mouth, Shiva,' snaps the man beside him. 'Negativity is the last thing we need. We're more than halfway through. We have to push on.' He tries to sound positive but it falls flat.

'Anyway, we need to get this over with. It's almost light now, and I can't wait to get home.'

Despite their protests, everybody gets back on their feet. Picking up their respective branches and their sloppy bedsheets, they get to work again, shouting their 'Jari Mata' slogans.

'How dramatic can this get,' thinks Shiva, as he tries to hoist the trunk back on his shoulders.

His vision keeps blacking out; he loses track of time, and after what seems like ages—it could really just be a few minutes—the trees start to thin out. The morning rays now fall on their weary feet as they lumber along. He can hear the bells on the bullocks' necks now.

Almost there... Almost there... Aaand...we're through!

Shiva feels like lying down and just sleeping there forever, but he knows that's not an option. The men line the bullock carts up like kindergarten students, load them with their hard-earned prize and head back home for some well-deserved rest.

Shiva quietly makes his way to the last cart in the line and manages to find just enough space for himself to sit in. His eyes hurt. He closes them and, almost immediately, falls asleep. The rhythmic tinkling of the bells acts as the perfect lullaby.

❖

The familiar sound of drumrolls wakes Shiva from his slumber. He feels refreshed, although it couldn't have been more than half an hour that he'd dozed off. He jumps off the cart and walks to the front.

The path has been lined with lime. The village awaits them, just a few steps away now. The people ogle at the size of the future pole, and Shiva feels proud. Men and women of all ages dance to the beat of the celebratory drumrolls. Shiva sees his mother crying happy tears, and a wave of satisfaction sweeps over him. All of his work has, after all, paid off. They get a hero's welcome. Shiva is smothered with hugs and pats, both from those he knows and those he barely does, and is almost choked with welcome jaggery shoved down his throat.

Liquor flows freely and it seems like nobody has plans to go to work that day.

Shiva laughs—a loud, happy laugh. He can't seem to stop; he has done it. He has become part of the history and heritage of the village. He has, with literally his sweat and blood, given the village its Jari back.

❖

Here he goes... Hmm... The girls seem pretty tough. I see what they mean by girl power... Ah! He's through... Whoa! Come on... Ooh, that must have hurt... No, no no, don't slip, don't slip!

The newly erected Jari is being climbed and Raghu finds himself giving a nail-biting commentary inside his mind as Salil puts his masculinity to the test in front of the entire village to get the money from the top of the slippery pole.

No! Come on! Show them what we boys can do! That's it... That's it... You can do it! Almost there.

Just when Salil really starts putting his back into it, a roaring engine sounds at the back of the crowd. Salil is now halfway up, but at the sudden sound loses his grip, slipping an inch or two.

Beeeeeep!

The horn tears through the air. The crowd goes silent, as everybody turns to stare wide-eyed at the outrageous disturbance. Salil slides down the pole when he sees the grim-looking uniformed man sitting behind the green jeep's wheel; nobody notices Salil landing on the ground with a soft thud. Everyone turns pale when they realize who the man is. They know in an instant that their celebrations haven't just been disrupted but now stand cancelled for the day—and perhaps forever.

'What is going on here?' enquires the man, jumping off the jeep. It's only now that it hits Raghu—the man is the forest range officer.

Panic engulfs him. The sea of people fidget around, talking and whispering, not really knowing what to do with themselves.

Beeeeeep!

It's that terrible, terrible horn again.

'Don't waste my time. I am not here to look at your faces,' he barks. 'Fetch me your sarpanch.'

Before long, Hiraman presents himself to him, his face wrinkled with worry. 'Namaste, saheb,' he says, sounding surprisingly composed.

'What do you think you are up to? We need to talk,' comes the stern reply.

'Ji saheb.'

'Now, I will ask you a few questions and you will be honest with your answers.'

'Ji saheb. No lies.' Hiraman's confidence surprises not just himself but the entire village. Raghu actually finds himself looking to the man to save the day. True, all Hiraman does at school is mess around, but in matters such as this, he's always the tough village sarpanch.

'Nice pole,' says the forest officer, eyeing the Jari.

The sarpanch raises an eyebrow. 'Yes, a real beauty.'

'Where did you get it from?' the officer demands.

'Saheb, don't take this the wrong way. We needed to do this, or else it...'

'Spare me the misery. Cut to the chase. Just tell me the truth.' He stares at Hiraman unblinkingly. The air is thick with tension. 'I will ask you only one more time. Where did you get the pole from?'

Hiraman exhales. 'From the other side of the border.'

'Hmm... That territory isn't under my jurisdiction. But since I'm here now,' he glances at the pole, 'why did you do it? Was it from a reserve forest?'

'I am not very sure. But I think it was from an allegedly ill-reputed valley of Temni, not very far from here.'

The officer nods. 'That is reserved. The reason doesn't matter, and ignorance is a silly excuse. You've gone against the law and you will be prosecuted. I have to take action.'

The people wait soundlessly for the verdict to be announced.

'Give me the names of all those who went to get it. Quick.'

Raghu's heart jumps right up to his throat. *'Baba...'*

One of the panchayat members scurries away to do as ordered.

'And you, sarpanch saheb,' the officer stares Hiraman down, 'you are in deep trouble. Also, did I mention? I'm sorry but I'm going to have to take your dear pole away.'

This tips the villagers over the edge. The elderly start wailing and thumping their chests, men and women start yelling and children start complaining. Everyone is shouting and cursing the officer with the worst things they can think of. Hiraman walks up to him to make him see some reason. They seem to be having a civil discussion, which soon turns into a heated debate.

'Sorry! You don't sound very sorry to me!' Raghu bellows, but he doubts anyone even a foot away can hear him. That doesn't stop him, however, from yelling out a few more things that his mother wouldn't be very proud of.

All around him, the hue and cry is beginning to get out of hand. The officer presses the horn yet again for an annoyingly long time but it has an effect opposite of what was intended. Instead of quietening down, the roar of the crowd gets louder. The officer looks to the sarpanch, his confident eyes now tinged with worry. He doesn't seem to want to ask for help but Hiraman understands that he needs it nevertheless. The sarpanch gestures to him to sound the horn once more, and steps in front of the crowd himself. He raises his hands and shouts out, 'Calm down, everybody!'

It takes Hiraman a mammoth effort—and countless false assurances—to just get the crowd to be less noisy, which is in no mood to listen to his entreaties.

'I have made my decision,' the officer shouts.

A sudden silence falls upon the crowd, as everyone looks on.

'I have talked to your sarpanch and he has told me all that I need to know. I see that the teak tree was felled for the village's good, for a community purpose. Therefore, I will take no, or rather minimal, action. You people have no reason to be agitated.'

Relieved murmurs sweep through the crowd.

'However,' he continues, and Hiraman thinks he sees him hesitating, 'I simply cannot ignore the fact that you people chose to steal from a reserve forest without the consent of the Forest Department. I still need the list of those who were involved in the felling of the tree, in case my seniors decide to do something about it, which, again, isn't worth troubling your minds with.'

He looks at Hiraman, who politely smiles back at him.

'I will also need the surety that this will not be repeated, no matter what. Or else, let me warn you, mercy will not be shown twice.'

'I give you my word, saheb,' promises Hiraman. 'You won't have to visit our humble village again.'

'I do hope so.'

The officer stares at Hiraman for a moment longer than would be usual.

'What now?' Raghu thinks.

But the officer just nods and climbs back into his jeep, looking thankful to be getting out of the place. He drives away, leaving in his wake a stream of black smoke.

'Hiraman, who do you think ratted on us?' asks an upset panchayat member.

'I have a feeling, a very strong one at that, that this is Rao's mess.'

'At least this got you in people's good books. You have risen in everyone's esteem. The next election will be easy for you,' comments another.

'Shh!' Hiraman scolds. 'Don't say all this in public.'

◆

As the sun sets over the hillside, Raghu leans against a wall, looking at the Jari. He can see the silhouette of the little bundle tied at the top, still intact, the way it had been in the morning. Raghu is awfully aggravated by the drama adults create sometimes.

Why can't they just live and let live? What fun is it to spoil everybody's day? It seems to Raghu that Rao is probably the biggest wretch in the village. He has discussed with his friends the happenings of the day, and it seems everyone has reached the same conclusion—it must have been the landlord. It had to be. Why else would he not be there when the officer had come? Why had he, being the head of the opposite party, not taken active part in bringing the Jari to the village? Let alone participation, he hadn't even said so much as a word on the matter. His neutrality on the subject has made him a highly suspicious character in the eyes of the entire village.

Raghu saunters back home, his mind troubled by the unnecessary game of politics. With each step he takes, he kicks a pebble, taking it all the way to his house, his mind brimming with thoughts.

Reaching his doorstep, he senses something wrong. He can hear faint sobbing sounds—definitely Dadi—and a soothing, consoling voice he can recognize just about anywhere—his mother's. He knows that going inside will mean putting a stop to whatever is going on, or is about to commence.

'... Shiva... It was supposed... sunset... Really miss... Jari... bad...'

He waits outside.

Before long, Shiva walks into the house without so much as giving his son a glance.

'Arre! What's wrong now?' his father exclaims.

'There you are,' she sniffles.

'What happened?'

'Oh, you know... the Jari. It's supposed to be taken down before sunset, and it's almost 8 now. This is a terrible sign, Shiva, it's an appalling omen,' she wails.

'So this is what it's all about. I should've known,' thinks Raghu.

But that's not it; there's something more, something he never could've thought was coming.

'I just realized, Shiva... It never occurred to me before, but... See, I'm an old woman now,' she controls her sobs enough to speak through them, 'and there's no telling when I...' she continues after a pause. 'You know.'

'Oh, Ma,' Shiva breathes out.

'No, let me finish. So I was wondering, if you just...if you could just climb the Jari once, in my presence... If I could just see you... My life will have had real meaning, Shiva... It will be the one true homage you can pay your father.'

'Hmm... Let's see,' Shiva thinks to himself. *Salil and the others have already climbed part of it before, so a lot of the grease must've come off. That should make it easier. It'll earn me a good name in the village too. Plus, Ma will be content.*

It's so silent that Raghu can hear his own heart thumping wildly. *What's it going to be?*

Shiva takes a deep, long breath and exhales equally elaborately. 'I'll do it, Ma. Stop crying, please; you're breaking my heart.'

◆

Shiva is caked with grease—his arms, his vest, his legs and even his face is coated in dirty olive green. Be that as it may, there is no stopping Raghu's proud grandmother from embracing her son. Shiva hands her the lump of grimy red cloth with twinkling eyes and a delighted grin. Both mother and son untie the knot together. Shiva picks the crisp green notes from inside and holds them up, displaying to the villagers his pride.

'Woohoo! Alright! Well done, Shiva!'

While the villagers cheer on, Raghu sits in a corner with his head against somebody's door. He catches sight of his mother, clapping her hands, laughing and just looking so happy. He smiles. Looking at her has always made him smile. But then he also notices something else—his Ma seems to be on the sidelines, neglected by his father in his moment of glory. And just as suddenly, Raghu's smile fades away.

He sees her coughing yet again, receding from the public eye. He worries for her a lot... And sometimes, it feels like he is the only one.

Raghu keeps sitting there as the people disperse and the sun sinks behind the hills. Ansh comes by to congratulate Raghu on his father's achievement but he brushes it off as pure luck. They talk for a while before Ansh also leaves.

Raghu usually doesn't like being alone, because then it becomes hard for him to keep away the thoughts that inevitably come his way. But now that he is by himself, there is no escaping them.

He thinks back to how...natural...his father had been with the villagers earlier that day—joking and laughing, chewing paan with them, folding his hands to thank everyone who congratulated him—how everyone kind of gelled along with his personality, without any fuss. If everyone finds Baba easy to be with, maybe there's nothing wrong with him. Maybe something's off with his own self. *Maybe that's why I don't get along with Baba.*

Okay, no. Enough.

He gets up, brushes the dirt off his shorts and starts walking home. He tries to keep his mind blank all through the way, or else he knows he will not be able to sleep that night.

◆

Just as he is about to enter the house, he overhears the elders' conversation yet again.

'See? He did it!' Ma's sweet voice tinkles in Raghu's ears, finding its way straight to his heart. He looks in through the window. 'I knew—'

'I did it only for you, Ma,' Shiva smiles.

Ma was talking, right? Why did he have to interrupt her like that?

His grandmother gazes at her son's face with eyes so full of love it makes Raghu sick.

Yashoda just stands there, fumbling for something to do or say. 'I'll go make some tea,' she blurts out, darting out of sight.

As they are left alone in the room, Shiva's mother takes her son's hands in hers. A tear rolls down her cheek. 'Even if I die this instant, I'll die in peace. Thank you.'

'*Oh God,*' Raghu rubs his forehead.

He steps into the house and, ignoring Shiva, heads straight to the kitchen.

7

Tang

'OYE, HURRY UP!'
'Ruuuuunn!'
'Raghu! Wait for us!'
'Move it, you oaf! I don't want to miss it because of you.'
'Good lord, how is he so fast?'
'Do you want to see it, or do you want to waste time yakking about how fast he is?'
'He's right. Let's go.'

The chase is on. A slight rev is all that's needed to have them racing. They see a shiny new creature approaching the school ground, which slows down in front of the gate and sits purring contentedly. Clenching their fists, they pour all the energy from every fibre of their being into the last few metres of the sprint.

As they close in on the heavenly creature, the real blow of its beauty hits them. Their hearts start galloping; even though their feet seem to have frozen, they can feel the heat in their flushed cheeks. Their chests, their temples, their palms, their whole bodies thump with excitement.

The clean silver lines on the dusty white body of the Ambassador are the most lavish treat possible for their eyes. The sunlight bounces off the flawless bonnet and dazzles them. They run their nervous, excited hands along the sides of the car, the slippery tinted glass of the windows and over the perfect handles of the doors with extreme care, as if any harshness on their part would scare this dream-like creature away. The joy of the moment, though, vanishes when a callous voice interrupts their trance.

'Hey! Don't touch the car, get away!'

'Can we sit in it, just for a moment? Please?' asks a quivering voice.

While the others wait for the driver's reply, Raghu is lost in his newfangled game of dust-graffiti.

The driver doesn't budge. 'Do you want a tight one under your ears, all of you? Don't fool around with me, okay? I want to take a nap. Don't even breathe near the car. Understand?'

The boys give him the dirtiest glare they can manage and cheekily touch the metal of the car one last time, which earns them another earful from the driver. They scamper away before the driver can make good on his threat.

Reaching the gulmohar tree a little distance away, a spot from where they can still see the car, they squat around in the heavenly shade of its delicate yellow branches. It is one of those places where the summer heat magically changes into a pleasant breeze, refreshing the senses.

'You know what? I caught a glimpse of the man sitting inside one of the classrooms,' Ansh starts off excitedly. 'He was wearing a deep blue shirt. And guess what?'

'What?' ask the others in unison, their curiosity piqued.

'He. Was. Wearing. Sunglasses.'

'Really? You saw them?' Raghu is lying on his back, with both his hands under his head. 'Living the lush life, I see. He must be rich.' The sunlight weaves through the flowers and falls on his face.

Just then, a long, loud beep cuts through the air. The car is leaving the school grounds.

Raghu looks at the bumper longingly and Ansh gives him a knowing wink.

'I bet I can do it before you,' Ansh says, with a smile on his lips.

They take off their frazzled slippers and race after their target. The car is jolting around on the earthy pathway, not fit to even be called a kuchcha road. They spot the bumper through the golden dust and run behind it relentlessly till their eyes hurt with the invading dirt and their feet can't take the assault of pebbles any more.

◆

The shrubs and trees are slowly transforming from a lush, happy green to a dull olive and brown. The sun lashes out at the barren earth. Birds rarely come out from the shelter of their nests any more. The cruel sun spares no one. The relentless heat burns everyone's skin, be it man or animal.

But the children don't care. They don't bother about sunburns or heat strokes. Their full concentration that afternoon is on the mammoth tamarind tree in the gothaan. They collect handfuls of stones and pebbles, close one eye and aim for the pods on the tree. Sadly, the children don't hit many. Aiming at pods just five inches long from over thirty feet away isn't easy, after all. They set to gathering pebbles again, and Chintu slumps down on the ground, defeated.

'I can't do this any more. My back hurts—and it is so hot! I can barely open my eyes against the sun,' he wails.

'Oh, stop your constant whining. Get up!' Rehan commands him.

Chintu makes a face at him.

'That's it. Enough is enough,' Raghu complains, siding with Chintu. 'Who has this much patience? I sure don't.'

'What now, then?' Ansh moans.

'Something I should've thought of right at the start.'

'You'll land us all in trouble,' says Ansh. 'I know that look of yours very well.'

'You can trust me. I promise.'

'I've heard that one before,' Rehan rolls his eyes.

'Let's get to work, boys!' Raghu rubs his hands in glee. His mood has gone from irritated to thoughtful; his furrowed brows reveal how hard his brain is working to concoct something outrageous and, of course, extremely fun. 'We need a bamboo with a hook at one end. We'll need to sneak it away from someone in the village. I think we can probably find one at Harish's. Let's all go look for it. We'll split up in pairs to save time.'

He snaps back to his animated self. 'Rehan, you go with Chintu and look in all the courtyards near the temple. Ansh and I will look around the houses surrounding the gulmohar tree.'

'Oho! Don't pair me up with him!'

'His snide commentary never ends!'

'He's completely useless!'

'I can't work with him! Don't make me!'

'Please!'

Rehan and Chintu flare up at each other.

'I see everyone's ready, then. I am happy to see how enthusiastic you all are!' Every syllable Raghu utters reeks of mockery. 'Come on now, no more grumbling. Let's do this.'

He winks at Ansh and they both dash off together, giggling and hooting, leaving no choice for the other two but to sulk and obey.

❖

Ansh holds the trophy in his proud hands. Rehan and Chintu had been a little too busy settling their differences to actually make themselves useful.

Raghu, now readying himself for the task at hand, rubs soil on his palms for a better grip.

Rolling his pants up, he instructs Ansh to hand over the bamboo stick to him when asked. He then digs his fingers into the crevices in the bark of the tamarind tree as high as he can and directs his friends to hoist him up. He scales the trunk till he has easy access to the fruit-bearing branches and, as soon as he gets comfortable, shouts, 'Now!' Ansh tosses him the bamboo stick.

Raghu catches it and uses it like a sword to hack at the stalks from which the pods hang. Tamarind rains down upon the exhilarated children below, who can't seem to get enough. They stuff the pods into their pockets till they overflow. When all the pods in Raghu's proximity run out, the ambitious boy extends his reach towards those a little far out.

'We have more than enough now, Raghu. Why don't you climb down?' calls Rehan.

'Just...a few more,' Raghu says, twisting his body around the branches and extending his arm, 'Let me just...get at tha...aaaah!'

It happens quickly. He plummets twenty feet down with a frightful thud. The hook of the bamboo stick swings just a metre away from Rehan's eyes.

'*Hay bhagwaan*! Raghu! Are you okay?' Ansh shouts, sprinting towards his friend and crouching down beside him, scared stiff. Chintu is muttering to himself about how much that would have hurt, while Rehan is just thankful that both his eyes are still intact.

Raghu feels a throbbing ache beginning to creep up from his lower back and spread to the rest of his body. It hurts, but he also feels numb at the same time. Blotches of black blot out his vision.

'I'm okay,' he manages to utter.

'Are you sure? Should we take you home?'

Raghu sits up and glares at Ansh. 'Do you or do you not want to finish what we started?'

Ansh sighs. 'Fine, then. Let's go to my house.'

'What are we waiting for?' Raghu leads the way, somehow dealing with the pain.

A whole year has passed since they last tasted tamarind. They sit on the cot in a circle and empty their pockets. Cracking open the shells, they separate the seeds and the fibres from the delicate flesh, which they collect in a bowl. Chintu is told to get up and go out in the sun again to find the right sticks, which are then washed hurriedly. Meanwhile, Ansh brings out the spice box from the kitchen—spiced tamarind balls make for juicy lollipops.

They suck happily at their hard-earned treats, deciding to go over to Salil's paan stall for some gossip. They slowly make their way to the shop, savouring the tang, but as the adrenaline rush fades, the soreness in Raghu's limbs starts to flare up.

The laughter and the chit-chat at the paan stall help him drown the pain, but not for long.

◈

Raghu gasps as the pain grips him in the wee hours of the morning. He has not told anyone at home about his misadventure earlier in the day, but now that the left side of his body feels paralysed in a pulsating ache, he creeps up to his mother to tell her.

'Shh... Quiet now, it's okay. I've told you not to act like a monkey before, haven't I?' his mother whispers and ruffles his dishevelled brown hair. 'It isn't a big deal, nothing to cry about. Shh... Stay quiet, child. Don't wake your father up.'

They hear the rustling of sheets behind them, and freeze—his head in her lap and her hand hovering over his hair—when they hear Shiva's voice.

'What is it? What's the matter?' the hoarse voice is dangerously close.

'N-nothing. It's nothing,' Yashoda stutters. 'Raghu can't seem to fall asleep.'

'Great. Now tell me what's really cooking here,' Shiva says, sitting up. He has always been able to see through people.

As if the quiet that follows isn't bad enough, he arches his eyebrows and commands, 'Speak.'

Raghu obeys and gets up from his mother's lap. 'The thing is... My friends and I went tamarind hunting and we couldn't get any down with stones, so I...I climbed the tree.'

'And then, let me guess, the inevitable happened—you fell and hurt yourself. Correct?' He looks at them with frighteningly red eyes.

'Um...yes.'

'Thought so,' he says, nodding aggressively. 'Have you done anything constructive today?'

'Well, that depends on persp...'

His mother pinches him hard. He exhales.

'No.'

'You really are a blockhead, aren't you? How many times have I told you to come out of your dreamworld and study a little, just for a change? Or have you decided to be useless for the rest of your life?'

Raghu ignores the second question. 'Many times,' he says, through gritted teeth.

'And why did you feel the need to climb up the thing? Stone-throwing seemed too tame for your liking?'

'It's not that, Baba, I...'

'Of course it's that. All you ever want to do is prove that you're different from the rest, that you're the best, that nobody can ever match you. Well, you're far from close—miles from it. You won't know how to survive in the real world, how to swim in the crowd, stay afloat. Even if you're the best, there will always be someone better than you. Stop trying to prove your worthless point and start working towards doing something that's worth doing.' He jabs a thick finger into Raghu's chest, as he spits out the words. It adds to the hurt but Raghu just sits still and quietly bears it.

'Now, I don't care if your arms, or your legs, or your entire body is hurting; you still have to come to the field tomorrow. There's a lot to be done.' Shiva dismisses them and goes back to bed, as if nothing has happened.

Raghu wishes, not for the first time, that he had been born in another house, but with the same mother—he loves her too much. He gets blamed for something he didn't do—Baba doesn't care. He almost drowns—Baba doesn't care. He falls off a tree—Baba doesn't care. Baba just never cares. He's dreamt of it many nights; what a sweet deal it would be, to not have to deal with the only hindrance he's ever faced.

He hates his father for doing this to him, to them. All he had wanted to do that day was have a good time. Was that really so bad, wanting to have fun? Baba didn't have to react the way he did. He's the only reason the house is always so tense and, for the most part, joyless.

He thinks about how his mother would react if she could hear him now. She has always stood up for Baba, no matter what. *'Is this what you think of your father, Raghu?'* she would say. *'Is this what I've taught you?'* Dismay would lace her usually cheery voice, like spring and drought braided together.

Raghu feels tears welling up in his eyes but controls himself before they can spill out.

Just last night, they'd had another session of bickering. Baba had called Raghu names, said that he was unworthy of anything he was being given. He had said a lot more but Raghu had blocked him out. Fresh tears had dampened his eyes as he had walked away mid-sentence and lain down on the mattress, at the very edge, silently crying himself to sleep.

8

Mail

THE TINKERING OF the postman's bell reverberates through the village lanes, announcing the arrival of a letter. The cycle halts right in front of Raghu's house. The postman discovers Yashoda sitting at the door, grinding sorghum to make porridge for dinner.

She coughs and wheezes as she gets to her feet, looking up at the messenger hoping for good news. The postman, who couldn't care less, rips open the envelope and reads out its contents to the ailing woman, who is trying not to cough on his face. As he reads, tears glisten in her eyes: news that she is now the grandmother of not just one, but two baby girls starts to sink in. Kavita has given birth to twins. She giggles and tells the postman to wait for just one moment, as she rushes into the house and comes out with her hands loaded with jaggery. She gives the biggest portion to the postman and starts handing out small lumps to anyone who crosses her line of sight. It's only when the postman complains that he is a busy man and has other deliveries to make that Yashoda stops. She apologizes and tries as patiently as she can to listen to the rest of the letter.

But just as the postman begins again, Yashoda spots Shiva in the distance. His sweaty clothes are caked with mud and it seems like he had fallen into a puddle. That he is walking with a slight limp supports her assumption. Cutting the postman off, she shouts out to her husband to run up to them as fast as he can. Shiva tries to sprint but trips on the way and almost falls down again. He walks up sullenly to his wife but his mood changes to that of elation when he hears the happy news. Husband and wife are just short of singing and dancing, when the postman interrupts their little private celebration.

'Should I continue reading, or do you want me to come back especially for you two again?'

'No, no, sorry. Go on.' Shiva and Yashoda are way too happy to let the postman's sarcasm bother them.

The rest of the letter is just about how everything is fine at Kavita's end and how she yearns for them to come and visit her. She misses everybody in the village and everything about it; above all, she misses them both, and even Raghu and his misdeeds.

When the postman is done, he places the letter in the happy mother's outstretched palm, nibbles on his jaggery and bids them a relieved farewell.

◆

'Come on, now! We need to pack! Get moving, we'll be leaving tomorrow itself,' Shiva tells his wife, who happily obliges.

They throw their bare necessities into the only cloth bag they own and force the zip shut.

'Raghu, you'll be staying back with Dadi. She cannot be left alone.'

'What? No, why? Let me come too! I really want to go.'

'Yashoda, tell him,' Shiva sighs.

She rests her hand on Raghu's shoulder. 'Dadi is too old to travel, son. Please understand. Sorry, we'll take you some other time, okay?'

'...Okay,' he agrees grudgingly.

The family gulps down the porridge, so they can sleep early that night and catch up on the rest they know they will need to brave the journey next day. As soon as the crickets announce the arrival of the night, Shiva forces himself, Yashoda and Raghu into bed.

However, Yashoda is so overwhelmed with happiness that she can't sleep. She smiles in the darkness, as euphoria wells up in her chest. She risks violating Shiva's command and speaks to her equally awake husband.

'Psst...listen,' she whispers.

He immediately turns to face her. She can tell that he had been waiting for her to break the silence, not wanting to go against his own word. 'Hmm?'

'We're grandparents!'

Shiva gives out a laugh; it's a deep, genuine laugh, the kind that's hard to restrain. It's the most blissful laugh she has heard from him in years. 'I still can't believe it. It only seems like yesterday that Kavita was bawling in the midwife's arms, and now she has wailers of her own.'

Right then, at that moment, Yashoda feels like she needs nothing more from life, like all she had ever wished for has somehow transformed into reality—her daughter, happily married, has beautiful baby girls now, and prosperous days ahead of her; Raghu is her life; her husband is in high spirits, which means he will not turn grouchy and dictatorial any time soon. Agreed, they don't have much money, but they have learnt, over the years, to manage with what they have; her relations with the villagers are healthy enough to be called friendship; and as for Yashoda herself, she's as happy as can be.

◆

Out of breath, Yashoda reaches out for Shiva's shoulder with one hand and massages her aching back with the other. At long last, the ageing couple have finally reached the sari shop. Yashoda has heard that they sell the best saris in the entire town. They push open the glass door and step inside, refreshed by the cool air from the fan.

'One glass of water?' Yashoda asks, slumping down on a stool. She coughs into her handkerchief, and then fans herself with it. 'Show us your best designs. That is, the best you can manage within ₹100.'

'Well, there isn't much choice in that range, but I can assure you that you won't go back disappointed,' says the plump-faced salesman pleasantly.

'I really hope so,' Yashoda heaves. She is determined to find what she is looking for in this very shop, having run out of patience and stamina. The next thing she will lose in this stifling heat, she thinks, is her mind.

A few agonizing indecisions later, Yashoda decides to raise the budget. 'Okay, fine, since you have decided not to show me anything worth my while, I will be forgiving and allow you ₹50 more. So ₹150 is the deal now—and that's my last offer. You show me something good, or else we walk. You wouldn't want that, would you?' she says, although both Yashoda and Shiva know well that she means none of what she said. There is no way they are going to face the sun again without first getting what they came here for.

However, Yashoda finally ends up buying an irresistible maroon sari at ₹175, after haggling with the salesman to bring it down from ₹200; the idea of her daughter draped in the soft, rich cloth is far too tempting to forego.

Satisfied, she follows her husband's lead as he steps out, and hisses as the full fury of the sun hits them again. Their next destination is the garment store, where they are to buy clothes for their newborn grandaughters.

Yashoda stops midway, exhausted. First the hour-long bus ride, then the walk to the sari shop, and now this. She wonders if she'll be able to reach her daughter's home alive.

'Come, come, you can do this. It's right across the road,' Shiva encourages.

'I know, but it...' she pants, 'it seems much...' She squeezes her eyes shut for a moment, then croaks, 'much farther'.

They are greeted at the door with the sound of wind

chimes. Everything that Yashoda lays her eyes on she wants to buy. Yashoda strikes up an easy conversation with the saleswoman at the shop and manages to buy a couple of pretty little frocks at a discount.

They now set off for their daughter's home. It takes the restless, worn-out couple all their inner strength and willpower to hike up to the house, which is just a few lanes ahead, opposite the sarpanch's concrete house. Even though it is only a matter of five more minutes, they can't seem to be able to stay on their feet any more.

They knock on the door, out of breath but expectant, anticipating a cheery welcome. They wait and wait, but nobody seems to be at home. There is silence inside. Where have all of them gone?

They knock again. Kavita's mother-in-law opens the door, all the while cursing her aching old back.

'Oh, yes, Kavita told us to expect you,' she says dryly.

Yashoda isn't sure, but she senses disappointment in the woman's tone. She leaves the door open, goes back to lie down on a mattress and promptly closes her eyes.

'Can we come in? Is something the matter?' enquires Shiva, looking between the woman and his wife.

'Cats and dogs don't seem to need permission to enter this house. Are you special?' snaps the sleepy grouch. 'The things I have to put up with...' she mutters.

A wide-eyed Yashoda looks at the offended Shiva and steps into the house, her gait now uncertain. Shiva follows her in.

'So, um...where's Kavita? Where are the babies?'

'Hmph. The babies... They're a pity, really, the three of

them. They're in the room inside. Kavita is with them, as usual, not doing any gainful work. What a waste.'

Shiva's temper threatens to flare up but Yashoda pats his shoulder. She looks at his resentful face, warning him not to do anything they will regret. He nods, and for once in his life, follows his wife's directions.

Their breath falters when they step inside the room. The newborns are napping in a makeshift hammock made from an old sari hanging from the ceiling and Kavita is asleep on a cot beside them. They lean over to look at the infants—their rosy cheeks, those cherry lips, the tiny fingers and toes, the rhythmic rise and fall of their chests, the tranquil closed eyes. Above all is the knowledge that the sleeping beauties before them are theirs. The babies make the couple forget the disrespect from moments ago, as their hearts melt into a puddle of emotion.

Yashoda walks over to her daughter and strokes her forehead. Kavita wakes up with a jolt.

'Ma!' she beams. 'Oh, thank god you're here. Baba!' she says in a loud whisper, not daring to disturb the peaceful quiet in the room.

'H-how have you been, Kavita?' Yashoda stammers. Shiva is still transfixed by the babies.

'I'm fine, Ma. I'm sorry I couldn't receive you at the door; these two keep me up all night. Anyway, you both sit, I'll make you some tea.'

'No, no, we're not here to eat and drink, Kavita. I don't want to miss out on time with you and the girls.'

Kavita laughs. 'Yes, Ma, I understand. But I know how much you must be craving a cup of tea now. Here, come with me to the kitchen. We'll talk there. Baba can wait here.' She looks at her father and smiles, who is now brushing the babies' cheeks with his fingertips.

'Yes, I think he can manage that,' giggles Yashoda. 'And,' she continues with a sideward grin, 'isn't there anyone else you want us to meet, except for that old hag?'

'Ma!' Kavita looks taken aback. 'Mind it!' she pretends to scold her mother in the typical sweet tone that Yashoda misses so much back home. 'He has gone out for work. He'll be back around 7. Till then, my time is all yours,' Kavita adds.

Yashoda follows her daughter to the dimly lit kitchen. The cool floor soothes her tired soles. The walls have been painted a deep aqua shade.

'So tell me now, Kavita.'

'Hmm?'

'How have you been, really?'

'Oh, Ma. You and your worries. I told you already, I'm just...I'm fine.'

Yashoda frowns. 'Yes?'

'Never mind, it's nothing.'

'I will not rest until you answer me. You know you can tell me anything.'

'It's nothing, forget it.'

Kavita busies herself making tea, as Yashoda looks on. But finally, Kavita relents.

'Well...' she hesitates, 'sometimes...okay, maybe a little more than sometimes, he comes home a little...drunk. But it's no big deal, Ma. It's normal, everyone does it.'

'And you're telling me not to worry!' Yashoda gets a little

worked up. 'Promise me, the second you think you smell any sort of trouble, you will immediately write to me. Am I clear?'

'Yes, you are.' Kavita clasps her mother's hands. 'Now let's not ruin your visit here with a problem that I'm not even sure *is* one.'

Yashoda exhales. 'You're right. I'm here to enjoy every single moment and I'm going to make sure I do that.'

'That's the way, Ma. How's your cough?'

'The same.'

She sighs. 'Right. Now, I'm assuming you want your tea with ginger, like always?'

'Yes.'

'And lots of sugar?'

'Two spoonfuls.'

'And do you still want Baba to have bland, tasteless tea?'

Yashoda cracks into a smile. 'It's for his own good.'

◆

Dinner is laid out in the common area. Everybody sits on bedsheets spread out on the floor, chewing their food quietly and minding their own business. Kavita goes back and forth from the kitchen to the babies to the diners, serving chapati to one, water to another. If it is quiet for too long, she offers more potatoes and dal—especially to Roshan, whose plate is already full.

'So...Roshan,' starts Shiva.

'Hmm?' Roshan looks up.

'I understand you had to sell two of your buffaloes. How

did that come about?'

'Hmm.' Roshan continues munching his potatoes, without offering any answer.

Looks are exchanged. Yashoda takes over. 'We were just wondering why you had to do that. Are things getting difficult?'

Roshan is quiet for a while, as if thinking about whether to answer, then mutters something incomprehensible between chewing his food and gulping down water, trying not to spit out the contents of his mouth. Yashoda and Shiva look at Kavita for an explanation but all they get is a little chortle and a shrug.

'Hmm...' says Shiva, nodding his head and trying to sound polite. Kavita breaks out in an embarrassed laughter this time.

Roshan now looks full. He leans back against the wall with a hand on his stomach and looks up at the ceiling. Taking deep breaths, he hauls himself off the ground in an indication that his meal is over.

'Arre, Roshan beta! What about your rice?' Yashoda looks at his plate, which is still loaded with food.

'What about it?' He heads off to wash his hands.

'...Okay then.' Yashoda can bear stuffing food up till her throat but wastage is something she can't tolerate.

Giving up all efforts to try and make conversation, she spends the rest of the evening contemplating how she hadn't realized what cranks she had given her daughter to.

◆

'Goodbye, Ma,' Kavita says, bending down to touch her mother's feet. Roshan bends too but doesn't seem to be able to reach farther down than her knees.

It is a bittersweet adieu, not to mention a teary one.

'Goodbye, Baba,' Kavita sniffles.

'Look after yourself. And the little ones.' He rests his hand on her head in blessing.

'I will,' she smiles.

'Where's your mother, Roshan? I wanted to meet her before leaving,' Yashoda looks around, although she knows exactly where the old hag is.

'Oh, she couldn't sleep very well last night, you know, so she said she felt like sleeping in.'

'I see, I see,' says Yashoda, trying her best to look sympathetic, and turns towards Kavita, who looks down at her feet sheepishly.

'Sorry,' she says, frowning.

'Don't fret. Her sleep is way more important—everybody's is,' she looks at Roshan, who nods gravely.

'Well, anyway, you all come visit us whenever you can, okay?' Yashoda cups Kavita's face in her hands.

'Yes, Ma, we'll come at the earliest.'

'We must be off now,' Shiva waves, as they start their walk to the nearest bus stop.

◆

Two months fly by. And although Yashoda is a little sceptical about Kavita's mother-in-law and thinks her son-in-law is a dimwit, she still believes there is scope for happiness for her daughter, with the children lighting up the place with their frolic.

There is a knock on the door. Yashoda gets up, broom in hand, and goes to receive the untimely visitor.

'Oh! It's you!' Yashoda's face lights up, as the broom drops to the ground.

'Oh no…it's you,' the postman gets off his bicycle and pulls it into the shade. He takes his cap off, squats down and unfolds the letter now in his hands. 'Ah… This will take time.' He sighs.

'I can't have you sitting outside now. Come in. Have some poha.'

'Oh, thank you, thank you. Who would've known you could be nice?'

The old man sits down inside, under the straw ceiling. The postman hungrily gobbles down the poha Yashoda offers him, chillies and all. When he is done—and has had three glasses of water—he lets out a loud burp.

Yashoda laughs. 'Now I know for sure you liked it. Do you mind?' She points to the letter, which he had thrown aside in his haste to eat.

'You actually want me to read it?' exclaims the postman, pretending to be surprised.

She makes a face.

'Okay, okay. And don't interrupt.'

'Hurry up, start now.'

As the postman reads what Kavita has written, Yashoda sits unmoving, gazing up at the straw ceiling without any sign of either sorrow or happiness. Once he's done, he sets the paper down on the floor and thanks her again for her hospitality. He gets up, heading towards the door. When he looks back, he sees her sitting in the exact same way she had throughout the time he had read the letter. 'I'm sorry for what's happening,' he says. 'I hope things get better.' He leaves, but Yashoda does not even acknowledge that.

She just sits on the floor, thinking and thinking about how to help her daughter escape her shackled life. She picks up the letter, folds it, then unfolds it. She considers throwing it away, wanting to believe that none of it is true. Helpless, drained, she picks herself up and makes her way to the one person she knows will have an answer, no matter what.

She knocks on Anjani's open door. As the lady of the house emerges from the kitchen, wiping her hands on her sari, she smiles at Yashoda, but immediately senses something is not right when it is not reciprocated as usual.

'What happened?'

'Nothing good.'

'I'm listening.'

'It's Kavita…'

'What's wrong?'

'I got a letter. The babies…' she cries through strained breaths. 'She says she hadn't wanted children so soon into her marriage but that there was p-pressure. But now t-they're blaming her for not having a son. They say all she's doing is burdening them. The children… My girl, she's going through so much all by herself.'

Anjani gulps. 'It'll be f-fine, it'll be fine, shh…'

'Will it?'

'I've seen her grow into a mature young woman, and so have you. She's strong, she'll manage. You know that better than me.'

'But that's not all. Hear me out. They've had to sell all their cattle. Why? Because that rogue husband of hers never feels like going to work!'

Anjani looks on with furrowed brows.

'She takes care of everyone, all alone, Anjani—but who takes care of her? No one!' She gags, coughing, then speaks. 'She never complains, but what does she get in return? Bruises! That man beats her up! My little girl...'

Anjani finds herself staring at the ground, wide-eyed. 'I understand your worry, Yashoda. But believe me, things will sort themselves out. I am sure of that.'

Yashoda keeps her head on Anjani's shoulder. 'No, you're not. How could you possibly be?'

'Shh... It's okay. Kavita is a strong girl. She'll take care of everything.'

'Stop saying that!' Yahoda snaps. 'It doesn't happen that way, Anjani. You know it doesn't! All that fellow can ever hope to be is a walking piece of ill-mannered, good-for-nothing meat.'

'Look, Yashoda, if you are thinking that Kavita should leave or divorce her husband, know that it will just make things tougher than they already are. You know that. Her life will become hell.'

'But what other choice does she have?' the helpless mother argues, although deep down she knows Anjani is right. Kavita is on her own in this.

Anjani pats Yashoda's arm. 'Shh... Have faith. It'll be okay.'
'It won't be!'
'Calm down, keep faith... Shh... Calm down.'

9
Tamasha

AFTER A HARD day's play, they decide to retire to the paan stall. There are quite a few men gathered around in small groups, talking animatedly. The boys scoot up closer to one of the clusters, keen to know what the excitement is about.

'For me, I can't wait for that song, you know, the one that always comes along... How does it go? That-that famous one...'

'*Apsara Aali?*'

'Oh yes, that one, yes. It's really got a beat that makes you get up and shake a leg. Every time it comes on, the cheers from the crowd are unimaginable. The rhythm is irresistible.'

'Agreed. They usually play it last, so they can end with a bang.'

The conversation then takes a turn towards gossip about neighbours, but the boys get enough of that from their mothers, so they move away and head towards Salil. However, seeing that he has his own congregation going, they head homeward. On the way, discussion starts.

'So what do you say? I really wish we could make it, you know…to the tamasha. The way those people are talking about it makes me want to go. What do you all say?'

'Well, why not? Let's sneak out in the night, run all the way up to Mahugiri and then come back when the tamasha is over. Nobody will get to know. It's a perfect plan,' Rehan says in jest.

'That's a great idea! Let's do that! Once everyone at home is asleep, come to the gulmohar. We'll go on from there,' Raghu chimes in.

'Wait! Raghu, I wasn't serious. At all! Plus, we have an exam tomorrow.'

'Oh, come on! Don't be a chicken, Rehan. Are you afraid? No courage?' Ansh taunts.

'I'm not sure if I want to…'

'It's not a matter of whether you want to. You *have* to.'

'Hmm… I'll see,' Rehan says, not wanting to sound like a spoilsport. 'But it depends on the situation at home. I mean, I can't help it if my sister decides to stay up late and study.'

'Stop making excuses. You're just plain scared,' Ansh smirks.

'I'm not.'

'Okay, okay, come on, you two, don't start. I'll see you there. Under the tree, I mean. Bye for now.' Raghu takes the turn that'll lead him home.

◈

He is accompanied for an early dinner by his father. Shiva had been in a good mood when he came back home from work but Raghu had known that it wouldn't last—Baba would go back to sulking once they would sit for dinner. 'It has become like a ritual in their house to sulk during mealtimes', Raghu thinks.

He barely notices what he's eating; his mind is somewhere else altogether. Ma is attempting to make polite conversation, as usual, putting in a few good words for him, which he knows is more for her own peace of mind than anything else, to make herself believe that the bunch of people sitting together to eat is a family and not just strangers who have been forced to sit together and shove food down their throats.

Excitement has made Raghu jittery; he can hardly contain himself. It seems impossible to sit without fidgeting, thanks to the adrenaline coursing through his veins. The plan that had been concocted earlier has to be kept hidden from his family.

His mother's food is as delicious as always, but tonight he just can't bring himself to swallow it. This is just one of the many problems he faces whenever he feels like he has more energy in his bones than usual, which is already considered abnormal by most. More often than not, he manages to sit without moving too much while eating, but it seems like too much work when you can very well be jumping around instead.

'Stop fiddling, you fool, and don't eat like an animal. God knows where you learn your manners from,' rebukes Shiva, although his expression isn't stern; in fact, it's softer than usual. Perhaps it is because he is actually considering the possibility of what Yashoda has been telling him. Perhaps it is the blossoming of hope in his heart that there might be better days to come.

Raghu meets his gaze for a fraction of a second and

then quickly lowers it, concentrating on his chapati, which is suddenly looking interesting.

The lights go off.

'Hay bhagwaan! Not again!' Shiva whines.

'I'll put the lamps on.' Ma stands up.

Raghu is thankful his father can't see him smile.

This should make it easier. God is with me tonight.

When dinner is all wrapped up, they disperse for bed. All the kerosene lamps in the house, except for the one in the kitchen, are doused, and within a few minutes, Shiva starts to snore like a bear. Yashoda washes the utensils and keeps them in a wire tub so they can dry off, and then goes to sleep as well. All this while, Raghu closes his eyes and tries to lie as still as he can manage.

Stay calm, Raghu. You just have one goal ahead of you. Act. Dead. When the time comes, you'll be a free bird. But till then...patience. It is a virtue. Shouldn't be too hard, right?

But he doesn't know how wrong he is. It is now that the thrill of what he is about to do gets into his naughty head. He knows he is moving way too much in his sheets, but he can't seem to help it.

Dead, Raghu, you are dead!

About an hour and a half passes, and Raghu is 100 per cent sure that there is now no risk involved. He surreptitiously gets up from his mattress in the middle of the night, picks up his slippers so they don't make any noise, tiptoes to the door and, like a professional burglar, soundlessly opens the latch. He closes the door behind him, puts on his slippers and then sprints up to the gulmohar tree, its bare branches beckoning him to a night of sin.

Raghu sees his friends waiting for him, leaning against the trunk. Their faces light up when they see him running towards them. Rehan has come too. Raghu sees that he is the last to arrive. All of them seem to have run out of the very last drop of self-restraint, and so, without any acknowledgement whatsoever and without wasting any more precious seconds of the night, they run on along the moonlit path, with the distant lights acting as their guide.

They run with all their might to the adjoining village of Mahugiri and, even without looking at each other, they know that each one of them is experiencing the same all-too-familiar tingling feeling that comes before any act of mischief.

Within the next fifteen minutes, they find themselves at the border of Mahugiri and can see the excited commotion of the tamasha in the distance. The catchy drumbeats and the jingling of ghungroos reach their ears. A raised platform in front of a house is hosting the night's cherished guests. The music artistes are important parts of the show, but the real crowd magnet, the very reason the tamasha is such a big deal in the village, is the nacha, whose nimble feet, swaying waist, graceful hand motions, soft, swan-like neck and riveting expressions engage everyone in the story she performs. Astounded by the grace with which she carries herself on the stage, all eyes, including the boys', follow her around, taking in her every movement with rapt attention. But perhaps 'astounded' is a word far too mild for an audience that wild. The men who have swarmed to the tamasha to watch the spectacle are acting like demented baboons—hyperactive, hyperventilating, hyper-everything. The constant whistling, hooting and jeering is expected to continue for the rest of the night.

There is a short break, when the nacha is permitted some rest. While she catches her breath, a burlesque interlude, put up by the lauded Dhamkya, is presented in the form of a monologue before the audience to keep it occupied. A part of the crowd seems interested, and even refreshed with the change in the mood, but the rest couldn't care less for slapstick humour and noisily demand that the dancer return. Bored and waiting on edge for the minutes to pass, the group starts blabbering about the show. The boys listen in.

'You know what? I bet you don't... The nacha all of you have been ogling at...' the man pauses for dramatic effect. It is only when the group starts getting restless does he continue, 'She is...wait for it...wait for it...she isn't a woman at all!' He finishes with a flourish.

All the people within hearing range look at the speaker with wide eyes, gaping.

'You ungrateful rascal! How dare you!' says a drunken friend, much louder than necessary.

'It's true! Believe it if you want to, else get out of my face. She's a transgender, that's what she is. An insider told me,' he fires back. 'You try to open people's eyes, do good for the world, and they...' He mutters something unintelligible. The children, however, are not interested in his gibberish any more. They turn to each other with wide smiles. Their faces are red, caused by a mixture of the heat emanating from the crowded gathering and, of course, unadulterated elation at being able to run away from home to watch the tamasha.

Some spectators who had overheard the conversation have disheartened looks on their faces, the same one would find on the face of a toddler when his favourite toy is taken away. The boys, however, aren't complaining; this has probably been the most extraordinary thing they have witnessed in the 15 years of their existence.

They had already been straining in their places, craning their necks left and right to get a better view, but they agree unanimously to pay—if it is possible—even more attention to the show. An announcement is soon made by the main singer, the shahir, that the audience's patience has been worth its while—the real part of the show is yet to blow them all away. Hoots and whistles erupt from the crowd, rending the night. The boys join in, howling and shouting, having the time of their lives.

The shahir guides them through the story of the nacha's romantic adventures and the boys look on with spellbound concentration, afraid to even blink, seized by the fear of missing out something important.

'*Apsara Aali*,' the shahir echoes in a booming voice.

"Here comes the nymph, down from the heavens,
Bringing with her the colours of dawn; her body is studded with jewels.
Laughing and singing, she lights up the stage.
Here comes the nymph, drenched in the moonlight."

◆

116 *Tamarind Ache*

The night seems to have turned colder as Raghu makes his way home. There's an uncomfortable nip in the air and he finds himself dreading what awaits him. His eyes are overflowing with self-pity and he feels exactly the opposite of how he had a little while ago. Now that the tamasha is over and morning is creeping up on the sky, Raghu doubts fate will be on his side like it was when he had left home the previous night. He somehow calms his heart, which is going crazy with worry, hoping his parents would not have noticed his absence during the night; maybe he can slip inside as quietly as he had slipped out, without disturbing their slumber, and then go back to lying down on the mattress like nothing had happened.

But he has a feeling that that isn't going to be the case. Fear and guilt have him in a vice-like grip, refusing to let go.

Of course, he pretends as if his father's scoldings don't hurt him, as if the beatings don't affect him beyond the physical ache. But they do. And they always would. Baba is his parent, after all. There's no escaping that.

But even though it all does matter, Raghu shoves it aside as an act of defiance against his father for demeaning him, for letting him down countless times, for inflicting so much pain on his mother, for being such a killjoy in everybody's otherwise blithe lives.

Raghu knows, though, that he cannot put all the blame on Baba. He himself has been a nuisance to a lot of people, particularly his parents.

But after last night's outing, he plans to change things. Although he cannot disagree with the fact that what he and his friends had done was fun, he knows that he has been immeasurably out of line this time. So to set things straight, he resolves not to lie to his parents about it—his mother, to begin with, and then when he musters up enough courage, he would tell Baba as well.

For now, how the next hour turns out to be depends entirely on Baba. Raghu feels uncertain; he knows too well that there's only so much Ma can do to rescue him. He has a hunch, and it's not a good one.

Dry leaves crunch under his shuffling feet. Every little sound seems amplified. Every step he takes feels unnaturally heavy. He stares at the closed wooden door ahead of him. He looks at the cracks on the worn wooden door with extreme concentration for the very first time. The door stares back. There are no sounds coming from inside. He starts to think of excuses to save himself from the inevitable misery.

No. No lies.

Just then, he hears the clicking of the latch and the door slowly opens. His mother is standing there with an expression Raghu doesn't quite understand, and ushers him in. Raghu complies as soundlessly as he can.

But the creaky door has done the job. Baba is now wide awake. Raghu closes his eyes, ready for the flogging. The seconds drag on.

'Where were you?' Shiva growls.

A lump forms in Raghu's throat. He tries to speak, but words always seem to desert him when he needs them the most.

'What have you been up to?' His father's fiery eyes drill into him.

'N-nothing. We were just... I mean, I was...' He fumbles

for something acceptable to say. He looks at the floor, as if that's where they will appear to help him out.

'Don't mumble, boy. Look me in the eye and tell me.'

Raghu obeys.

'Now speak.'

'We had gone to the tamasha, Baba.' The words tumble out.

An ominous silence follows for what seems like an eternity.

'Hm...I'd figured as much,' says Shiva. 'You do know you have an exam today?'

'Y-yes, Baba.'

Shiva clears his throat. 'It amazes me sometimes, you know, how small, little things can bother people so much. A fly buzzing in your ear at night, a rainy day that makes you cancel your plans... Things like that. I'm sure you get what I'm talking about. They make me really, really angry.'

Raghu isn't sure where his father is going with this, but he's sure about one thing: whenever parents pretend to be calm about things that otherwise have the potential to get you kicked out of the house, know that you have landed yourself in a mess. And it's not just any common, everyday mess—it is the kind of trouble that sits prickling your conscience, tormenting you, so you never forget what you have done.

'But it's only when it comes to the big issues,' Shiva continues, as plainly as before, 'that you understand what anger really is. Blue bulls feasting on a crop for which you poured out your sweat and blood, your father dying before your own eyes as you helplessly look on, your son not abiding by anything he's ever told to do, your wife...' His voice falters. He glances at Yashoda for a moment, who is sitting in one corner and pretending not to exist, and then looks at the ceiling, clearly pained. 'And when the big issues keep happening over and over again, day in and day out, that's when you lose control.'

Sadness washes over Raghu; the feeling is so strong that it wipes away all trace of fear from his heart. He doesn't believe it at first but he feels like what he's channeling towards Shiva is pity. The person sitting in front of him doesn't look like the fuming image he has of his father. Instead, he sees a man who has lost a great deal, a man who has been pushed around too much. He sees a man who, sometime in the future, he could even befriend. Not for his own sake but solely for the man's, so he can finally have someone he can rely on, someone he can share his smiles with, a shoulder he can cry on.

'I truly believe that there is a better world out there, on the other side of the village boundary. I wanted you to go and study there when you grew up, but I see that the chances of that happening are close to nil. Maybe you know it already—I think you do—but let me remind you anyway that you're, by far, the *sole* reason my temper ever flares. And since you happen to live under the same roof as I do, that happens every hour, every minute, every second of the day, every day.'

Raghu feels the pang of newfound shame hit him hard. He wants to fall on his father's feet and weep, telling him how very sorry he is, but he also wants to walk up to him and hug him like nobody's ever hugged him before.

However, all he manages to do is mutter a subdued apology and say that he genuinely means it this time.

'Oh, please. You don't need to put on that I-am-from-this-instant-a-changed-boy act any more. My worries end tonight,' Baba beams, or rather, tries to. It seems forced to Raghu. 'I've thought about it, and I've come up with the perfect solution.'

Raghu waits to hear about this genius plan, eager to know how he can help.

Instead, Baba grabs him tightly by the arm and stands staring at Ma for a while. As for her, she looks like her worst fears have just come true.

Raghu isn't feeling very good about this. Is Baba going to lock him up? Is he going to beat him so that Ma, or anyone at all, can't save him? Is he going to starve him?

All of a sudden, Yashoda breaks down. 'Please! My poor child! Don't do this to him, please! I know he's committed mistakes, lots of them, but this isn't how to deal with it! Oh god, please, listen to me. He's just a boy,' she wails, as she tries to get Baba's hands off him.

'I can't handle him any more, Yashoda. He's a rotten little scoundrel, and it's all your fault! Who told you to treat him like a pet, huh? "You can do that; it's okay, dear; it doesn't matter",' he does a bad mimicry of her in falsetto.

His iron grip on Raghu's arm doesn't loosen; his muscles tense and his fingernails turn white.

The noise has awoken the neighbourhood, and to make the already awful situation worse, Raghu now has an interested audience, ready as always for a tamasha.

Both Raghu and his mother know that this time, Shiva will neither hear, nor see reason. Raghu has given up, surrendering himself to the mercy of the man he calls 'Baba' and letting go of the couple of strands of optimism that he'd been holding on to all this time. His mother, however, keeps fighting gallantly, trying to hold her husband back, trying to break his unyielding grip on her son's arms, calling for help from the whispering onlookers. Trying and trying.

'It's too late now. He has left me no other option. It'll either be him or me in this house.'

Baba shoves him out of the door. Raghu trips and falls on all fours, scraping his hands and knees, bleeding from where the gravel has rubbed against his skin too hard.

But it doesn't hurt there, not at all. Where it does hurt is in the core of his chest. It almost feels like somebody's spiteful fingers are wrapped around his throat, squeezing with all their might. Oxygen seems to have left his lungs—he can't seem to be able to breathe.

That's when the realization of what's actually happening hits him. He can't even begin to imagine what his tomfoolery has cost him this time. What has he done? He starts to get up on his feet, crying. He looks at his father, his vision blurry, and sees a man so wounded that he has turned into a monster. There is nothing that can be done now. This time, Baba will not sway.

'Baba, just...please just don't...' He chokes through incessant sobs. 'I swear I won't do a single thing to disappoint you ever again. Just...let me stay. I'll be good, I promise. All of my energy... I'll use all of my energy the right way, your way. I'll...I'll do anything you want me to... I'll make you proud... Please...let me just stay, please. I won't...won't be able to...to live without you both, Baba. Where will I go?'

'Look here, listen,' Ma pleads with watery, yet determined

eyes. 'Your head is not in the right place. He's the sweetest, kindest boy a mother could ever want; all you need to do is give him another chance. Just one more chance to prove himself to you; the Lord Almighty is witness, and I know he won't let you down.'

Shiva does nothing; he just stands there, filling the doorway with his mighty frame and looking down at Raghu unblinkingly. Nobody has the courage to stand up to him. His eyes are red, brimming with anger and tears.

Raghu knows what he's thinking. *That ship's already sailed.*

He thinks back to the day he had put itching fronds on the teacher's chair. That day when he had received heaps of compliments from his friends about how genius his brainwave was. That day his parents had been called to school and told about the last warning he was being given before they would throw him out. He remembers all the days he had let his father down. His father's reaction had been a gradient from disappointed to angry to disappointed again. Through all these instances, his father had shown no signs of reconciliation—but Raghu hadn't tried either.

'Where did I lack?' Shiva says softly, almost talking to himself. The silence stretches on. His eyes go from furious to sorrowful. He looks down at his feet, deep in thought.

'Here you are, coming back home at dawn. Trust me, I've thought about it a lot, but I can't seem to understand, I am not even close.' He finally looks up at Raghu. 'I can't comprehend what you want to achieve through your actions. Tell me, Raghu,' he says, staring at him hard, 'what *do* you get from doing all this? Amusement? Thrill? Satisfaction? Oh, I'm sure that's it. You feed off the satisfaction of sucking the very life out of me, you little demon. I gave you everything you needed that was within my power and means, didn't I? I think I deserve to know why you turned out to be so crooked. Look at you! You're such a deplorable, useless creature! I had so many hopes, so many dreams from you, but you...' he heaves, 'you squashed them all. *You* are at fault for what's happening right now, Raghu, not me. If people didn't know otherwise, nobody would believe that it's my blood that courses through your veins.'

Shiva takes deep breaths to calm himself. He steps forward. 'Every child is precious, Raghu. Every child is a gem. But you're no commonplace boy. You are a curse. You're a disaster waiting to happen. Tell me, Raghu, where did I lack?'

Shiva spits out all the poison that has built up in him over the years. His eyes pool over. Yashoda's tears silently run down her cheeks, as she stands behind her towering husband. Her current situation can be perfectly condensed into one word—devastation. Shiva never had much love for Yashoda, and she knows that. But she had her children. Once Kavita had left, Raghu had been the force that drove her through the day, every day. But now that he is being made to leave too, Yashoda's life seems to have lost all meaning and purpose.

When Raghu doesn't speak, Shiva heads back into the house. He emerges a few moments later with all of Raghu's belongings that he can collect in one handful, and throws them on the ground. 'Well, there you have it. You've caused enough damage here. Now you can't do anything more. You don't know how good it feels to see you so powerless. Don't dare to step inside my house before you make something of yourself—if you do, that is. Good luck. And goodbye.'

The door bangs shut on his face. Raghu can hear his mother's muffled cries and pleas still coming from inside. The spectators murmur among themselves for a while but, soon, even they start to go back to their homes to get a few more hours of sleep before they start their day. It hurts Raghu to see how the world is already moving on without him, like his absence doesn't even matter to anybody. He has been feeling that way a lot lately.

He feels numb all over.

'What you lacked was love, Baba,' he whispers. Raghu doesn't sound anything remotely like his usual rampageous self.

'You lacked love,' he sobs.

Raghu sits by the front steps of the house in a daze. For how long, he doesn't know.

Dadi, who is still deep in sleep, has not a hint of an idea that she probably won't see her grandson in this life again.

Once the situation starts to sink in, Raghu picks up his only belongings in the world and sits underneath a street lamp, thinking about what to do next.

He considers knocking on his friends' doors, but then thinks the better of it. That way he'll have to encounter his parents, especially Baba, pretty often, and that doesn't seem like a very good idea.

Now what?

His head is a mixture of emotions—sorrow, panic, exhaustion, regret. Guilt. Every bad memory of his life comes rushing into his mind. Raghu realizes with a start that all of them involve Baba in one way or another.

Just then, he feels a tingling at the back of his mind. *What had Baba said? 'There's a better world out there, on the other side of the village boundary.'*

That's it. That's what he'll do. He'll take a bus to Bhimpur and start from scratch. He'll go to Haridas's dhaba. He'll find work there. He'll beg, if all else fails. But he'll survive.

◆

Raghu sits on top of the haystack, legs folded, staring wide-eyed at the ground. His belongings lie in his lap. The refreshing morning breeze blowing from near the gulmohar tree gently nudges him out of his daze. He cracks his knuckles and rolls his shoulders; he has a mission to pull off.

The dusty bus screeches to a stop, its exhaust pipe sending a blast of gas and smoke right in Raghu's face. He chokes, but stays put. He's in the perfect position to execute his plan—the ladder attached to the back of the bus is just half a foot away from him. He waits till the engine roars back to life, and then some more.

Of course, if he had the money, he would have bought a ticket, but since he doesn't, Raghu is more than happy to add another accomplishment to his résumé.

Okay, it starts in three...two... Raghu lunges for one of the rungs with one hand, holding his possessions in the other. It's a close call, but he manages to get a grip tight enough to keep him dangling above the ground. With a final effort, he manages to latch on firmly, all four limbs secure on the metal ladder, and starts climbing.

Once he gets to the top of the bus, he squeezes in between the metal bars running across the length of the roof and holds on for dear life as the bus speeds away to what is to be his new home.

10
Reminisces

You did well, don't worry about it. That boy was a pest.
But he's your son, your own flesh and blood. How could you?

All that he ever would have done is sit around and do nothing anyway. How would that have made you feel? At least you don't have to see him waste away now.

What if it's you who's at fault? You were never the father you should've been to him. You know Yashoda is right, he's just a boy. There's still time. Bring him back inside, talk it out. This isn't the way it has to be.

No way. It's done. No more thinking about it.

You first lost her, Shiva. Now you're losing him too.

Walking back to his mattress, Shiva feels a terrible ache growing inside him, spreading like a black splotch of venom, tearing him from the inside out, burning his soul.

Do well, Raghu.

He lies down and turns to face the wall, not wanting anything to remind him of what he has just done, of what has been happening over all these years. His warped life has, somehow, managed to become even more twisted—a cloud without a silver lining. He has failed to handle the only thing that matters in the end—the people he loves. He wants to forget every minute of the past two decades that have gone by, about the misery he has inflicted and undergone. About the person he has become.

He's your one chance, Shiva. One chance to right the wrongs. Do it for yourself, if not for him. Take him back.

He can hear Yashoda wailing but he can't make out what she's saying. He tries to focus on the words, but they seem hazy. She seems to be in a different world altogether.

All these years, it was not that he didn't love Raghu—he loved him too much. So much that every scrape felt like a razor wound and every caress an elixir. The scrapes just happened to be more than what he could handle. He'd raised his hopes so high that when they fell, they bled to death, permanently scarring him.

It's not like I would've benefited. I did it all for him.

But what he doesn't want to admit, even to himself, is the irony of it all. He did all that he had done for Raghu so that he could do well, like...like *her*—even thinking about her hurts—so that he could make money and settle down, have a satisfying life and just be happy; something he himself had miserably failed at. But he knows it was more for his own sake, to convince himself that raising his son would be the one thing he would do right. Here they are, though—he, the villainous father, and Raghu, the homeless son.

He wishes he could go back to the days when life wasn't so damn wicked, when looking back didn't feel so suffocating; he wants to go back to the time when life was, impossibly, a friend, not a fiend.

He thinks about the time he had with Suchita, the sweet seconds that had ticked by ever so slowly. His memory snakes its way back through the years, to the web-laden details of his distant past, back to the days when she used to grace the school with her presence. He remembers the way her long, thin hands enveloped her study gear as she made her way across the stony pathway and into class. He recalls how Suchita's deer-like grace used to fascinate him, how her glossy black hair used to shine in the sun, how her perfect hazel eyes could hypnotize anyone, how her petite frame made her look almost breakable, and yet how strong she really was; how her wit used to flabbergast everyone but unnerve him at the same time, how her comicality caused him to laugh his lungs out, how her simplicity made him melt, and how she was someone to learn from in almost every way.

She used to live with her maternal uncle but she wasn't from anywhere around. She had, in fact, shifted with her mother from a place called Gondipur when her father had passed away. Interestingly enough, Shiva and Suchita had first bonded over this very truth—neither of them had known the love of a father. Her uncle had given her everything, of course, and she was grateful, but it wasn't quite the same.

When the school ran out of grades, the one in Mahugiri

saw the arrival of the few who'd decided to study more; Suchita was one of them, Shiva was not.

Aah, I should have gone too.

It was only later that this decision had come back to bite him.

At that time, though, the sole reason for him to be upset was that he would have to spend those many school hours away from Suchita, though he sought solace in the fact that, at least, at the end of the day, he had someone he could go to, share the happenings of the day with, laugh and prattle with.

But then, as gradual as the process was, the most terrible thing had happened. Suchita had become successful.

She had been dogged about pursuing medicine ever since he'd known her, her eyes fixed on the doctor's coat. It was more than any girl—or boy, for that matter—from their cluster of villages had ever aspired to be.

She'd sprinted up to him one evening with feverish hysteria, wanting to spill it all out, but not knowing where to start. When she broke the news to him—she'd managed to get accepted into a top-ranking college in Bhimpur—Shiva didn't know how to react. Of course, he was happy for her—but Bhimpur?

'H-how long?' Shiva had blurted out, catching Suchita off-guard.

'Hmm? What?'

'For how long will you be gone?'

'Five years,' she'd replied, somewhat apologetically.

'F-five years?' Shiva's voice had faltered. 'Isn't that too much? Don't you know enough already?'

'It doesn't work that way, silly,' she'd laughed. 'Don't you worry, I'll make it a point to keep bothering everyone here with my letters and visits.'

'I'll miss you,' he'd said, his voice quivering. Till date, he doesn't think she'd taken note of how deeply he meant those words. He still believes that if she had, she would've stayed.

Who am I kidding.

'I know. I will miss you too,' she'd replied, and then added with a wink, 'if I get the time, that is.'

Shiva had just looked on, for Suchita seemed to be awfully pleased with what she was doing. He'd worried for her, though. Would she be able to manage in the concrete jungle alone?

When he'd asked her this, she'd retorted mockingly, 'Need I remind you, mister, that I'm a fully grown, independent woman who knows quite well how to fend for herself.' But then, something in her had loosened up and she'd said, softly, 'Please don't worry. I'll be fine, I promise.'

She had told him how the idea of a city with smooth, straight roads lined with concrete buildings daunted her too, but that she couldn't think of a life that didn't include a proper job that earned her enough money and satisfied her need to be useful in the world. She had to do this—she really had no choice.

A feeble 'okay' was all he could muster then, his lips forming a weak smile.

The day she had had to leave dawned sooner than Shiva had expected. He'd been looking forward to spending at least a month more with Suchita before she left for half a decade. As the bus had driven away, and her beaming mother and uncle had waved from the edge of the road, Shiva had stayed hidden behind the gulmohar tree that marked the stop, trying his best to keep his knees from buckling.

Once Suchita had left, life for Shiva had become a dreary, grey smear, deprived of all the joyful colours her company had brought. Waking up with the sun, working all through the day till he couldn't feel his legs, coming back home, eating, sleeping, and then waking up again the next day to do the same things all over again—this was what his life had become without Suchita, mechanical and meaningless.

A few months after her departure, Suchita's mother couldn't bear being away from her daughter any longer and insisted on going to the city. She talked of nothing else. She would work as a domestic help if she had to, she'd said, if that meant she could stay with her daughter. Her relentless whines had finally convinced her brother and he had let her leave the following morning without saying a word to anyone else.

How Shiva had wished he could do the same.

◆

One fine day, Shiva's restlessness had aggravated beyond all measure. His field was far out, on the periphery of the forest. Blue bulls had invaded the area the night before, feasting on Shiva's soya bean crop, leaving only the ruined stubs as a surprise for him in the morning. The farmers had been aware—they had, in fact, planned to build a fence to keep the animals out, but it had still been in the initial stages and hadn't been fully thought out. So without anything to stop them, the bulls had laid to waste Shiva's days of hard toil.

One look at the trampled field, and something had snapped inside Shiva. Without wasting even a minute, he'd caught the first bus to the Forest Department office. He'd jogged into the bottle-green building and asked a couple of people for the Range Forest Officer's room. Following a few vague directions, he'd found it and barged straight into the shabby office.

'Sir, help me. Please, sir. The blue bulls, those abhorrent creatures, have eaten up my crop, sir, and that was my only way to earn. Do something, sir, they're big trouble for everyone in Nimkhedi. I say just kill the beasts in cold blood, sir. The whole problem will get solved in the blink of an eye. I will get compensation, right, sir?'

'Calm down, mister, calm down. First, we can't just kill animals like that—it's against the law. Secondly, you surely will get your compensation. However, you must do as I say.'

Shiva had looked on as the officer broke into a mechanical drone of instructions, almost as if he'd rehearsed those very words on countless farmers before.

'Bring a written application, along with a picture of the blue bull inside your field. Mind you, the picture must also depict a landmark of your field, so that we know it's yours and that you're not trying to pull off a fraud here.'

'A picture? This doesn't make any sense. How do you expect me to do that? I'm sure the wretched thing won't conveniently pose beside a landmark for a photograph.'

'I'm telling you what I have told everyone else. These are the orders that I got. There's nothing I can do about it, I'm sorry.'

'But what if...'

'No ifs or buts, please. Now if you'll excuse me, I have to get back to work. Please leave.'

Devastated, he'd walked back to the bus stop and sourly waited for his ride back home. He'd had no choice then but to hunt for work; the next sowing season was still a long time away. It was late afternoon by the time he had managed to get the job of a labourer with a meagre pay, but he had been in no condition to turn it down. He'd been looking all day and had known that was the best he'd ever get.

Reaching home, he'd found a letter waiting for him. He remembers how he'd felt the blood rush to his face. He'd thanked god then, for it was from Suchita. The day hadn't fared that dismally after all. He had sat himself down on a chair and started to read.

It had clearly been written in high spirits, in the eagerness to get the message across. The hurriedly misspelt words had been scribbled off and the handwriting was not nearly as calligraphic as he'd remembered it to be. Shiva could almost see Suchita smile through the letter, hear her laugh.

My dearest Shiva,

I crave you.

I feel alone. I mean, I do have friends and oh so much work, but what are they compared to your company?

Shiva had read the words over and over again. He'd touched the paper, run his fingers over the words, which seemed almost embossed, and giggled like a girl. He had often teased her about the excessive pressure she applied on the pen when writing. 'You know, even if I close my eyes, I can read what you've written. I just need to run my fingertips over the words,' he would say. 'Oh, come on, it's not *that* bad,' she would reply in mock anger.

He had sniggered like he had back then.

Anyway, the holidays are coming up and you have no idea how much I'm longing to come back home. The thing is, I've still got mountains of work to do and I have no clue how to manage without putting in late hours too. It might sound like it, but I'm not complaining, trust me. I've wanted this for so long, I can't believe I'm actually here.

Hey, I know just what to do. How about you come visit me? That'll be great! My god, I'm a genius.

Her exact address had been mentioned below. Of the two of them, she had always been the organized one.

Also, I almost forgot to mention. Be a darling and get a box of sesame laddoos for me, will you? I can't find them anywhere here.

I hope I see you soon!

Love,

Suchita

When Shiva was done reading, he had kept staring at the floor and smiling like an idiot. He'd hidden the envelope beneath a pile of clothes, wanting to keep it to himself. He hadn't heard from her since the day she'd left, and it had felt like Suchita had forgotten about life in the village. Until that moment. His smile had widened as he'd realized that his future wife was on her way to becoming an awe-inspiring doctor.

And, there he was, a small-time farmer who couldn't even handle a few plants. How could he possibly be good enough for Suchita?

'No,' he'd thought, 'no more of these thoughts.'
He would go to bed, and that would be it.

◈

Hff.

He had let out a long, deep breath as the bus had started for Bhimpur. He wanted to shout out Suchita's name in his excitement. He could feel his heartbeat grow faster; it was so loud he could almost hear it.

He was on his way to the city. To Suchita. Finally, after a year and a half, he would get to see her pretty face again. He could hardly wait. He almost felt like singing out loud and dancing around the bus. Instead, all he could actually do was fiddle with his fingers and then with the hem of his kurta. He'd been sitting at a window seat, facing the full lashing of the equally excited wind. He'd squinted at the sun, which glared down at him, but he had been determined to spot the first signs of the city. Whenever he'd felt like they were in the proximity of one, he would dart out of his place and stand in front of the bus's door ready to get off. When it turned out that it was not Bhimpur, he would sheepishly ask the conductor 'How much more time?' and then, on getting an exasperated reply, would walk back to his seat. The cycle had continued, till finally, the bus had reached.

Shiva had wasted no time—not a single second—in jumping out.

◈

Back at his village, the next few days had passed in slow, moping cycles, until one last blow had slammed him into the pits of dejection. An announcement had been made. A man pounding a spoon on a metal plate had been made to shout at the top of his voice, informing all villagers of a job opening. Anyone who had passed the tenth grade and was willing to work as a forest guard was to assemble at the gram panchayat office the following morning.

Shiva's heart had sunk. His crop had been destroyed by the wild, roving varmints, he was stuck in a pretty much useless place and, as the announcement had made clear, he wasn't even good enough for the job of a low-ranking guard.

For some reason, he had thought of Suchita then. There she was, a strong, self-sufficient woman in a big, formidable city, busy flourishing; and there he was, a lost cause, frantically trying to put the pieces of his fragmented life together.

This is what we've boiled down to? Social status, of all things?

He had decided to not go to work that day; he would tell his employer that he had fallen sick. He had sat in his room, mulling over his sad state of affairs.

Don't. Even. Think about it.

Oh, come on, it's the obvious thing to do.

You're in love. So is she. What you have is magical; it's hard to come by. Don't ruin it.

Ruin it? What's there to ruin? She's out there in the big city and you are here. You two barely talk. She'd said she would write to you but, guess what—she's busy.

Pause. Wash your face. Then slap yourself hard a couple

of times and get to work. This is stupid. You are being stupid.

No, wait. It's only rational. Half the time you don't even know what you are doing. Maybe she has realized that too.

Then why would she have called you to visit her? She seemed excited to see you, didn't she? Let's end this now.

That's exactly my point. You have to end it. She's not even your type, and you know it too. She's always blabbering about stuff you aren't even interested in. Her college canteen? Really? And what was she thinking when she introduced you to her friends in English? She knows you're not comfortable with the language.

Okay, now you're just making things up. You love listening to her stories—what are you talking about? And it's not like she asked you to speak English, she was the one talking.

You have never really fancied her much anyway. And now, it's like she doesn't even care any more. You're strangers. She clearly doesn't want to trouble her precious mind with your small world. Don't you get it? That's why she hasn't been writing!

What rubbish! What is even wrong with you? Are you sick? Of course, you must be sick. Everything is going perfectly alright, Shiva. Then why are you so set on fabricating a catastrophe out of happy times?

He had got up from that spot after a long time, though he couldn't tell how long. He had walked to the door, only to discover the sun already on its way behind the hills. His mother had been sitting on the doorstep, staring at the purple sky.

Shiva had taken in a deep breath. Yes, he had thought about it hard enough. His decision was a sensible one. There had been no doubt in his mind. Sure, it would be hard, not just for him but for both of them, but it would be for the best. As he had sat thinking about it, he had wondered how it hadn't come up for so long.

'Oh, so you're finally up! Are you okay? Or do you not plan to answer me yet?'

'Yes, I'm fine, Ma.'

'Well, what was all that about, then?' She'd raised her eyebrows, anxious.

'I want to get married.'

'Oh Shiva, you've finally said the magic words! I'll start looking for a girl right away.' There had been a certain curiosity on her face. 'But why this sudden decision?'

'Just be quick about whatever you do, okay? I'm going out. I won't have dinner, so don't wait for me.'

He had stomped away from the scene of crime, where he had ruthlessly just slaughtered his own heart. He'd wanted to head to some place, any place, where he could bury the corpse. He had kept walking, searching for somewhere he could pour his misery out. Hot tears had gushed down his angry face.

He had kept walking till he had reached the edge of the village. He had thought he could sit down there but people were still milling around. His strides had kept getting longer and his pace had kept increasing in his desperation to get away. But soon, he had not been able to contain himself any more and had sat down and cried like a child. His legs rebelled from walking so far so quickly but Shiva had got up and kept moving. Where he had been heading to, he hadn't known.

The sky had become dark and fog had settled on the ground, covering everything under its malicious blanket. The night was cool and the silence pressed against Shiva's eardrums, but the pain he felt inside him had raged harder than ever, louder than ever, deafening him, defeating him.

He had kept walking until he had found a spot for himself that was so untouched he could call it his own. It had been on the far side of the forest that stretched over the hills. An old tamarind tree had stood at the edge of a small crater, too big to be called a depression but too small to be called a pit. The withered trunk of the tree had blended in almost seamlessly with the edge of the crater, creating a perfect backrest.

How such a wonderful place had been left untouched by the human race he did not know; humans, in his mind, barely let go of any chance at sabotaging natural beauty, not caring that this very attitude would lead to their ultimate destruction.

Shiva had thought, back then, surprised by the accidental comparison, that Suchita's case was not too different. She was to him like any other miracle of nature, and he, thus, felt that she needed to be protected from him. They unquestionably had to stay apart, because his closeness to her would most certainly lead to her ruin.

Shiva realizes now that he hasn't been there in a while. He really feels like spending the day there, just like old times.

He had gone to the tree so many times after that day to sit quietly in its solitude. He knows he has never really been a people's person, but after his marriage to Yashoda, he had receded even further into his shell.

Yashoda, his wife, was a responsible, youthful woman. She was jovial, selfless, good at household chores and skilled at work on the field too. She was dedicated to him and good to his mother, and was always trying to come up with new ways to please him. But she wasn't *her*, the one who refused to get out of his head, no matter how hard he tried, the one who tormented his sleep at night, the one he wished could be by his side. No matter how impeccable his wife was, she wasn't Suchita, and could never be. He tried to humour her, though, but how long could he keep the show up? Nothing made sense any more—and the artificial life with Yashoda was no exception.

That day, after his marriage, he had pressed the bottom of the brown glass bottle so forcefully against his palm that it had left a deep, painful impression.

What did I tell you? Don't do it.

He had thought about it then, like he had on countless other occasions, and taken a big swig of the bitter, intoxicating liquid. His throat had burnt but he had taken another gulp.

Don't you dare start again. It's been done, and it's for the best.

He sighs, pulling the ratty blanket over his face. His finding that spot had been quite a coincidence, but he had always believed it had been created especially for him. Whenever life had felt like tumultuous waves, that place had been his shore; it calmed him, helped him think. The fresh air, the withering tree, the sailing clouds, all content in their own existence, oblivious to the chaos that raged inside him. They reminded him that no matter what happened to him, life would move on; that even if he was going through the worst of times, the world would still be the same—the sun would rise every day, the moon and the stars would continue to shine, birds would sing, and that no matter what his own problems were, the rest of the world would be happy. It made him realize that there were things far greater than himself, which made his problems seem trivial. Almost.

11
Stiff

'RAGHU! I'M LEAVING!'
'Coming!'
He leaps down the stairs, taking them two at a time. Haridas is standing in the evening sun, straining to look at him come out the door.

'Yes, Dada.'

'You know what to do. Lock the door at night, okay? Don't forget. And if Rasul comes in even a minute late tomorrow, give him a couple of whacks.'

Raghu sniggers.

'I'll be back tomorrow evening. You take care, boy. Keep an eye on the place.'

'Don't worry about it.' He waves, as the man walks across the road, away from this home and towards that which now seems so far removed from Raghu.

'I'll tell your mother you said hello!' the man yells from afar.

'Thank you, Dada!'

He smiles, waving at Haridas, the man he owes everything to.

He walks back in, through the mostly empty tables, through another small door and into the kitchen at the back, where he's greeted with the sound of the exhaust fan whirring against the strains from an old Bollywood song, seeking dominance over it. A young boy in a dirty brown vest is blocking his view to what's cooking on the stove.

'What are you making, Rasul?'

'Oh! You scared me! Has Dada left?'

'Yes. What're you making?'

'Naan. You want some? Come make some.'

'Always the rascal,' Raghu shakes his head. 'Serve all the customers, then we'll see. Don't stretch it, we'll have some time before the moon comes out.'

'Yes, boss,' Rasul salutes.

Rasul, who is Rehan's elder brother, has been working for Dada ever since he'd inaugurated the dhaba; it would be incomplete without him.

Rasul continues with his work, alongside his singing, while Raghu sits down at the top of the stairs and rests his head against the wall.

He has so often wondered what it would be like if he were to tag along with Dada sometime on his trips to Nimkhedi. He wonders if Baba will be happy to see him. He wonders if things could ever go back to the way they were.

It had been exactly three years that he had left home. He had known Dada as Haridas back then. Dada had unquestioningly taken him in, provided him with all that he had needed—a roof, food, clothes, even a job. Raghu now washes the dishes at the dhaba for ₹120, although he knows that's just a formality. Dada has even been helping pay his school fees.

On top of that jolting bus, while trying to keep his hold steady on the iron rails, Raghu had realized something. It had just clicked, fallen into place. He had remembered what his headmaster had said about lotuses. He had remembered the neat wooden boards put up in every classroom back in school. 'Education is power.'

Power. That's what he would need to be able to look his father in the eye again.

He remembers the surprise on Dada's face when he'd told him he would be enrolling himself in a school.

'I don't understand you, Raghu. I mean, good, it's great, but... I don't understand you,' he had said, smiling and shaking his head.

Raghu knows that he can never repay Dada's debts.

'Oye!'

'Huh?' Raghu looks up.

Rasul is holding two cups of tea and looking down at him.

'You brought me tea.'

'See? I'm not such a rascal, after all,' Rasul grins.

'Hmm.'

They sit two steps apart, sipping silently.

'Dada has gone to the village after a very long time,' Rasul tries to start a conversation. 'I wonder what news he'll bring this time around.'

'I don't see how it matters, really.'

Sip. Sip. Sip.

'It was today, wasn't it?' asks Rasul.

'Yes.'

'What does it feel like? I never could bring myself to ask you, but... What does it feel like?'

'It's fine. I guess I deserved it.'

'You know you don't mean that.'

'I know I do.'

'Anybody there?' a voice calls out from somewhere below.

'Well, I guess the moon is out.' Raghu clears his throat, springing to his feet and—*thump!*—hitting his head on the ceiling.

'Oh, ouch, that must have hurt. Your life is a mess, isn't it?' sniggers Rasul.

'Like I said, always the rascal.'

◈

Twenty-four hours later, Raghu finds himself sitting on the floor with his head between his knees, trying to block everything out. He feels Haridas pat his head on the back and walk away silently, leaving him with his thoughts.

He imagines Ma back at home, lying on the cot with her eyes closed. Just lying there. The skin under her droopy eyes would've darkened even more, her sleep, earlier disturbed, would have by now been driven away completely by blood-spewing coughs. His father had sold everything he could have, including their land, Haridas had told Raghu, to collect money for her treatment. Raghu imagines Baba sitting close beside her, or pacing up and down the room, tense, trying to think of something that can make her better, something he hasn't already thought of, his mind as empty as the house he's in.

Ma is sick. She has never been this sick before. Baba can do nothing more; there's no one else he can approach, nowhere he can go. All anyone can do now is wait.

Neither Haridas, nor Rasul come to check on him, or to ask if he wants dinner; they know better than to disturb his solitude—and he is grateful.

Raghu has never known anybody quite like his Ma. She had been a good mother, of course, but he had also found in her a fierce friend. Besides him and Kavita, she was about the only other person who truly knew what it was like to fall prey to Baba's outbreaks. All those years they had spent saving each other's necks from the guillotine of his cusses, thinking of ways to rescue each other from his bashes; all those years together in arms; and here they are now, kilometres apart... Defeated, after all those years of perseverance.

He gets up and lets himself drop down on his bed.

He doesn't think it fair of the universe to make a person so lovely fall this sick. His longing for her sweet kisses, her warm caresses, has never been so strong. All he wants to do is run into her arms and stay there forever. He misses her so much, it physically hurts.

He's sweating, but he covers his head with the sheet anyway. He hasn't felt this low since his grandmother passed away the previous year.

He imagines a parallel world, one where everything is exactly as it should be—exactly like it isn't in this one. Ma comes into the room, fit as a fiddle, and serves Baba tea and biscuits. She then sits down on the ground too and the three of them have a nice, hearty conversation. They talk about how it would be great if Kavita could be with them that moment. And although she can't hear much, Dadi pitches in too. Baba asks Raghu how his day has been because he actually cares. Raghu tells him how he did wonderfully at a test in school and Baba pats him on the back. Baba loves the tea and makes it a point to tell Ma that. He imagines his parents exchanging smiles between sentences, conveying unsaid things. Baba cracks a joke and the happy little family laughs till their stomachs ache.

Raghu giggles. Oh, what glorious days they could've had. All the *could haves* and *should haves* are killing him. He would give the world to live that life.

He has no idea how late into the night it is, or if it's late at all. He stretches his memory as if to remember a blurry dream, right back to the time Baba used to sit him on his shoulders and walk around the village. A dream, that's what it seems like now. Raghu used to wave at everyone, teasing them about how short they were. Mischief had been a good friend back then.

'I guess it's alright when you're a kid,' he thinks.

He is reminded of his friends then, how naive they had all been. He hopes, not for the first time, that at least the drama that his life is has taught them to mend their ways. It sure did teach him.

Raghu doesn't feel like going to school the next day. It's not a question of sincerity—he just knows he won't be able to pay attention. And the people... There isn't anything particularly wrong with them—they're all just quite dull. The fact that he had been thrown out of his house and now works at a dhaba is too much for their puny little minds to comprehend, because all they ever do is point at him and talk in whispers like he's some sort of a museum exhibit. He's sure he'll have red eyes the next morning, which he knows will just make matters worse... Funny how it has to be this way when he's finally trying to change.

He remembers what Rasul had said the previous day. *Your life is a mess, isn't it?*

If it is, so be it. How much worse can it get?

◆

Brrrr.

From his brain to the world, everything's vibrating. He sees the sun dipping behind the hills; it's been a while since he's seen it do that. Even though it's hard to open his eyes against the wind, he sees lights in the distance from his window. Lights he has come to fear, but lights he has been dreaming of every night nonetheless. But these aren't the circumstances he had planned to see them again in.

Ansh's hand rests on Raghu's shoulder and a resigned smile finds its way to his haggard face. His partner-in-crime has changed so much, it's almost disturbing. He turns back to see Rehan staring blankly at the seat in front of him. Just having them around in such a time is comforting, and Raghu is grateful for their presence. It's nice of them to have come all the way to fetch him.

They're getting closer and closer.

Halt.

Palak is waiting under the gulmohar tree. They all walk to his house in silence. What a long, long walk it is, like a pilgrimage, except that there's nothing holy about it. It's far from any sort of piety. But there is peace, yes. Peace that follows wreckage.

There she is, lying on the cot. His Ma. Just like he remembers, but not quite the same. He has cried over this woman for more nights than he can remember.

'Raghu...' he hears Baba whisper.

She has become a little old. Faint wrinkles have encroached on her beautiful face. She looks tired, though—he doesn't quite remember exhaustion ever being reflected on her face.

She's wearing her favourite sari—blue with multicoloured flowers. She seems stiff, almost like she's uncomfortable with all those eyes on her.

He still can't believe that she is right there, in front of him. After so many nights of longing to be in her embrace, he can finally touch her, but he can't seem to be able to move. Without warning, tears trace a path down his cheeks; he is surprised he still has some to spare. She has taken up too big a chunk of his sorrow, too big a piece of his heart; it's unfair.

And yet, he cries.

He cries because he's lost her. He cries because he couldn't be there for her, not even *with* her. He cries because he never got a chance to say goodbye, because he'd been forced to miss her even before she was gone.

Gone, that's what she is now. This is what reality is going to be like from now. Him minus her.

He cries because he simply doesn't know what else to do.

◆

He sees his little boy, almost a man now, on his knees, weeping, clutching her hand. Something crumples inside him, and Shiva doesn't know what to do with the emptiness he feels inside. The knowledge that he has more than contributed to his son's anguish fills him with self-loathing. A deep-rooted revulsion for his own self clutches him, numbing his senses, but amplifying the pain.

He has blood on his hands. Yashoda was doing fine when Raghu was home; it was only later that things started to go downhill. He had separated a sick mother from her son. What had he done?

The scene triggers more wails from the village women. Kavita breaks down all over again.

All he wants to do is hold his son in his arms, but he knows their relationship is not as simple as that.

'Goodbye, Ma,' he hears Raghu say, as he gets up on feet, walking right past Shiva into his sister's embrace.

Oh, hell.

He takes a step towards Raghu, when he hears a voice: 'It's time, Shiva.' Sitaram looks at him and nods.

The procession.

As he lifts his wife's limp body, he understands the true

depth of his loss. As he lays her down on the last bed she'll ever know, a wooden platform built to carry her, he realizes what she had meant to him. To all of them. As he walks with the body on his shoulders, helped by three other men, the village following close behind, he for the first time appreciates the true burden life will be without her. As they set her down on the logs, the full blow of his loss hits him.

And as the malicious flames lick hungrily at her skin against the starless night, the little fortitude he has left in him withers away and he succumbs, inconsolably, to the devastation.

◈

Raghu is leaning against the trunk, talking to Kavita, squinting against the early-morning rays. He's grown taller, more confident. He's sobered up, undoubtedly, but he looks like he's been frowning too much. Shiva has never seen that expression on his son's face before, except…except when he was to blame.

'This can be undone. You just have to ask.'

He knows Raghu's peripheral vision has detected him coming. He also knows he's trying hard not to look at him directly. And he does a good job of it too, except for one little slip. Shiva can sense Raghu becoming edgy as he gets closer, can almost see every inch of his son screaming at him to stay away. Raghu is only just pretending to be listening to what Kavita is saying; Shiva knows all his attention is really on him.

But when he stands beside him, Raghu's nerves dissipate. He draws on some inner reserve, straightens up, looks at Shiva and acknowledges him. 'Baba.' The word takes him by surprise.

'Raghu.'

Kavita just stands there.

'Where are you going this early?' Shiva asks.

'Back to Bhimpur. I can't afford to stay away from work much longer.'

'I see.'

No reply.

'So how's it going with you?'

Just ask, Shiva.

'Things are quite alright.'

'Hmm...good.'

After three years of neither hearing from nor seeing each other, this is what they do. They make small talk.

Shiva doesn't even realize when the bus arrives.

'I must leave now,' says Raghu. He hadn't bothered bringing any luggage along. 'Take care, Kavita. Look after yourself.' He pats her lightly on the cheek. 'And take care of the girls.'

Ask. Now.

'Baba,' he nods, boarding the bus.

Shiva tries to see which seat his son sits on—he had always liked the window ones.

Sure enough, it is a window seat.

In no time, the bus starts again, and Raghu waves at them.

'You should've asked, you know,' Kavita says, watching as the bus disappears into a trail of dust.

'Huh?'

'You should've asked him to stay.'

His mouth is dry; he struggles to tell Kavita that he tried,

tried to tell his son to stay and that he was sorry—but he just couldn't. It is as if his mouth is filled with sand.

'He wouldn't have,' he manages.

As father and daughter stand looking at the receding bus, now just a speck in the distance, the gulmohar tree stands above them, old and shrivelling.

12

Marooned

'TINA! HOW MANY times have I told you? Don't stuff your fingers into your nose! Rina, do you want to be late? Hurry, you two! Ugh.'

She drags them to the school gate just in time, bending to give them each a kiss on the forehead.

'Bye bye, Ma,' Tina waves, while Rina plays with her ponytails and giggles.

'Be good, okay? Eat your tiffin!'

Phew. One job done.

She fans herself with her pallu. The mornings are getting warm.

She hurries back home; Roshan had said he'd go to work today, and she still has to prepare breakfast. What will she make him? Poha? No, he had said he's bored of that. Some vegetable rice, maybe. Or will that be too much?

Perhaps she'll just give him a couple of laddoos. Yes, that should be fine.

'What do you have for me, Kavita?' Roshan sounds annoyed.

On second thoughts, maybe she shouldn't experiment today, save it for some other time.

'Poha.'

'Again?'

'I'm…I'm sorry. It won't take long. I will be as quick as I can.'

'Your apology won't get me decent food. What a dull mind you have, so devoid of ideas.'

She goes about the kitchen, swallowing the insult—something she never had to do back at Nimkhedi. Oh, how she misses home, even after all these years.

'Move quickly now, woman. I'm hoping you can at least do that.'

Clang! She drops a steel plate.

Great. Ma had always playfully rebuked her, saying she had holes in her palms.

And, as expected, the commentary begins.

'Good god, did that mother of yours not teach you a thing? Holding a utensil isn't *that* hard, you know. How you are supposed to manage the house, I have no idea. Five years, and you still haven't learnt a thing!'

Sigh.

'I'm trying, Ma.'

'Don't you dare call me that!' she looks at her angrily, moving towards her son.

That old bat. Doesn't move an inch, but that tongue of hers runs a million miles a second.

Fumbling, she bolts to the porch with the plate of poha in her hand, feeling victorious that she had managed to make the poha so fast. But then...

'Look at this, Ma—look at it! Even an animal won't eat this.' Roshan points at her efforts and makes a face, as if it's the most appalling thing he's ever seen.

'W-what's wrong?' Kavita enquires. She's sure she has done everything right.

'My dear Kavita,' the wrinkled cow says, with a mocking smile, 'do you see any potatoes on this plate? Are you aware we don't eat poha without potatoes in this house? And are you out of your mind or just shameless to be serving something so piteous to your husband?'

'He was in a hurry, so I thought...'

'Your mind is the size of a pea, Kavita. Do us all a favour and stop thinking, okay?' Roshan hisses. 'It ruins near about everything. Now go get me a slice of lemon.'

And as her husband quietly tells his mother how the poha is actually pretty okay, Kavita sits inside the kitchen with her head in her hands, wondering what would become of her in this house. She can't even stand seeing their faces, and she's supposed to spend the rest of her life caring for them! How good can this get?

'Kavita!' Roshan shouts.

'Yes?' she shouts back.

'Come here, you slug!'

Here we go again.

'Take this,' he shoves his now-empty plate at her.

'You're supposed to bring water along with the food. Please tell me you know that much,' says his mother.

Pfft.

She rolls her eyes when they're not looking.

With the breakfast drama finally over, Kavita starts sweeping the floor, thinking about what to make for lunch. She's about to start mopping, when she realizes mother and son are still chatting outside.

She stands by the door and clears her throat, hoping to catch their attention.

Bull's eye.

'You'd said you would go to work today.'

'That was the plan, but your rotten cooking has forced me to change my mind.'

She gives him a murderous glare, making no effort to hide her contempt this time.

'What are you looking at? Never seen me before? Go wash a spoon or something. Don't you have any work to do?' he spits, going back to gossiping with his mother, a conversation that obviously seems to be more important than earning a living.

She storms in, locks herself in a room, throws herself down on the bed and screams for all she's worth into a pillow. Exhausted, she wonders what she has gotten herself into.

◆

'Ma?'

Thump, thump.

'We're back, Ma. I'm hungry.'

She wipes her face and sniffs. She shouldn't have shown her anger, shouldn't have, shouldn't have. The girls will have to witness the drama now. She imagines his belt on her, now an old acquaintance, biting into her arm, or maybe her back, leaving behind souvenirs of red.

'Have I not told you before to stop thinking? When will you learn?' she imagines him yelling at her, imagines herself screaming.

She's scared. The girls will get afraid. She's scared the girls will get afraid.

'I'm coming. One minute.' She hasn't even started making lunch yet. What is wrong with her?

What a life.

Sitting alone in a room now seems like the only act of rebellion she's capable of.

Okay, take deep breaths.

She opens the door.

She finds Tina on the floor, digging her nose, and Rina playing with...a box of matches! She rushes to her, snatching her new toy away and making her howl in indignation.

Why isn't that old hag around? She thinks she can just leave the children alone like this?

'Shh, you'll get hurt, Rina. Here,' she says, handing her a bowl, 'go play with this.' And her daughter's tears stop as if nothing had ever happened.

Kavita smiles at Rina's theatrics. She's such a faker.

'Where's Dadi, Rina?'

'Dadi said she's going out,' Rina drools.

'Hmm.'

She couldn't care less about where Roshan could be either; she's just happy both of them are away from home.

'Why didn't you come to school to pick us up, Ma?' asks Tina. 'I don't like walking home without you. The big kids are mean.'

She replies with a timid 'sorry'.

Kavita has no idea what she'd do if it wasn't for these two.

By late evening, neither does Roshan return, nor that pig of a woman. Kavita waits for them, sitting by the front door, as the world moves on around her. It's calming to see everything happening just like it always does: the women walking back home with pots of water resting on their waists, the elderly chatting, the goats and cows ambling through the streets.

Khapa bothers her, suffocates her. She feels trapped in the silk of neighbourhood gossip, clucking hens and clanking bronze bells. It all feels too much like a prison. She wonders if she's going to be marooned here for the remainder of her existence; the very thought is depressing.

She looks back at the girls, who are by now deep in slumber. Surprisingly, Kavita has actually had a good day. The three of them had spent their afternoon tickling each other's bellies, laughing and chatting about the twins' school. After that she had made them sit and learn the alphabet. 'No wonder they're exhausted', she thinks.

She realizes how much of a rarity good days have become. How happy they all used to be a decade ago. Raghu was little, Baba was fine, Ma was still breathing, and she herself was oblivious—to any other possibility other than that life.

She suddenly springs to her feet; she brushes Tina's sole with her fingers and softly blows in Rina's ear, evoking slightly annoyed 'mmms' from them. She smiles and gets to work.

She's not quite sure what's fuelling this upsurge in her—whether it is the frustration, the anxiety or the monotony—but she starts quickly piling her clothes up on the floor, followed by the girls'. Roshan is definitely not going to like this. Then she dumps all of it in a bag.

Maybe it's the rage.

'Come on, girls. I'm taking you out,' she says, picking them both up in her arms and shaking them awake.

'Maa...' they complain.

Or maybe it's the stress.

They walk quickly to the bus stop.

Roshan is right across the road, idling away time with a couple of other loafers like himself, all of them sitting on cracked and broken plastic chairs.

She sees him see her.

Just in time, the bus pulls to a stop in front of her and the girls.

'Kavita! Where do you think you're going?' she hears him bellow.

She shoves the kids in, followed by the bag, then quickly hoists herself up. As the bus starts moving again, they make their way to a few empty seats at the back.

'Hey, wait! You crooked, shameless woman! You wait and watch...'

His shouts fade in the distance as the bus picks up speed.

There's only one thing this can be called. Revolt.

'It's dark, Ma.' 'I want to sleep.' 'I'm hungry.' 'Where are we going?'

'Home.'

◆

Fate seems to have a thing against him. First he managed to lose the one true love of his life. Then, he, with his own cruel hands, shooed his son away. He failed to save his wife, the woman who had been with him through thick and thin. And now, there she is at his doorstep, his daughter, whom he had married off to that good-for-nothing sloth of a boy. His two little, beautiful granddaughters are stuck with an unworthy father, and he, their grandfather, doesn't even have enough money to buy them new dresses.

Shiva has started thinking a lot these days, and even though it drives him insane, ironically, it is also the one thing that keeps him anchored to reality. He feels like with every passing phase of his life, he takes it up a notch—his unworthiness.

He looks at Kavita sitting facing the children in their house, smart and confident. Maybe Shiva should have pinned all his expectations on Kavita and not on Raghu—she may have taken it better.

'In which year did India gain its independence? Raise your hands, whoever knows the answer.'

The children do as they are told.

'Okay, Bunty. Tell me.'

'But I didn't raise my hand.'

'Which is why I'm asking you. Tell me.'

'Uh... 1950...'

'1950? Are you sure?' She raises her eyebrows, crossing her hands.

'Uh,' he replies.

'1947!' A few of Bunty's friends whisper collectively.

'Quiet!' Kavita booms, silencing everything in the room, even the clinking pencils and the sharpener sounds.

'Oh, don't be so strict, Kavita... He'll do better next time,' Shiva tries to placate her, sitting on the book-sprawled cot nearby.

It still bewilders her how much Baba has changed. If only this could've happened when Raghu was home.

But then, it wouldn't have if he was.

She inhales. 'Alright, fine. All of you will revise the chapter and come prepared tomorrow, okay? I don't want to look at blank faces.' She eyes Bunty, who has turned pink.

'I will learn my chapter, Teacherji,' Bunty says in a voice so small Kavita breaks into a smile.

'Ooh, did I miss any drama?' Anjani walks in against the small tide of children rushing outside.

'Hah, not too much, I'd say.'

'I'm happy this tuition thing is going well, Kavita,' Anjani chirps. Like everyone else in the village, time has changed her once youthful features. But unlike everybody else, she's fought it well. Her only affliction is that she dyes her hair black twice a month.

'All thanks to you,' a horizontal Shiva says from the cot.

'Please don't give me credit. It's Kavita's hard work that has paid off.'

Among all the things Kavita had yearned for at Khapa, Anjani was the one she had missed the most. And, in the end, it had been Anjani who had sat Kavita down and talked her into tutoring the village kids; Shiva could really do with some cash in his pockets, she had said.

'Anyway,' says Shiva, getting up, his legs feeling a little weak. 'When...' For a second, he loses his balance, blinking hard.

'Careful, Baba, careful,' Kavita holds him by the waist.

'What's wrong?' asks Anjani.

'I-I don't know, I kind of felt...giddy. I'm fine now.' He gently puts Kavita's hand away. 'It's okay, it happens sometimes these days. I'm sure it's nothing to worry about. Well, as I was saying,' he breathes in, 'Raghu.'

Both Kavita and Shiva know Anjani is about to leave for Bhimpur in Haridas's second-hand ferrying machine—he'd bought a jeep recently. She has come to bid them goodbye, along with an offer to take any messages to Raghu.

'Umm...' Anjani's not quite convinced Shiva is alright but decides not to press the issue. Instead, she asks, 'Yes, what about Raghu?'

'Tell him I said...' he thinks, and then thinks some more.

'Tell him the girls miss him. They haven't seen him in a while,' Kavita saves them the awkwardness.

Shiva sighs. 'Just tell him I'm sorry.'

'Light-bulb moment! Hmm, this could work,' Kavita thinks.

'Wait, how about...' she closes one eye, as if thinking up some plan, 'how about we accompany her to Bhimpur, Baba?'

'Oh yes, please! That'll be great. Come on, Shiva, say yes... Say yes!'

'Uh, really? I don't think that's a good idea. I mean, I...'

'Oh please, Baba, I'm begging you. Please come. We can sort this thing out; he's still a boy—and your son—after all.'

Shiva looks at the two wide-eyed women.

'This could set it all straight.'

Shiva scratches his head.

What's it going to be, Baba?

'Okay.'

Kavita squeals, hugging Anjani. 'Thank you!' she beams.

'Well, come on then, Haridas is waiting,' says Anjani, grinning happily.

'I'll just go get the girls,' Kavita runs out.

'You two go ahead. I'll be there, just give me a minute.' Shiva shuffles over to the kitchen.

'You *are* alright, aren't you?' Anjani asks.

'Yes, yes, don't worry. Let me just have a glass of water and I'll join you two. I won't be long.'

'Come on, we'll get late!' Kavita bellows from outside.

'You go join her, Anjani,' Shiva says.

'Fine, I'm coming. Relax, Kavita.'

'There you are. What took you so long?'

'And there are my girls!' Anjani holds their sweaty little faces in her palms. 'You've been running around, huh?'

'Where's Baba?' Kavita is getting fretful now.

'Oh, he's just coming. Tina, how old are you, my darling?'

'I'm four years old.'

'You didn't ask me!' Rina puffs out her cheeks.

Laughing, Anjani turns to her. 'Oh, I'm sorry. How old are you, Rina?'

She wipes away a small tear. 'I'm four years old too.'

Kavita silently giggles at her daughter. She keeps her hands on top of both their heads. 'Don't you just love them?'

Anjani smiles. 'More than life itself.'

'I'm telling you, I'm thinking of never going back to Khapa. Everything's perfect here. I'm earning too. So who needs a husband?'

'You don't really mean that.'

Kavita closes her eyes, letting out a sigh. 'No, I don't. One thing's for sure, though—my husband and his mother will not be very happy to see me again.'

'You can't run from them forever, you know.'

'Oh, I know. It's not like I have much choice.'

'Anyway, we'll worry about that later. Shiva said he was just having a glass of water. I'm sure it doesn't take that long. I feel like I'm getting cooked in the sun.'

Kavita furrows her brows. 'Stay with the girls, okay? I'll go check on him.'

Kavita wipes the sweat off her chin with a finger. The heat is outrageous.

'Baba?' she calls from the door.

No answer.

'You'll make me come in? Fine!' She walks straight into the kitchen, and the first thing she notices is the deep red smeared all over his mouth. Shiva is on the floor, right in the middle of the room, the glass of water lying spilt beside him. His eyes have rolled back into his lifeless head.

She screams.

13

A Lucky Stroke

RAGHU IS CLEANING the tables after a busy afternoon when he hears the jeep approaching.

'Rasul! Dada's back! Get more plates!' he calls. 'He's late today, his companions will be starving.'

He strains to look out at the furnace, expecting Dada to walk in any second with a fleet of hungry travellers. It was Haridas's genius mind that had come up with the idea—the jeep drops the passengers on the road across the dhaba, so whoever's hungry, which most of them are, can come right in. Good for business.

But he sees now that Dada has no intention of coming home just yet. The jeep just whooshes past. Raghu is curious—he's pretty damn sure the jeep is Dada's.

So he stumbles through the haphazardly kept chairs and rushes out to the blistering asphalt, pursuing the vehicle with his eyes. It neither halts at the pharmacy, nor at the tailor's. It bypasses the sweet shop and the turn for the petrol pump too. He sees a head inside, bobbing up and down to the rhythm of the potholes.

Is that...Kavita?

Its rear lights up in an angry auburn, telling him that the car is finally coming to a stop—in front of the hospital. Dada gets down from the driver's seat in a frenzy and barges in through the hospital door.

Raghu throws down the napkin he is holding in his hands and runs like he has never run before. He's only halfway through when he sees people—dressed in gentle shades of green, as if it's a happy place they're coming from—rush to the car with a metal platform. A stretcher.

A body Raghu is all too familiar with is pulled out.

He runs faster. He can hear his own breath coming in deep, heavy gasps; his eyes seem to have turned into frosted glass.

The face is lathered with blood. He has never seen so much red before.

His lungs burn, they're on fire, but he doesn't remember the last time he had felt this chilly.

Baba.

Kavita steps out next from the car, her sari stained in the same red. She spots him running towards them and, though already in pieces, now visibly falls apart.

◆

'Hypertension caused the stroke,' they had declared.

'The bleeding too. He might need surgery, but consider that a last resort—it's better to wait and see if the body can cope. Once all the blood's been sucked out of the cranium, we'll get him on medications. Massaging is...'

But he'd stopped listening.

Last resort, they'd said. It could come to that.

A week later, the words still swim in his mind like sharks preying on his sanity, tearing at it bit by bit. Baba has still not opened his eyes; he still does not know that his son has been sleeping three hours a night by his bed, has still not cared to acknowledge anything that the white coats are doing for him, is still as indifferent as ever. The thoughts set ablaze whatever little composure he has left, until he feels like falling to the ground, a frostbitten leaf, helplessly ready to face the next acrid gale.

'That wasn't me,' he thinks, willing his father to listen.

The 'me' you knew, that wasn't me at all.

Funny how it had taken being kicked out of the house to realize that.

I want to show you who I am now. Come back, please.

He'd missed out on those years he could've spent with Ma; he couldn't lose the few days he could have with Baba too. He should've begged Baba to let him stay when he'd gone to the village for Ma. He should've held his feet and wept, should've pleaded with all that he'd got. Maybe the three years away from home could've bought him enough pity to be granted back his home.

He had only just discovered this side of himself. He had been wishing with all his soul that one day, no matter how distant it may be, his father would be pleased to call him his son. He knows there's still so much of him his father hasn't seen yet.

He realizes that he hasn't been the same since Ma died. Cruel old Ma had left him alone in this world to fend for himself, but she had taken a part of him. He wonders if Baba, too, will do the same.

His gaze moves from Baba's battle-ridden, shaved head, to his shut lids, slides down his nose to his chapped, slightly parted brown lips, to the incision in his throat and the flurry of embellishments—pipes, tubes—snaking around his neck, into his nostrils, down his oesophagus. The beeping monitor kept beside him is the only thing that tells him his father is still breathing.

It's remarkable how much has happened in such little time. Things were finally getting a little better when life had again thrown them a curveball.

He looks around the room. Every bed seems blanketed in an aura of gloom, of loss. Ironically, however, it gives him the sense of solidarity he has been seeking. The agony of suffering, the fear of impending loss, binds them all together; but there is still hope of a silver lining.

He's been resisting looking at the bed beside Baba's for a while now, but he can't help but sneak a glance at it now. The woman on it seems to have shrunk in size since the previous day, her half-open eyes dimmer than he last remembered— just like that of the young man sitting beside her, who Raghu assumes is her son. He is distraught, holding one of her limp hands in his, pressing his temple into it. His bloodshot eyes and stubble make it look like Raghu has it easy.

Parents are such invaluable parts of our life, Raghu thinks. He suddenly realizes that this young man is the only one to have come in to visit the old woman on the bed. All the other beds always have a bunch of people hustling around, but this woman does not seem to have anyone else to worry for her.

A nurse in the same green overall walks in to check on her, upping her dose and taking notes.

'She's... I don't know. I try to get her to speak... But all she does is stare at the ceiling or tilt her head sometimes to look at me.'

Raghu realizes the man is not as old as he had initially thought; worry has made him age. His boyish voice is the only giveaway.

Raghu waits for the nurse to finish speaking.

'How long have you been here?' Raghu asks the boy.

'Nearly three weeks now, I think.'

'I hope she gets better soon.'

'Yes, me too.'

They both turn to her together, and find her with the same empty gaze she has worn for the past few days.

The boy sighs.

The nurse looks at him now with an expression Raghu recognizes as pity.

'I'm sorry.'

'Hmm.'

She rattles off a slew of medical terms and Raghu doesn't even try to keep up.

He hears a woman on the opposite side of the room, near the door, wailing—a frequent sound these days—ringing out in the silent hospital gloom. Once again, Raghu sees relatives weep on each other's shoulders as nurses push out yet another body on a trolley, its face covered with a sheet.

The boy looks as unsettled as Raghu feels, and he knows both of them are thinking the exact same thing—what if their own is next?

Raghu is still just staring at the scene when Kavita comes in. She pulls him into a hug. 'Go home. Get some rest,' she insists.

He sees the nurse leave the boy to himself and head out of the ward to chat with face he knows. Her jet black hair is cropped short. She has a longish face, fair skin, thin lips.

Maya.

What is she *doing here?*

◈

Raghu races against the sun, wanting to get to Baba's window before it does. Dada has been up all night by his bed, giving Kavita a chance to be with the girls at the dhaba and Raghu an opportunity to catch up on some sleep. Gratitude is too small a word to use in such a situation, too clichéd for either Kavita or Raghu to use. From the hospital bills to a place to rest to something as irreplaceable as his presence, Dada is helping them with everything they can possibly ask for.

Raghu rushes into the hospital room and places his hand on Dada's shoulder just as dawn breaks. With a few pats on his back and encouraging words, Dada heads out, leaving Raghu to his glum solitude. He is just about to settle down, when he sees Maya walking towards him with a frown. That same striking contrast between her hair and her fair skin leaves him looking at her for a second longer than he would have wanted.

'Raghu, what happened?'

Maya is in his class at school. She's adopted—that's about all he knows of her.

'My father had a stroke. Blood pressure.'

'This is why you haven't been coming to school! Everyone has been wondering where you are.'

'I see.'

'Where's your family? Are you here alone?'

Family. God really seems to loathe mine.

'No, no, they're back at the dhaba. My sister's little girls have also had to come, so someone has to stay back with them.'

'Oh, alright. I'm guessing you take turns.'

'Yes, we manage.'

'Well, alright. Let me know if you need anything.'

Now what's that supposed to mean?

'Uh, sure. Thanks.'

'I'm really sorry. I'll pray for him.'

He nods as she walks away. He can bet that he's seen her somewhere, even before Bhimpur.

No sooner is she gone than he feels a nasty urge to throw up, drag Baba's bed right out of this cursed place and take him far away to some corner of the world where things are better. It's like Death itself is sitting like a predator in this ghastly room, inching closer to Baba.

He imagines the poor man all alone in their village house,

bearing the weight of his mother's absence all by himself, praying to not snap, praying that his knees don't give way—for the weight he bears surpasses a million earths, and he a million Atlases.

The neighbouring bed, he notices, is empty.

◆

'Rasul! Hurry up, man! One last order to go. Then play all you want.'

Dada has had to leave for the village for another round of ferrying, so Raghu is now left to manage the dhaba with Rasul. Having the girls around is really not helping, Raghu thinks, with a pang of guilt. Raghu knows that it's been a while that Rasul has had the company of children, but that's surely no reason to be dancing with them in the kitchen at peak hours.

'Okay, enough is enough,' Raghu pulls him away from their little circus and pushes him towards the counter. The twins hold their stomachs and laugh.

'Fine, I'll get back to work. There's no need to manhandle me. Hmph... I tell you, how times have changed,' he mutters, as he begins rolling out a chapati.

Dada can handle him when he comes back. For now, Raghu has somewhere else to be.

Walking down the same scorched road to the hospital, he sees a distant scrunched-up nose waiting for him. A nose he realizes he has been seeing quite often, but not in the past few days.

He still hasn't had a chance to ask her.

'Hello,' she says.

'Hello. Seeing you after some time.'

'Yes, I was out of town with my grandmother. Ma's been out on one of her trips for a while now, so we thought a change of scenery would be good till she came back. Come, let me walk with you.'

'Where had you gone, if I may ask?'

'Nimkhedi, if you know where that is.'

They take a left.

'What? Really? That's my village!'

'You're joking! You're from Nimkhedi?'

'Yes! I am. Rather, I was... Do you go there often?'

'I've only been there once before, briefly.'

That's why! Now I get it.

She smiles.

He smiles back.

'This is where I leave you. I have to go that way.' She points in the opposite direction.

'Okay, see you.'

'Sure.'

'Just a minute, wait.' Raghu decides to ask her. 'Why *do* I see you here? A hospital isn't a very pleasant place. Is anyone you know admitted here?'

'No, no. My mother, she's—'

'*There* you are, Maya. I've been looking all over for you!' A woman perhaps as old as Shiva strides into view from across the hallway. 'I'm starting on my rounds now, so I will take some time. I won't be seeing you till lunch. But stay around.' She's wearing one of those white coats. 'I see you have company,' she raises a brow.

Maya laughs. 'As I was saying, my mother's a doctor here.'

He sneaks a look at her name pin. Suchita Kulkarni.

'This is Raghu, Ma. We're classmates.'

He greets her with a timid hello.

'Is someone you know a patient here, young man?'

'My father, he had a stroke.'

'Really? Well, then, I'll be seeing him in a while. What's his name?'

'Shiva.'

'Shiva what?'

'Shiva Shirsat.'

The woman stares at him like he's wearing socks on his ears. He, in turn, gives Maya a look as if to say, 'Did I do something wrong?'

It takes Suchita a few moments to catch her breath. 'Okay, I'll look him up. Come along, Maya.' She walks away.

14
Unfinished

She stares at the ink that spells out that bittersweet name—a name she'd doodled on to all her notebooks as a girl, a habit she'd unwillingly carried on well after it was no longer hers to doodle; a name that had made her drive away all the proposals that had come knocking on her door; a name that could blow the wind out of her whenever it wickedly fleeted across her mind; a name that had made her cry so many times it was ridiculous. And yet she'd craved to call it out one more time. She had thought she had gotten over it, that that chapter in her life had ended, and yet, after all these years, scribbled carelessly on that yellowing piece of paper in her shaking hands, there it is, waiting for her to call it out one more time.

'Shiva.'

One little droplet from her eyes disappears into the sheet.

Even after the oceans she's poured out for him, he's still demanding more.

'This is real.'

Suchita checks the date of admission. *27 April.*

That's a lot of time; this is not good.

Haemorrhagic stroke, she reads. *Room No. 6. Bed 4.*

Before she realizes, she's running across the corridors, flying past rooms and patients, quivering, breathless. She's not sure what the outcome of this is going to be—it had taken a lot out of her to banish thoughts of him from her mind—but here she is, tossing all of that out with the trash and tearing right through the hallway.

She stops right outside the smooth metal of the door, her hand poised to push it open, but she doesn't have the stomach to.

'I can't.'

She should've known.

'Excuse us, doctor.' An old couple shuffles past her, into the ward.

And though she tries to look away, she sees him.

It's still just like the good old days. All the life in her, right from the small of her toes to the tips of her fingers, gathers up in a ball inside her belly, making her dizzy. She sees his son too, crouching beside him, looking into his still face.

Shiva is here. At her hospital. Ten feet away from her.

And he's far from alright.

Okay, easy. One step at a time.

She walks towards him.

For thirty-five years she had managed to stay away from her former life—but it had finally caught up with her. She hadn't even gone back home since then, using work as an excuse. But she had woken up every day of those thirty-five years feeling she wasn't enough. For anything. For *anyone*. Maya was her biggest, most selfish gamble, but she'd longed for someone to fall back on, someone who would accept her, turning a blind eye to all her shortcomings.

She still stands at the sink every morning trying to wash the sadness off her face, till she realizes that no matter how much she wants it gone, wants *him* gone—from the look on her face to the sneakiest corner of her mind to her new uptight self—he isn't going anywhere.

She walks up to his bed and calls to a nurse for his details.

'Comatose for forty-three days. Vitals have been improving, though. Increased recent movement. Previously under the care of Doctor Meshram.'

'Please tell me he'll be okay, doctor.' The boy—Maya's friend—looks disconsolate. 'Tell me he'll be fine. No matter how long it takes.'

Throughout her career, Suchita has seen a lot of tears. But this boy's tell a different story.

'So much has happened,' his voice cracks. 'If he doesn't open his eyes, I won't know what to do with myself.'

Maybe it's just because he's his son... Of course he's upset.

'I've got too much to prove, too much to lose. You have to do something, please...'

'I'll do my best.'

She can't run from it this time. He's in a coma and yet has her cornered.

◆

She finds herself in front of his door, just staring at the metal.

God, why is this still so hard? Get a grip, Suchita.

'Aren't you going in, doctor?'

She turns around. It's his daughter. She's a real beauty.

'Y-yes, just been thinking.'

Kavita nods, looking at her expectantly. Neither of them says anything.

'Um, Doctor Suchita?'

'Yes?'

'Could you move a little to the side? I need to go in.'

Suchita flushes. 'Yes, I'm sorry, I was a little distracted...' she mumbles, following Kavita in.

Great. Just great.

Suchita stands across from Shiva's bed, staring at his feet. Three days have passed and he's still wearing that poker face. Stubborn fellow.

The monitor proclaims all vitals to be normal. *What am I missing?*

'When will he wake up, doctor?' the boy's voice trembles. 'It's been more than a month and a half.'

He has sweet children. And yet just thinking about them leaves her mouth sour.

'What do I say, he should've been conscious by now. But... let's see. We will just have to give him time.'

Raghu presses his lips together. 'It's been a while since we've been hearing that. I wish someone would give us better news.'

She squeezes her eyes shut. 'Yes, I understand.'

Shiva has not shown any signs of anything medically significant for quite some time now.

'Shiva, can you hear me?' she rests her hand on his arm. 'Shiva, I need to know if you can hear me. I need you to open your eyes, if you can.'

The wait feels like aeons.

Nothing.

She massages the bridge of her nose and sees Raghu rubbing his forehead.

'Try calling out to him. Though it doesn't seem like it, he can hear us. You'll have to tap into his conscious brain and he'll start responding.'

A barely audible 'okay' comes from Raghu, as he continues rubbing his forehead mechanically.

It's as if Raghu has given up the prospect of having an actual conversation with his father again.

That would mean failure. Suchita is the doctor, after all; it's her job to heal people. If she fails at this, she knows she will never be able to heal herself all over again either.

'Shiva, listen to me. You *have* to wake up. Your family's been waiting for you. You have to take them home. Get up. For them.'

Nothing.

Get up for me.

'I'll keep trying, doctor.' The boy's hollow words are piercing. 'Thank you.'

She nods. 'Alright then.' She leaves the boy to wallow in his desolation.

Back in her room, she slouches in her chair, rolling around a pencil in her fingers. What's happening is still too hard for her to digest.

Yes, she has done everything in her power to erase all that can lead back to him. Yes, she has tried a million times to convince herself that he'd betrayed her. But no, not for one second has she ever truly believed that. Yes, he had deserted her, but...

Ugh. She has tried before too, to look for an excuse to hate him. But she has always failed.

At least he has taught her one thing—there's no such thing as certainty. She is almost thankful she learnt this early in her career. She had been so sure, so utterly confident that he would always be there.

God help me.

Bringing all this back from the dead is like tearing open a scar into a gaping, dripping wound.

On top of all this, his son and her daughter turn out to be in the same class! The universe plays such twisted games. The children are so completely unaware of the history their parents share, it almost feels criminal.

There's a knock on her door.

That must be Maya.

'Come on in!'

Maya's petite figure makes its way across the room and plops down on the sofa. She dumps her bag beside her on the floor. Her sweaty face has turned pink from the heat outside.

'There you are. How was school?'

'The same old drab. I don't even know why you still bother to ask.'

'Oh, well, a mother can hope.'

They share a smile.

Another knock, more urgent this time.

A nurse. 'Patient No. 34, Doctor. Shiva Shirsat. He's just opened his eyes.'

Within seconds, Suchita finds herself at his bedside.

Those eyes.

'Oh, Baba, you're with us!' Raghu wails. 'Do you know how much you scared us all! I am right here.'

Those eyes. Adjusting to the light.

They stare right through his son.

Kavita's face is wet with tears. They stream down her face, unrestrained, dripping on her father's arm. She doesn't say anything—or maybe she can't.

Those eyes. Now clueless, blank, lost. They're horrifying.

Suchita wipes away the wetness from her own cheek as swiftly as she had allowed it to materialize. 'Hello, Shiva.'

He turns to her.

That's a response.

Thank god.

'Hello, Shiva. Can you hear me?' she tries to push the words into his consciousness.

That same empty stare.

'Baba, look, it's me. It's me, Raghu,' the boy cries, his sobs worsening with the lack of response. 'Baba, it's me.'

'It's alright, Raghu,' Suchita pacifies him. 'Your father's fine. That's what matters. He can only get better now. It's just a matter of days.'

◆

Days turn to weeks, and the weeks inch towards a month. Sooner or later, the hospital will have to release him.

'It's Suchita again, Shiva,' she shifts her position so her face is right in his line of sight. 'I wish you'd say something. You've trifled with us enough.'

All you need to do is speak. Just one word. Any word.

Almost as if in response to her thoughts, she hears a voice. That same tantalizing voice that makes her knees buckle even today.

'Suchita,' he croaks.

Could it be?

She spins around. Kavita is gawking at his face.

She drops the pen she has been holding.

'How is...what...' It seems as if as soon as Shiva has found his tongue, Kavita has lost hers.

'Why is she crying, Suchita?' Shiva is pointing at Kavita, his eyes big and innocent. Just like in the days gone by. 'Was it something I did?'

'Oh, Baba! How does he know you, doctor?' The situation is too much for Kavita to understand.

'I was meaning to tell you, Shiva and I go way back. We're... Uh,' she falters, hoping Kavita won't notice. 'We used to be friends when we were children.'

Suchita continues to look at her strangely. Shiva, however, seems strangely calm. No surprise, no shock. It is as if having Suchita on one side of the bed and his daughter on the other is the most natural thing in the world. Suchita hadn't really expected anything from him, but she had never thought it would mean nothing to him, that seeing her after so many years would mean nothing to him.

'Why aren't you answering me, Suchita?' She can see he's really puzzled.

It is at that moment that Raghu walks into the ward and stops short at the scene in front of him, eyes wide and mouth slightly open. No words come out.

'The boy...I've seen him before somewhere. Please don't cry. Who are you? What have I done to you? I'm sorry.'

In that moment, the world stops turning for all of them. It is as if everything has frozen, suspended in time.

No...

Kavita holds Raghu's hand tightly.

'He doesn't even recognize me,' Raghu whispers, as Shiva turns back to Suchita with a lopsided smile.

◆

Suchita watches from the door as Haridas shares a joke with Shiva and they both break into grins.

'You're funny. We could be good friends,' she hears Shiva say.

Kavita and Raghu stand on one side of the hospital room. Though they now know bits and pieces of the past Suchita shares with Shiva, they don't know all of it. Suchita couldn't bring herself to tell them the entire truth. Maybe she will tell Maya someday.

She exhales.

It's astounding how much he has forgotten. Tracing what's left of his memory has been quite a task in itself.

'Do you remember that time, Suchita,' Shiva had giggled, 'when I was trying to throw a paper ball at you in class and it hit the teacher instead?'

'So Baba had been no better than me, huh,' Raghu had elbowed Kavita, who'd let out a little smirk.

'What drama ensued!' Shiva had continued. 'You all should've been there to see. Fun times they were.'

'Yes, they really were.' Shiva had got Suchita reminiscing with him. Rather surprisingly, he had remembered those times from his childhood, the people even more so, with such utter clarity that it was hard even for her to keep up at times.

'Do you still like sesame laddoos?' he'd asked her another time. 'I could ask Ma to make you some. If she ever plans to visit me, that is. I wonder what's more important than her own sick child,' he'd fumed, while his children exchanged nervous looks.

'Do you know anyone called Yashoda, Baba?' Kavita had dared to ask.

'Why does she keep calling me that, Suchita? "Baba". Tell her to stop, it annoys me,' he'd snapped. 'And tell her I've never known anyone by that name. Yashoda. Never heard of anyone by that name.'

Kavita had fumbled for something to say but had come up empty.

'Wife?' Suchita had asked.

'Wife,' Haridas had affirmed.

Yashoda. The woman who'd been what I couldn't be.

A nurse pulls the IV drip out of the back of his swollen hand.

Kavita spots Suchita looking at them. Adjusting her pallu on her shoulder, Kavita walks up to her, pulling Raghu along.

'Thank you so much, doctor, you've been very kind,' she says.

Suchita looks at them. Smiles.

'Yes,' Raghu concurs. 'You're most welcome at the dhaba any time. We would love to have you over.'

'Thank you, Raghu.'

Shiva is carefully lifted off the bed—with Raghu's help—and is helped into a wheelchair, one side of his body slumping a little more than the other. And though she knows it's all going to be fine now, Suchita can't help but worry. Half-paralysis is a monster to deal with.

Fate, in its macabre sense of irony, has finally given Shiva what he most desired. To forget.

That, along with his childhood a second time over.

Suchita feels a weird guilt. *She's* the one encroaching upon his memory while he shoves his own children away whenever they call him 'Baba'.

She who is about the only one he remembers—and he about the only one she can't forget.

'Will he be like this forever?' Kavita asks through Suchita's daze.

'He might improve, as time goes by. Keep engaging him in conversation, remind him of milestone events in his life.'

'Milestone events, hmm. Maybe we'll alter those just a little bit. He hasn't been in such high spirits for a while now,' says Raghu, trying to lighten up.

'You know what they say. When your father has a stroke, nearly dies and forgets his life, weave him a new one,' Suchita smiles.

Kavita laughs.

'You people have a lot of catching up to do.'

'Lots.'

Suchita turns to face Shiva as he is about to be wheeled out of the room. Thirty-five years later, she finds herself at a similar juncture yet again. Only this time, he's on a wheelchair. Ready to leave her. Yet again. She looks him in the eye this time, though; she doesn't run away or hide, like she had done the last time. He unabashedly does the same. Yet again, she finds one of them still looking forward to spending more evenings with the other. One of them still optimistic, blind to the impossibility of things. One of them still hopeful. This time, though, it doesn't have to end in tears. This time, they will wave each other off with smiles, expecting, not in vain, to see each other again someday.

And as they dive into this sea of colourful fancies and heartfelt promises, they're careful to not let words break something so heart-wrenchingly beautiful.

The silence speaks volumes.

Acknowledgements

Writing this book has been the most testing, yet amazing thing I have done so far. I want to thank my dad for the nights he stayed up late reading and editing with me, and for keeping me in check the few times I lost patience. My brother, Dikshant, and my mom have also extended nothing but love and support throughout the process, and have always come through with ways to make my work better. My grandparents have shared countless village stories with me and been one of my main sources of inspiration. The people of my village in Maharashtra have been more than cooperative, and I thank them for being as candid with me about their lives as they have been.

I am also truly grateful to Mr Raghavendra Singh, who, with his timely help, has been instrumental in the publication of this book. A very special thanks to Ms Sanjana Roy Choudhury for her diligent editing, and Ms Puneet Sodhi for not only her edits but also her heart-warming encouragements.

My gratitude extends to Mr Ruskin Bond for his beautifully written foreword; I absolutely cannot believe his words are between the covers of my book. Finally, I thank the team at Rupa who made this book what it is today.